Policy-Driven Climate and Development Finance

Policy-Driven Climate and Development Finance

Strategies for Equitable Solutions

Edited by
Mahmoud Mohieldin

DE GRUYTER

This book is published in an open access edition and released on University Press Library Open (UPLOpen. com) as part of the 'UPLOpen Climate Change Collection.' UPLOpen is an initiative of Paradigm Publishing and the De Gruyter eBound Foundation.

ISBN 978-3-11-159028-8
e-ISBN (PDF) 978-3-11-159048-6
e-ISBN (EPUB) 978-3-11-159080-6
DOI https://doi.org/10.1515/9783111590486

Library of Congress Control Number: 2025942647

Bibliographic information published by the Deutsche Nationalbibliothek
The Deutsche Nationalbibliothek lists this publication in the Deutsche Nationalbibliografie; detailed bibliographic data are available on the internet at http://dnb.dnb.de.

© 2026 the author(s), editing © 2026 Mahmoud Mohieldin, published by Walter de Gruyter GmbH, Berlin/Boston, Genthiner Straße 13, 10785 Berlin
The book is published open access at www.degruyterbrill.com.

Cover image: Eoneren/E+/Getty Images
Typesetting: Integra Software Services Pvt. Ltd.

www.degruyterbrill.com
Questions about General Product Safety Regulation:
productsafety@degruyterbrill.com

To the veterans of climate and development finance around the world, and to the memory of Saleemul Huq OBE and Ambassador Bernarditas de Castro-Mueller, whose work continues to inspire

Acknowledgments

The journey of preparing and editing this book has been deeply enriched by numerous engagements with scholars, practitioners, policymakers, and other stakeholders in the climate and development finance field over the past few years. The idea behind this book originated nearly three years ago, in the lead-up to COP27, during which the editor served as the UN Climate Change High-Level Champion. The development of this work has benefited enormously from insights shaped through global forums, conferences, negotiations, and seminars that addressed the structural challenges of financing climate and development goals.

The editor would like to express sincere thanks to Dr Mona Elbahtimy and Miral Shehata for their invaluable contributions. Their input into the design of the book, along with their exceptional research efforts and meticulous attention to detail, was instrumental in bringing this work to completion.

Special thanks are due to Yasmine Kamel for her valuable assistance and outstanding support during the initial planning stages of the book.

The excellent copyediting of the manuscript by Oonagh McQuillan is also gratefully appreciated.

The authors and the editor wish to extend their appreciation to the De Gruyter Brill team. In particular, they are grateful for the dedicated support and patience of Ashley Fritsch, Content Editor for Social Sciences.

Finally, support from Beyond Progress in facilitating research assistance for this book is gratefully acknowledged.

Disclaimer

The ideas and views expressed in this book are those of the contributors and should not be attributed to any institutions that they are affiliated with.

Foreword

By Nicholas Stern

Climate finance is defined by its purpose. It is finance for the investments that drive climate action forward, both mitigation, or emissions reduction, and adaptation, or building resilience to the climate change that is occurring and will occur. Investment that is necessary for delivery on the Paris agreement in the context of the Sustainable Development Goals (SDGs). This important book argues, convincingly, that these investments will drive development forward. They can deliver growth in incomes, greater security, better health, and more protection and opportunity for poorer people who are particularly vulnerable to climate impacts. They will: transform energy systems, making them cleaner, cheaper, and more secure; improve economy-wide efficiency; reduce damage to people and productivity from pollution; and improve the functioning of city, energy, transport, and land systems. The adaptation investments will foster resilience and support growth by reducing output fragility and future losses, and increasing confidence to invest. Thus, climate finance is not some pot to be filled in and then divided up by some procedure or others. It is finance for a purpose: to finance the investments that will drive forward sustainable, resilient, and inclusive growth. And different investments will need different forms and combinations of finance.

There is no horse race between climate action and growth and development; on the contrary, climate action drives growth and development forward. Further, much of climate action, for example, public transport, restoring degraded land, decentralised solar, mangroves, provides all three of mitigation, adaptation, and development together.

It is also important to recognise that climate action is, or should be, closely integrated with action on biodiversity. Climate change undermines biodiversity, and biodiversity loss creates climate change. Further, the two have many causes in common, including the burning of fossil fuels. And climate action is at the core of the achievement of the SDGs. Climate action is nested within action for the SDGs.

An understanding of the importance and necessary structures of climate finance must begin with an understanding of the intense urgency of action. And the necessary scale of action. The next decade and the nature of the investments we make as a world, particularly on infrastructure, both physical and natural, will be vital to our function on this planet. Climate action is an *imperative: action to reduce the immense risks of climate change is urgent. And it is, of crucial importance, a great opportunity:* the investments and innovation will create a new and more attractive path of growth and development, than the dirty destructive models of the past.

The first priority is therefore to create the conditions for investment in both private and public sector. This means building and strengthening economic and financial institutions that can give potential investors, and potential financers of investment, confidence that the revenues can be realised, costs managed, and practical problems resolved. The book is clear and strong on the importance of the necessary institutions for both regulatory and policy clarity and policy stability. Government policy and institutional structures should provide strategic confidence in the sense of direction and in the recognition of structural and systemic changes that are necessary.

The strategies should have within them policies to reduce the key market failures that make the current system so inefficient and damaging. Thus, policies should include: carbon pricing or management; the promotion of R and D and innovation; measures to reduce and manage risks in markets, particularly in capital markets; fostering the provision of networks (e.g. public transport and grids) and so on. Sound public policy, credibility, and strategic clarity will drive investment forward. That is the principal motivation for what we now call "country platforms".

That investment must, however, be financed, with different investments requiring different combinations of instruments. That is the second priority. And actions on the two priorities are closely related. The book demonstrates clearly and strongly both how different forms of finance can be scaled up and how they are mutually supportive. Domestic resource mobilisation is crucial for public investment and to give confidence in the future of fiscal policy and macro stability. And crucial for critical infrastructure, including natural infrastructure. But for many emerging market and developing economies, substantial external finance will be needed. Further, for some countries that are in real debt difficulties, international action to reduce and resolve debt issues will be vital if the necessary external investment finance is to be realised.

External finance for the required investment will be in large measure from the private sector. But that private finance will not be forthcoming on the scale and cost-of-capital necessary without international action to manage and reduce risk. Development banks and financial institutions, both multilateral and national, have a crucial role to play here. The book sets out carefully and analytically how those financial institutions can use different kinds of instruments, including guarantees and equity, to help manage and share risk and thus enable private finance to flow at the necessary scale and at reasonable cost-of-capital. Reducing that cost-of-capital is critical to investment and its finance and the book shows how that can be achieved.

The book also shows clearly the essential role of concessional capital, including overseas development assistance, philanthropy, and voluntary and official carbon markets. Many activities including adaptation, a just transition, and natural capital, will require highly concessional financing. That is one reason why new forms of revenue sources are crucial. There is great potential in, for example, international taxation of shipping and aviation. If pursued in a high-carbon way, these activities damage the climate and biodiversity. They are, in large measur,e untaxed. There is potential too in the creation of Special Drawing Rights from the IMF and their allocation to poorer countries.

The book goes beyond financing at the national level to include regional issues. Climate impacts and land, water, transport, and energy systems, for example, go beyond the confines of one country. Responses must be at a regional as well as a national level. Similarly, much of the action must take place at the sub-national level, including provinces within a nation, and cities. In each of these cases, institutional structures and external support are likely to play a critical role.

The book covers the above difficult and complex issues with admirable clarity and a powerful sense of purpose. Mahmoud Mohieldin has assembled many of the very best analysts, practitioners, and policy makers across the world who are working on climate action and climate finance. It is an extraordinarily impressive line-up of major figures in this area.

We owe a real debt of gratitude to Mahmoud Mohieldin for his outstanding contributions as a researcher, writer, and practitioner, studying and creating policy responses to the most important problem of our time. His work combines experience, wisdom, practicality, political acuity, and rigorous analysis in a most powerful and effective way. Mahmoud's body of work on these issues is of great importance. He has been tireless, prolific, and rightly influential. The essays assembled here by such key authors, together with the editor's thoughtful commentary and structuring, provide a book of real insight and importance. It should be read and studied by all those working on these critical issues.

We can, as a world, find a new and more attractive path of development and growth. One that is sustainable, resilient and inclusive. There are special opportunities now, unique in history, for developing countries to leapfrog the dirty, destructive, and inefficient paths of the past. This immensely valuable book shows us how this new path of development can be created and financed.

Contents

Part Three: **Means to Close the Climate Finance Gap**

Part Four: **Climate Finance from Regional and Local
Perspectives**

About the Contributors

Amr Osama Abdel-Aziz is the Chairman of Integral Consult since 2004. He has more than 30 years of experience, including on climate mitigation projects in the energy, industry, and waste sectors. He led the implementation of hundreds of projects in these fields including evaluation of policies to reduce GHG emissions, technology, and finance needs. He has worked on mitigation projects with international institutions, such as WB, AfDB, UNDP, UNIDO, UNFCCC, DG CLIMA, and GIZ. Dr Abdel-Aziz is a former co-chair of Sharm El-Sheikh Mitigation Ambition and Implementation Work Program under the Paris Agreement. He is also the advisor to the Egyptian Minister of Environment on climate change issues since 2014. Dr Abdel-Aziz is a member of the Methodologies Panel of the CDM Executive Board since 2005 and the Methodologies Expert Panel of Article 6.4. He was a lead author for the IPCC WGIII AR5 report (Industry chapter, waste section), IPCC WGIII AR6 report (Emissions drivers and trends), and the 2019 refinement for the IPCC 2006 Guidelines. He has a PhD in Environmental Engineering from North Carolina State University, USA in 2003.

Adriana Erthal Abdenur is co-President of the Global Fund for a New Economy (GFNE). Between 2023 and 2005, she was Special Advisor in international affairs in the office of President Lula. A Brazilian policymaker and scholar, she co-founded Plataforma CIPÓ, a think tank headquartered in Rio de Janeiro and dedicated to issues of international relations, climate change and sustainable development. Dr Abdenur earned a PhD in sociology of development from Princeton University and an AB in East Asian Studies from Harvard University. She has taught at universities in the United States, Brazil and France and has published widely on global governance, sustainable development and peacebuilding. She sits on the Advisory Board of a number of UN entities, including UNITAR and UNU-CRIS, and served two terms on the ECOSOC Committee on Development Policy.

Jean-Paul Adam is the Director for Policy, Monitoring and Advocacy in the Office of the Special Adviser on Africa to the United Nations Secretary General. He joined the United Nations in January 2020 and served as the Director for Technology, Climate Change and Natural Resources Management in the United Nations Economic Commission for Africa up until June 2023. Mr. Adam previously served in several Cabinet positions in the Government of Seychelles including Minister of Finance, Trade and the Blue Economy (2015–2016) where he negotiated a debt for climate change adaptation swap in 2015 which placed 30 per cent of Seychelles oceanic space under protection and launched the process for Seychelles to become the first issuer of a Blue Bond. He also served as Seychelles' Minister of Foreign Affairs (2010–1015) and Minister of Health (2016–2019).

Razan Khalifa Al Mubarak is a global leader in nature conservation and climate action, serving as President of the International Union for Conservation of Nature (IUCN) and previously as UN Climate Change High-Level Champion for COP28 UAE. She is the first IUCN President from West Asia and only the second woman to hold the position. For over two decades, Razan has shaped environmental policies in the UAE and beyond, championing species conservation and climate resilience. She is the founding director of the Mohamed bin Zayed Species Conservation Fund, which has supported over 3,000 projects worldwide. She is also the Managing Director of the Environment Agency – Abu Dhabi and Emirates Nature-WWF. On the global stage, she is the UAE Sherpa for the High-Level Panel for a Sustainable Ocean Economy, and Co-Chair of TNFD. Razan holds an MSc in Public Understanding of Environmental Change from University College London, UK and a BA in Environmental Studies and International Relations from Tufts University, USA.

Sabrina Bachrach is a senior advisor for global policy and finance at the Atlantic Council's Climate Resilience Center, where she leads work on global financial policy and private-sector mobilization for adaptation and resilience. She also serves as a technical advisor to the UNFCCC and PwC on innovative financial instruments for adaptation. Previously, she was the adaptation and resilience finance lead for the UN Climate Change High-Level Champions. She has worked at a cutting-edge innovator for adaptation finance, YAPU Solutions and led initiatives such as the Scale for Resilience, and the Women in Resilience Finance mentorship program. Bachrach has also worked on nature-based solutions in Borneo and Costa Rica with Fairventures Worldwide and the International Analog Forestry Network. Her work on adaptation finance has been featured in major global reports and policy publications. She holds a BSc in communication and media studies from the University of Hohenheim.

Hisham Badr currently serves as the Assistant Minister for Strategic Partnerships, Excellence and Initiatives at Egypt's Ministry of Planning and Economic Development, and as National Coordinator of the National Initiative for Smart Green Projects. Ambassador Badr previously held the position of Egypt's Plenipotentiary Ambassador to Italy and Japan, and Permanent Representative to the United Nations and other international organizations in Geneva. His multilateral leadership includes serving as President of the Executive Board of the World Food Programme, Chair of the African Group at UN agencies in Rome, and President of the UNHCR Executive Committee. He also served as Assistant Minister of Foreign Affairs for Multilateral Affairs and International Security. Ambassador Badr has represented Egypt in key international forums and chaired numerous UN committees. He holds master's degrees from Oxford University and the American University in Cairo, where he also taught political science and diplomacy.

Barbara Buchner is the Global Managing Director of the Climate Policy Initiative (CPI), where she leads global efforts to drive investment in climate, energy, and sustainable land use. Recognized among the 20 most influential women in climate change and the 100 most influential people in climate policy, Dr Buchner is a trusted advisor to leaders worldwide. Barbara directs the Global Innovation Lab for Climate Finance, which has mobilized over USD 4 billion for low-carbon, climate-resilient development. She also leads CPI's flagship Global Landscape of Climate Finance report and co-authored the seminal OECD-CPI study on the USD 100 billion goal. Barbara plays a central role in high-level policy dialogues, from the G20 to COPs, and holds advisory positions with institutions including SOAS, the Schwarzenegger Climate Initiative, and the UNFCCC. Originally from Austria, she holds a PhD in Economics and is based in San Francisco.

Sagarika Chatterjee is Director, Climate Finance for the UN Climate Change High-level Champions. Sagarika has supported the UN High-Level Climate Champions, particularly the Champion for COP27, in areas of climate finance since 2022. She serves on the World Economic Forum's Global Future Council on Climate and Nature Governance and the advisory board of the Imperial College Business School Centre for Climate Finance and Investment. In her last role at PRI, Sagarika co-headed the UN-convened Net Zero Asset Owner Alliance secretariat. She contributed to establishing GFANZ with the COP26 Private Finance Hub. Sagarika worked at F&C Asset Management, as an investment committee member for the Joseph Rowntree Foundation and as a trustee at Earthwatch. Sagarika holds an MSc in Development Studies from the University of London, a post-graduate diploma in Management Studies from the University of Oxford and a BA in Social and Political Sciences from the University of Cambridge.

Mona Elbahtimy is a career diplomat and has practical experience in multilateral human rights and climate diplomacy. She served as Senior Advisor to the COP27 Presidency and to the UN Climate Change High-Level Champion for COP27. Previously, she was the Vice-President of the Technical Secretariat of the Supreme Standing Committee for Human Rights in Egypt and consultant to the Arab Human Rights Committee within the League of Arab States. She has a number of publications in the area of human rights, including her manuscript "The Right to Protection from Incitement to Hatred: An Unsettled Right" published by Cambridge University Press in 2021. Dr Elbahtimy holds a PhD from the University of Cambridge.

Nermin Eltouny is a climate change consultant at Integral Consult, specializing in implementation projects across Africa and the MENA region. Her expertise includes developing MRV systems, conducting assessments to inform climate policy and strategy, designing mitigation planning, and preparing project materials to access climate finance, including project prioritization in programmatic planning. She has also supported international negotiations under the Just Transition and Mitigation Work Programs for COP28 and COP29. Nermin contributed to Egypt's National Climate Change Strategy and Low Emission Development Strategy and served on the internal technical review team for Egypt's Biennial Transparency Report. She holds a PhD in Analytical/Environmental Chemistry from McGill University.

Patricia Espinosa is the Founding Partner and CEO of onepoint5, a consulting firm specializing in ESG strategy and climate change. Ambassador Espinosa is also the Chair of the GFANZ Latin America & Caribbean Advisory Board. With over 35 years of experience in diplomacy and international relations, she is a globally respected leader in multilateral negotiations. From 2016 to 2022, she served as Executive Secretary of the United Nations Framework Convention on Climate Change, where she played a key role in advancing the Paris Agreement. Her previous roles include Secretary of Foreign Affairs of Mexico and Ambassador to Germany, Austria, Slovakia, and Slovenia. In 2012, she was named Ambassador Emeritus of Mexico, the country's highest diplomatic honor. Ambassador Espinosa has been decorated by numerous governments and is widely recognized for her leadership on sustainability, gender equality, and human rights. Through her work at onepoint5, she continues to shape global climate policy and support organizations in building a more resilient and equitable future.

Zaheer Fakir is a South African national who has more than 30 years of experience in the world of international politics, finance, and development. He has been at the forefront of negotiations on several major multilateral outcomes, most notably, the Sustainable Development Goals (SDGs) and Agenda 2030, the Paris Agreement, the Green Climate Fund, and the Fund for Responding to Loss and Damage. Mr. Fakir has also served as the finance coordinator for the developing countries (G77 & China) in the UNFCCC negotiations for several years. He is also a board member and Co-Chair of the Board of the GCF, GEF, Climate Investment Funds, and the Adaptation Fund. He currently serves as Senior Advisor to the Energy and Sustainability Division at the Ministry of Foreign Affairs of the United Arab Emirates. He previously held the position of Chief Policy Adviser for International Relations at South Africa's Department of Forestry, Fisheries and the Environment.

Susanna Gable oversees global development finance and inclusive sustainable economic development for the Development Policy and Finance team at the Gates Foundation. Previously, Susanna held the Chief Economist position at Sida. She was the Chair of OECD-DAC CoP on Poverty and Inequality, co-founder of the global OECD-DAC Chief Economist Network, co-founder of the CoP on Country Diagnostics, and member of the Global Council on SDG1 and the Development Committee of the Global Innovation Fund. Before joining Sida she was at the World Bank, working on growth diagnostics and economic transition, private sector development and trade, public expenditures and debt, poverty reduction, the Sustainable Development Goals and financing for development. Susanna has a PhD in Economics, focused on economic and political reforms, economic growth and the environment.

Jorge Gastelumendi is Senior Director of the Atlantic Council's Climate Resilience Center, where he leads efforts across three strategic pillars: the extreme heat initiative, global climate policy and finance, and the gaming initiative. He joined the center in 2020 and has also served as co-lead of the UN Race to Resilience under the High-Level Climate Champions. A recognized leader in climate and environmental policy and finance, Gastelumendi brings decades of global experience in policy design, multilateral negotiations, and climate finance. Prior to joining the Council, he was Managing Director for External Affairs at The Nature Conservancy, where he also led the International Climate Finance Team. He served as Chief Advisor and Negotiator to the Government of Peru during its UNFCCC COP20 Presidency and co-chairmanship of the Green Climate Fund Board, playing a central role in the adoption of the Paris Agreement. Earlier in his career, he managed carbon funds at the World Bank and worked for a decade as a natural resources lawyer in Peru. Originally from Peru, Gastelumendi holds a JD from Peru's Catholic University, a master's in energy and the environment from the University of Calgary, and an MPA from Harvard's Kennedy School of Government.

Clara B. Gurresø is a Junior Fellow at The New Institute. She has worked in international climate policy for over a decade and held roles in civil society, government and research. Among other things, she was actively engaged in the UNFCCC negotiations on the New Collective Quantified Goal on Climate Finance and acted as the climate finance coordinator for the UNFCCC's research constituency, RINGO. She holds a PhD in Political Science from Kiel University, an MSc in Global Development from the University of Copenhagen and an MA (Hons) in Geography from the University of Edinburgh. Her research explores the decision-making procedures that shape the international and subnational allocation of climate adaptation finance with a particular focus on Small Island Developing States.

Juan José Guzmán Ayala is an economist and sustainable development specialist with expertise in climate finance, nature-related risk, and economic policy. As co-founder and co-director of Strata Advisors, a Colombia based consultancy, he works with corporations, financial institutions, and governments to design financial and policy strategies that address climate and nature-related risks while advancing low-carbon business models, particularly across emerging markets. He also serves as senior advisor for policy and finance at the Atlantic Council's Climate Resilience Center, contributing to global initiatives on climate adaptation, disaster risk finance, and resilience. For more than eight years Guzmán has advised Fortune 500 companies, governments, multilaterals, and financial institutions across the Americas, Sub-Saharan Africa and Asia on a wide array of issues. These include the development of financial structures for sustainable agriculture, sovereign debt strategies aligned with climate objectives, corporate sustainability frameworks, just energy transition finance, and the integration of fiscal and monetary policy into climate and nature risk management. His work bridges disciplines to develop economic solutions that support both planetary and human wellbeing. Originally from Colombia, Guzmán holds a Bachelor of Arts in economics and sustainable development from Columbia University, where he also obtained a master's in public administration and a master's in public health.

Stéphane Hallegatte is the Chief Climate Economist of the World Bank Climate Change Group. Mr. Hallegatte is the author of dozens of articles published in international journals in multiple disciplines and of several books and World Bank reports including *Shock Waves: Managing the Impacts of Climate Change on Poverty* in 2015 and *Rising to the Challenge: Success Stories and Strategies for Achieving Climate Adaptation and Resilience* in 2024. He also led the development of the Resilience Rating System, a tool of monitor and report on how resilience is included in public or private investments. More recently, he has supervised the new World Bank diagnostic, the Country Climate and Development Reports, and has co-led the CCDRs for Turkey and Brazil. Mr. Hallegatte holds an Engineering degree from the Ecole Polytechnique (Paris) and a PhD in Economics from the Ecole des Hautes Etudes en Sciences Sociales (Paris).

Stephen Hammer currently serves as Founding CEO of the New York Climate Exchange, an NGO working to speed and scale climate solutions at both the local and global levels. Dr Hammer has 30+ years of international experience working on climate change and climate finance issues. Hammer joined The Exchange after spending 11 years at the World Bank as a Senior Climate Policy Advisor, where he led on all major global climate partnerships (with the UNFCCC, UN Secretary General's team, G7, and G20) and represented the Bank as a technical advisor to the UNFCCC's Transitional Committee charged with setting up the new global fund on Loss and Damage. Dr Hammer was previously on the faculty at MIT and Columbia University, where his research focused on urban energy systems and urban climate resilience. Dr Hammer holds degrees from the London School of Economics, Harvard University, and UC Davis.

Navid Hanif is the Assistant Secretary-General for Economic Development in the Department of Economic and Social Affairs (DESA). He is also the UN sous Sherpa to the G20 finance and main tracks. He was Senior Policy Adviser in the Division for Sustainable Development. He served as Director in the Office for Economic and Social Council (ECOSOC) and Director for Financing for Sustainable Development Office. He has held many leadership roles at the United Nations, including Committees of the General Assembly, ECOSOC and High-Level Committee on Programming. He currently leads analytical and policy work ranging from sustainable development, financing for development, digital transformation to social inclusion and economic analysis. He has contributed several articles on financing and investing in the SDGs in various journals and reports. He holds MIA, International Political Economy, Columbia University (NY), MA, English Literature, Government College University (Lahore). He has done numerous courses in international finance, institution building, foresight and technology.

Eoin Jackson is Chief of Staff/Legal Fellow of the Climate Governance Commission and a PHD Candidate in Law at the London School of Economics where his research focused on rights-based approaches to corporate climate accountability. He is also a Research Assistant with the Grantham Research Institute for Climate Change & the Environment, the Irish Rapporteur for the Sabin Center for Climate Change Law, Research Chair for Law Students for Climate Accountability, and an Attorney of the New York State Bar. His work on climate law and governance has featured in Review of International, European & Comparative Law, the Cambridge Journal of Climate Research, the Hibernian Law Journal, and LSE Law Review among other publications, and Eoin has also published op-eds in the Irish Times, the Indian Express, and Irish Legal News among other outlets. He holds an LLB (Law) from Trinity College Dublin where he was elected a Foundation Scholar and an LLM (Law) from Harvard Law School.

Martin Kessler is the Executive Director of the Finance for Development Lab. Previously, he worked as an economist in the Development Cooperation Directorate of the OECD, focusing on trends of development finance for developing countries, and debt risks in particular. Prior to this, Martin worked at the World Bank on development dynamics in East Asia and held research positions at the Brussels-based economic think-tank Bruegel and the Peterson Institute for International Economics in Washington DC. His publications cover topics on the financial consequences of trade wars, hyper-globalization and economic convergence, as well as on the internationalization of the RMB. Martin is a graduate of the Harvard Kennedy School MPA/ID programme and the Paris School of Economics.

Kalpana Kochhar is Director, Development Policy and Finance at the Bill and Melinda Gates Foundation. Prior to taking this position in October 2021, she spent 33 years at the IMF, in various leadership positions in the Asia and Pacific Department, Strategy Policy and Review Department and the Research Department. Between 2010 and 2012, she was seconded to the World Bank as the Chief Economist for the South Asia Region of the World Bank. Ms. Kochhar's professional work has been focused on emerging markets and developing countries, jobs and inclusive growth, gender and inequality issues, structural reforms, and regional integration. She holds a PhD and an MA in Economics from Brown University and an MA in Economics from Delhi School of Economics in India. She also holds a BA in Economics from Madras University in India.

Arend Kulenkampff is an economist and policy expert specializing in sovereign debt, government technology, climate and nature finance. His career has spanned sovereign advisory, sovereign credit ratings, sovereign credit trading, macroeconomic research, insurance and disaster risk finance, and digital financial inclusion. Arend leads Innovative Finance for Nature and the Sustainable Sovereigns Debt Hub at NatureFinance. He was part of the sovereign advisory unit at Citigroup, where he helped governments manage a wide range of public financial management challenges. He also designed innovative tools for financial authorities while working at BFA Global. Arend was a Director of Sovereign Ratings at Fitch Ratings, a macroeconomist at Swiss Re, and an investment banker at Standard Bank. He holds a BA from McGill University and an MSc from the London School of Economics and Political Science.

Rachel Kyte is a Professor of Practice in Climate Policy at the Blavatnik School of Government and special representative on climate for the UK government. Rachel served as special representative of the UN secretary-general and chief executive officer of Sustainable Development for All (SEforALL). She previously was the World Bank Group vice president and special envoy for climate change, leading action on climate finance in the run-up to the Paris Agreement. Rachel served as an advisor to the UN secretary-general on climate action and the crisis response to the invasion of Ukraine, chaired the Rwandan Green Fund (FONERWA) and advised the UK government on COP26. Rachel is currently co-chair of the Voluntary Carbon Markets Integrity Initiative (VCMI) working to build high integrity voluntary carbon markets, member of the board Private Infrastructure Development Group with responsibility for ESG, and a member of the G20 Expert Group on MDB reform, appointed by the Government of India. Rachel is an advisor to General Atlantic's Beyond Net Zero fund and a member of the board of the Carbon Policy Initiative. Rachel is an advisor to AIIB, JBIC and served as a member of IDB-Invest's Blue Ribbon Commission.

Penny Mealy is a Senior Economist at the World Bank, a Research Associate at the Institute for New Economic Thinking and the Oxford Smith School of Enterprise and the Environment, and an External Applied Complexity Fellow at the Santa Fe Institute. Her work applies various methods from complex systems and data science to analyze the interrelated challenges of climate change and economic development. Penny completed a PhD at the Institute for New Economic Thinking at Oxford University. She has held various research fellow roles at the Oxford Martin School, the Oxford Smith School of Enterprise and the Environment, the Bennett Institute for Public Policy at Cambridge University, and SoDa Labs, Monash University.

Ravi Menon is Singapore's first Ambassador for Climate Action and Senior Adviser to the National Climate Change Secretariat at the Prime Minister's Office. He is Chairman of the GFANZ Asia-Pacific Advisory Board and the Global Finance and Technology Network, and a member of the GFANZ Principals Group. He also serves as a Trustee of the National University of Singapore (NUS) and Chairman of its Innovation and Enterprise Committee. Mr. Menon is Chairman of ImpactSG and a Board Member of The Majurity Trust. Prior to his current roles, Mr. Menon served for 36 years in the Singapore Public Service. As Managing Director of the Monetary Authority of Singapore (2011–23), he oversaw monetary and macroprudential policies, reformed the financial regulatory framework, and developed Singapore as a green finance center and a global FinTech hub. On the international front, he served as Chairman of the Network of Central Banks and Supervisors for Greening the Financial System and Chairman of the Financial Stability Board Standing Committee on Standards Implementation. As Permanent Secretary at the Ministry of Trade & Industry (2007–11), Mr. Menon helped to steer the economy during the global financial crisis. As Deputy Secretary at the Ministry of Finance (2003–07), he oversaw fiscal policy and government reserves. Mr. Menon holds a master's in public administration from Harvard University and a Bachelor of Social Science in Economics from NUS.

Justin Mundy is the Chairman of the Earthna Centre of the Qatar Foundation, the co-founder and co-Managing Director of MPS Global, Chairman of SLM Partners, Chairman of the Sustainability-linked Sovereign Debt Hub, Chairman of Cibus Fund's Advisory Board and Chairman of TRAFFIC International. From 2007 to 2018, he was the Director of HRH the then Prince of Wales's International Sustainability Unit (ISU). In the last few years, he has also been the Commonwealth Secretary General's Special Envoy, a Distinguished Fellow at the World Resources Institute and a Trustee of WWF-UK and of Global Canopy. Prior to his role at the ISU, he worked as an Adviser to the UK Government and the European Commission and had also held positions at Deutsche Bank and Aon, having previously managed the World Bank's forestry and biodiversity programs in Russia and Central Asia and having worked on first debt for nature swaps in the 1980s.

Mohamed Nasr is the Ambassador of Egypt to Austria and Permanent Representative to the UN and International Organizations in Vienna. Previously, he was the lead negotiator for the Climate Change Presidency Team for COP27 and Director of the Climate, Environment, and Sustainable Development Department in the Egyptian Ministry of Foreign Affairs, as well as a member of the senior management unit for organizing and managing COP27. Prior to his current role, he served as Ambassador to Somalia from 2019 to 2021 and as Counsellor at the Mission of Egypt in Geneva, responsible for the development portfolio. He also served in Egyptian missions and embassies in Australia and Togo. He has been part of the Egyptian delegation to climate negotiations since 2008, a member of the Lead Coordinators group for Africa since 2012, Chair of the African Group of Negotiators (AGN) in 2018–2019, and has coordinated the AGN Finance negotiating team under the UNFCCC process since 2010. He is also an adviser to Green Climate Fund African board members, a member of the Standing Committee of Finance, and a member of the Transitional Committee operationalizing the Loss and Damage Fund. He is a member of the official Egyptian delegation to the meetings of the African Ministers Responsible for the Environment (AMCEN) and the African Heads of State and Government on Climate Change. He was involved in the processes of establishing the African Renewable Energy Initiative and the Africa Adaptation Initiative. He served as a member of the Compliance Committee under the Kyoto Protocol and as a UNFCCC Bureau member. He also served as a member of Egyptian official delegations to WMO, UNDRR, WTO, BRS Conventions, UNEA, INC for Plastics, and UNCTAD, among others. He was a member of the core G77 team negotiating the Sendai Framework under UNDRR, the WMO Global Framework on Climate Services, and the UNCTAD strategic document UNCTAD16.

Dileimy Orozco is an Independent Advisor working on reimagining the role of finance in tackling climate change and enabling transformative action. She works closely with senior leaders across international and national institutions to influence financial reforms that support resilience, decarbonization, and inclusive growth. Her work spans diverse geographies and political contexts, including Latin America, Africa, Southeast Asia and the EU and UK. Previously, she worked at E3G, a climate change think-tank, leading the work on macroeconomics and economic governance, and was head of development finance in the COP26 Unit at the UK Cabinet Office. She has contributed to frameworks developed for the Coalition of Finance Ministers for Climate Action. She currently serves as a technical advisor to Grupo Financiamiento Climático para América Latina y el Caribe. Dileimy is currently one of the technical leads for the Circle of Finance Ministers' report on the Baku to Belém Roadmap, an initiative led by Brazil's Ministry of Finance that serves as a key input to COP30 Presidency.

Avinash Persaud is Special Advisor on Climate Change to the President of the Inter-American Development Bank. Persaud has over 30 years of experience in finance, public policy, and academia. Prior to this appointment in January 2024, he was Special Climate Envoy to the Prime Minister of Barbados and an architect of the "Bridgetown Initiative" that played an instrumental role in helping to set the international financial reform agenda in recent years. Persaud is a member of the High-Level Expert Group on Climate Finance of the COP26, 27, and 28 Presidencies and a member of the Independent Expert group on Debt, Nature and Climate, established by the Governments of Colombia, France, and Kenya. He previously served as Chairman of the Caribbean Community's Commission on the Economy and Commissioner of the UN Commission on Financial Reform. Prior to his public policy roles, Persaud was a senior executive at several major banks including J. P. Morgan, State Street and UBS. Persaud has authored multiple academic publications with particular emphasis on financial policy. An Emeritus Professor of Gresham College in the UK, he is 2024 Perry World Fellow at the University of Pennsylvania, former Nonresident Senior Fellow at the Peterson Institute and winner of the Jacques de Larosiere Award in Global Finance for his work on financial risk management and systemic crises.

Mohamed Farid Saleh has served as Chairman of Egypt's Financial Regulatory Authority (FRA) since August 2022 and is a Board Member at the Central Bank of Egypt. Internationally, he chairs IOSCO's

Growth and Emerging Markets Committee and serves as Vice Chair of the IOSCO Board, the GFANZ Africa Network Advisory Board, and Africa Reinsurance Corporation. Previously, he was Executive Chairman of the Egyptian Exchange, during which he held various regional and global leadership roles, including Chair of the Federation of Euro-Asian Stock Exchanges, Arab Federation of Capital Markets, and the Emerging Markets Working Group at the World Federation of Exchanges. He also served on the board of the African Securities Exchanges Association. Dr Farid worked with the World Bank Group as an External Consultant on Venture Capital and Financial Leasing. He also served as a visiting lecturer for Financial Markets, International Finance, and Financial Derivatives at the American University in Cairo and the Arab Academy for Science, Technology and Maritime Transport. Dr Farid holds a PhD in Financial Economics from Cardiff Metropolitan University; a master's in law in International Financial and Commercial Law from King's Collage London; an MSc in Quantitative Finance from Bayes Business School, City St George's, University of London; an MSc in Economics from York University, UK; and an MBA from the Arab Academy for Science, Technology and Maritime Transport, Egypt.

Miral Shehata is an independent economics researcher specializing in climate finance and financing for development, with a broader interest in economic policy. She has experience in economic development, public policy design, and macroeconomic modeling. Miral is the co-author of *Business, Government and the SDGs: The Role of Public-Private Engagement in Building a Sustainable Future*, which explores the intersection of public and private sector efforts in sustainable development. She has contributed to various publications on financing strategies for sustainable transitions and the role of governance in climate and development finance. Miral holds an MSc in Economics for Development from the University of Oxford and a BA in Economics from the University of Chicago.

Puninda Thind is Finance Nature Lead with the UN Climate Champions Team focused on catalyzing and mobilizing global finance sector action to address biodiversity loss and nature-related risks and opportunities. Puninda is deeply committed to building a sustainable, prosperous, equitable future. She has previously worked at the intersection of sustainable investing and climate resilience for 10+ years. She is also a member of the Global Shapers Community, an initiative of the World Economic Forum. Puninda has been previously recognized as one of Canada's top sustainability leaders, and as a Clean50 honoree for her contribution to the advancement of climate action. She holds a Bachelors of Environment and Business (Honors) from the University of Waterloo and an MSc Sustainability, Enterprise, and Environment from the University of Oxford.

Nidhi Upadhyaya is the Deputy Director for Global Policy and Finance with the Adaptation Finance and Policy pillar of the Atlantic Council's Climate Resilience Center. She leads the center's global policy and finance pillar and its engagement in India and South Asia. Prior to joining the Climate Resilience Center in 2019, Upadhyaya was an associate director at the Atlantic Council's South Asia Center. She contributed to the center's policy research initiatives and programmatic tasks. She has also held roles with the policy consulting firm, Bower Group Asia, and with the Indian business news channel ET NOW. As part of the United Nations' Race to Resilience campaign in 2021, she supported systems transformation solutions to achieve the campaign's goal of building the resilience of four billion people most vulnerable to climate change. Upadhyaya has contributed to publications on trade, climate finance, and resilience, including at the Atlantic Council and in collaboration with the Climate Policy Initiative. Originally from Mumbai, India, Upadhyaya graduated with a master's degree in international affairs from the George Washington University's Elliott School of International Affairs in 2017 and also holds an MBA in media with a post-graduate in journalism from India.

Simon Zadek is the co-founder and managing partner of Morphosis, an adaptation solutions business, and is Senior Advisor to the Paulson Institute and the Taskforce on Nature-Related Financial Disclosures and a member of the Steering Board of International Advisory Panel on Biodiversity Credits. Simon's work over four decades has focused on creating, catalyzing, and shaping markets and their enabling policy environment to address sustainable development goals. He has had many roles, including his founding leadership of NatureFinance and AccountAbility, his senior advisory roles on sustainable finance to the UN Secretary General and the World Economic Forum, his co-Chairing of China's first Green Finance Taskforce and steering of the G20's work on green finance under the Chinese, Argentinian and German Presidencies, to positions in leading academic institutions in China, Europe, the US, and Southern Africa. Simon is widely published including the award-winning book The Civil Corporation and most recently "Time to Plan for a World Beyond 1.5C". Dr Zadek holds a PhD in Economics.

Dina Zayed is a policy strategist, researcher, communicator, and facilitator. Her expertise straddles climate adaptation politics and finance, international development, and public participation in climate governance. An interdisciplinary social scientist and participatory action researcher, Dr Zayed is currently an independent consultant and advisor. She is an Associate Fellow at the Carboun Institute, the Middle East and North Africa's first independent climate and energy policy think tank. A participatory action researcher and practitioner, Dr Zayed is a former Program Director with the Climate Emergency Collaboration Group (CECG), a philanthropic pooled fund focused on leveraging multilateralism for greater and more just international climate ambition. She led CECG's work on climate impacts and resilience, as well as the organization's equity and inclusion strategy and grant making. She currently serves on the Editorial Advisory Council of Alliance Magazine, a leading nonprofit publication covering philanthropy and social investment worldwide. She is also a Board Member of ACTS Foundation Kenya, a community-based organization focused on promoting social justice, equality, and the protection of human rights through community-driven development. Dina holds a PhD from the Institute of Development studies, an MSc in Environmental Change and Management from the University of Oxford, and a BA in Political Science from the American University in Cairo.

Professor Nicholas Stern is the IG Patel Professor of Economics and Government, Chairman of the Grantham Research Institute on Climate Change and the Environment, and Head of the India Observatory at the London School of Economics. President of the British Academy, July 2013–2017, and was elected Fellow of the Royal Society in 2014. Professor Stern has held academic appointments in the UK at Oxford, Warwick, and the LSE and abroad, including at the Massachusetts Institute of Technology, the Ecole Polytechnique and the Collège de France in Paris, the Indian Statistical Institute in Bangalore and Delhi, and the People–s University of China in Beijing. He was Chief Economist of the European Bank for Reconstruction and Development, 1994–1999, and Chief Economist and Senior Vice President at the World Bank, 2000–2003. He was Second Permanent Secretary to Her Majesty's Treasury from 2003–2005; Director of Policy and Research for the Prime Minister's Commission for Africa from 2004–2005; Head of the Stern Review on the Economics of Climate Change, published in 2006; and Head of the Government Economic Service from 2003–2007. He was knighted for services to economics in 2004, made a cross-bench life peer as Baron Stern of Brentford in 2007, and appointed Companion of Honour for services to economics, international relations, and tackling climate change in 2017. He has published more than 15 books and 100 articles. He holds 13 honorary degrees and has received the Blue Planet Prize (2009), the BBVA Foundation Frontiers of Knowledge Award (2010), the Leontief Prize (2010), and the Schumpeter Award (2015), amongst many others.

Mahmoud Mohieldin

Climate and Development Finance: Insufficient, Inefficient, and Unfair

Abstract: This introductory chapter sets the stage for a critical examination of the global climate finance architecture, arguing for urgent action to reform the existing institutions, standards, and practices that govern climate finance flows on the international and national levels. Despite growing global awareness of the climate crisis and rising climate-related investments, current climate finance remains insufficient, inefficient, and unfair – particularly for developing countries that are most vulnerable to climate impacts but least responsible for emissions. The chapter highlights the massive and rising financial needs for mitigation, adaptation, loss and damage, and nature-positive development, which far outpace available resources. It examines systemic inefficiencies – such as complex access procedures, prolonged disbursement timelines, and limited institutional capacity – and inequities in the distribution of climate finance. The chapter calls for a new framework that integrates public and private finance, aligns international and national financial reforms, and centers justice and equity. It introduces the book's core premise: transformative action – through policy reform, institutional redesign, and innovative financial instruments – is essential to bridge the climate finance gap and achieve a sufficient, efficient, and just climate response within an integrated framework for development that captures the essence of the relation between climate and development finance.

Keywords: Climate finance, Emerging markets and developing economies, Debt, Adaptation, Loss and damage, Global financial architecture

Introduction

Finance is an indispensable enabler in addressing the climate crisis. Although scientific evidence confirms that climate change is accelerating – and that the window of opportunity to secure a sustainable future is rapidly closing – climate finance remains insufficient, inefficient, and inequitable (Lewis 2022).

At the national level, the success of climate policies and actions depends on mobilizing adequate financial resources, which often exceed the capacities of most developing countries. Within the multilateral climate process, climate finance remains a central pillar of negotiations at the annual Conferences of the Parties (COP) to the United Nations Framework Convention on Climate Change (UNFCCC), yet it continues to be one of the most contentious topics.

In recent years, the complexities associated with articulating and implementing climate finance policies – both nationally and internationally – have been further exacerbated by challenging geopolitical conditions. These have negatively impacted climate finance budgets and official development assistance flows. Moreover, the current silent debt crisis in low- and middle-income countries imposes additional constraints on prioritizing climate finance, as shrinking fiscal space limits both climate- and development-related expenditures (Mohieldin 2024).

This book is informed by the ongoing, often complex discussions surrounding the challenges of climate finance. Drawing on experiences as the United Nations Special Envoy on Financing the 2030 Sustainable Development Agenda since 2020, the UN Climate Change High-Level Champion for COP27, a facilitator of the second replenishment process of the Green Climate Fund (GCF), Chair of the Glasgow Financial Alliance for Net Zero (GFANZ) Africa Network Advisory Board, and, more recently, leading a high-level expert group appointed by the UN Secretary-General to advance policy responses to the global debt crisis, the editor brings a deeply engaged and nuanced perspective to the topic.

Through its 21 chapters, this book argues that a practical climate finance framework must evolve to incorporate structural changes, policy reforms, and innovative solutions aimed at transforming the global climate finance architecture. This architecture includes the network of institutions, standards, and practices that govern both international and national climate finance flows.

A critical yet often underexplored dimension is the intersection of climate finance, development finance, and policy formulation. The book seeks to examine this interface by proposing a range of interventions – across multiple levels – for mobilizing and deploying climate finance at the appropriate scale and in the appropriate form, with particular emphasis on efficiency, accessibility, affordability, and equity. The various chapters highlight the many opportunities that must be leveraged to overcome the current impasse.

Insufficiency

Despite the multiplicity of definitions in use for climate finance – particularly in the context of aggregate accounting and reporting – the inadequacy of current climate finance flows to effectively address the climate crisis is well-established.

Global climate finance has grown in recent years. According to the Climate Policy Initiative (CPI), global climate finance reached approximately USD 1.46 trillion in 2022, up from USD 653 billion in 2019/2020 (CPI 2023; CPI 2024). However, this still falls significantly short of the estimated needs.[1] CPI projects that annual climate finance requirements will rise steadily from USD 8.1 to 9 trillion[2] through 2030. The Independent High-Level Expert Group on Climate Finance (IHLEG) estimates a need for USD 5.8–6.2 trillion annually by 2030 – comprising USD 2.4–2.6 trillion in advanced economies, USD 1.1 trillion in China, and USD 2.3–2.5 trillion in emerging markets and developing economies (EMDEs) excluding China[3] (Bhattacharya et al. 2024).

Financial requirements reported in the Nationally Determined Contributions (NDCs) of developing countries are estimated at USD 5.1–6.8 trillion through 2030 (UNFCCC 2024a, para. 3). COP29 called for climate finance to developing countries to scale up to at least USD 1.3 trillion annually by 2035 (UNFCCC 2024a, para. 7). Additionally, around USD 4.3 trillion per year must be invested in clean energy in developing countries until 2030, increasing to USD 5 trillion annually from 2030 to 2050 to reach net-zero emissions by mid-century (IEA 2023).

Adaptation finance needs in developing countries are estimated at USD 215–387 billion per year until 2030 – an amount 10–18 times greater than current international public finance flows (UNEP 2023, 30). For loss and damage finance, estimates place the required funding at USD 300 billion annually by 2030, rising to over USD 400 billion by 2035 (Bhattacharya et al. 2024). The establishment and operationalization of the new funding arrangements, including a dedicated fund for loss and damage, represents a critical milestone in bridging this gap. In parallel, to avoid further nature loss, global nature finance flows must rise to USD 400 billion per year by 2030, with the majority allocated to EMDEs (Bhattacharya et al. 2024).

Bhattacharya et al. (2024) estimates that from 2030 to 2035, climate finance must increase to USD 3.1–3.7 trillion annually to meet intensifying challenges. CPI further projects that global climate finance needs will exceed USD 10 trillion per year from 2031 to 2050 (CPI 2023). Any failure to meet climate investment needs before 2030 will compound financial pressures in the subsequent decades – a cost that must be avoided.

---

1 Reports containing an estimate of needs include the: UNFCCC Standing Committee on Finance Needs Determination Report, the Independent High-Level Expert Group on Climate Finance (IHLEG) report, previous acknowledgements in G20 declarations, and the UN Environment Programme Adaptation Finance Gap Report.

2 According to COP28 UAE leaders Global Climate Finance Framework, investing USD 5–7 trillion annually in greening the global economy by 2030 will be critical to achieving climate goals.

3 According to the third report of the Independent High-Level Expert Group on Climate Finance (IHLEG), the lower estimates reflect the investment outcomes that are achievable given the real-world constraints and challenges associated with mobilizing resources and implementing climate projects (Bhattacharya et al. 2024).

Inefficiency

The increasing number of climate funding sources does not necessarily translate into easier access for developing countries (The Commonwealth Secretariat 2022). Multiple constraints, challenges, systemic inequities, and barriers hinder access to climate finance – both concessional and non-concessional – including the high cost of capital, co-financing requirements, and burdensome application processes (UNFCCC 2024a, para. 21). Inefficiency is further evident in the protracted funding process, which can take several years from agreement to disbursement. This is particularly problematic when funds are needed urgently for adaptation, resilience, and loss and damage.

Administrative and bureaucratic deficiencies within financial institutions also contribute to delays. Moreover, limited human, institutional, and technical capacities in many developing countries to design and advance project proposals through complex stages exacerbate these delays (The Commonwealth Secretariat 2022). Multilateral climate funds must therefore assume greater responsibility in building the capacities of developing countries.

Heavily indebted countries face compounded difficulties in accessing climate-related funds. Addressing the burden of existing debt is thus vital to improving access to climate finance. Enhanced coordination among climate finance actors is needed to improve efficiency and streamline access to bilateral, regional, and multilateral finance for developing countries (UNFCCC 2024a, para. 21). Priority must be given to improving the predictability, flexibility, transparency, affordability, and speed of disbursement.

Unfairness

The current climate finance landscape is unfair, particularly due to the inequitable geographical distribution of international financial flows. Moreover, the growth in global climate finance is uneven across mitigation, adaptation, and loss and damage, with the majority focused on mitigation within G20 countries (Guilanpour, Kosma, and Pourarkin 2024).

The United States, Canada, East Asia and the Pacific, and Western Europe together account for 84% of total climate finance (CPI 2023). The observed growth in global climate finance largely stems from significant increases in clean energy investments in advanced economies and China, which attracted 85% of total investments in this sector. In contrast, EMDEs – home to two-thirds of the global population and abundant in solar, wind, and critical mineral resources – received just 15% (IEA 2024).

Despite possessing the highest solar potential globally, the Middle East and Africa accounted for less than 3% of clean energy investment in 2023 (Bhattacharya et al. 2024). To rebalance the allocation of financial resources, adaptation finance must be significantly scaled up to support the urgent need for resilience-building in developing countries (UNFCCC 2024b, paras. 86, 100). Additionally, there remains a significant finance gap in addressing the increasing scale and frequency of loss and damage and the associated economic and noneconomic impacts (UNFCCC 2024b, para. 128).

With regard to nature finance, although over 70% of the global investment need in natural capital is concentrated in EMDEs, excluding China, only 20% of finance flows are directed to these countries (Center for Global Commons 2023).

Rising to the Climate Finance Challenge: Transformative Action Is Urgently Needed

This book focuses particularly on the dilemmas faced by countries in the Global South. These countries have contributed the least to the climate crisis, yet they are on the front lines, experiencing its most severe impacts – an unjust and harsh irony. The financial requirements for fostering climate-resilient, low greenhouse gas emission and nature-positive development far exceed the capacities of most developing countries. These nations face a substantial gap between available and required climate finance flows to meet their NDCs – a gap that must be urgently bridged.

While there is sufficient global capital to close the investment gap, that capital must be redirected toward climate action (UNFCCC 2024a, para. 4). Mobilizing the necessary finance to confront the climate emergency demands leveraging the synergies across multiple sources: local, national, regional, and global finance; public and private sectors; and concessional – particularly for adaptation and loss and damage in developing countries – and non-concessional finance. Innovative financial instruments must be explored, utilized, and scaled up. These include first-loss instruments, guarantees, local currency financing, foreign exchange risk hedging tools, voluntary carbon markets, and debt-for-climate swaps.

Developing countries encounter numerous obstacles and disincentives that constrain their ability to close the climate investment gap. These include compounded macroeconomic challenges, high capital costs, limited fiscal space, unprecedented debt levels, and high transaction costs and conditionalities for accessing climate finance (UNFCCC 2024a, para. 6). These barriers help explain why developed countries significantly outperform developing countries in mobilizing domestic resources for climate action (CPI 2023) and why the share of international climate finance received by developing countries remains disproportionately low.

A new framework for action is urgently required to overcome the limitations of the existing climate finance architecture – which includes the institutions, standards, and practices governing international and national climate finance flows. Reforming both the international financial architecture and national-level climate finance policies is essential. These reforms must be complementary and indispensable to catalyzing climate investment in developing countries.

At the international level, the Paris Agreement and its core principles of justice, equity, and common but differentiated responsibilities and respective capabilities necessitate that developed countries provide financial resources to assist developing nations. International public finance – both concessional and non-concessional[4] – must ensure that the growing momentum for climate investment is not restricted to advanced economies. Instead, they should prioritize countries that are particularly vulnerable to climate change and face significant capacity constraints. These funds must also focus on areas of climate impact that do not attract sufficient private investment, particularly adaptation and loss and damage. Addressing the uneven distribution of finance across mitigation, adaptation, and loss and damage is critical.

Nonetheless, delineating financial responsibilities and commitments among developed countries remains a politically sensitive issue in climate negotiations. In 2009, developed countries pledged to mobilize USD 100 billion annually to support climate action in developing countries. Setting a new climate finance target under the multilateral regime has proven contentious, with key disagreements over burden sharing – advocated by developing countries to ensure accountability – and expanding the contributor base, as some developed countries argue that other economies now have the capacity and responsibility to contribute (Pettinotti, Kamninga, and Colenbrander 2024, 1–4).

At COP29, following three years of negotiations on the New Collective Quantified Goal on Climate Finance (NCQG), parties agreed to set a target of at least USD 300 billion per year by 2035 for developing countries, to be drawn from a wide range of sources – public and private, bilateral, and multilateral – with developed countries taking the lead (UNFCCC 2024a, para. 8). This new target must act as a catalyst for climate action while addressing the delivery failures of the previous USD 100 billion commitment. Although public international climate finance constitutes only a small share of the total solution, it is vital to advancing the principles of justice, equity, and common but differentiated responsibilities, and to leveraging additional private investment in developing countries (Guilanpour, Kosma, and Pourarkin 2024, 6).

Transformative action is also required in the realm of debt relief, suspension, and restructuring, along with expansion of concessional financing instruments. These steps are essential to free up fiscal space and reduce risk for developing nations. Multilateral development banks (MDBs) must align their operational models and financing tools with the demands of addressing the climate crisis. Similarly, multilateral cli-

---

4 Public domestic finance is driven by national budgets, public international finance is driven by international public funding, including grants as well as bilateral and multilateral contributions, private domestic finance is driven by access to the domestic financial system, and private international finance is driven by domestic policies and international support.

mate funds should take decisive action to enhance coherence, complementarity, streamlining, and access.

Any reforms to the international financial architecture must account for the developmental context of climate goals and the principle of a just transition. Economic growth and climate action must go hand in hand. No country should be forced to choose between eradicating poverty and achieving financial stability on one hand, and taking climate action on the other.

At the national level, creating a supportive macroeconomic environment is essential to boosting public domestic resource mobilization and increasing both domestic and international private sector engagement. Aligning policies, laws, and regulatory frameworks with climate finance objectives is also critical. The World Bank has estimated that an additional 2.7 percentage points of GDP must be mobilized domestically by 2030 to meet climate financing needs (World Bank Group 2023). Unlocking this potential will help create the fiscal space necessary for increased climate investment.

Given the limitations of public sector financing and donor contributions, private finance is indispensable for achieving the scale of investment required for climate-resilient and low-carbon development. However, developed countries are far more successful in mobilizing private finance. In 2023, less than 3% of global climate finance – around USD 30 billion – went to or within Least Developed Countries (LDCs), while only 15% went to or within EMDEs, excluding China (CPI 2023).

Scope of the Book

Climate finance in this book covers local, national, regional, and global financing that supports mitigation, adaptation, resilience, and loss and damage actions required to address the adverse impacts of climate change. The book provides an understanding of concepts and tools that address a broad range of issues within climate finance, including adaptation, mitigation, loss and damage, nature finance, domestic resource mobilization, international climate funds, multilateral development banks (MDBs), climate technology, nature-based solutions, debt-for-climate swaps, blended finance, carbon markets, green bonds, carbon credits, and climate risk insurance.

This volume brings together the perspectives, experiences, and knowledge of internationally renowned practitioners and experts from various geographical and professional backgrounds who are directly involved in exploring solutions to the bottlenecks affecting climate financial flows. The diversity of contributions melds practice, theory, and research into a coherent and critical analysis of climate finance conundrums and solutions.

The book provides policymakers and practitioners in the public and private sectors, philanthropic organizations, and civil society – those involved in and concerned with the good governance of climate finance – with a toolkit of actions for mobilizing the necessary financial resources. These actions emerge from a wide variety of sources, instruments, and channels, drawing from lessons learned through actual implementation. Real-world case studies – spanning global, regional, national, and local climate finance initiatives – and empirical evidence are integrated across the chapters to offer practical strategies and actionable solutions. These initiatives reflect the latest shifts in the policies and practices of institutions involved in climate finance, as well as the evolving priorities of international climate finance negotiators.

The book aims to advance debates with global, regional, national, and local relevance by offering critical perspectives that illuminate innovative policy solutions. These solutions are intended to support the articulation of an effective and equitable approach to climate finance. Accordingly, the book serves as a resource for policymakers, practitioners, and researchers working or conducting research in climate and development finance, particularly those seeking practical, implementable insights to foster an enabling and effective ecosystem for the mobilization of climate finance.

Structure of the Book

The book is divided into four thematic parts. *Part One* presents an integrated approach to climate and development finance. In Chapter 1, *"Different Paths, Same Goals: A Transition Approach to Climate and Development Finance"*, Susanna Gable and Kalpana Kochhar propose a methodology for prioritizing investments and allocating resources to address the intertwined challenges of development, climate mitigation, and adaptation. The chapter outlines a transition framework developed by the Gates Foundation and assesses the investments required to achieve global development and climate goals. It highlights the importance of aligning financing tools with investments based on their risk-adjusted returns and expected timeframes. Additionally, it introduces key principles to enhance coordination, efficiency, and the scaling up of climate and development funding.

Technological innovation has, in recent years, shifted the dynamics of addressing climate change. The greatest challenge now lies in ensuring that these technologies reach the countries that need them most, at the lowest possible cost. In Chapter 2, *"Working Together to Promote Greener and Better Technologies for All"*, Stéphane Hallegatte and Penny Mealy discuss emerging global trends reshaping the development and deployment of green technologies. The chapter emphasizes the need for global cooperation to overcome current challenges in technological innovation and diffusion, especially regarding R&D funding, experimentation, and knowledge sharing. It also underscores the need for international cooperation in green industrial policies and trade measures.

In Chapter 3, titled *"A Compass to Guide Climate Finance Integrity"*, Dileimy Orozco, Barbara Buchner, and Rachel Kyte examine the concept of climate finance integrity, identify systemic barriers to its implementation, and analyze ongoing efforts to enhance accountability within a fragmented and complex financial ecosystem. Additionally, the chapter introduces a pragmatic tool designed to sustain integrity by tracking progress and aligning reform efforts, thereby fostering momentum. The chapter argues that achieving integrity will require a coordinated, whole-of-system approach to redirect global financial flows toward climate and the Sustainable Development Goals, laying the foundation for a more resilient and prosperous future.

In Chapter 4, titled *"Enhancing Transparency and Accountability in Climate Finance Mobilization from Developed to Developing Countries"*, Clara B. Gurresø and Eoin Jackson explore the discrepancy between reported climate finance flows from developed countries and the actual needs of developing countries. They critique the current reporting systems and offer recommendations for improving transparency and accountability.

Part Two focuses on financing climate action, specifically by addressing the financing of mitigation, adaptation, nature, and loss and damage.

In Chapter 5, *"Financing Mitigation, Including Just Energy Transitions"*, Amr Osama Abdel-Aziz and Nermin Eltouny examine current trends and disparities in the deployment of mitigation technologies and investments. They explore opportunities to scale up these investments and barriers to finance – particularly in developing countries. The chapter highlights challenges such as the cost of capital, high upfront investment requirements, public debt burdens, insufficient public financing, weak domestic resource mobilization, and limited private-sector involvement. It also addresses the negative impacts on fossil fuel-based economies and the cost of energy transitions, while proposing a range of solutions to overcome these hurdles.

In Chapter 6, *"Financing the New Adaptation Economy"*, Sabrina Bachrach, with Nidhi Upadhyaya, Jorge Gastelumendi, Juan José Guzmán Ayala, and Puninda Thind, defines adaptation and resilience finance, arguing that current investment levels are inadequate. The authors challenge three prevailing narratives: that the private sector is absent from adaptation and resilience efforts; that adaptation is not a systemic issue; and that adaptation represents a burden rather than an opportunity. By addressing these misperceptions, the chapter identifies actionable steps to scale up adaptation finance. It concludes with a forward-looking vision for a financial system capable of effectively mobilizing adaptation and resilience finance and provides recommendations for achieving this goal.

Nature and climate crises are, in many ways, two sides of the same coin. In Chapter 7, *"Financing a Global Nature-Positive Economy"*, Razan Khalifa Al Mubarak and Simon Zadek argue for an urgent transformation toward a nature-positive economy by aligning global financial flows with the goals of the Global Biodiversity Framework. The chapter discusses the challenges to this transformation and proposes a series of interventions to facilitate alignment.

The scale of funding required to address climate-induced losses and damages is not currently matched by sufficient, harmonized, and predictable financial flows. In

Chapter 8, titled *"Financing Loss and Damage*, Mohamed Nasr and Zaheer Fakir define the scope of loss and damage, highlight the realities of climate-related impacts, and provide an overview of how international negotiations have addressed the issue. The chapter discusses the establishment and operationalization of the Loss and Damage Fund and concludes with recommendations to ensure the fund's successful implementation.

Part Three presents several financing tools to close the climate finance gap, including domestic resource mobilization, debt management, debt swaps, de-risking instruments, support from MDBs, voluntary carbon markets, and philanthropic capital.

In Chapter 9, titled *"Domestic Resource Mobilization"*, Navid Hanif highlights a broad range of fiscal, monetary, administrative, capacity-building, and regulatory measures necessary to fully leverage domestic resources for climate action. He argues that an enabling international economic and financial environment, along with targeted development cooperation, is crucial to support countries in achieving their full potential.

In Chapter 10 titled, *"Managing Debt Vulnerabilities to Allow for Climate Action"*, Martin Kessler provides an updated assessment of debt challenges amid increasing climate investment needs. He outlines the financing conditions developing countries are likely to face and their impact on debt projections. The chapter identifies two main policy challenges: rising debt service flows triggering concerns from the IMF and World Bank and reduced fiscal space. Kessler explores options for debt management in high-risk countries.

Jean-Paul Adam, Justin Mundy, and Arend Kulenkampff, in Chapter 11, titled *"Connecting the Virtuous Circle: From Debt-for-Development Swaps to Sustainability-Linked Sovereign Finance"*, advocate for a comprehensive approach to the debt crisis. They argue that debt swaps are effective in aligning sovereign finance with the SDGs and climate goals and call for their integration into a broader, programmatic framework that includes diverse finance instruments and aligns with public financial management systems.

Chapter 12, titled *"De-risking Macro-Finance and Unblocking the Green Transition in Emerging Economies"*, by Avinash D. Persaud, examines the high cost of capital in developing countries. He attributes this to macroeconomic risks such as sovereign credit ratings and currency volatility. Persaud emphasizes the need to address both micro-level project risks and systemic macro risks and proposes integrated platforms involving governments, MDBs, and financial markets to scale up investment in renewable energy.

In Chapter 13, titled *"Multilateral Development Banks' Support for Climate Action: A Story of Evolution, Rather than Revolution"*, Stephen Hammer provides an overview of how MDBs have established climate finance targets and aligned with the Paris Agreement, with varying goals based on sectoral needs and country priorities. The chapter discusses critiques of the MDBs' climate performance and concludes by recognizing their progress while emphasizing the need for transformative measures, including shifts in funding priorities, stricter alignment criteria, and a greater focus on adaptation and resilience.

In Chapter 14, titled *"What Can MDBs Do for Climate Adaptation?"*, Adriana Erthal Abdenur argues that MDBs can and should be part of the solution by improving the scale, access, effectiveness, and equity of adaptation finance.

Chapter 15, titled *"Voluntary Carbon Markets: Promise or Peril in Global Climate Action"*, by Mohamed Farid Saleh, explores the potential of carbon markets in mobilizing finance for climate action. He begins with an examination of cooperation mechanisms under Article 6 of the Paris Agreement, outlining foundational principles of international carbon trading. The chapter then surveys emerging trends in voluntary carbon markets (VCMs), assesses key challenges, and discusses Egypt's Regional Carbon Frontier and the role of its Financial Regulatory Authority in creating a regulated VCM.

In Chapter 16, titled *"Shaken or Stirred? Mobilizing Philanthropy for Climate Finance"*, Dina Zayed contends that, in the face of a widening international climate finance gap, philanthropy has a significant role to play in unlocking finance flows. Drawing on interviews with philanthropic leaders and her own experience, Zayed examines various forms of philanthropic interventions and proposes a basic typology of current approaches.

Part Four shifts the focus to regional and local climate finance initiatives.

In Chapter 17, titled *"The Regional Platforms for Climate Projects (RPCP): Lessons Learned for Mobilizing Climate Finance for Tangible Climate Projects"*, Sagarika Chatterjee argues that climate finance discussions often neglect regional priorities and investment opportunities. She explains how the RPCP initiative fosters collaboration among regional public and private stakeholders and highlights key outcomes and lessons from its implementation.

In Chapter 18, titled *"GFANZ Regional Networks for Africa, Asia-Pacific, and Latin America & the Caribbean"*, Patricia Espinosa, Ravi Menon, and Mahmoud Mohieldin review the work of the three regional networks of the Glasgow Financial Alliance for Net Zero (GFANZ), a private-sector-led initiative aiming to mobilize capital and remove investment barriers in the global transition.

In Chapter 19, titled *"Mobilizing Local Climate Finance"*, Hisham Badr presents Egypt's "National Initiative for Smart Green Projects". He outlines its objectives, structure, achievements, and challenges in mobilizing investments for local climate action.

We cannot afford the cost of delay in meeting climate investment needs. The longer the delay, the higher the toll on our planet and livelihoods.

The concluding chapter titled *"Towards Sufficient, Efficient, and Just Climate and Development Finance"*, outlines a new policy and practical framework for effectively mobilizing climate finance. This framework integrates the tools, principles, and instruments discussed throughout the book and underscores the roles of governments, local authorities, MDBs, climate funds, and philanthropic institutions. Its goal is to reinvigorate confidence that climate finance will be available, accessible, and affordable – supporting a low-carbon, climate-resilient, and nature-positive future.

References

Bhattacharya, Amar, Vera Songwe, Eléonore Soubeyran, and Nicholas Stern. 2024. *Raising Ambition and Accelerating Delivery of Climate Finance*. London: Grantham Research Institute on Climate Change and the Environment, London School of Economics and Political Science.

Center for Global Commons. 2023. *Financing Nature: A Transformative Action Agenda – A Discussion Paper*. December 2023. Accessed December 16, 2024. https://sdgtransformationcenter.org/news/nature-finance.

Climate Policy Initiative (CPI). 2023. *Global Landscape of Climate Finance 2023*. November 2023. Accessed December 16, 2024. https://www.climatepolicyinitiative.org/wp-content/uploads/2023/11/Global-Landscape-of-Climate-Finance-2023.pdf

Climate Policy Initiative (CPI). 2024. *Global Landscape of Climate Finance 2024: Insights for COP29*. October 2024. Accessed January 3, 2025. https://www.climatepolicyinitiative.org/publication/global-landscape-of-climate-finance-2024/

Guilanpour, Kaveh, Eda Kosma, and Leila Pourarkin. 2024. *Rising to the Climate Finance Challenge*. Center for Climate and Energy Solutions. September 2024. Accessed January 3, 2025. https://www.c2es.org/wp-content/uploads/2024/04/rising-to-the-climate-finance-challenge.pdf.

International Energy Agency (IEA). 2023. *World Energy Investment 2023*. Paris: International Energy Agency. https://www.iea.org/reports/world-energy-investment-2023.

International Energy Agency (IEA). 2024. *World Energy Outlook 2024*. Paris: International Energy Agency. https://www.iea.org/reports/world-energy-outlook-2024.

Lewis, Aidan. 2022. "Egypt Climate Champion Calls for New Metric on Climate Finance." *Reuters*, September 12, 2022. Accessed January 3, 2025. https://www.reuters.com/world/middle-east/egypt-climate-champion-calls-new-metric-climate-finance-2022-09-12/

Mohieldin, Mahmoud. 2024. "Dealing with the Bane of Debt." *Ahram Online*, December 10, 2024. Accessed January 8, 2025. https://english.ahram.org.eg/NewsContentP/50/536744/AlAhram-Weekly/Dealing-with-the-bane-of-debt.aspx

Pettinotti, Laetitia, Tony Kamninga, and Sarah Colenbrander. 2024. "A Fair Share of Climate Finance? The Collective Aspects of the New Collective Quantified Goal." ODI Working Paper. London: ODI. https://odi.org/en/publications/a-fair-share-of-climate-finance-the-collective-aspects-of-the-ncqg.

The Commonwealth Secretariat. 2022. *Toolkit to Enhance Access to Climate Finance: A Commonwealth Practical Guide*. March 17, 2022. Accessed December 11, 2024. https://unfccc.int/documents/461219.

UNFCCC. Conference of the Parties serving as the meeting of the Parties to the Paris Agreement (CMA). 2024a. *Draft decision -/CMA.6: New collective quantified goal on climate finance*. FCCC/PA/CMA/2024/L.22. United Nations Framework Convention on Climate Change. November 24, 2024. Accessed January 2, 2025. https://unfccc.int/sites/default/files/resource/cma2024_L22_adv.pdf.

UNFCCC. Conference of the Parties serving as the meeting of the Parties to the Paris Agreement (CMA). 2024b. *Decision 1/CMA.5: Outcome of the First Global Stocktake*. Report of the Conference of the Parties serving as the meeting of the Parties to the Paris Agreement on its fifth session, held in the United Arab Emirates from 30 November to 13 December 2023. FCCC/PA/CMA/2023/16/Add.1. March 15, 2024. Accessed January 2, 2025. https://unfccc.int/documents/636132.

United Nations Environment Programme (UNEP). 2023. *Adaptation Gap Report 2023: Underfinanced. Underprepared. Inadequate investment and planning on climate adaptation leaves world exposed.* Nairobi: United Nations Environment Programme. https://doi.org/10.59117/20.500.11822/43796.

World Bank Group. 2023. *The Big Push for Transformation through Climate and Development: Recommendations of the High-Level Advisory Group on Sustainable and Inclusive Recovery and Growth.* Washington, DC: World Bank.

Part One: **Development and Climate Finance: An Integrated Approach**

Susanna Gable and Kalpana Kochhar

Chapter 1
Different Paths, Same Goals: A Transition Approach to Climate and Development Finance

Abstract: Countries' economic policies and investment priorities change as they achieve development milestones and transition to higher levels of income, as does the available mix of financing flows. Today, two factors are complicating this picture. First, all countries – advanced and developing – have to find a new playbook that reduces dependence on activities that generate unsustainable amounts of greenhouse gas emissions. Second, public financing is severely constrained, with governments facing multiple urgent demands arising from recent shocks. Against this background, the chapter highlights the need for a development and climate transition financing framework that: (i) allows countries to prioritize investments that are needed to improve the lives of people, while adapting to climate change and safeguarding the planet; and (ii) provides the basis for discussions on not only how to mobilize additional resources but also how to allocate scarce resources to these different investments, based on the sector in question and the level of development of the country. This framework is relevant to low-income countries as well as middle- and high-income countries, allowing for different pathways, depending on the starting point and capabilities, without compromising the global goals of development, poverty reduction, building climate resilience, and limiting future climate change. The framework also highlights potential co-benefits and trade-offs of different types of investment over time and how different types of financing flows and instruments create opportunities as countries develop. The chapter disaggregates the debate for each country's income group, from the general level to the sector level, spells out key actions needed for development, mitigation, and adaptation, and emphasizes the connection to different financing flows, modalities, and instruments.

Keywords: Sustainable Development Goals, Development finance, Poverty reduction, Climate adaptation, Climate mitigation, Economic transition

Introduction

Over the past two decades, the global community has convened on multiple occasions to establish ambitious goals for development and climate change. Policymakers worldwide face three critical but interlinked imperatives. First, they must accelerate economic development and poverty reduction, while meeting the associated Sustainable Development Goals (SDGs). Second, they need to mitigate the burden of climate change resulting from past emissions, particularly those impacts that disproportionately affect the poorest populations and lower-income economies. Third, global emissions of greenhouse gases must be significantly reduced, in alignment with the Paris Agreement.

Despite some progress on all three imperatives, the pace has not been sufficient to achieve the agreed global targets. A major constraint has been the persistent shortfall in funding required to meet these goals. The annual SDG funding gap has risen dramatically, from an estimated USD 2.5 trillion in 2014 to USD 4.2 trillion in 2023. This increase reflects setbacks in development caused by the COVID-19 pandemic, the shocks to food and fuel prices, and the intensification of climate-related disasters (United Nations, Inter-agency Task Force on Financing for Sustainable Development 2024; UNCTAD 2023). Public finance is increasingly constrained as donor governments face tight fiscal conditions and competing demands on their aid budgets (Kenny and Gehan 2023). Simultaneously, public funding in developing countries is under significant pressure, compounded by a sharp rise in global interest rates that has made market financing more expensive. Lastly, the policy, regulatory, and institutional changes necessary for sustainable progress, particularly in low- and lower-middle-income countries (LICs and LMICs), have been slow to materialize. Addressing these challenges requires a multipronged strategy: increased financing, more efficient allocation of resources, stronger and sustained policy reforms in LICs and LMICs, and accelerated innovation to reduce the costs of low-carbon economic activity.

The global discourse on resource allocation has become increasingly polarized, often pitting advocates for climate action against proponents of development in a zero-sum competition for scarce resources. This polarization manifests in two primary ways. First, policymakers, donors, and commentators frequently fail to account for the varying stages of development across countries, overlooking the fact that a one-size-fits-all approach is unlikely to succeed. The recognition of differing country contexts is embedded in both the SDGs and the Paris Agreement, which emphasizes the primacy of national priorities. Second, even within individual countries, climate and development priorities are often perceived as competing objectives. This framing overlooks opportunities for synergistic investments and the need to analyze potential trade-offs carefully. Addressing these dynamics is crucial to advancing global goals with urgency and efficiency.

We need a framework for decision-making that enables all countries to view themselves as integral parts of the global system, both in selecting investments to achieve global goals and in financing those investments. Crucially, in the face of financing constraints, progress toward global goals necessitates acknowledging that countries are at varying stages of economic development. Consequently, their pathways and urgency in addressing both development and climate goals will differ.

This chapter builds upon the Gates Foundation's framework for development and climate finance, offering a methodology to prioritize investments and allocate resources to address the intertwined challenges of development, climate mitigation, and adaptation. It begins by outlining the Foundation's transition framework, followed by an evaluation of the investments required to achieve global development and climate objectives. The chapter underscores the importance of aligning financing mechanisms with investments, considering their risk-adjusted returns and expected timeframes. Furthermore, it introduces key principles to enhance coordination, efficiency, and scalability in climate and development funding. The chapter concludes by stressing the necessity of recognizing countries' diverse priorities, capacities, and access to financing across the development and climate spectrum, as these factors are essential for driving meaningful global change.

Toward a Fit-for-Purpose Financing Framework

The Gates Foundation's paper, *Climate and Development Finance: A Transition Framework for All* (Gable et al. 2023; Gates Foundation 2023), advocates for a "fit-for-purpose" financing framework to guide the allocation of resources for development, climate mitigation, and climate adaptation. This framework emphasizes sensitivity to a country's position along the continuum from low- to high-income status as they implement policies and projects aimed at accelerating progress on three critical global imperatives: economic development, transitioning to a green economy, and building resilience to current and future climate risks. The paper also argues that countries' priorities should shape their policies within the boundaries of these global imperatives. Furthermore, different types of financing flows must align with the nature of investments, taking into account the availability of alternative financing sources and the risk–return profiles of investments.

This chapter builds on these ideas, drawing on the follow-up paper, *Principles for Allocating Finance for Development and Climate Goals* (Gates Foundation 2024). It develops a methodology to:
i. Prioritize investment needs across climate mitigation, adaptation, and economic development, including poverty reduction, across various countries and sectors.
ii. Identify the highest-priority actions to address those needs, including potential overlaps among investments.
iii. Allocate different sources of financial resources to match priority investments, based on their risk and return considerations.

While countries' priorities are shaped by a complex interplay of internal and external economic and political factors, this framework focuses on prioritization based on their contributions to global development and climate goals, objectives that nations have collectively committed to achieving. With global goals as a benchmark, the chapter examines the concept of efficiency from both a global perspective and an individual country perspective, concluding that these perspectives often align.

This framework builds on existing work in climate-development financing, including:

i. The report of the Independent High-Level Expert Group on Climate Finance, also known as the Songwe-Stern report (Songwe, Stern, and Bhattacharya 2022).
ii. The World Bank's Country Climate and Development Reports (CCDRs) (World Bank Group 2023).
iii. The UN's Integrated National Financing Frameworks (INFF) (INFF n.d.).

The Songwe-Stern report calls for a comprehensive financing strategy that leverages the complementary strengths of various financial pools to ensure appropriate scale, type, and cost of financing. It highlights the importance of combining external financing sources – private finance, private finance with risk mitigation, long-term financing from multilateral development banks (MDBs), concessional finance (both bilateral and multilateral), and grants – based on the expected risk–return profile of each investment.

While this chapter aligns with the Songwe-Stern report's call for additional financing from these sources, two key distinctions exist:

i. It adopts a broader perspective on the development imperative, beyond investments in sustainable agriculture.
ii. It addresses the question of prioritizing investments to maximize progress toward the Sustainable Development Goals and Paris Agreement objectives, particularly in scenarios where financing remains constrained.

The World Bank Group's CCDRs serve as a diagnostic tool to help countries identify high-impact actions that reduce greenhouse gas emissions, enhance adaptation and resilience, and advance broader development goals. The CCDRs recognize the need for governments to translate diagnostic findings into prioritization and sequencing exercises that consider overlaps, co-benefits, and trade-offs. Unlike the CCDRs, this framework explicitly considers the types of financing best suited for different investments in a context of constrained resources, focusing not only on mobilizing climate financing but also on ensuring its alignment with risk–return profiles.

The Integrated National Financing Frameworks outline the full range of domestic and international financing sources, spanning public and private finance, to enable countries to develop strategies that increase investments, manage risks, and achieve sustainable development priorities. They are tools to strengthen policies, processes, and institutions to overcome barriers to financing SDGs at the national level. In this chapter, INFFs are framed as a resource for developing detailed, country-specific reforms to maximize financial flows for investment needs. They complement the broader approach discussed here by providing actionable recommendations at the national level

Assessment of the Actions Needed

The analysis[1] of the investment needs required to achieve global goals across country-income groups and individual countries yields four key insights. In this context, investment needs[2] are measured as the distance from achieving the respective global goal. Development investment needs are illustrated by the number of people living below the international extreme poverty line, mitigation investment needs by the projected trajectory of GHG emissions, and adaptation investment needs by the population-weighted exposure index derived from six adaptation indicators in the Notre Dame (ND) Gain dataset (Notre Dame n.d.).

First, the types of investments required to achieve global goals vary significantly across income groups. Figure 1.1 illustrates the three indicators – poverty reduction, mitigation, and adaptation – across different income categories. The greatest need for poverty reduction and human development is concentrated in LICs and LMICs, which collectively house over 90% of the global poor.[3] By contrast, the challenge of mitigating emissions is most acute in high-income countries (HICs) and middle-income countries (MICs).[4] Together, HICs, upper-middle-income countries (UMICs), and India account for 85% of current GHG emissions, a share projected to decline modestly to 78% by 2050 under existing policies. In terms of adaptation, investment needs are more evenly distributed across all country groups. At first glance, this might seem counter-intuitive, given that the tropical and subtropical regions, where most LICs and LMICs are located, experience the greatest climate impacts. However, this conclusion stems from using population-weighted data to measure adaptation needs and does not yet account for the need for financing support, which could alter this analysis.[5]

---

1 As with any analytical framework, we make a number of assumptions to make the analysis and discussion tractable. The conclusions are, of course, sensitive to the selection of indicators and thresholds; for this reason, the conclusions should be interpreted as an illustration of principles to consider when making decisions, rather than firm directions for action.

2 Note that this part of the analysis is not about the allocation of finance—it is only about identifying the actions needed to achieve the three imperatives of human development, climate adaptation and climate mitigation. The framework to consider the allocation of different types of finance for different actions and countries is addressed in the next section.

3 Using the poverty line of USD 2.15 per day should be seen as the lower bound when assessing the investment needs for development. People whose income is only slightly above that threshold remain extremely vulnerable to shocks and setbacks.

4 Under the Network for Greening the Financial System (NGFS) current policies scenario, the GCAM6.0 downscaled model projects emissions from all gases across energy, agriculture, and land-use systems.

5 It is important to make a distinction between the need for adaptation actions and the allocation of financing for these actions. Even if their global population weight is low, LICs rise in priority for financing at the most favorable terms when climate change exposure is combined with the proportion of the country's population affected by climate change and with their economic and financial readiness to handle the effects of climate change.

Size of bubble = value of relevant metric in each area (smaller is better in each column).

	Development	Adaptation & resilience	Mitigation	
	Size of the population living under the international poverty line *M people, total within country group*	Population weighted exposure index based on ND Gain exposure indicators *M people, total within country group*	Total CO2e emissions from energy, agriculture and land use systems *Gt CO2e, total within country group*	(% of global total)
			Today 203 205 0 0	
High income countries (Population = 1.1b)	4M	531M	11.9 (24%)	9.5 (18%)
Upper middle-income countries (Population = 2.7b)	45M	1,267M	25.5 (52%)	25.7 (48%)
Lower middle-income countries (Population = 3.3b)	390M	1,591M	10.6 (22%)	17.2 (32%)
Low-income countries (Population = 1.2b)	251M	294M	1.0 (2%)	1.7 (3%)

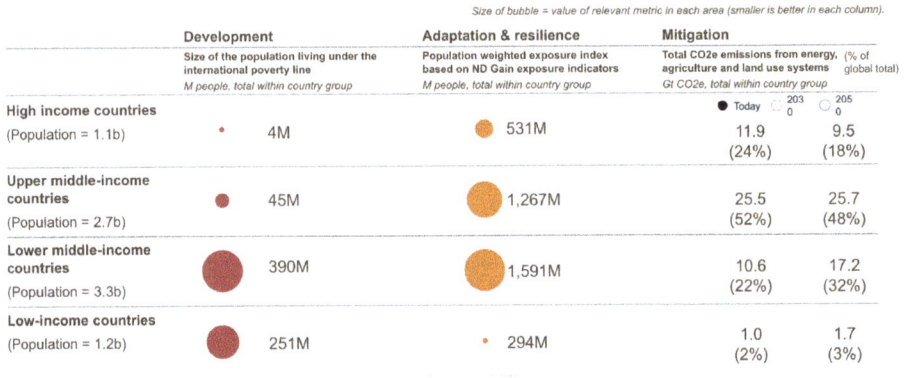

Figure 1.1: Needs assessed across development, adaptation, and mitigation.
Source: Development indicators from SDSN Sustainable Development Report 2023 (Sachs et al. 2023), full indicator database; Adaptation population exposure based on ND Gain Adaptation Country Index (12 'exposure indicators' from ND Gain dataset were averaged by country and weighted by population); Emissions from EDGAR database and NGFS and includes CO_2 and non-CO_2 gases. Non-CO_2 gases use a conversion factor. Global Warming Potential (GWP) 100, from IPCC Assessment Report 5 (IPCC 2014). Emissions growth rates under the "Current Policies" scenario.

Second, an examination of individual countries reveals that targeted investments in a relatively small subset of nations could significantly accelerate global progress across all three imperatives. Figure 1.2 shows that just 23 countries account for 80% of global mitigation investment needs, 29 countries account for 80% of adaptation investment needs, and 18 countries represent 80% of development investment needs. Given some overlaps, a total of 40 countries represent 80% of the global investment needs across all three imperatives. Within this group, an even smaller subset of 11 countries – including China, Indonesia, and the Democratic Republic of Congo (DRC) – accounts for more than 50% of the combined investment needs for mitigation, adaptation, and development. An important caveat is that while these countries represent outsized needs, this does not imply that all financing should be concentrated exclusively on them. Nonetheless, accelerating progress in these countries will be critical to achieving global goals in a timely manner.

Third, the majority of the 40 "high-contribution" countries significantly impact one or, at most, two global investment needs. LICs such as Ethiopia and Uganda primarily face development challenges, while HICs and UMICs are predominantly focused on mitigation efforts. MICs, in particular, have significant needs spanning both development and adaptation. Countries like India and Brazil have substantial investment requirements across all three imperatives. In such cases, financial resources must be carefully balanced to ensure investments in one area do not undermine progress in others. Managing potential tensions between these imperatives will be critical.

Finally, each country faces a unique mix of investment needs to address the overarching goals of development, mitigation, and adaptation. For most LICs and LMICs,

Countries with over 1.5% of global total across all three objectives

Development – countries in top 80%
Population under the international poverty line, % of global total

Country	%
India	20.3%
Democratic Republic of the Congo	9.6%
Nigeria	9.5%
Ethiopia	4.7%
United Republic of Tanzania	4.1%
Madagascar	3.4%
Bangladesh	3.3%
Mozambique	3.0%
Uganda	2.8%
Kenya	2.2%
Malawi	2.0%
Niger	1.8%
Brazil	1.8%
South Africa	1.8%
Zambia	1.7%
Pakistan	1.6%
Angola	1.5%

50%

Adaptation – 29 countries in top 80%
Population weighted exposure index based on ND Gain exposure indicators, % of global total

Country	%
India	21.8%
China	17.1%
United States	4.3%
Indonesia	3.8%
Pakistan	3.1%
Brazil	2.9%
Nigeria	2.6%
Bangladesh	2.4%
Japan	1.8%
Russia	1.7%
Mexico	1.7%
Ethiopia	1.5%
Philippines	1.5%
Viet Nam	1.3%
Dem. Rep. Congo	1.2%
Egypt	1.1%
Turkey	1.0%
Thailand	0.9%
Tanzania	0.9%
Iran	0.8%
Germany	0.8%
Myanmar	0.8%
Kenya	0.7%
France	0.7%
United Kingdom	0.7%
Italy	0.7%
Colombia	0.7%
South Africa	0.7%
Korea, Republic of	0.7%

50%

Mitigation – 23 countries in top 80%
Country emissions, energy and agriculture emissions (excludes land use) CO2e Gt/year, % of global total

Country	%
China	30.2%
United States	11.4%
India	7.3%
Russia	5.0%
Brazil	2.6%
Japan	2.3%
Indonesia	2.2%
Iran	1.8%
Germany	1.5%
Saudi Arabia	1.5%
Mexico	1.5%
Canada	1.4%
South Korea	1.4%
Türkiye	1.3%
Australia	1.1%
Pakistan	1.1%
South Africa	1.1%
Vietnam	1.0%
Thailand	0.9%
France	0.9%
United Kingdom	0.8%
Nigeria	0.8%
Poland	0.8%

50%   80%

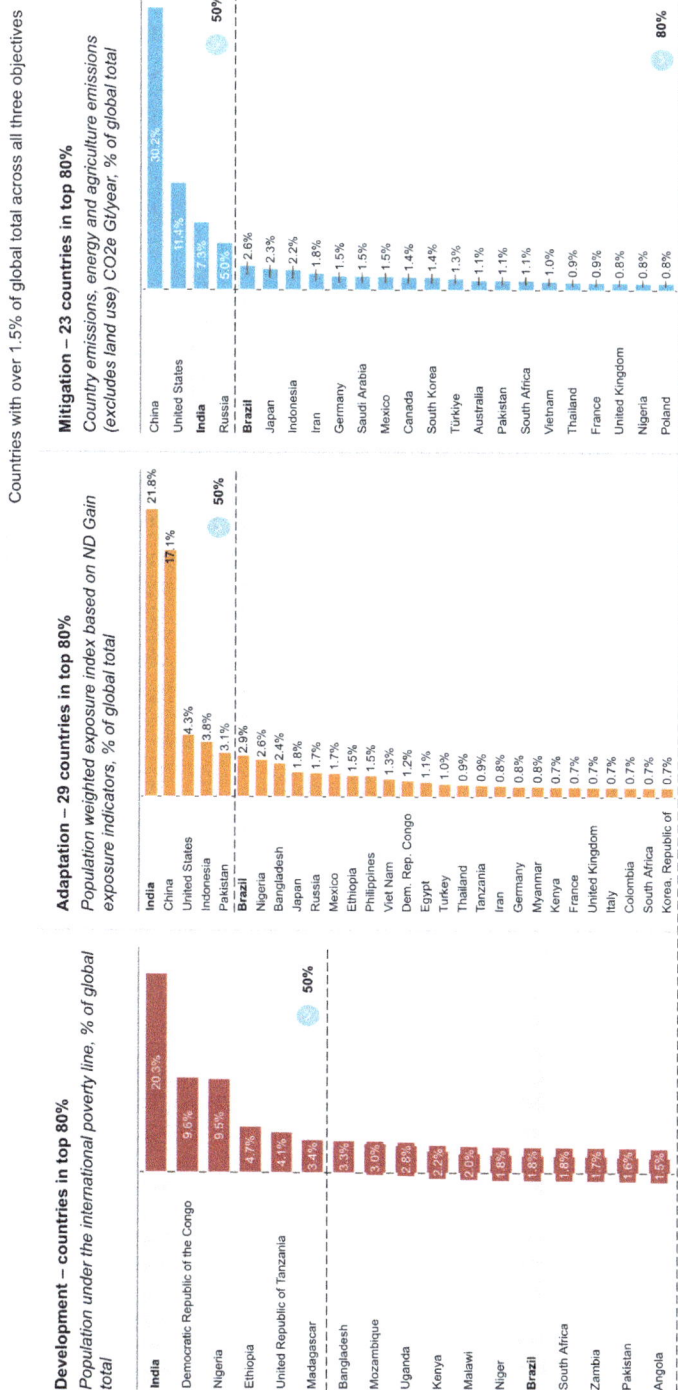

Figure 1.2: 11 countries represent the majority of the needs across development, adaptation, and mitigation.
Source: Development indicators from SDSN Sustainable Development Report 2023 (Sachs et al. 2023), full indicator database; Adaptation population exposure based on ND Gain Adaptation Country Index (12 "exposure indicators" from ND Gain dataset were averaged by country and weighted by population); Emissions from EDGAR – no land use estimates included given the high uncertainty about country level land use emissions. Non-CO2 gases use a conversion factor. Global Warming Potential (GWP) 100, from IPCC Assessment Report 5 (IPCC 2014).

durable poverty reduction requires significant investments in human capital and physical infrastructure, including energy and access to clean water. While mitigation remains essential, it should complement the primary objectives of development and poverty reduction. For example, consider an LIC investing in a primary healthcare center in an underserved area. The choice of energy source for the facility, such as solar power or a fossil-fuel-based, demonstrates the potential for dual benefits. If the solar option is more cost-effective, it not only fulfills the primary development objective but also contributes to climate change mitigation.

When determining how to prioritize climate and development actions from the perspective of a specific country, it is essential to evaluate investments that would yield the most significant contribution to the global goals for that nation. This process begins with an assessment of each country's contribution to global needs as a proportion of the worldwide total. For instance, Ethiopia accounts for 4.7% of the global impoverished population, 0.4% of global greenhouse gas emissions, and 0.8% of the world's population-weighted exposure to climate change. Based on these figures, investments targeting poverty alleviation and economic development emerge as the most impactful strategies for Ethiopia to advance both national and global objectives.

In contrast, India presents a different profile, contributing 8% of global emissions, 22% of population-weighted exposure to climate hazards, and encompassing 20% of the world's impoverished population. Consequently, India faces the imperative to allocate resources across all three dimensions – emissions reduction, climate resilience, and poverty alleviation – to achieve meaningful progress.

Sources of Finance and Efficient Allocation

Two main funding challenges highlight the critical importance of using the right forms of capital to finance different investments. First, the overall magnitude of global and domestic financing is currently substantially below what is required to achieve the SDGs and climate goals. Second, domestic or international public sources of funding are likely to be even more constrained in the future.

Efficiently allocating scarce finance requires matching financing and instruments based on the risk-adjusted return of the investment and the time horizon over which it is expected to accrue. Figure 1.3 presents a theoretical framework for allocating capital by risk and return characteristics. Figure 1.4 outlines an example of a mapping exercise for the three imperatives to the investment return and impact profile. While not an exhaustive set of actions, this figure demonstrates how the most critical actions to address climate and development goals fall across the financing spectrum – from "public goods", typically suitable for grants or highly concessional flows (such as public primary school education and the early retirement of coal power generation capac-

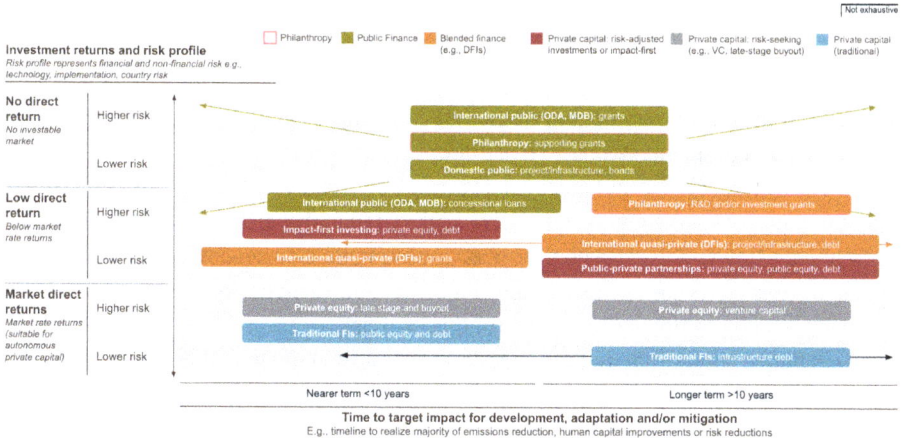

Figure 1.3: Financing sources: Different types of investments may be best suited to different types of capital.
Note: The figure does not provide an exhaustive list of investments.
Source: Gates Foundation (2024).

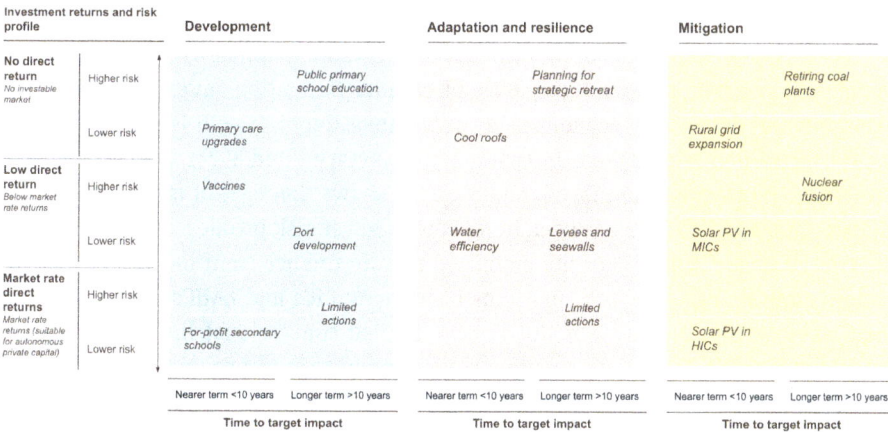

Figure 1.4: Understanding the investment characteristics of actions to address development, adaptation, and mitigation.
Note: The figure does not provide an exhaustive list of actions.
Source: Development indicators from SDSN Sustainable Development Report 2023 (Sachs et al. 2023), full indicator database; Adaptation population exposure based on ND Gain Adaptation Country Index (12 "exposure indicators" from ND Gain dataset were averaged by country and weighted by population); Emissions from EDGAR. Non-CO_2 gases use a conversion factor. Global Warming Potential (GWP) 100, from IPCC Assessment Report 5 (IPCC 2014).

ity), to opportunities attractive for autonomous private capital (such as the development of solar power generation capacity in high-income countries).

Figure 1.5 presents a high-level illustration of the sources of funding that might be suitable for various investment areas across each imperative. It was developed by assessing each action's investment return and timeline to impact, mapping that to the sources of capital, shown in Figure 1.3. Figure 1.5 shows a stylized view of what such a "capital map" looks like when actions are aggregated and matched to broad categories of financing flows. The returns profile of investments can be significantly impacted by a country's governance, institutional capacity, and the certainty of the policy environment, which are not accounted for in this exercise.

This figure shows that actions to address the most acute global needs for LICs and LMICs – to accelerate human capital development and build resilience to climate change – will need to rely mostly on grants and the most concessional forms of loans from Official Development Assistance (ODA) and philanthropic capital, especially where domestic public and private funding capacity is limited. This is because many of these investments concentrated on development and adaptation needs, have low financial returns, accrue benefits over long time horizons, or represent avoided loss or damage. Some examples of high-impact development investments include primary health clinics and schools, while high-impact adaptation investments include flood-resilient public infrastructure, sea walls, and urban cooling shelters.

Turning next to the role of private capital, it is estimated that by 2030, the private sector will need to cover roughly 80% of climate mitigation investment needs in emerging and developing economies, as public investment growth is projected to remain constrained and limited (International Monetary Fund 2023). Organisation for Economic Co-operation and Development (2024) shows that 68% of mobilized private climate finance 2016–2022 has been in MICs with lower risk profiles, and 48% went to the energy sector. Only 3% of the mobilized private finance went to LICs. Private investors often do not view the environment in many LICs and LMICs as conducive to their risk-bearing capacity. For this reason, limited concessional financing is better used in most LICs and LMICs to support governments in improving the underlying enabling environment, strengthening institutional and regulatory frameworks, and creating markets that would draw in private capital over time. However, there may be cases (like India, Brazil, and Nigeria) where some concessional financing should be used to crowd in private financing for high-impact investments to hasten the transition away from carbon and accelerate emissions reductions. There are also cases where mobilizing private capital is indeed possible, even for the type of development issues faced by LICs or LMICs, and where higher risk profiles could foster improvements in the underlying enabling environment.

When considering how to prioritize climate and development actions from the perspective of a particular country, we measure the investments that would deliver the specific country's biggest contribution to any of the global goals. To do this, each country's contribution to each need is assessed as a share of the global total. For ex-

Indicative and high level only, exceptions will exist

Legend:
- Preferably capital that is channeled through government budgets (sourced from either domestic revenues or international aid – MDBs and philanthropy)
- Blended finance (e.g., DFIs)
- Private capital: risk-seeking (e.g., VC, late-stage buyout)
- Private capital (traditional)
- Not among highest priority needs

		Example Investments	LICs	LMICs	UMICs	Rationale
Development	No poverty	Invest in rural infrastructure to support small-scale farmers e.g., irrigation, roads, market access				Typically limited financial returns, investment in public good, low risk but typically no/limited return
	Zero hunger	Improve distribution of nutrient rich foods				
	Good health and well-being	Diagnostic tools and technologies for tuberculosis, child and maternal health facilities				
	Quality education	Improving learning practices (e.g., tablets, teaching to level, structured lesson plans)				
	Gender equality	Invest in programs to help women enter the workforce				
	Clean water and sanitation	Build toilets, and improve sewage management and sanitation practices				
	Affordable energy	Invest in distributed energy solutions (e.g., microgrids) for remote/isolated communities				Some financial returns in infrastructure projects possible, needs for risk mitigation for some countries
	Decent work and economic growth	Expand access to banking and financial services				
	Industry innovation and infrastructure	Invest in road, rail, port and aviation network development and improvement				
	Reduced inequality	Invest in policy advocacy and design that progressively achieves greater equality				
	Sustainable cities and communities	Invest in development and repair of public transport infrastructure				
Mitigation	Power – Generation	Install intermittent renewables (wind, solar PV, solar CSP)				Possible financial returns possible, needs for risk mitigation for some countries
	Transmission & dist.	Upgrade grid and transmission & distribution capacity to facilitate higher VRE				
	CCUS	Install carbon capture and storage on fossil fuel generation facilities				Early stage, low financial returns
	Transport – Vehicles	Phase out fossil fuel vehicles and encourage adoption of zero emission vehicles				Financial returns as market rate possible
	Infrastructure	Expand public and private charging infrastructure for zero emission vehicles (EVs/hydrogen)				Public good, needs high coordination
	Industry – Efficiency	Upgrade energy efficiency of existing infrastructure				Mostly proven technology, needs for risk mitigation for some countries
	Electrification	Electrify industrial energy requirements where possible (e.g., EAF steel production route)				
	Processes	Reduce process emissions from emissions via scrubbers/alternative technologies				Early stage, possibly high risk high return
	Power/transport/industry R&D	Invest in R&D activity that reduces the emissions intensity and increases energy efficiency				Typically needs public support
	Agriculture Productivity – R&D	Invest in R&D for alternative protein sources				Typically use proven technologies, R&D and transfer need some public support
	Productivity – transfer/scale	Invest in technology transfer of low carbon livestock breeds				
	Low carbon farming	Invest in developments in fertilizers, irrigation, and farming practices such as low-/no-tillage				Early stage, possibly high risk high return
	Buildings – Efficiency	Install energy efficient lighting and heating, better insulation				Financial returns as market rate possible
	Electrification	Install or replace gas boilers with electric heat pumps				Financial returns as market rate possible
	Waste	Invest in recycling programs to reduce volume of waste going to landfill				
	Fuel exploitation	Reduce methane emissions from coal, oil and gas power through efficiency/leak detection and repair				Likely done by private investors
Adaptation	Heat – Emergency response and planning	Implement better forecasting and early warning systems				Public good nature of the returns (avoided damages), typically low/no financial returns – some exceptions
	Urban planning and infrastructure	Reduce urban heat island effect through passive cooling (white/green roofs, cool building design)				
	Exposure management	Permanent shift in working hours to be during cooler parts of the day or at night				
	Drought – Agricultural R&D	Invest in agricultural R&D for drought-tolerant livestock breeds and crops				
	Water efficiency	Install/convert to efficient individual irrigation systems (sprinklers, drip/micro irrigation, last mile)				
	Flooding – Emergency response and planning	Enhanced weather and climate services including equipment (infrastructure) and forecasting				
	Urban planning and infrastructure	Invest in flood proofing existing buildings (wet floors, dry floodproofing)				
	Wildfire – Emergency response and planning	Invest in early warning systems for fire events				
	Urban planning and infrastructure	Invest in energy grid hardening by burying power lines				
	Exposure management	Increase healthcare system capacity for fire related health conditions (e.g., asthma)				

1. Priority needs: Development: lowest (red) and second lowest (orange) attainment band. Adaptation: band in top 90% of population weighted ND gain exposure index. Mitigation: band in top 90% of emissions.

Figure 1.5: Optimal capital sources flowing to the highest priority needs across country income groups. Note: Indicative and high-level only. Exceptions will exist. Priority needs: Development: lowest (red) and second lowest (orange) attainment band; Adaptation: band in top 90% of population weighted ND gain exposure index; Mitigation: band in top 90% of emissions.
Source: Gates Foundation (2024).

ample, consider Ethiopia: it is home to 4.7% of the global impoverished population, 0.4% of global emissions, and 0.8% of the world's population-weighted exposure to climate change. Using these measures, we posit that investments aimed at poverty reduction and economic development represent the greatest opportunity to advance both for Ethiopia and the world. By contrast, India contributes 8% of global emissions, 22% of population-weighted exposure to climate hazards, and 20% of the world's impoverished population, and thus needs to invest across all three imperatives.

Transition Finance Principles

The approach described here is one illustration of the more granular analysis needed for meaningful conversations about investment priorities and the allocation of different types of financing as countries transition and global goals are met. We propose a financing framework anchored in several principles to improve coordination, efficiency, and the scaling-up of climate and development finance:

i.   **Expand available financing**: The global community should identify ways to expand the available pool of financing by elevating the ambition for reforms in the domestic and international development finance ecosystem, enhancing domestic resource mobilization, and making stronger efforts to mobilize private capital through improvements in the enabling environment and innovative financing methods to lengthen the investment horizon and reduce the risks of relevant investments.

ii. **Prioritize areas of greatest need**: In the face of constrained financing and capacity, investments should be prioritized in areas of greatest need at the country level, with a view to making the most meaningful contributions to global goals. Recognizing that the locus of decision-making on investments lies with individual countries, and that country ownership of priorities is a critical success factor, investment priorities should be selected based on their impact on each imperative for the country in question. Choosing an investment that addresses a country's largest investment need is often consistent with making the most meaningful contribution to global goals. In cases where the priorities chosen by countries do not align with those that would help make the most rapid progress against the global goals, the gap will need to be bridged through dialogue, cooperation, and incentives.

iii. **Maximize impact across the prioritized imperatives**: For each selected high-impact investment, it is important to explore co-benefits, provided the cost of the investment remains reasonable. However, the selection and design of investments to achieve co-benefits should not come at the expense of making investments that significantly impact only one of the goals.

iv. **Efficiently match financing sources and instruments to their best uses**: This may, for example, require public finance institutions to prioritize concessional financing – the scarcest form of capital – to support the most acute development and climate adaptation needs of lower-income countries. Concessional financing should be used to crowd in private investments, only in cases where there is a realistic expectation of significant effects on capital mobilization or improvements in the underlying investment environment.

v. **Drive down the "green premium"**: Even with more financing and better matching of financing to development and climate investments, progress toward global goals will require stronger efforts to drive down the "green premium". The global community should make concerted efforts to accelerate technological innovation to lower the costs of interventions in all sectors, reducing the overall funding needed.

To underpin these principles, three critical areas of reform are essential:

1. **Sound policies and governance**: All countries should put in place sound pricing policies, regulatory frameworks, and governance arrangements to encourage and sustain large-scale, long-term investments.

2. **Improved tracking of needs and capital flows**: Better measurement and tracking of needs and capital flows are necessary to foster a more coherent and globally aligned climate and development finance agenda.

3. **Global agreement on carbon pricing**: Although the political path to this action is not yet clear, reducing fossil fuel subsidies and reaching a global agreement on putting a price on carbon emissions (possibly through a carbon tax or cap-and-trade system) is critical for achieving long-term climate goals.

Conclusion

Different countries have different roles to play in addressing global challenges. With constrained resources and a real sense of urgency, it is essential to avoid wasteful investments that will have limited impacts on both country priorities and global goals, or ineffective financing of the multiple challenges we are facing. The key to change is to recognize that different countries face different priorities among the three imperatives, possess different potential to contribute to progress on each of these goals, and have varying access to types of financing. Therefore, supporting countries in their specific transition paths toward inclusive and sustainable economic development will ensure that we maximize the impact across all three imperatives and meet the goals with the needed urgency.

References

Gable, Susanna, Florence Bayat-Renoux, Maria A. Gonzalez-Perez, Jamal Saghir, Kevin C. Urama, and Bambang Widianto. 2023. *A Transition Approach to Poverty Reduction and Climate Finance: The Missing Link to Implementation*. Global Council on SDG1 and UNESCWA. https://www.unescwa.org/publica tions/transition-approach-towards-poverty-reduction-climate-finance.

Gates Foundation. 2023. *Climate and Development Finance: A Transition Framework for All*. https://www.gate sfoundation.org/ideas/articles/melinda-foreword-climate-and-development-finance-framework.

Gates Foundation. 2024. *Principles for Allocating Finance for Development and Climate Goals*. https://docs. gatesfoundation.org/documents/gates_foundation_principles_finance_for_development_and_cli mate_goals.pdf

Sachs, Jeffrey, Guillaume Lafortune, Grayson Fuller, and Eamon Drumm. 2023. *Sustainable Development Report 2023: Implementing the SDG Stimulus – Includes the SDG Index and Dashboards*. Paris: SDNS, Dublin: Dublin University Press.

Songwe, Vera, Nicholas Stern, and Amar Bhattacharya. 2022. *Finance for Climate Action: Scaling Up Investment for Climate and Development*. London: Grantham Research Institute on Climate Change and the Environment, London School of Economics and Political Science.

Integrated National Financing Framework (INFF). n.d. *Integrated National Financing Framework Knowledge Platform*. Accessed September 14, 2024. https://inff.org/.

International Monetary Fund (IMF). 2023. *Global Financial Stability Report 2023 – Financial and Climate Policies for a High-Interest-Rate Era*. Chapter 3: Financial Sector Policies to Unlock Private Climate Finance in Emerging Markets and Developing Economies. Washington, D.C.: International Monetary Fund. https://www.elibrary.imf.org/display/book/9798400249686/CH003.xml.

Intergovernmental Panel on Climate Change (IPCC). 2014: *Climate Change 2014: Synthesis Report. Contribution of Working Groups I, II and III to the Fifth Assessment Report of the Intergovernmental Panel on Climate Change*. Geneva: IPCC.

Kenny, Charles, and Zainab Gehan. 2023. *The Future of Official Aid Flows*. Washington, DC: Center for Global Development. https://www.cgdev.org/sites/default/files/future-official-aid-flows.pdf.

Notre Dame. n.d. *Notre Dame Gain (ND Gain) Dataset*. Accessed September 14, 2024. https://gain.nd.edu/.

Organisation for Economic Co-operation and Development (OECD). 2024. *Climate Finance Provided and Mobilised by Developed Countries in 2013–2022, Climate Finance and the USD 100 Billion Goal*. Paris: OECD Publishing.

United Nations, Inter-agency Task Force on Financing for Sustainable Development. 2024. *Financing for Sustainable Development Report 2024: Financing for Development at a Crossroads*. New York: United Nations. Accessed September 16, 2024. https://developmentfinance.un.org/fsdr2024.

United Nations Conference on Trade and Development (UNCTAD). 2023. *SDG Costing*. Accessed September 14, 2024. https://unctad.org/sdg-costing.

World Bank Group. 2023. *The Development, Climate, and Nature Crisis: Solutions to End Poverty on a Livable Planet – Insights from World Bank Country Climate and Development Reports Covering 42 Economies*. Washington, DC: World Bank. http://hdl.handle.net/10986/40652.

Stéphane Hallegatte and Penny Mealy

Chapter 2
Working Together to Promote Greener and Better Technologies for All

Abstract: The global response to climate change is unfolding against a rapidly shifting backdrop of technological, economic, and political change. Over the past decade, the landscape of climate action has been transformed by three key developments: rapid technological progress in renewable energy and electric mobility, increasing trade fragmentation and geopolitical tensions, and the rise of green industrial policies. These developments present both opportunities and challenges for advancing mitigation, adaptation, and resilience, highlighting the urgent need for greater global cooperation and strategic policymaking at the intersection of climate, trade, and industrial policy. This chapter explores how these forces are shaping the future of climate action and examines the role of global cooperation and trade openness in accelerating the development and diffusion of green technologies while ensuring that the benefits of the green transition are equitably shared.

Keywords: Trade, Technological development, Diffusion, Industrial policy, Global cooperation, Green transition

Introduction

For the first time, the transition to a low-carbon economy is not only technologically feasible but also economically attractive. Solar photovoltaics, onshore wind, and battery storage have all seen dramatic cost reductions over the past decade, making renewable energy more competitive than fossil fuels in many markets. These developments mark a major shift in the economics of climate action, but technological progress alone does not guarantee a smooth or equitable transition. Many of these technological advancements remain out of reach for many, as low- and middle-income countries struggle with high capital costs and inadequate infrastructure, which limits their ability to scale up clean energy investments.

At the same time, the geopolitical and economic context for climate action is becoming more complex and uncertain. Trade, which has historically played a critical but underappreciated role in driving global economic growth and technological diffusion, is increasingly under pressure from supply chain disruptions and growing geopolitical tensions. The rise of green industrial policies further complicates this picture. Once overlooked in favor of economy-wide approaches like carbon pricing, industrial policies have gained prominence as governments seek to boost domestic clean technology industries while ensuring security of access and even strategic economic advantages through the green transition. While these policies can accelerate climate action, they also risk distorting markets, exacerbating trade disputes, and limiting technology access for developing economies. The intersection of these forces raises urgent questions about how to balance national interests with the need for global cooperation in advancing an equitable low-carbon transition.

As policymakers confront an economic, technological, and political landscape markedly different from that which shaped the Paris Agreement, global cooperation remains indispensable for achieving net-zero emissions. This chapter explores the critical role of international collaboration in addressing contemporary challenges across three key domains. First, regarding trade, it emphasizes the necessity of inclusive dialogue, partnerships, and coordination through key international bodies to design trade measures that harness the benefits of free trade while mitigating unintended consequences. Second, in the area of technological development and diffusion, it identifies several avenues where enhanced cooperation – in research and development (R&D) funding, experimental approaches, and knowledge sharing – could significantly accelerate progress. Finally, concerning green industrial policies, it draws on key lessons from past successes and failures to underscore the importance of globally coordinated efforts in minimizing the risks of inefficiencies or adverse outcomes.

Recent Developments in Technology, Trade, and Green Industrial Policies

Technology has always played a critical role in the fight against climate change, but three recent global developments are creating new challenges and opportunities in the race to develop and deploy green technologies around the world.

First, the incredible progress in renewable energy and electric mobility technologies has fundamentally changed the economics of climate action. Over the past decade, the cost of solar photovoltaics has dropped by 90%, while onshore wind has fallen by 70%, and battery prices have decreased by over 90% (Ritchie 2024). Transforming the world's carbon-intensive energy system into a clean one was once thought to be prohibitively expensive (Nordhaus 2018). However, as renewables have become cheaper than fossil fuels, rapidly transitioning to a clean energy system is now more likely to save countries significant sums of money compared to maintaining their existing emissions-intensive systems (Way et al. 2022).

Key challenges remain in bringing affordable green technologies to where they are most needed. High capital costs in low- and middle-income countries continue to hamper investment in critical green technologies and supporting infrastructure for grids and storage (World Bank Group 2023a). Meanwhile, although batteries, green hydrogen, and other power-to-X solutions show promise for ensuring stable and reliable clean energy systems, uncertainty remains over the most cost-effective and scalable long-term storage solutions. Beyond electricity, further innovation is needed to decarbonize hard-to-abate sectors such as shipping, steel, and cement, as well as to reduce methane and other greenhouse gas emissions from agriculture and food production. Further, political economy barriers such as entrenched fossil fuel interests are hampering transformations, even when they are highly desirable from an aggregate perspective (Hallegatte et al. 2024).

Second, the shift toward a more fragmented world has the potential to slow – or even stifle – technological transfer. In part as a response to the supply-chain disruptions caused by COVID-19 and rising international tensions in many regions, countries around the world are increasingly favoring and supporting production on their national soil or from their geopolitical allies. Almost 3,000 trade restrictions were imposed by countries in 2023, a fivefold increase compared to restrictions in 2015 (Kose and Mulabdic 2024). This is not without economic consequences: The International Monetary Fund (IMF) estimates that trade-related fragmentation could result in permanent losses of 2–7% of global economic output, with low-income countries facing the highest impacts (Bolhuis, Chen, and Kett 2023). Reduced trade openness can hamper the diffusion of green technologies, with particularly adverse consequences for smaller, lower-income countries that are not strong competitors for frontier technologies but depend on the technological advances and cost reductions achieved in larger, more advanced economies. Many of these countries benefit from cost reductions driven by investments of high-income economies in greener technologies and products, such as subsidies for solar power and investments in low-cost production, notably in China. Less integrated supply chains risk making access to green goods and services more expensive, making the transition harder and costlier (Hasna et al. 2023; World Bank Group 2024).

Third, the rise of green industrial policies around the world is creating both risks and opportunities for the development and diffusion of green technologies. Once largely shunned by the economic and policy communities that made carbon pricing the cornerstone of their recommendations, industrial policies targeting green objectives and other goals, such as energy security, have become increasingly popular policy tools. From a market failure perspective, there are strong grounds for introducing green industrial policies. Given the knowledge and environmental externalities associated with the development and diffusion of green technologies, markets are unlikely to provide the socially optimal amount of green innovation and deployment, especially under the tight timeline to achieve global climate objectives. From a political economy perspective, green industrial policies can also be advantageous. Since these policies provide concrete and highly visible short-term benefits to specific firms and households, they can build coalitions of supportive actors who can then advocate for more climate action, including using other tools like carbon pricing (Meckling et al. 2015).

However, such policies pose significant risks. Governments have a poor track record of picking technological winners, and political capture can lead to wasteful subsidies and inefficiencies. Furthermore, many countries simply do not have sufficient public finances to afford grants, subsidies, or tax credits and to compete with wealthier nations. The sheer abundance of green industrial policies interacting on the global stage also presents new types of risk. For example, interventions tend to allocate production to nations with the deepest pockets, potentially creating wasteful subsidy races and excluding lower-income countries with limited fiscal capacity. They can also distort trade, further exacerbating trade fragmentation.

These three forces – technological progress, trade fragmentation, and the rise of industrial policy – are shaping the trajectory of climate action in ways that are both promising and precarious. The challenge ahead is ensuring that green technologies remain widely accessible, that trade policies facilitate rather than hinder climate cooperation, and that industrial strategies are aligned with the broader goal of a just and effective global transition to a low-carbon economy. Addressing these issues will require a balance between national economic priorities and international collaboration, ensuring that climate action is not undermined by geopolitical divisions or protectionist impulses.

Cooperation to Capture the Benefits of Trade and Ensure All Countries Can Participate

While green technologies are becoming increasingly affordable, ensuring equitable access to them remains a significant challenge, particularly for low- and middle-income countries. Today's technologies can deliver more than 80% of the emissions reductions required by 2030 to remain on track for a 1.5 °C target (IEA 2023). However, this will require a significant increase in investment in resilient, low-carbon development, with estimates for incremental needs ranging from a few percent in upper-middle-income countries (UMICs) to more than 5% of GDP in low-income and lower-middle-income countries (LICs and LMICs), as shown in Figure 2.1. These investment needs include large expenditures in infrastructure, such as for renewable power generation and electric grids, urban transit and e-mobility, water and sanitation, efficient and resilient buildings, and many other sectors.

Trade policies play a critical role in determining the cost and accessibility of these investments. For years, efficient global supply chains helped drive down the cost of clean technologies, but the recent resurgence of tariffs in global markets are reversing some of these gains. In particular, higher duties on clean energy equipment, components, and critical minerals are adding costs and uncertainty to green transitions worldwide. These measures can slow deployment, deter investment, and fragment supply chains. At the same time, many low-income countries continue to maintain relatively high tariffs on environmental goods, which can also raise the cost of their transitions (Hasna et al. 2023; World Bank Group 2024). For instance, Cambodia's

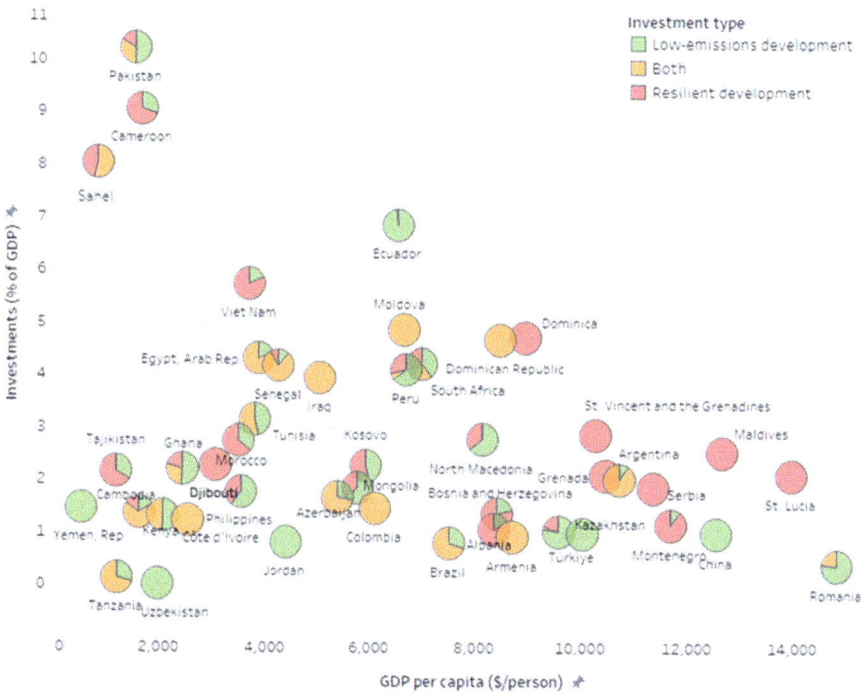

Figure 2.1: Investment needs for resilient and low-carbon development identified in Country Climate and Development Reports.
Source: World Bank Group (2024).

tariffs on final environmental goods, parts, and components are higher than both the world average and those of its regional peers, undermining its competitiveness and participation in value chains for low-carbon goods (World Bank Group 2023b).

Trade barriers can also reduce the environmental gains from trade, which arise when countries specialize in their environmental comparative advantage. Environmental gains from trade occur when countries specialize in what they are relatively "green" at – that is, what they can competitively produce with the least environmental harm. Some studies suggest that the environmental gains from trade could be significant, accounting for more than one-third of the emissions reductions associated with a worldwide carbon tax (Le Moigne et al. 2024). However, poor countries could be disproportionately affected by the transition due to their current industrial structure and technologies, which tend to be more emissions intensive. Still, many low- and middle-income countries have large potential for cheap renewable energy and, with sufficient investment, could develop new important sources of environmental competitiveness in the future, including in energy-intensive goods and services like steel, fertilizer, or aluminum. The challenge, of course, will be overcoming the higher cost of capital in these countries.

Designing appropriate trade measures that leverage the benefits of trade without driving unintended consequences is challenging and requires open dialogue and a collaborative approach. For countries with ambitious emission reduction goals, the imposition of national climate policies, such as a carbon tax, can harm the global competitiveness of trade-exposed, emissions-intensive sectors like steel or chemicals. Recent trade measures, such as the EU's Carbon Border Adjustment Mechanism (CBAM), aim to help countries sustain high levels of ambition and reduce emissions leakage – where emission-intensive activities move to places with laxer regulations. However, such policies need to be carefully designed to avoid unintended impacts on poor countries' development prospects[1] and to prevent creating new constraints for technology transfers across countries or increasing the price of green goods and services. A collaborative approach is essential. For example, additional reporting requirements for firms and countries can create barriers to their participation in global value chains. Standardizing and harmonizing reporting requirements across jurisdictions, as well as simplifying them, when possible, can reduce compliance costs and avoid unintended impacts on low-income countries and small firms. These standardization and harmonization processes could be led by existing international bodies such as the United Nations Framework Convention on Climate Change (UNFCCC), the World Trade Organization (WTO), or the United Nations Conference on Trade and Development (UNCTAD) and considered by relevant working groups in the G7 and G20. Dedicated channels of financial and technical assistance are also needed to support compliance in countries with more limited administrative capacities or those that require more time to adapt – for instance, to create robust land registries and halt illegal deforestation.

The global community can also cooperate to build resilience in global value chains that are critical for the green transition. For the world to reach net-zero emissions by 2050, the global deployment of technologies such as solar photovoltaics and wind turbines needs to increase by around 3 to 5 times by 2030. Electric vehicles would need to increase by around 18 times (IEA 2021). However, the production of these technologies, along with their parts and components, is geographically concentrated in a few countries and is more vulnerable to domestic policy changes or supply chain disruptions, such as those caused by natural disasters, pandemics, or other geopolitical events. An effective global response to these challenges would first involve strengthening the logistical and transport systems needed for these chains to function. A second, complementary approach is to diversify these value chains across countries, particularly in those with latent comparative advantages in the relevant supply chains (see, for example, Figure 2.2).

---

1 A recent estimate suggests that climate-related trade regulations alone could reduce some of the poorest countries' exports by 10% and reduce GDP by 1% (Keane 2023).

Cooperation to Drive Progress on Green Technological Development and Diffusion

While the costs of key mitigation technologies have been falling, international cooperation could help drive these costs down even faster. Technologies such as solar photovoltaics, wind turbines, batteries, and electrolyzers have the convenient property that the more they are produced globally, the more their costs decline (Way et al. 2022). The low cost of solar energy today is, in large part, due to successive rounds of investment and policy support from the United States, Japan, Germany, and China over the past few decades. Although these countries incurred the costs of this sustained learning process, the benefits of cheaper renewable energy accrue globally, including to the lowest-income countries.

However, not all technologies follow this trend. Due to greater project complexity, less technological modularity, and more limited historical investment, nuclear energy and carbon capture and storage technologies have shown more limited potential for cost improvement (Malhotra and Schmidt 2020). Higher-income countries could, therefore, collaborate to provide greater policy support and investment for green technologies that are experiencing declining cost curves (Way et al. 2022). This could take the form of pooling funding through joint ventures and concentrating efforts on technologies with a greater likelihood of cost reduction. More collaborative approaches to knowledge sharing could also avoid unnecessary duplication of R&D efforts, help countries manage the risks and uncertainties inherent in technological development, and accelerate global progress on decarbonization.

Adaptation and resilience offer a stark illustration of the need for global coordination to develop technologies and make them available to those who need them most. An assessment of innovation for resilience and adaptation conducted in 2020 showed that technological innovation in these fields is concentrated in a limited number of relatively high-income countries (Dechezleprêtre et al. 2020). China, Germany, Japan, the Republic of Korea, and the United States together account for nearly two-thirds of all high-value inventions – those seeking patents in more than one country – filed globally between 2010 and 2015. Worse, these technologies rarely diffuse to the countries with the highest needs: transfers of patented inventions for adaptation occur mostly between a small set of high-income economies and China, which accounts for 85% of global technological flows (see Table 2.1). Diffusion is particularly low for agriculture and coastal adaptation technologies, and there is virtually no diffusion to low-income countries. While this problem is not unique to adaptation and resilience, it is especially concerning given the high adaptation needs in these countries. A more collaborative approach could help by ensuring that high-income-country R&D and investments in innovation also address the needs of lower-income countries – such as those related to tropical agriculture or diseases – and by providing mechanisms to facilitate the diffusion of such innovations to the countries that need them most (e.g., through technology transfers, training programs, or dedicated financial instruments).

Table 2.1: Distribution between country income groups of patented inventions of technologies for climate change adaptation, 2010–15 (percent).

Origin country	Destination country		
	High income	**Middle income**	**Low income**
High income	66	27	0
	(69)	(24)	(0)
Middle income	5	1	0
	(7)	(<1)	(0)
Low income	<0.1	<0.01	0
	(<0.1)	(<0.01)	(0)

Source: Dechezleprêtre et al. (2020). Calculations are based on World Patent Statistical Database (PATSTAT) data, European Patent Office. Note: Distributions are the percentages of patents filed in both an origin country and at least one destination country. Results for all technologies appear in parentheses.

Innovation is urgently required for the hard-to-abate sectors. Sectors that are most challenging to decarbonize – such as cement, steel, chemicals, heavy-duty freight, and aviation – are collectively responsible for around 20% of the world's emissions (IRENA 2024). While progress on decarbonizing these sectors has been fairly slow to date, the increasing cost-competitiveness of renewable energy and other enabling technologies are opening up new possibilities. For example, performance and cost improvements in battery technologies are unlocking greater opportunities for electric trucks in road freight. Similarly, energy-saving technologies, like high-efficiency propellers, wind-assisted propulsion, and waste heat recovery systems, could drive significant emission reductions in shipping (potentially 20% of the needed reductions by 2050) (IRENA 2024). Electrification is also making progress in industrial processes in ways that were not anticipated only a few years ago (Rissman 2024). However, the economic viability of various solutions remains highly uncertain.

Global coordination on R&D investment, experimentation, testing, and demonstration of new technologies can accelerate progress. By coordinating efforts during the initial and uncertain testing phases of technology development and ensuring that the learning from these tests is widely shared, countries can accelerate innovation while maintaining or enhancing the incentives for the industry to invest in this process. The deployment of green technologies can also be sped up through coordination on standards, reporting requirements, green procurement, and credible commitments on the phase-out of carbon-intensive technologies (e.g., thermal vehicles). For instance, governments' commitment to procure a certain quantity of electric vehicles, heat pumps, or high-efficiency cooling systems (with clear definitions and internationally accepted criteria) would create a strong signal that a large market exists, which is attractive to new entrants and investors (Hasna, Jaumotte, and Pienknagura 2023). It also creates a level playing field where low-carbon innovators are not undercut by emissions-intensive incumbents (Victor et al. 2019).

Cooperation to Reduce the Risks of Today's Green Industrial Policies

Today's industrial policies differ from those of the past. Historically, industrial policies were primarily used to stimulate economic diversification, promote industrialization, and protect infant industries. More recently, however, industrial policies have expanded to target a broader range of economic and noneconomic objectives, including national and energy security, supply chain resilience, geopolitical concerns, and the green transition (Rodrik, Juhasz, and Lane 2023). While industrial policies were once more prevalent in emerging economies, recent interventions have been driven by large economies such as the U.S., China, and the European Union (Juhasz et al. 2022).

Industrial policies, however, should not be viewed as substitutes for other tools in the climate policy "toolbox", such as R&D subsidies, direct investment in infrastructure, carbon pricing, or standards and regulations. Achieving a transition to green technologies requires success across the full chain, from technology creation to final widespread adoption. This includes early-stage actions like R&D and technology creation, followed by demand support and the creation of niche markets through regulations, green procurement, or tax incentives. The next stage involves learning by doing and economies of scale for cost reduction and scaling up, culminating in adoption by and adaptation to local market contexts through training, capacity building, trade, and worker migration. Industrial policies play an essential role in this process, but they must be coordinated with other strategies, including on the demand side. For instance, China's support for solar power production would not have resulted in reduced costs without the global demand generated elsewhere. An important implication of this is that industrial policies and pricing policies should not be seen as substitutes, as they are often presented in academic literature, but rather as complementary or sequenced strategies of increasingly ambitious policies (Fay et al. 2013; Mealy et al. 2025).

Several key lessons from past industrial policies can help mitigate the risks of repeating previous mistakes. These lessons, derived from both the successes and failures of nongreen industrial policies, are also applicable to green industrial policies. For example, industrial policies should not simply aim to accelerate the development of a sector but should be designed to correct specific market failures or to target latent comparative advantages.

While identifying a country's latent comparative advantages has traditionally been challenging, new methodologies and data sources now offer valuable insights.

Although picking "winning" sectors will always involve uncertainty and be prone to political capture, recent analytical approaches can help policymakers and industry leaders objectively map out areas where a country may have untapped potential to successfully enter global value chains for key green technologies. Drawing from countries' current export profiles, Figure 2.2 identifies countries that are more likely to be able to expand production within key green technology value chains. This is assessed along two dimensions: the average alignment of their current exports with the needs of green value chains (x-axis) and the number of different products for which they show emerging export potential (y-axis). These figures illustrate the potential to diversify green value chains, making them more resilient, as well as the opportunity for many countries to benefit from the global decarbonization process by generating jobs and income from the expected high growth in global demand.

Governments also face political challenges in applying a portfolio approach to industrial policies. With significant uncertainties regarding the potential of various technologies and firms, an industrial policy is expected to experience a significant rate of failure. However, governments often struggle to manage these failures and interrupt support when a firm or technology does not show the expected progress and performance. To address this, common recommendations include that governments should subject firms to competition when possible and have clear, verifiable, and predictable sunset clauses to ensure they do not provide endless support to failing firms or technologies. Even with the right approach, a portfolio strategy will be easier to deploy in large countries with the resources to support multiple sectors or technologies. For smaller and poorer countries, the lower ability to diversify industrial policy makes it a much riskier and less appropriate instrument.

While industrial policy is most often discussed in the context of sunrise industries, it has also been used to manage the phase-down of sunset industries, keeping social and economic costs manageable. Such policies have been used, for instance, in shipbuilding to ensure that the least-productive producers close first. They have also been used to ensure that labor demand declines progressively and is anticipated, facilitating social support, worker retraining, and reskilling alongside local development policies. Given the concentrated impacts of climate policies on certain communities and regions, especially those dependent on coal, place-based policies will need to be implemented to facilitate the transition of these areas toward new and greener activities. Once again, lessons from the past will be crucial. In particular, the need for integrated and participatory approaches is essential (Hallegatte et al. 2024). Successful strategies combine structural reforms with more targeted support. For example, adopting structural policies to improve access to financial instruments and borrowing, strengthen social safety nets, critical infrastructure, and related services, as well as healthcare; facilitate greater labor market flexibility and mobility; and create alternative employment by incentivizing economic innovation and diversification. Targeted policies aimed at supporting affected workers, such as early retirement, financial and reemployment support, and skills training, should be complemented by

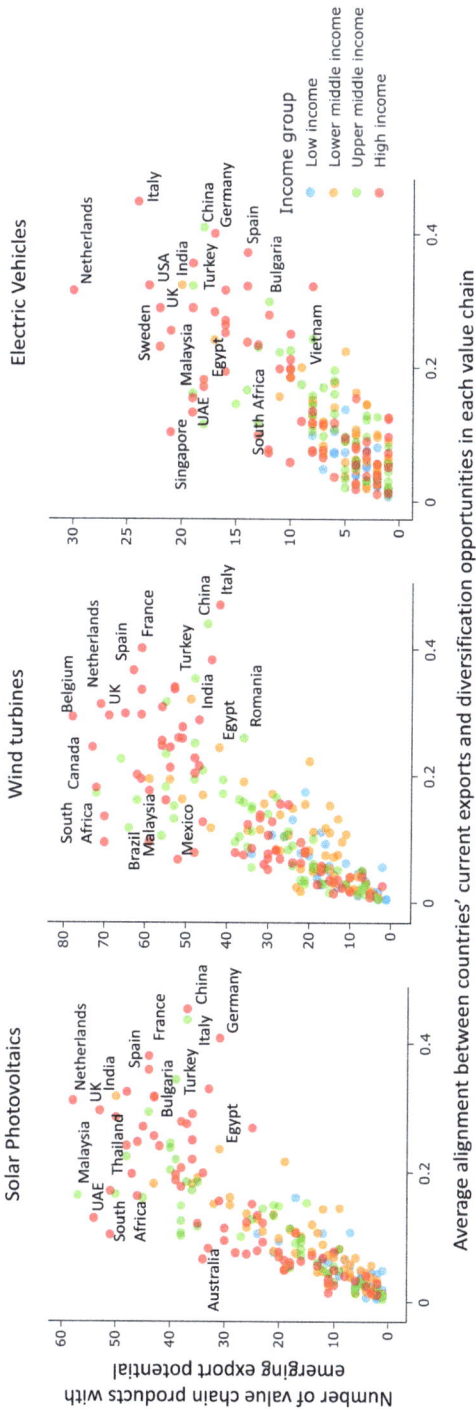

Figure 2.2: Countries with the potential to participate and diversify the global value chains associated with solar PV, wind turbines, and electric vehicles based on their latent comparative advantage.
Source: Rosenow and Mealy (2024).

broader community-level interventions. These might include investments in human capital, local economic development programs, and environmental regeneration. Many countries have begun developing coal transition strategies, but low- and middle-income countries will require increased support from the international community.

Conclusion

Although the global policy arena has become more complex to navigate since the signing of the Paris Agreement, there is now much greater clarity on the availability of technological solutions. The central challenge is no longer about innovation alone but about ensuring that these solutions are widely accessible, equitably distributed, and deployed at the scale and speed necessary for meaningful climate action. This requires not only lowering costs but also creating the right conditions for green technology diffusion, particularly in countries that lack financial and industrial capacity. A coordinated and collaborative international approach is essential to overcoming these barriers and maximizing the benefits of decarbonization worldwide.

Three critical areas of action can help accelerate this transition. First, expanding green technology production capabilities in regions with latent comparative advantages can help diversify global supply chains, enhance resilience, and ensure that more countries benefit from the economic opportunities of the green transition. Supporting green industrial development in emerging economies through targeted investment, technology transfer, and appropriate trade policies will help create a more geographically distributed and robust low-carbon industrial base. Second, strengthening absorptive capacity is vital to ensure that all countries, not just those leading in green technology innovation, can integrate and scale up these solutions. This means investing in infrastructure, regulatory frameworks, workforce training, and institutional capacity to facilitate the widespread adoption of green technologies as they become more affordable.

Lastly, but perhaps most importantly, building bridges across geopolitical divides will continue to be crucial for accelerating green innovation and diffusion and for transitioning toward a more livable planet. Cooperation can make innovation quicker and more efficient, ensuring appropriate exploration of all technology options and preventing wasteful subsidy wars. It can also ensure that the poorest countries have access to the green technologies they need to accelerate their development – such as affordable solar panels and batteries – and that they can participate in green value chains, thus contributing to and benefiting from the global transition toward a more resilient and greener development path.

As the world moves into the next phase of climate action, balancing national interests with international cooperation will be key to success. Green technologies have the potential to fuel economic progress and strengthen climate resilience, but realizing this vision will depend on a sustained commitment to working together.

References

Bolhuis, Marijn A., Jiaqian Chen, and Benjamin R Kett. 2023. "Fragmentation in Global Trade: Accounting for Commodities", *IMF Working Papers* 2023, 073. https://doi.org/10.5089/9798400236563.001

Dechezleprêtre, Antoine, Samuel Fankhauser, Matthieu Glachant, Jan Stoever, and Sarah Touboul. 2020. *Invention and Global Diffusion of Technologies for Climate Change Adaptation: A Patent Analysis.* Washington, DC: The World Bank.

Fay, Marianne, Stéphane Hallegatte, and Adrien Vogt-Schilb. 2013. "Green Industrial Policies: When and How." *Policy Research Working Paper*, vol. 1, no. 6677. Washington, DC: World Bank.

Juhasz, Reka, Nathan Lane, Eric Ohelson, and Valeria C. Perez. 2022. "The Who, What, When, and How of Industrial Policy: A Text-Based Approach." SSRN. https://papers.ssrn.com/sol3/papers.cfm?abstract_id=4649813.

Hallegatte, Stéphane, Catrina Godinho, Jun Rentschler, Paolo Avner, Ira Irina Dorband, Camilla Knudsen, Jana Lemke, and Penny Mealy. 2023. *Within Reach: Navigating the Political Economy of Decarbonization.* Washington, DC: The World Bank Group.

Hasna, Zeina, Florence Jaumotte, Jaden Kim, Samuel Pienknagura, and Gregor Schwerhoff. 2023. "Green Innovation and Diffusion: Policies to Accelerate Them and Expected Impact on Macroeconomic and Firm-Level Performance." *IMF Staff Discussion Notes* 2023, no. 008. Washington, DC: International Monetary Fund. https://doi.org/10.5089/9798400256950.006

International Energy Agency (IEA). 2021. *Net Zero by 2050: A Roadmap for the Global Energy Sector.* Paris: IEA. https://www.iea.org/reports/net-zero-by-2050.

International Energy Agency (IEA). 2023. *Net Zero Roadmap: A Global Pathway to Keep the 1.5 °C Goal in Reach.* Paris: IEA. https://www.iea.org/reports/net-zero-roadmap-a-global-pathway-to-keep-the-15-0c-goal-in-reach.

International Renewable Energy Agency (IRENA). 2024. *Decarbonising Hard-to-Abate Sectors with Renewables: Perspectives for the G7.* Abu Dhabi: IRENA.

Keane, Jodie. 2023. *The Green Squeeze: An Explainer.* ODI. https://odi.org/en/publications/the-green-squeeze-an-explainer/.

Kose, Ayhan, and Alen Mulabdic. 2024. "Global Trade Has Nearly Flatlined. Populism Is Taking a Toll on Growth." *World Bank Blogs.* Accessed September 15, 2024. https://blogs.worldbank.org/en/voices/global-trade-has-nearly-flatlined-populism-taking-toll-growth

Le Moigne, Mathilde, Simon Lepot, Ralph Ossa, Marcos Ritel, and Dora Simon. 2024. "Greening Ricardo: Environmental Comparative Advantage and the Environmental Gains from Trade." *WTO Staff Working Paper ERSD-2024-07.* https://www.wto.org/english/res_e/reser_e/ersd202407_e.htm.

Malhotra, Aarti, and Tobias S. Schmidt. 2020. "Accelerating Low-Carbon Innovation." *Joule* 4 (11): 2259–2267.

Mealy, Penny, Michael Ganslmeier, and Stéphane Hallegatte. 2025. "Climate Policy Adoption: Path-Dependency and Feasibility Frontiers." *World Bank Policy Research Working Paper 11094.* Washington, DC: World Bank.

Meckling, Jonas, Nell Kelsey, Eric Biber, and John Zysman. 2015. "Winning Coalitions for Climate Policy." *Science* 349 (6253): 1170–1171.

Nordhaus, William. 2018. "Projections and Uncertainties About Climate Change in an Era of Minimal Climate Policies." *American Economic Journal: Economic Policy* 10 (3): 333–360.

Rissman, Jeffrey. 2024. *Zero-Carbon Industry.* New York: Columbia University Press.

Ritchie, Hannah. 2024. "Solar Panel Prices Have Fallen by Around 20% Every Time Global Capacity Doubled." *Our World in Data*. Accessed September 15, 2024. https://ourworldindata.org/data-insights /solar-panel-prices-have-fallen-by-around-20-every-time-global-capacity-doubled

Rodrik, Dani, Reka Juhasz, and Nathan Lane. 2023. "Economists Reconsider Industrial Policy." *Project Syndicate*. Accessed September 15, 2024. https://www.project-syndicate.org/commentary/new-economic-research-more-favorable-to-industrial-policy-by-dani-rodrik-et-al-2023-08.

Rosenow, Samuel Kaspar, and Penny Mealy. 2024. "Turning Risks into Reward: Diversifying the Global Value Chains of Decarbonization Technologies." *World Bank Policy Research Working Paper 10696*. Washington, DC: World Bank.

Victor, David G., Frank W. Geels, and Simon Sharpe. 2019. *Accelerating the Low Carbon Transition: The Case for Stronger, More Targeted and Coordinated International Action*. Brookings Institution. https://www. brookings.edu/wp-content/uploads/2019/12/Coordinatedactionreport.pdf.

Way, Rupert, Michael C. Ives, Penny Mealy, and J. Doyne Farmer. 2022. "Empirically Grounded Technology Forecasts and the Energy Transition." *Joule* 6 (9): 2057–2082.

World Bank Group. 2023a. *Scaling Up to Phase Down: Financing Energy Transitions in the Power Sector*. Washington, DC: World Bank. https://openknowledge.worldbank.org/server/api/core/bitstreams/ d0c0c6a2-f331-4bb9-b9d1-638d1f039e7d/content.

World Bank Group. 2023b. *Cambodia Country Climate and Development Report*. Washington, DC: World Bank Group. http://documents.worldbank.org/curated/en/099092823045083987/ P17887106c6c2d0e909aa1090f3e10505c1.

World Bank Group. 2024. *People in a Changing Climate: From Vulnerability to Action – Insights from World Bank Group Country Climate and Development Reports Covering 72 Economies*. Washington, DC: World Bank. http://hdl.handle.net/10986/42395.

Dileimy Orozco, Barbara Buchner, and Rachel Kyte

Chapter 3
A Compass to Guide Climate Finance Integrity

Abstract: Climate finance is often described as "the great enabler" of global climate action. However, persistent gaps between financial commitments and actual disbursements threaten to erode trust and diminish ambition. As the need for climate-related resources intensifies, ensuring the integrity of climate finance – by fostering transparency, accountability, and alignment with intended outcomes – has emerged as a defining challenge. This chapter examines the concept of climate finance integrity, identifies systemic barriers to its implementation, and analyzes ongoing efforts to enhance accountability within a fragmented and complex financial ecosystem. Additionally, the chapter introduces a pragmatic tool designed to sustain integrity by tracking progress and aligning reform efforts, thereby fostering momentum. Ultimately, achieving integrity will require a coordinated, whole-of-system approach to redirect global financial flows toward climate and sustainable development goals, laying the foundation for a more resilient and prosperous future.

Keywords: Climate finance integrity, Accountability, Transparency, Governance, Climate Finance Reform Compass, Financial system reform

Introduction

In the global effort to combat climate change, finance is frequently termed "the great enabler". Trillions of dollars are required to transform key sectors and mitigate the most severe impacts of a warming planet. Encouragingly, there have been notable developments in climate finance. Since the Paris Agreement, both governments and the private sector have steadily increased their focus on this area. Annual climate finance surpassed USD 1 trillion for the first time in 2021 (CPI 2023). Each year, new commitments are announced, targeting ever-higher levels of finance. These ambitious commitments are essential to closing the gap between current financing levels and what is required to transition toward more equitable and sustainable economies.

Despite these positive trends, a persistent gap remains between pledged and delivered funds. As global temperatures rise, the resulting economic losses and social harms underscore the urgency of closing this gap. Addressing this challenge requires not only more financial pledges but also a stronger emphasis on integrity, accountability, and oversight in both public and private sectors.

This chapter explores why climate finance integrity is crucial, the barriers impeding its realization, and emerging initiatives aimed at fostering greater accountability. Practical tools, such as the Climate Finance Reform Compass, are introduced as mechanisms to track progress and guide reforms. Fundamentally, this chapter argues that embedding integrity into climate finance is essential to maintaining trust, accelerating cooperation, ensuring timely implementation, and achieving the ambitious goals necessary to confront the climate crisis.

Defining Climate Finance Integrity

Climate finance integrity refers to the transparent and accountable management of financial resources committed to climate action, ensuring they remain aligned with their intended goals and result in meaningful, measurable outcomes. A key component of integrity involves the ability to trace financial flows from pledges to tangible impacts.

Although no universally accepted definition of climate finance integrity exists, several prominent institutions have outlined its essential characteristics. The United Nations Framework Convention on Climate Change (UNFCCC) Standing Committee on Finance emphasizes transparency and accountability as foundational to building trust in climate finance flows (UNFCCC 2022). Transparency International's longstanding Climate Finance Integrity Programme (Transparency International 2014) frames integrity as safeguarding climate funds from corruption and misuse through robust governance and public oversight. Similarly, the Organization for Economic Co-operation and Development (OECD) underscores the importance of consistent and transparent reporting to uphold credibility in public climate finance (OECD 2023).

In the private sector, integrity increasingly pertains to the credibility of climate-related financial claims. This involves ensuring that investment strategies, net-zero targets, and financial instruments are genuinely aligned with science-based pathways (CPI 2023). The International Sustainability Standards Board (ISSB) reinforces this through the establishment of global standards for sustainability and climate-related disclosures. Frameworks such as IFRS S2 aim to ensure that information on climate risks, governance, and performance is consistent, comparable, and reliable. Across these perspectives, a common principle emerges: climate finance must be trustworthy, accountable, and effective, with integrity institutionalized as a core feature. Without integrity, commitments risk devolving into empty promises, undermining trust and international cooperation (International Sustainability Standards Board 2023).

Identifying the Integrity Challenge

At first glance, ensuring climate finance integrity may appear straightforward. An entity makes a public commitment, and stakeholders should, in theory, be able to verify whether that commitment has been fulfilled. In reality, however, integrity in climate finance is far more complex.

Efforts to track and uphold commitments occur alongside broader financial system reforms. Public and private initiatives, operating at both international and domestic levels, address these challenges through a patchwork of policy, regulatory, and voluntary frameworks. The fragmented nature of these efforts makes it difficult to monitor progress comprehensively and understand how disparate elements interconnect.

Surveying and harmonizing these efforts are only the first hurdle. Political, economic, and social pressures further complicate the fulfillment of financial commitments. Politically, regulatory uncertainty and shifting climate policies – particularly during election cycles or under new administrations – can cause private actors to hesitate or retract commitments. Economically, factors such as market volatility, tightening credit conditions, and recession fears often lead companies and investors to prioritize short-term returns over long-term climate investments.

Recognizing these challenges, key forums for reform, including those focused on reshaping the International Financial Architecture (IFA), are increasingly integrating the interconnected issues of climate, nature, and development into their agendas. For instance, there is a growing emphasis on leveraging limited international development funds to strengthen local financial institutions, mobilize domestic capital, minimize reliance on market-rate debt, and support investments that avoid exacerbating climate impacts.

Moreover, many pledges to enhance both the volume and quality of climate finance necessitate structural changes within institutions and across systems. Initiatives such as multilateral development banks (MDBs) capital optimization, prudential regulation reforms, debt relief mechanisms, and new risk-sharing instruments introduce substantial complexity. This complexity makes it difficult to assess whether meaningful progress is being made or if commitments remain unfulfilled.

Specific Challenges and Gaps in Climate Finance Integrity

Several specific challenges and gaps contribute to the persistent issues undermining climate finance integrity:

- **Accountability:** Many financial pledges lack robust monitoring and enforcement mechanisms, resulting in delays, underfunding, or complete nondelivery. Financial needs are cumulative and often fail to adequately consider long-term commitments. A significant portion of pledges are made through voluntary platforms and alliances, which are proving unsustainable in the current political–economic environment (Bryan and Mundy 2025).

– **Transparency:** Outside of public finance, reporting remains limited or nonexistent. Issues such as overstatement, double-counting, and insufficient oversight of internal reforms hinder the ability to track whether financial flows reach their intended targets (Jessop 2024). Institutions may publish headline figures without providing properly tagged and disaggregated data that reflects on-the-ground realities. Although new tracking initiatives are emerging, the absence of clear, uniform reporting standards and independent verification mechanisms obscures whether financial commitments are genuinely impactful.[1] This is further compounded by definitional inconsistencies, underscoring the need for a systemic approach that addresses both quantitative and qualitative aspects of financial flows.

– **Structural Challenges:** Proposals to reform the IFA often require large institutions to overhaul decades-old financial models and decision-making processes. For instance, MDB reform agendas include calls for increased shareholder capital contributions, expanded mandates, enhanced capital efficiency, new financing mechanisms, and improved country engagement. For a single agenda item, at least 40 reform areas have been identified, illustrating the magnitude of this challenge (Lee and Matthews 2024). Furthermore, electoral cycles and leadership transitions frequently disrupt continuity, complicating the pursuit of sustained, long-term reforms.

– **Complexity**: The IFA reform agenda is fragmented across multiple roadmaps and processes, with decision-makers dispersed across diverse institutions and reform tracks. As shown in Figure 3.1, numerous initiatives have emerged over the past decade to advance sustainable finance across the public and private sectors. Public institutions – including finance ministries, central banks, MDBs, and other development finance organizations – have formed networks to promote green financial strategies. Similarly, private sector groups have coalesced around net-zero goals, bringing together asset owners, asset managers, banks, insurers, consultants, and service providers under various targeted alliances (CPI 2021).

The sheer breadth of climate finance reform needs across the ecosystem adds substantial complexity. This complexity fosters inertia, fragmentation, and delays, as overlapping priorities and governance structures hinder coordination. Decision-makers face an overwhelming volume of information, impeding timely and coherent actions.

Without clear mechanisms to assess progress and understand the interactions between different reform elements, financial commitments risk remaining theoretical

---

1 For example, CPI's Net Zero Finance Tracker brings together data from 50 sources to provide the most comprehensive assessment of private finance institutions' progress on aligning their activities with Paris Agreement goals and delivering net-zero impact.

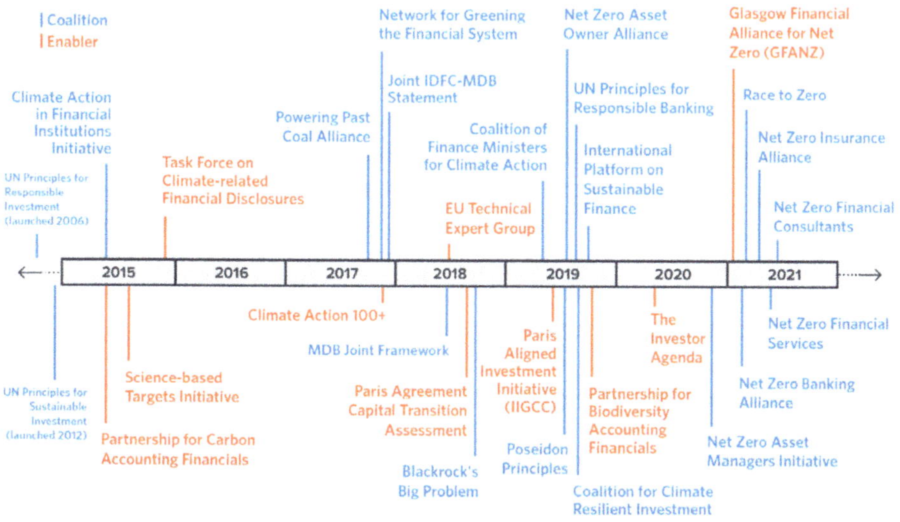

Figure 3.1: Sustainability coalitions and enabling initiatives in the financial sector.
Source: CPI (2021).

aspirations rather than materializing into tangible outcomes. This not only jeopardizes the integrity of existing commitments but also weakens the foundation for future pledges. Eroded trust in the climate finance system discourages cooperation and investment, while fostering duplication of efforts and fragmentation. Ultimately, this lack of confidence can stifle the ambition needed to drive systemic financial reforms, perpetuating a cycle of inaction.

Addressing the Integrity Challenge

Given these persistent challenges, and with the global community in the final stretch of the "Decade of Action", the need to transition from agenda-setting to full-scale implementation has never been more urgent. After years of setting targets and debating reforms, a fundamental shift in focus is required to deliver meaningful results.

This shift necessitates a comprehensive understanding of the key actors involved in ensuring climate finance integrity and the conditions required for successful implementation. Specifically, this involves identifying decision-makers, empowering critical actors, establishing appropriate incentives, equipping stakeholders with necessary tools and information, and instituting accountability mechanisms to guarantee that commitments translate into real-world outcomes.

In response to the information gaps and action inertia, a coalition of climate finance stakeholders launched the Climate Finance Reform Compass in 2024 (CPI 2024).

Developed by the CPI, with input from financial institutions, policymakers, and civil society organizations, the Compass addresses the need for coordinated climate finance commitments and accountability. It is a strategic tool designed to align priorities, build consensus around short-term goals, track progress, and drive action towards reforming the international financial system to meet global climate objectives.

The Compass offers a structured framework for governments, financial institutions, and the private sector to coordinate efforts and assess the status of key reforms. By facilitating data-driven, transparent monitoring and reporting, the tool supports the transition from commitments to tangible outcomes.

As the first comprehensive effort to systematically track climate finance reforms across the international financial ecosystem, the Compass organizes its work around nine thematic areas aligned with the UAE Global Climate Finance Framework established at COP28 (Ministry of Foreign Affairs, United Arab Emirates 2023). These thematic areas encompass critical elements such as increasing public and private investment, expanding fiscal space, enhancing MDB roles, scaling concessional finance, and boosting domestic resource mobilization. Additionally, the framework emphasizes the importance of carbon markets, just transition strategies, and country platforms as vehicles for channeling investment.

To ensure a systematic and outcome-driven approach, the Compass outlines 29 key reforms, each with defined targets and milestones to be achieved by 2030. As a dynamic tracking tool, it aligns reform priorities with major international climate and finance milestones, ensuring that high-level discussions translate into concrete outcomes.

The Compass also serves as the official accountability tracker for the Global Climate Finance Framework agreed upon at COP28, providing comprehensive architecture to guide negotiations and broader climate action. By consolidating information on ongoing initiatives and identifying gaps, the tool enables decision-makers to prioritize interventions, coordinate efforts, and measure progress towards a more effective and equitable global climate finance system.

Building the Integrity Process

Stakeholders place trust not only in the fulfillment of commitments but also in the systems that track progress, assess outcomes, and measure real-world impact. Tools like the Climate Finance Reform Compass contribute to these systems by providing cohesion and clarity; however, their success ultimately depends on the direct and sustained engagement of all stakeholders.

Each stakeholder group has a critical role to play:

- **Governments and policymakers** must continue evolving policies and strengthening the enabling environment to align climate, economic, and development objectives.

- **Financial institutions** should ensure that climate finance commitments are credible and translated into real-world impacts.
- **Private sector actors** must develop comprehensive implementation plans that are fully integrated into their strategic and operational frameworks.
- **Civil society and researchers** are essential in analyzing transparency, verification, and integrity through evidence-based, pragmatic approaches rooted in real-world conditions.

Cross-cutting action areas also require attention, particularly efforts to improve data quality through harmonized definitions, standardized sustainability reporting, mandatory disclosures, and enhanced capacity building and technical assistance. Together, credible and coordinated actions aligned with transparency and accountability mechanisms can build momentum for improving climate finance integrity.

If these efforts are maintained, they will reverberate through broader financial system reform initiatives – from COP finance negotiations to G20 actions – catalyzing the collaboration required to implement meaningful reforms across both public and private sectors. Enhanced interoperability among climate finance providers will ensure more efficient and effective use of limited resources, transforming commitments into tangible socioeconomic impacts.

Ultimately, realizing a scaled-up and impactful financial regime for climate action necessitates a holistic, whole-of-system approach. This involves reorienting all financial flows and capital in alignment with climate, biodiversity, resilience, and sustainable development objectives, thereby enabling the transformation of the global economy and societies.

Strong coordination across the financial ecosystem is fundamental to this transformation. Recent initiatives, such as contributions from major coalitions of financial stakeholders[2] to the UNFCCC's post-2025 climate finance processes, represent positive steps in this direction.

Conclusion

Ensuring the integrity of climate finance is critical to achieving global climate goals and fostering trust among stakeholders. Addressing persistent challenges – such as accountability, transparency, structural inertia, and systemic complexity – requires coordinated, outcome-driven reforms across the entire financial ecosystem. Tools like

---

2 This coalition includes the International Development Finance Club (IDFC), UNEP Finance Initiative (UNEP FI), the Mainstreaming Climate in Financial Institutions initiative, and Principles for Responsible Investment (PRI). For more details, see "Making Finance Work for Climate". https://www.idfc.org/wp-content/uploads/2024/11/joint-contribution-making-finance-work-for-climate-final.pdf.

the Climate Finance Reform Compass provide a practical framework to align efforts, track progress, and translate commitments into real-world impacts. However, lasting progress will depend on sustained collaboration, enhanced data transparency, and a collective shift toward a whole-of-system approach. By strengthening the foundations of climate finance integrity, the global community can unlock the scale and ambition needed for transformative climate action.

References

Bryan, Kenza, and Simon Mundy. 2025. "Banks' Climate Alliance Calls Vote to Ditch Pledge on Limiting Warming to 1.5C." *Financial Times*, March 11. Accessed April 1, 2025. https://www.ft.com/content/8087b0bc-1cd1-4581-9fe6-fa4f8ecf3b38.

Climate Policy Initiative (CPI). 2021. *Framework for Sustainable Finance Integrity: A Tool for Guiding Action across the Financial System*. https://www.climatepolicyinitiative.org/wp-content/uploads/2021/10/Framework-for-Sustainable-Finance-Integrity.pdf.

Climate Policy Initiative (CPI). 2023. *Global Landscape of Climate Finance 2023*. https://www.climatepolicyinitiative.org/publication/global-landscape-of-climate-finance-2023/.

Climate Policy Initiative (CPI). 2024. *Climate Finance Reform Compass*. Accessed April 1, 2025. https://www.climatepolicyinitiative.org/climate-finance-reform-compass/.

International Sustainability Standards Board (ISSB). 2023. "ISSB Issues Inaugural Global Sustainability Disclosure Standards IFRS S1 and IFRS S2." *IFRS Foundation*. Accessed April 1, 2025. https://www.ifrs.org/news-and-events/news/2023/06/issb-issues-ifrs-s1-ifrs-s2.

Jessop, Simon. 2024. "Insurers' Climate Alliance Relaunches after Member Exodus." Reuters. April 25, 2024. Accessed April 1, 2025. https://www.reuters.com/sustainability/climate-energy/insurers-climate-alliance-relaunches-after-member-exodus-2024-04-25/.

Lee, Nancy, and Samuel Matthews. 2024. *The MDB Ships Are Turning but Not Yet on Course: Results of CGD's Updated MDB Reform Tracker*. CGD Note 383. Washington, DC: Center for Global Development. https://www.cgdev.org/publication/mdb-ships-are-turning-not-yet-course-results-cgds-updated-mdb-reform-tracker.

Ministry of Foreign Affairs, United Arab Emirates. 2023. "UAE Announces $100 Million Contribution to Support Climate Resilience in Least Developed Countries and Small Island Developing States." Accessed April 1, 2025. https://www.mofa.gov.ae/en/mediahub/news/2023/12/1/1-12-2023-uae-devolep.

Organisation for Economic Co-operation and Development (OECD). 2023. *Climate Finance Provided and Mobilised by Developed Countries: Aggregate Trends Updated with 2021 Data*. https://www.oecd.org/climate-change/finance-usd-100-billion-goal/.

Transparency International. 2014. *Climate Finance Integrity: Global Corruption Report*. https://www.transparency.org/en/publications/climate-finance-integrity-global-corruption-report.

UNFCCC Standing Committee on Finance. 2022. Fifth Biennial Assessment and Overview of Climate Finance Flows. Bonn, Germany: United Nations Framework Convention on Climate Change (UNFCCC).

Clara B. Gurresø and Eoin Jackson

Chapter 4
Enhancing Transparency and Accountability in Climate Finance Mobilization from Developed to Developing Countries

Abstract: This chapter, developed as part of the Planetary Governance Program at The New Institute, chaired by the Climate Governance Commission, identifies and discusses key climate finance reform proposals to enhance transparency and accountability within climate finance governance. It first highlights the need for high-quality climate finance to be transferred from developed to developing countries and the lack of transparency in identifying the majority of climate finance contributions from developed countries. This lack of transparency has exacerbated the gap between existing climate finance needs and the actual level of finance that is provided by the developed world. As a first step toward addressing these issues, the chapter proposes key governance innovations that build off the Climate Governance Commission's 2023 landmark report, "Governing Our Planetary Emergency". These proposals include the establishment of common definitions of "climate finance", stricter accounting rules to tighten standards regarding what qualifies as "climate finance", the establishment of new climate finance accounting and reporting systems, and the full operationalization of Article 2.1(c) of the Paris Agreement.

Keywords: Climate finance reporting, Donor accountability, USD 100 billion goal, OECD Creditor Reporting System, Paris Agreement, UNFCCC

Introduction

The past decade is the warmest on record, with 2024 setting a new heat record, reaching an average global temperature of 1.6 °C above pre-industrial levels (Copernicus 2025). The rising temperatures are linked to an increase in the frequency and intensity of extreme weather events, such as storms and droughts, as well as slow-onset events, such as sea-level rise and desertification (IPCC 2019; 2021). Developed countries are

Note: The authors submit this contribution as part of the Planetary Governance Program at The New Institute. The Planetary Governance Program takes forward the work of the Climate Governance Commission by identifying, refining, and further developing key near-term and medium-term governance reform proposals to address the planetary emergency, building off the Climate Governance Commission's 2023 Report Governing Our Planetary Emergency (CGC 2023).

responsible for the majority of historical emissions that have contributed to climate change (Matthews 2014; Jones et al. 2023). However, the adverse effects disproportionately harm countries and communities in developing nations (IPCC 2023; Jones et al. 2023).

Due to their higher levels of economic development, developed countries[1] have the largest capacity to pursue and support climate mitigation and adaptation measures. These measures are also critical for supporting climate action and protection in developing countries, which, however, often lack the financial resources to implement them.

As a result of these economic circumstances and historical emissions, developed-country parties to the United Nations Framework Convention on Climate Change (UNFCCC) have agreed to mobilize financial resources to support climate mitigation and adaptation in developing countries (UNFCCC 1992; UNFCCC 2009; UNFCCC 2015a; UNFCCC 2024). The most recent agreement stipulates that developed countries will mobilize USD 300 billion per year by 2035 (UNFCCC 2024). However, there exists a significant gap between the amount of finance officially mobilized by developed countries and the needs of developing countries. Critics also argue that official climate finance reporting is exaggerated due to practices of overreporting and mislabeling climate finance contributions, combined with flaws in the accounting system. As a result, the actual volume of mobilized climate finance could be much lower than what is reported and committed to (Dasgupta et al. 2015; Carty, Kowalzig, and Zagema 2020; CARE 2021a, 2023).

According to the Climate Governance Commission, as identified in its 2023 report *Governing Our Planetary Emergency*, near- and medium-term governance innovations are needed to unlock new sources of climate finance and drive forward reform of the global financial architecture (CGC 2023). As a crucial first step, the focus of this chapter is on illustrating the need to ensure that developed countries fulfill the quantity and quality of climate finance they have promised. High-quality climate finance refers to finance that is accessible, predictable, and does not create additional burdens for recipient countries (Bhattacharya et al. 2023; G77 2024). Another step is to explore innovative sources of climate finance to bridge the remaining finance gap. Scholars, including contributing authors to this book, have already proposed such solutions (Songwe, Stern, and Bhattacharya 2022; Shirai 2022; Abdel-Aziz and Eltouny 2025; Al-Mubarak and Zadek 2025; Bachrach 2025; Nasr and Fakir 2025).

The challenge in delivering the promised level of climate finance is partly due to the lack of transparency in identifying the majority of climate finance contributions

---

[1] We use the terms "developed countries" and "developing countries" to refer to countries based on their commitments under the UNFCCC. These categories are based on countries' level of economic development when the Convention was established in 1992. "Developed countries" refer to *Annex II-countries*, while "developing countries" refer to *Non-annex countries* (UNFCCC n.d.). Some states traditionally viewed as developing countries, like China and India, have experienced rapid industrialization and become major emitters in recent decades, but this is not reflected in the Annex categories.

from developed countries. This lack of transparency has enabled many developed countries to inflate their reported climate finance contributions. Honig and Weaver (2020) argue that aid donors are motivated by their peer reputation. Based on this assumption, reforms to promote clear transparency and accountability mechanisms in climate finance could incentivize stronger performance. This chapter outlines the limitations of the current reporting and accounting system and provides recommendations for improving transparency and accountability.

What is Public Climate Finance?

International climate finance commitments, as articulated under the United Nations Framework Convention on Climate Change (UNFCCC), provide essential context for discussing the limitations and opportunities in climate finance accounting. The Convention commits developed countries to mobilizing financial assistance to support climate adaptation and mitigation in developing countries (UNFCCC 1992). This commitment was reaffirmed at the 15th Conference of the Parties (COP15) in 2009, when developed countries agreed to collectively mobilize USD 100 billion per year by 2020 (UNFCCC 2009). The finance was to originate from "a wide variety of sources, public and private, bilateral and multilateral, including alternative sources of finance" (UNFCCC 2009, art. 8). It was further stipulated that the mobilized finance should be "new and additional" to avoid redirecting aid from existing development budgets and that allocation should be "balanced" between adaptation and mitigation (UNFCCC 2009, art. 8). However, no formal definitions of "balanced" or "new and additional" were ever agreed upon by the Parties.

With the adoption of the Paris Agreement at COP21 in 2015, Parties agreed to extend the USD 100 billion goal until 2025, by which time they would establish a New Collective Quantified Goal (NCQG) (UNFCCC 2015b). The provision of climate finance from developed to developing countries, based on existing obligations under the Convention, is outlined in Article 9 of the Paris Agreement (UNFCCC 2015a). Additionally, Article 2.1(c) of the Agreement includes an objective to "[make] finance flows consistent with a pathway towards low greenhouse gas emissions and climate-resilient development" (UNFCCC 2015a). Unlike Article 9, this provision addresses broader financial flows and efforts to align the financial system with climate goals (Zamarioli et al. 2021). Consequently, Article 2.1(c) extends beyond Article 9 by encompassing financial flows between developed countries and at the subnational level. However, the Agreement did not specify how to operationalize this objective.

The NCQG was adopted at COP29 in 2024, where Parties agreed to triple the existing mobilization target to at least USD 300 billion per year by 2035 (UNFCCC 2024). The COP29 agreement further "calls on all actors to work together to enable the scaling up of financing to developing country Parties [. . .] to at least USD 1.3 trillion per year by

2035" (UNFCCC 2024, art. 7). The NCQG also recognized the need to address loss and damage (UNFCCC 2024, art. 19), marking the first instance of such recognition in a climate finance decision text. However, the mobilization and allocation of the USD 300 billion are described solely in the context of mitigation and adaptation.

Although the COP29 agreement demonstrates a commitment to scaling up climate finance, the goal remains insufficient to meet the needs of developing countries. Estimates of climate finance needs vary depending on methodology, data sources, temperature scenarios, and other factors. Based on an aggregate assessment of the costed mitigation and adaptation needs outlined in Nationally Determined Contributions (NDCs), the Standing Committee on Finance (SCF) (2024) estimated an annual requirement of USD 455–584 billion until 2030.

However, 57 out of 155 developing countries (nearly one-third) did not provide a cost estimate in their NDCs, indicating that the total climate finance needs are likely much higher (SCF 2024). Moreover, 79% of the costed needs in NDCs relate to mitigation, while only 16% pertain to adaptation and 5% to cross-cutting projects. This suggests an adaptation need of approximately USD 73–93 billion per year. However, the latest Adaptation Gap Report by the United Nations Environment Programme (UNEP) (2023) estimates that adaptation finance needs in developing countries will range from USD 215 billion to USD 387 billion per year until 2030. The Organisation for Economic Co-operation and Development (OECD) (2024a) provides a similar estimate, projecting adaptation-related investment needs between USD 200 billion and USD 400 billion annually by 2030. Adaptation costs are expected to rise due to increasing temperatures and associated adverse effects (IPCC 2023; UNEP 2023). Additionally, the OECD (2024a) estimates that mitigation-related investment needs in developing countries will range from USD 550 billion to USD 2.5 trillion annually by 2030. These figures highlight that the climate finance needs of developing countries far exceed the USD 300 billion mobilization target.

The gap between the climate finance target and actual needs is concerning because some mitigation and adaptation measures in developing countries depend on financial support. These are referred to as conditional contributions, contrasting with unconditional contributions, which countries can implement using their own resources. Of the costed needs listed in current NDCs, 48% are classified as conditional, 18% as unconditional, and 35% remain unspecified (SCF 2024). Thus, insufficient climate finance mobilization jeopardizes the achievement of mitigation and adaptation targets pledged under the Paris Agreement, including the collective goal of limiting global warming to 1.5 °C.

Beyond the shortfall in climate finance mobilization, two additional challenges persist. First, mobilization efforts have lagged behind political commitments. Official climate finance reporting from the OECD (2024b) indicates that developed countries failed to meet their USD 100 billion annual mobilization target by 2020, achieving it only in 2022 – two years later than promised. Second, critics argue that official climate finance reporting is inflated, and that the real volume of mobilized climate finance may be much lower than reported (Dasgupta et al. 2015; Carty, Kowalzig, and Zagema 2020; CARE 2021a, 2023). For example, an Oxfam assessment of climate finance reporting in 2017–2018 found that of the USD 59.5 billion officially reported, only USD 19–22.5 billion actually qualified as climate-specific net assistance (Carty, Kowalzig, and Zagema 2020). Similarly, Oxfam reported that climate finance reporting by the World Bank – the largest multilateral climate finance provider – could be overstated by as much as 40% (Farr, Morrissey, and Donaldson 2022). The same issue applies to adaptation finance from the Asian Development Bank, which may be overreported by up to 44% (Acharya, Sørensen, and Dejgaard 2024). Overall, Borst, Wencker, and Niekler (2023) estimate an overreporting rate of 32.03% across all providers' climate finance reporting. Disputes over the actual amount of mobilized climate finance arise partly from deficiencies in the reporting system and partly from disagreements over definitions and which financial instruments should qualify as climate finance.

Concerns also exist regarding the quality of climate finance provided to developing countries. Climate finance should be accessible and should not impose additional burdens on recipients. However, climate finance providers currently count all financial instruments – including grants, investments, and concessional and non-concessional loans – at face value, without considering potential future repayments (Carty, Kowalzig, and Zagema 2020; CARE 2021a). The role of loans in climate finance has increased over time: in 2013, loans comprised 52% of climate finance, rising to 67% by 2021 (OECD 2020, 2023). This increased reliance on loans raises concerns because it exacerbates the debt burdens of recipient countries, many of which already face high levels of debt that hinder economic development (Carty, Kowalzig, and Zagema 2020; Ciplet et al. 2022). Additionally, many subnational actors lack the creditworthiness or capacity to manage debt-based financial assistance (Colenbrander, Dodman, and Mitlin 2018; Bracking and Leffel 2021). Excessive reliance on loans thus restricts the ability of these actors to access climate finance effectively.

Another crucial aspect of climate finance quality is the speed at which funds are disbursed to recipients. The world's largest dedicated climate fund, the Green Climate Fund (GCF), was established to serve as part of the Financial Mechanism of the United Nations Framework Convention on Climate Change and to support the provision of climate finance to developing countries (UNFCCC 2011). Despite this mandate, the GCF has been criticized for its slow and complex funding process (Beasley 2023; Darby 2017; GCF 2021). Delays occur at multiple stages, including the initial accreditation process required for eligibility (Wilkinson, Treichel, and Robertson 2023), project approval (Treichel et al. 2024), and the final disbursement of funds (Djabare, Tovivo, and Koumassi 2021). These delays hinder the timely delivery of climate finance to recipient countries, impeding the implementation of critical mitigation and adaptation measures.

Current climate finance mobilization efforts fall short of official commitments in both quantity and quality, and the reporting system for climate finance remains flawed. The COP29 agreement seeks to scale up mobilization efforts to USD 300 billion; however, it fails to address issues related to the reporting system or the broader challenge of delivering high-quality climate finance. Ensuring that climate finance providers fulfill their commitments – both in terms of the quantity and quality of climate finance – is essential for meeting obligations under the Convention and addressing the needs of developing countries.

Lessons from the USD 100 Billion Goal

This section begins by unpacking issues related to the accounting system for climate finance, followed by a discussion on the quality of the mobilized finance. Climate finance mobilization is self-reported by developed countries in the OECD-DAC Creditor Reporting System (CRS), which tracks the objectives of the Rio Conventions[2] in development cooperation. Finance providers label the mitigation and adaptation components of their aid contributions through a three-score system: principal objective, significant objective, or no objective (OECD 2016). If projects have a principal climate objective, their full value is counted as climate finance; if they have a significant climate objective, donors apply a coefficient relative to the size of the climate component; and if they have no climate objective, they are not counted as climate finance (OECD 2024c).

However, this data is self-reported and lacks independent verification, making it prone to overreporting of projects' climate-related components (Weikmans and Roberts 2016). In an assessment of providers' adaptation finance reporting, CARE (2021a) shows that providers often exaggerate the climate-related component of projects or report non-climate-related projects as climate finance. For example, some providers, notably the Czech Republic, Iceland, Poland, and Slovenia, use a fixed coefficient of 100% for projects with a significant climate objective (OECD 2024c). This likely leads to a vast overestimation of climate finance. In addition to issues around donors' self-reporting, the design of the Rio marker system allows for double-, triple-, or even quadruple-counting of resources (Weikmans and Roberts 2016). This occurs when a project is labeled with more than one principal objective (OECD 2012). For this reason, the OECD has emphasized that the Rio marker system is suitable only for describing aid activities, not for tracking progress against a mobilization target (OECD 2012). Regardless, the Rio marker system remains the official approach for tracking international climate finance mobilization.

Another issue contributing to inflated climate finance reporting is the lack of an agreed definition or baseline for what constitutes new and additional finance (Mitchell, Ritchie, and Tahmasebi 2021; Stadelmann, Roberts, and Michaelowa 2011). If

---

2 The Rio Conventions were adopted at the 1992 Rio Earth Summit and consist of the UNFCCC, the Convention on Biological Diversity (CBD), and the Convention to Combat Desertification (UNCCD).

climate finance providers can relabel general development aid as climate finance, it risks displacing finance for other vital development sectors, such as health, education, or gender equality. For example, France and Japan have reported large increases in bilateral climate finance, yet there has been stagnation in non-climate-related aid contributions, suggesting that their climate finance is being drawn from development budgets (Mitchell, Ritchie, and Tahmasebi 2021; CARE 2023). To address this problem, it has been suggested that "new and additional" finance could be defined as "an increase compared to present and projected future development assistance" (Stadelmann, Roberts, and Michaelowa 2011). An even more ambitious definition would only count aid contributions above 0.7% of the provider's gross national income (GNI) as climate finance (Carty, Kowalzig, and Zagema 2020; Stadelmann, Roberts and Michaelowa 2011), since this is the level that developed countries have committed to providing as official development assistance (ODA) (UNGA1970, art. 43). In 2018, only five countries fulfilled the commitment to provide 0.7% of their GNI as ODA (Carty, Kowalzig, and Zagema 2020). Therefore, most of the currently reported climate finance would not qualify as such under this definition.

Disagreement also exists regarding the quality of climate finance provided to developing countries. Climate finance mobilization must be predictable and accessible and not carry high costs for recipients, such as the provision of loans at high interest rates. Yet, much of the finance mobilized by developed countries has been in the form of loans rather than grants (UNFCCC 2024). This is problematic because loans must be repaid and are often offered at high interest rates, which limits the capacity of developing countries to implement long-term adaptation measures. According to CARE (2023), 35% of reported climate finance from developed countries in 2021 consisted of loans rather than grants. These loans are often subject to strict conditionalities, such as economic liberalization and privatization reforms, which further undermine their effectiveness in supporting climate adaptation and mitigation (CARE 2021b).

Looking Forward

As outlined above, the current climate finance reporting system enables donors to overreport their mobilization efforts due to several structural issues: (1) the lack of independent verification of financial contributions, (2) the absence of a commonly agreed baseline and definition of "new and additional" sources of climate finance, (3) the failure to distinguish between high-quality climate finance that delivers tangible impacts and low-quality finance with potentially negative implications for developing countries, and (4) slow and complex disbursement procedures. According to Honig and Weaver (2020), donors are motivated by status and perceived legitimacy among their peers, and peer pressure can encourage poor performers to improve, at least to some extent. This suggests that governance reforms aimed at enhancing transparency and accountability in climate finance reporting could encourage climate finance providers to strengthen their mobilization efforts.

To address these challenges, several governance innovations can be pursued: first, establishing common definitions for key climate finance terms would greatly clarify what is meant by "climate finance". This is particularly important for the term "new and additional". As previously discussed, two distinct definitions for "new and additional" are proposed in the climate finance literature. The weaker option defines it as "an increase compared to present and projected future development assistance" (Stadelmann, Roberts, and Michaelowa 2011), while the more ambitious option considers only contributions exceeding 0.7% of the provider's GNI as "new and additional" (Carty, Kowalzig, and Zagema 2020; Stadelmann, Roberts, and Michaelowa 2011). We advocate for the latter option, as it would align commitments in both the development and climate regimes and significantly increase the financial support currently provided by developed countries to developing countries.

Second, stricter rules are needed regarding which financial instruments qualify as climate finance for accounting purposes. Loans have become more common in climate finance, but they often come with stringent terms and conditions favorable to developed countries. Loans are particularly disadvantageous for adaptation projects, which rarely generate financial returns and are harder to scale or replicate compared to mitigation projects. Mitigation projects, with their higher profitability and scalability, are more likely to attract private investment and repay loans. Small Island Developing States (SIDS) and Least Developed Countries (LDCs), which depend more on adaptation finance than mitigation finance due to their negligible emissions, are often the most resource-constrained and indebted, making it difficult for them to repay loans. We recommend that only grants be counted as adaptation finance, while concessional loans can be counted as mitigation finance. However, when loans are provided instead of grants for both climate mitigation and adaptation, the climate finance provider should be required to justify their choice of financial instrument, considering the project's economic plan and the recipient country's debt situation. Echoing the Bridgetown Initiative (2024), the recipient country's circumstances should not be evaluated solely in economic terms but also in terms of climate vulnerability, natural capital, and biodiversity conservation needs.

It is also essential to establish a new climate finance accounting and reporting system with more oversight and better mechanisms for tracking pledges. This system should include a new method for labeling aid contributions to prevent double-, triple-, or quadruple-counting of resources. The system should not rely solely on self-reporting by climate finance providers. Instead, an independent evaluation panel or committee could be established to monitor and verify that the aid contributions reported by developed countries indeed include a climate-related component. If aid contributions are reported as having a "significant" climate-related objective, the panel or committee should assess whether the reported coefficient accurately reflects the project's climate-related objective. For this purpose, climate finance providers must provide more detailed information on their aid projects and justify why they are considered climate related. Currently, the OECD-DAC CRS determines what information climate finance providers must provide. As an OECD system, only OECD member states have decision-making power over changes. A new climate finance and reporting system could be established under the UNFCCC, such as within the SCF, to ensure balanced decision-making power and transparency demands from both developed and developing countries. This new system would aim to prevent distortions in the reported contributions, which undermine the achievement of urgent global climate goals.

Finally, while not strictly part of the reporting and accounting system, the importance of operationalizing Article 2.1(c) of the Paris Agreement should be emphasized. This would help realign financial flows from fossil fuels toward renewable energy. The International Monetary Fund estimates that, in 2022, fossil fuel subsidies totaled USD 7 trillion globally (Black et al. 2023). Of this amount, 18% were explicit subsidies (involving undercharging for supply costs), while 82% were implicit subsidies (involving undercharging for environmental costs and missed consumption taxes) (Black et al. 2023). The distortion of the energy market by these vast subsidies significantly hampers the transition to green energy at the scale and speed required. Redirecting these subsidies toward renewable energy would have a transformative effect on the energy market and help achieve shared climate finance goals. A centralized mechanism could work with UNFCCC member states to identify strategies for realigning financial flows and providing pathways for the elimination of fossil fuel subsidies on a multilateral basis. Additionally, when developed countries explicitly subsidize fossil fuels, these subsidies could be subtracted from their climate finance contributions, as they undermine mitigation and adaptation objectives.

Conclusion

In 2022, developed-country parties to the UNFCCC claimed to have met their joint mobilization target of USD 100 billion per year to support the climate mitigation and adaptation efforts of developing countries (OECD 2024b). However, critics have raised concerns about the accuracy of these claims, pointing to flaws in the reporting and accounting system that may have inflated the mobilized finance figures. Allegations of overreporting and mislabeling of climate finance contributions, combined with issues such as double-, triple-, and quadruple-counting, have led to doubts about the true volume of mobilized finance (Dasgupta et al. 2015; Carty, Kowalzig, and Zagema 2020; CARE 2021a, 2023). Consequently, the actual mobilization efforts may be much lower than what climate finance providers claim.

In 2024, developed countries committed to increasing their joint climate finance mobilization target from USD 100 billion to USD 300 billion per year by 2035 (UNFCCC

2024). This new USD 300 billion goal, however, has two key limitations. First, it remains insufficient to meet the needs of developing countries. In response, scholars have suggested various innovative sources of finance to bridge the gap (Songwe, Stern, and Bhattacharya 2022; Shirai 2022; Abdel-Aziz and Eltouny 2025; Al-Mubarak and Zadek 2025; Bachrach 2025; Nasr and Fakir 2025). Second, the new climate finance mobilization target does not address the flaws in the reporting system that have led to the inflated accounting of previous climate finance contributions. Promoting transparency and implementing accountability mechanisms in climate finance reporting would help reveal the true mobilization efforts of climate finance providers, both in terms of quantity and quality. This could incentivize stronger performance by tapping into concerns over peer reputation and status.

To this end, we propose several reforms to the climate finance reporting and accounting system to foster transparency and greater accountability for climate finance providers. First, Parties to the UNFCCC should agree on a common definition for the term "new and additional". We support the definition proposed by scholars, which considers only aid contributions exceeding 0.7% of a provider's GNI as climate finance (Carty, Kowalzig, and Zagema 2020; Stadelmann, Roberts, and Michaelowa 2011), as this aligns with commitments made in both the development and climate regimes. Second, stricter rules should govern which financial instruments count as climate finance, limiting the role of loans. We propose that only grants be counted as adaptation finance, while concessional loans may be counted as mitigation finance. This would enable better tracking of high-quality finance and improve transparency regarding which categories of finance are directed to which projects. However, the use of loans in mitigation projects should be justified based on the project's economic plan, expected profitability, and the general debt situation of the recipient country. Third, a new accounting and reporting system for climate finance should be introduced, featuring independent oversight and more granular information from climate finance providers. This system should include a labeling mechanism that prevents double-, triple-, or quadruple-counting of resources. This new system could be set up under the UNFCCC, in place of the OECD, to ensure balanced accountability for both provider and recipient countries. Finally, Article 2.1(c) of the Paris Agreement should be operationalized with a centralized mechanism to help UNFCCC member states realign their financial flows and develop pathways to eliminate fossil fuel subsidies. Explicit fossil fuel subsidies by developed countries could be deducted from their climate finance contributions, as these subsidies undermine mitigation and adaptation objectives.

References

Abdel-Aziz, Amr Osama, and Nermin Eltouny. 2025. "Financing Mitigation, including Just Energy Transitions." In *Policy-Driven Climate and Development Finance: Strategies for Equitable Solutions*, edited by Mahmoud Mohieldin, Chapter 5. Berlin: De Gruyter.

Acharya, Sunil, Rasmus Bo Sørensen, and Hans Peter Dejgaard. 2024. *Unaccountable Adaptation: The Asian Development Bank's Overstated Claims on Climate Adaptation Finance*. Oxford: Oxfam GB.

Al-Mubarak, Razan Khalifa, and Simon Zadek. 2025. "Financing a Global Nature-Positive Economy." In *Policy-Driven Climate and Development Finance: Strategies for Equitable Solutions*, edited by Mahmoud Mohieldin, Chapter 7. Berlin: De Gruyter.

Bachrach, Sabrina, with Nidhi Upadhyaya, Jorge Gastelumendi, Juan José Guzmán Ayala, and Puninda Thind. 2025. "Financing the New Adaptation Economy." In *Policy-Driven Climate and Development Finance: Strategies for Equitable Solutions*, edited by Mahmoud Mohieldin, Chapter 6. Berlin: De Gruyter.

Beasley, Stephanie. 2023. "Devex Newswire: GCF's Slow Process Fails to Match Climate Urgency." *Devex*, November 15, 2023. Accessed February 3, 2025. http://devex.com/news/devex-newswire-gcf-s-slow-process-fails-to-match-climate-urgency-106573

Bhattacharya, Amar, Vera Songwe, Eléonore Soubeyran, and Nicholas Stern. 2023. *A Climate Finance Framework: Decisive Action to Deliver on the Paris Agreement – Summary*. London: Grantham Research Institute on Climate Change and the Environment.

Black, Simon, Antung A. Liu, Ian Parry, and Nate Verno. 2023. "IMF Fossil Fuel Subsidies Data: 2023 Update." IMF Working Paper WP/23/169. Washington, DC: International Monetary Fund.

Borst, Janos, Thomas Wencker, and Andreas Niekler. 2023. "Constructing a Credible Estimation for Overreporting of Climate Adaptation Funds in the Creditor Reporting System." In *Proceedings of the 7th Joint SIGHUM Workshop on Computational Linguistics for Cultural Heritage, Social Sciences, Humanities and Literature*, 99–109. Dubrovnik, Croatia: Association for Computational Linguistics.

Bracking, Sarah, and Benjamin Leffel. 2021. "Climate Finance Governance: Fit for Purpose?" *WIREs Climate Change* 12 (4): 1–18.

Bridgetown Initiative. 2024. *Bridgetown Initiative on the Reform of the International Development and Climate Finance Architecture*. Accessed February 12, 2025. https://www.bridgetown-initiative.org/bridgetown-initiative-3-0/.

CARE. 2021a. *Climate Adaptation Finance: Fact or Fiction*. The Hague: CARE.

CARE. 2021b. *Hollow Commitments: An Analysis of Developed Countries' Climate Finance Plans*. The Hague: CARE.

CARE. 2023. *Seeing Double: Decoding the 'Additionality' of Climate Finance*. Accessed February 2, 2025. https://careclimatechange.org/seeing-double-decoding-the-additionality-of-climate-finance/

Carty, Tracy, Jan Kowalzig, and Bertram Zagema. 2020. *Climate Finance Shadow Report 2020: Assessing Progress Towards the $100 Billion Commitment*. Oxford: Oxfam GB.

Ciplet, David, Danielle Falzon, Ike Uri, Stacy Ann Robinson, Romain Weikmans, and J. Timmons Roberts. 2022. "The Unequal Geographies of Climate Finance: Climate Injustice and Dependency in the World System." *Political Geography* 99: 102.

Climate Governance Commission (CGC). 2023. *Governing Our Planetary Emergency*. November. https://www.stimson.org/2023/governing-our-planetary-emergency/

Colenbrander, Sarah, David Dodman, and Diana Mitlin. 2018. "Using Climate Finance to Advance Climate Justice: The Politics and Practice of Channelling Resources to the Local Level." *Climate Policy* 18 (7): 902–915.

Copernicus. 2025. Global Climate Highlights 2024. Accessed February 2, 2025. https://climate.copernicus.eu/global-climate-highlights-2024.

Darby, Megan. 2017. "Green Climate Fund 'a Laughing Stock,' Say Poor Countries." *Climate Home News*. April 6, 2017. Accessed February 3, 2025. https://www.climatechangenews.com/2017/04/06/green-climate-fund-laughing-stock-ethiopia-bid-left-limbo/.

Dasgupta, Dipak, Shweta Rajasree Ray, and Salam S. Singh. 2015. *Climate Change Finance, Analysis of a Recent OECD Report: Some Credible Facts Needed*. Government of India Climate Change Finance Unit Discussion Paper. Accessed January 28, 2025. https://dea.gov.in/sites/default/files/ClimateChan geOEFDReport_0.pdf

Djabare, Komna, Kouassigan Tovivo, and Koffi Koumassi. 2021. *Five Years of the Green Climate Fund: How Much Has Flowed to Least Developed Countries?* Climate Analytics. Accessed January 28, 2025. https://ca1-clm.edcdn.com/assets/five_years_of_the_green_climate_fund.pdf?v=1679478104.

Farr, Jason, James Morrissey, and Christian Donaldson. 2022. *Unaccountable Accounting: The World Bank's Unreliable Climate Finance Reporting*. Briefing Paper. Oxford: Oxfam GB. https://doi.org/10.21201/2022.9554.

G77. 2024. *Ministerial Declaration Adopted by the 48th Annual Meeting of Ministers for Foreign Affairs of the Group of 77 (New York, 27 September 2024)*. Accessed March 3, 2025. https://docs.un.org/en/A/79/398.

Green Climate Fund(GCF). 2021. *Independent Evaluation of the Adaptation Portfolio and Approach of the Green Climate Fund. Report No. 9, February 2021*. Songdo: Green Climate Fund

Honig, Dan, and Catherine Weaver. 2020. "A Race to the Top? The Aid Transparency Index and the Social Power of Global Performance Indicators." In *The Power of Global Performance Indicators*, edited by Judith Kelley and Beth Simmons, 139–173. Cambridge: Cambridge University Press.

Intergovernmental Panel on Climate Change (IPCC). 2019. *IPCC Special Report on the Ocean and Cryosphere in a Changing Climate*. Cambridge: Cambridge University Press

Intergovernmental Panel on Climate Change (IPCC). 2021. "Weather and Climate Extreme Events in a Changing Climate." In *Climate Change 2021: The Physical Science Basis: Contribution of Working Group I to the Sixth Assessment Report of the Intergovernmental Panel on Climate Change*, 1513–1766. Cambridge: Cambridge University Press.

Intergovernmental Panel on Climate Change (IPCC). 2023. *Climate Change 2023: Synthesis Report*. Geneva: IPCC.

Jones, Matthew W., Glen P. Peters, Thomas Gasser, Robbie M. Andrew, Clemens Schwingshackl, Johannes Gütschow, Richard A. Houghton, Pierre Friedlingstein, Julia Pongratz, and Corinne Le Quéré. 2023. "National Contributions to Climate Change Due to Historical Emissions of Carbon Dioxide, Methane, and Nitrous Oxide Since 1850." *Scientific Data* 10 (1): 1–23.

Matthews, H. Damon, Tanya L. Graham, Serge Keverian, Cassandra Lamontagne, Donny Seto, and Trevor J. Smith. 2014. "National Contributions to Observed Global Warming." *Environmental Research Letters* 9 (1): 1–9.

Mitchell, Ian, Euan Ritchie, and Atousa Tahmasebi. 2021. *Is Climate Finance Towards $100 Billion 'New and Additional'?* CGD Policy Paper 205. Washington, DC: Center for Global Development.

Nasr, Mohamed, and Zaheer Fakir. 2025. "Financing Loss and Damage." In *Policy-Driven Climate and Development Finance: Strategies for Equitable Solutions*, edited by Mahmoud Mohieldin, Chapter 8. Berlin: De Gruyter.

Organisation for Economic Co-operation and Development (OECD). 2012. *Development Co-operation Report 2012: Lessons in Linking Sustainability and Development*. Paris: OECD Publishing.

Organisation for Economic Co-operation and Development (OECD). 2016. *OECD DAC Rio Markers for Climate: Handbook*. Paris: OECD Publishing

Organisation for Economic Co-operation and Development (OECD). 2020. *Climate Finance Provided and Mobilised by Developed Countries in 2013–18*. Paris: OECD Publishing.

Organisation for Economic Co-operation and Development (OECD). 2023. *Climate Finance Provided and Mobilised by Developed Countries in 2013–2021*. Paris: OECD Publishing

Organisation for Economic Co-operation and Development (OECD). 2024a. "The New Collective Quantified Goal on Climate Finance: Options for Reflecting the Role of Different Sources, Actors and Qualitative Considerations". Accessed January 28, 2025. https://one.oecd.org/document/COM/ENV/EPOC/IEA/SLT(2024)2/en/pdf.

Organisation for Economic Co-operation and Development (OECD). 2024b. *Climate Finance Provided and Mobilised by Developed Countries in 2013–2022*. Paris: OECD Publishing

Organisation for Economic Co-operation and Development (OECD). 2024c. "Results of the Survey on the Coefficients Applied to Climate Change Rio Marker Data when Reporting to the UNFCCC". Accessed January 28, 2025. https://one.oecd.org/document/DCD/DAC/STAT(2024)28/REV1/en/pdf.

Standing Committee on Finance (SCF). 2024. *Second Report on the Determination of the Needs of Developing Country Parties Related to Implementing the Convention and the Paris Agreement*. UN Framework Convention on Climate Change. Accessed January 28, 2025. https://unfccc.int/documents/640757

Shirai, Sayuri. 2022. *An Overview on Climate Change, Environment, and Innovative Finance in Emerging and Developing Economies*. Working Paper No. 1347. Tokyo: Asian Development Bank.

Songwe, Vera, Nicholas Stern, and Amar Bhattacharya. 2022. *Finance for Climate Action: Scaling Up Investment for Climate and Development*. London: Grantham Research Institute on Climate Change and the Environment.

Stadelmann, Martin, J. Timmons Roberts, and Axel Michaelowa. 2011. "New and Additional to What? Assessing Options for Baselines to Assess Climate Finance Pledges." *Climate and Development* 3 (3): 175–192.

Treichel, Pia, Michai Robertson, Emily Wilkinson, and Jack Corbett. 2024. "Scale and Access to the Green Climate Fund: Big Challenges for Small Island Developing States." *Global Environmental Change* 89: 102943. https://doi.org/10.1016/j.gloenvcha.2024.102943.

United Nations Environment Programme (UNEP). 2023. *Adaptation Gap Report 2023: Underfinanced. Underprepared. Inadequate investment and planning on climate adaptation leaves world exposed*. Nairobi: UNEP

United Nations Framework Convention on Climate Change (UNFCCC). n.d. "Parties & Observers". Accessed February 10, 2025. https://unfccc.int/parties-observers

United Nations Framework Convention on Climate Change (UNFCCC). 1992. *United Nations Framework Convention on Climate Change*. Accessed February 2, 2025. https://unfccc.int/files/essential_background/background_publications_htmlpdf/application/pdf/conveng.pdf.

United Nations Framework Convention on Climate Change (UNFCCC). 2009. *Report of the Conference of the Parties on its Fifteenth Session*. Accessed February 2, 2025. https://unfccc.int/resource/docs/2009/cop15/eng/11a01.pdf#page=4.

United Nations Framework Convention on Climate Change (UNFCCC). 2011. *Report of the Conference of the Parties on its Sixteenth Session*. Accessed February 24, 2025. https://unfccc.int/event/cop-16#decisions_reports.

United Nations Framework Convention on Climate Change (UNFCCC). 2015a. *Paris Agreement*. Accessed February 11, 2025. https://unfccc.int/sites/default/files/english_paris_agreement.pdf.

United Nations Framework Convention on Climate Change (UNFCCC). 2015b. *Report of the Conference of the Parties on its Twenty-first Session, held in Paris from 30 November to 13 December 2015*. Accessed February 11, 2025. https://unfccc.int/resource/docs/2015/cop21/eng/10a01.pdf.

United Nations Framework Convention on Climate Change (UNFCCC). 2024. *New Collective Quantified Goal on Climate Finance*. Accessed February 2, 2025. https://unfccc.int/documents/644460

United Nations General Assembly (UNGA). 1970. *A/RES/2626 (XXV)*. Accessed February 11, 2025. https://docs.un.org/A/RES/2626(XXV).

Weikmans, Romain, and J. Timmons Roberts. 2016. "Fit for Purpose: Negotiating the New Climate Finance Accounting Systems." *Policy Brief* 3/2016. Climate Strategies.

Wilkinson, Emily, Pia Treichel, and Michai Robertson. 2023. *Enhancing Access to Climate Finance for Small Island Developing States Considerations for the Green Climate Fund (GCF) Board*. Policy Brief. London: Overseas Development Institute.

Zamarioli, Luis H., Pieter Pauw, Michael König, and Hugues Chenet. 2021. "The Climate Consistency Goal and the Transformation of Global Finance." *Nature Climate Change* 11: 578–583.

Part Two: **Financing Climate Action**

Amr Osama Abdel-Aziz and Nermin Eltouny

Chapter 5
Financing Mitigation, Including Just Energy Transitions

Abstract: This chapter focuses on presenting the significant gap in the financing of mitigation actions and the urgent need to reconsider approaches in bridging this gap. Challenges and barriers associated with mobilizing finance for mitigation, including the integration of considerations for just energy transition, notably as crucial and decisive limitations for developing countries, are presented. The chapter identifies principal considerations related to socio-economic environments that hinder mitigation financing. In this context, a taxonomy of solutions, considering the promotion of sustainable development and socio-economic effects and informed by the dialogues and investment-focused events under the Sharm El-Sheikh Mitigation Ambition and Implementation Work Programme, is presented. Furthermore, the chapter highlights the need to reconsider the strategic direction for overcoming barriers related to access to finance, including increasing affordable finance, and reiterating the role and responsibility that developed countries must take to enable the scale-up of actionable solutions for mitigation actions, and limit warming to 1.5 °C.

Keywords: Mitigation finance, Just energy transition, Clean energy, New Collective Quantified Goal, Cost of capital, Paris Agreement

Introduction

Mitigation encompasses actions, policies, and measures aimed at reducing or avoiding greenhouse gas (GHG) emissions. Between 1850 and 2019, global cumulative emissions totaled 2,400 ± 240 GtCO$_2$,[1] consuming approximately four-fifths of the total carbon budget[2] necessary for a 50% probability of limiting the global temperature rise to 1.5 °C (IPCC 2023; UNFCCC 2023a). Observations indicate that the increase in global surface temperature between 1850–1900 and 2013–2022 was 1.15 °C, with land and ocean surface temperatures reaching 1.65 °C and 0.9 °C, respectively (IPCC 2023). From 2020

---

1 1 Gt = 10^{15} grams.

2 Carbon budget refers to "the maximum amount of cumulative net global anthropogenic CO$_2$ emissions that would result in limiting global warming to a given level with a given probability, taking into account the effect of other anthropogenic climate forcers. This is referred to as the Total Carbon Budget when expressed starting from the pre-industrial period, and as the Remaining Carbon Budget when expressed from a recent specified date." (IPCC 2022a).

onward, the remaining carbon budget for a 50% probability of limiting warming to 1.5 °C is 500 $GtCO_2$, while for a 67% probability of limiting warming to 2 °C, the budget increases to 1,150 $GtCO_2$ (IPCC 2023).

The concept of a "Just Transition" was first recognized in the Paris Agreement, which emphasizes "the imperatives of a just transition of the workforce and the creation of decent work and quality jobs, in accordance with nationally defined development priorities" (United Nations 2015). At COP27, a Just Transition work program was initiated and operationalized at COP28, aiming to establish equitable transition pathways. This program recognizes disparities between developed and developing countries, particularly in terms of socio-economic circumstances and development goals.

For many developing countries, fossil fuels remain critical as inexpensive and accessible energy sources that support development and, in some cases, constitute principal economic revenue streams. A just energy transition in these contexts must balance the need for decarbonization, with the imperative to prioritize poverty eradication and energy security. Resource limitations – primarily financial but also related to capacity and technology – mean that the transition to clean energy or low-carbon economies often competes with essential development priorities.

This chapter explores current trends and disparities in deploying mitigation technologies and investments, highlighting opportunities to scale up financing, while identifying barriers, particularly in developing countries where access to finance is limited.

Articles 2[3] and 3[4] of the Paris Agreement (United Nations 2015) on equity and common but differentiated responsibilities and respective capabilities (CBDR-RC) have thus far not been adequately considered or reflected in carbon budget burden shar-

---

3 "**Article 2.1**: This Agreement, in enhancing the implementation of the Convention, including its objective, aims to strengthen the global response to the threat of climate change, in the context of sustainable development and efforts to eradicate poverty, including by:

(a) Holding the increase in the global average temperature to well below 2 °C above pre-industrial levels and pursuing efforts to limit the temperature increase to 1.5 °C above pre-industrial levels, recognizing that this would significantly reduce the risks and impacts of climate change;

(b) Increasing the ability to adapt to the adverse impacts of climate change and foster climate resilience and low greenhouse gas emissions development, in a manner that does not threaten food production; and

(c) Making finance flows consistent with a pathway towards low greenhouse gas emissions and climate-resilient development."

Article 2.2: "This Agreement will be implemented to reflect equity and the principle of common but differentiated responsibilities and respective capabilities, in the light of different national circumstances."

4 **Article 3**: "As Nationally Determined Contributions to the global response to climate change, all Parties are to undertake and communicate ambitious efforts as defined in Articles 4, 7, 9, 10, 11 and 13 with the view to achieving the purpose of this Agreement as set out in Article 2. The efforts of all Parties will represent a progression over time, while recognizing the need to support developing country Parties for the effective implementation of this Agreement."

ing, emission reduction target determinations, and the associated financial support that should be provided to developing countries.

Current Trends in the Deployment of Mitigation Finance

The potential for mitigation, defined as "the quantity of net greenhouse gas emission reductions that can be achieved by a given mitigation option relative to specified emission baselines" (IPCC 2022a), has been assessed across various sectors. Agriculture, Forestry, and Land Use (AFOLU) represents the highest mitigation potential, estimated at 15 Gt CO_2e by 2030. This is closely followed by the energy sector, with a potential of just over 14 Gt CO_2e, as shown in Figure 5.1.

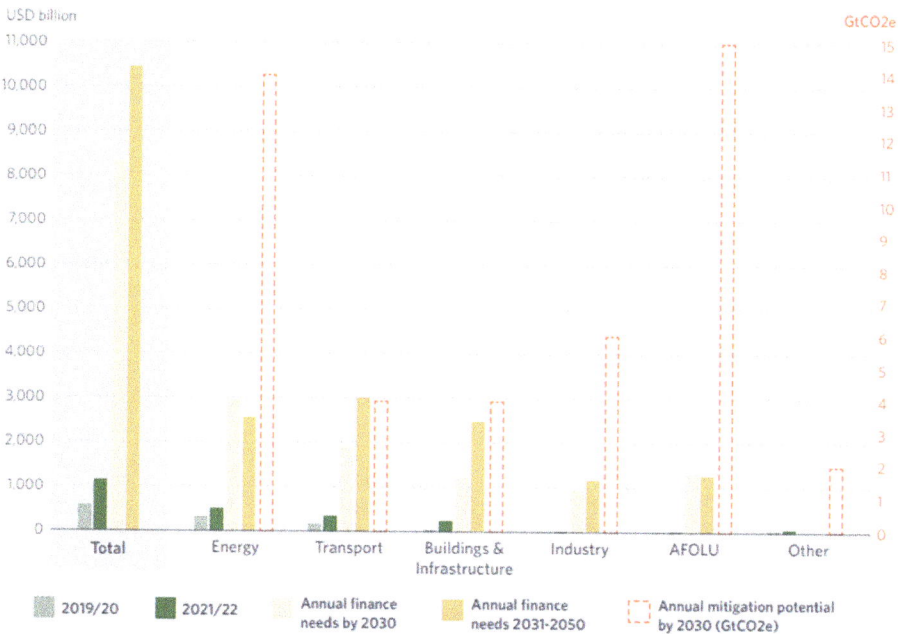

Figure 5.1: Climate finance flows in major mitigation sectors, finance needs, and mitigation potential. Note: Historical finance flows (2019–2022) are expressed in nominal USD. Climate finance needs for 2023–2050 are expressed in 2022 USD. Average mitigation potential is sourced from IPCC 2022b. Source: CPI (2023).

Achieving a global energy transition necessitates the rapid deployment of new technologies (IRENA 2023). Electrification is essential for leveraging renewable energy, with the share of electricity in final energy consumption needing to increase from

20% to 50% by 2050 to meet the 1.5 °C target. Significant infrastructure development is required for green hydrogen production, grid expansion, and energy storage to connect clean energy supply and demand (IRENA 2023). Despite rising investments in battery storage and hydrogen technologies, these have yet to reach their full potential (CPI 2023).

In terms of carbon capture and storage technologies, the global technical geological storage capacity – estimated at 1,000 Gt CO_2 – exceeds the storage needed to limit temperature rise to 1.5 °C through 2100 (IPCC 2023). However, current capacity is limited, with approximately 50 million tons of CO_2 captured annually by the 40 operational commercial facilities worldwide. To meet net-zero targets, global capacity must increase to between 350 and 1,200 Gt CO_2 (UNFCCC 2023b).

Significant regional and sectoral disparities exist in the deployment of mitigation technologies and financing. Between 2019/2020 and 2021/2022, global mitigation finance flows increased by USD 439 billion. However, 90% of clean energy investments were concentrated in developed countries, China, Brazil, and India. Total mitigation finance for 2021/2022 amounted to USD 1,150 billion, representing the bulk of the USD 1.27 trillion in global annual climate finance flows (CPI 2023). Most finance was allocated to energy systems (USD 515 billion), transport (USD 336 billion), and buildings and infrastructure (USD 240 billion). In contrast, agriculture and industry received less than 4% of total finance despite their significant mitigation potential (CPI 2023).

Increased investments in advanced economies are partly driven by the declining costs of renewable energy installations, which have reduced the levelized cost of electricity (IRENA 2023). Conversely, the Least Developed Countries (LDCs) and emerging markets (excluding China) received only 3 and 15% of global climate finance flows, respectively (CPI 2023).

For developing countries, reliant on fossil fuels, transitioning to renewable energy necessitates significant capacity expansion due to differences in energy generation efficiency. For instance, replacing 4 TWe of fossil fuel generation with renewable sources requires an installed capacity of 12 TWe[5] of solar and wind energy, highlighting the scale of infrastructure needs and financing required (Bolson, Prieto, and Patzek 2022).

Large disparities are evident in reported climate finance contributions from developed to developing countries. According to the Organisation for Economic Co-operation and Development (OECD), climate finance grew to USD 115.9 billion in 2022, with mitigation finance at USD 69.9 billion (OECD 2024). In comparison, UNFCCC estimates for climate-specific contributions to developing countries averaged USD 51.6 billion annually for 2019–2020, with climate-specific contributions alone totaling USD 40.2 billion (UNFCCC 2023c). Oxfam estimates suggest the real value of financial support for climate

---

5 1 TWe $= 10^{12}$ W.

action in 2020 was significantly lower, between USD 21 and 24.5 billion, compared to the USD 83.3 billion reported by climate finance contributors (Zagema et al. 2023).

Mitigation measures can promote socio-economic development through green job creation, workforce upskilling, and environmental benefits such as reduced air pollution (UNFCCC 2023b). However, trade-offs may arise, particularly in developing countries, where the transition to green energy could negatively affect vulnerable populations, such as through the removal of fossil fuel subsidies or carbon pricing. Ensuring a just transition requires assessing these impacts and increasing financial and technological support for developing countries (UNFCCC 2023b).

Global Outlook: Projected Financing Needs and Mitigation Targets

Despite mitigation finance reaching USD 1.15 trillion in 2021/2022 (CPI 2023), projected needs are significantly higher. The Standing Committee on Finance (SCF)[6] reported total cost estimates, including adaptation and cross-cutting needs, of USD 5.04–6.88 trillion based on NDCs as of June 2024, with USD 3.96 – 3.97 trillion allocated to mitigation (UNFCCC Standing Committee on Finance 2024). The global energy transition alone will require USD 5 trillion annually through 2050 (IRENA 2023), while climate finance needs are projected at USD 8.1 trillion annually through 2030 and up to USD 10 trillion for 2031–2050 (CPI 2023). According to IPCC projections (2022b), achieving a temperature rise limit of 1.5°C to 2°C between 2020 and 2030 requires investments that are 3 to 6 times higher than current levels.

By sector, the highest financing needs are in energy, followed by industry, transport, forestry, ecosystem and biodiversity, agriculture and food, and waste management (UNFCCC Standing Committee on Finance 2024). For a 1.5 °C scenario, half of the investments must focus on renewable energy and electrification, with one-third allocated to energy efficiency and the remainder to fossil fuel mitigation and CO_2 removal technologies (IRENA 2023).

More ambitious mitigation targets also increase financing needs, including funds to address potential socio-economic impacts to ensure a just transition. Developed countries' mitigation targets often fail to account for historical responsibility, shifting the burden disproportionately to developing countries. The U.S. and EU alone account for 47% of historical emissions from 1750 to 2017, with per capita emissions of 17.6 t CO_2e and 7 t CO_2e in 2019, respectively (Ritchie 2019; Vigna and Friedrich 2023). By contrast, India, with a per capita emission of 2.5 t CO_2e, and many developing nations remain low emitters but face significant pressure to increase their targets. Developing

---

6 Reported needs are based on the UNFCCC Standing Committee on Finance (2024).

economies with high per capita emissions, such as Qatar (41 tCO_2e per capita) and Kuwait (32 tCO_2e per capita) from 1990 to 2019 (Vigna and Friedrich 2023), have contributed only 0.12% and 0.17%, respectively, to global historical emissions from 1750 to 2019 (Ritchie 2019).

The NDCs communicated prior to COP26 indicate that the 1.5 °C limit is likely to be exceeded during the twenty-first century (IPCC 2022b). Recent analyses indicate that global carbon budget allocations disproportionately favor developed countries. Under equity-based models,[7] 89% and 11% of the remaining global carbon budget[8] should be allocated to non-Annex I and Annex I[9], including EU 27 (Alcaraz et al. 2023). Analyses of equity considerations in IPCC global modeled scenarios reveal significant and persistent inter-regional disparities. These include lower-than-average GDP per capita and substantially reduced primary energy consumption per capita for developing countries. Projections indicate that Sub-Saharan Africa, South Asia, Latin America, and the rest of Asia will remain below the energy sufficiency threshold of 79 GJ per person. Meanwhile, fossil fuel consumption per capita is higher across all Annex I regions, with the majority of CO_2 emissions reductions, through sequestration, originating in developing countries (Kanitkar, Mythri, and Jayaraman 2024).

Moreover, historical emissions linked to colonialism, including early deforestation and later fossil fuel combustion, significantly inflate developed countries' contributions. When emissions are reassigned from colonized regions to colonial powers, the historical shares of countries like the United Kingdom and the Netherlands more than double and triple, respectively (Evans and Viisainen 2023).

This misallocation exacerbates financial burdens on developing nations and hinders their ability to implement equitable mitigation strategies, perpetuating disparities in addressing climate change impacts.

Barriers to Financing Mitigation and a Just Energy Transition

Achieving the global potential for meeting mitigation targets and facilitating an energy transition requires overcoming significant barriers, including insufficient financing and economic constraints, particularly in developing countries. Enabling domestic policies is also essential to advancing these goals.

---

7 Defined in terms of responsibility, capacity, equality, and right to development.
8 This assumes a remaining global carbon budget of 400 $GtCO_2$ corresponding to 67% probability of achieving 1.5 °C.
9 Party included in Annex I to the Convention and Party not included in Annex I to the Convention.

Economic and Financial Barriers

1. Cost of Capital

Developing countries face significantly higher capital costs for clean energy projects, which limits access to funding (IRENA 2023). A survey[10] of risks perceived by investors, when considering Africa, which contributes to the application of high risk premiums, revealed several key concerns: limited exit options (62%), currency risk (56%), a less attractive risk–return profile than other markets (35%), political risk (35%), and non-enabling regulatory environments (32%) (Hill et al. 2024). Moreover, the higher perceived risk compared to the actual risk, as estimated by credit rating agencies, increases the cost of capital in developing countries (UNFCCC 2024). For instance, the risk profile of a project in a developing economy can be five or six times higher than that in an advanced economy (IRENA 2023). The cost of capital for utility-scale solar photovoltaics is 4% in Western Europe, while it is 8.7% in the Middle East (excluding the GCC) and Africa (IRENA 2023). There is also a significant disparity among developing countries with the same risk rating. For example, the cost of debt for climate-related projects is 20% in South Africa compared to 8% in Brazil (Gautam, Purkayastha, and Widge 2023).

2. High Upfront Capital Costs

Clean energy systems typically involve higher infrastructure costs compared to non-climate-friendly infrastructure (IRENA 2023). Despite decreases in the overall costs of installations, costs remain prohibitively high in developing countries. Additional challenges include investment risks arising from investment lock-ins and delays in developing countries. Green investments for power generation often involve asset-specific investments and contractual risks due to weak enforcement of contracts, which leads to counterparty risks. For instance, decreases in electricity costs due to the increasing development and deployment of green technologies can lead electricity buyers to opt for the least costly option, even if they are bound by contracts with higher-cost options. In such cases, investments are locked in, and the investor is held hostage by the contract. Counterparty risks contribute to the reluctance to invest or demand higher risk premiums (Ryan 2021).

3. High Public Debt

Developing countries face rising public debt, especially in Africa, where many nations are experiencing debt distress (UNFCCC 2024). Public debt for developing countries increased from 16% to 30% of global debt between 2010 and 2023. Combined with rising interest payments, these countries have fewer resources available for development goals and climate action. In emerging and developing countries, public expenditure

---

10 Survey conducted by African Private Equity industry survey referenced by BCG (Hill et al. 2024).

on interest payments (2.4% of GDP) was higher than spending on climate investments (2.1% of GDP) in 2019 (UNCTAD 2024).

4. Insufficient Public Finance and No-Cost/Low-cost Financing Instruments

Public finance constitutes just over half of all global climate finance. Development finance institutions (DFIs) are a crucial financing source, providing 57% of all global public finance, estimated at an annual average of USD 640 billion for 2021/2022. National DFI sources and state-owned enterprises, predominantly comprising domestic commitments in East Asia and Pacific institutions, contributed 37% of the total. Contributions by governments, multilateral DFIs, state-owned financial institutions (FIs), bilateral DFIs, and multilateral climate funds were 16%, 15%, 9.5%, 5%, and 0.5% of global public climate finance, respectively (CPI 2023).

5. Multilateral Development Banks and Financial Institutions

Multilateral development banks (MDBs) are an important source of financing for developing countries. However, their effectiveness is limited by the low quantum of funding and financial instruments ill-suited to the economic realities of borrowing countries. According to the OECD, MDBs provided USD 46.9 billion in multilateral public finance and mobilized USD 10.7 billion in private finance, totaling USD 57.7 billion in 2022. In comparison, in 2019–2020, MDBs reportedly provided USD 30.5 billion and USD 33.2 billion, respectively (OECD 2024). Loans represented 89% of the finance provided by MDBs (OECD 2024). For low-income economies, loans accounted for 35% and grants for 64% of public climate finance. In contrast, for low-middle, upper-middle, and high-income economies, loans represented 85%, 87%, and 92% of public climate finance, respectively (OECD 2024). Specifically, for mitigation finance, project-level market-rate debt (43%) and equity (32%) were the main financial instruments (OECD 2024). Insufficient capital increases for MDBs to support governments further reduces an already insufficient level of public and affordable finance (UNFCCC 2024).

6. Discrepancies in Reported Climate Finance Values

Developed countries committed to providing USD 100 billion per year by 2020 to developing countries. According to a recent OECD report, this goal was achieved in 2022, with developed countries providing and mobilizing USD 115.9 billion, mostly through public finance in multilateral (USD 50.6 billion) and bilateral (USD 41.0 billion) channels, with a smaller contribution from mobilized private finance (USD 21.9 billion) and other export credits (USD 2.4 billion) (OECD 2024). However, estimates based on the climate relevance of finance for previous years suggest that this goal has not been met, with contributions to climate finance often being overestimated (Zagema et al. 2023). In 2020, the reported climate finance provided and mobilized amounted to USD 83.3 billion (OECD 2024). Oxfam re-estimated climate finance values reported by the OECD based on different accounting principles – namely, climate relevance (referred to as climate-specific net assistance or CSNA) and the real support value of provided finance based on grant-equivalent value.[11] Using these principles, estimates of climate finance considered as support ranged from USD 21 billion to USD 24.5 billion in 2020 (Zagema et al. 2023).

For MDB-reported climate finance, estimates indicate that of the USD 31.7 billion reported for 2019–2020, only USD 6 billion were climate-relevant funds (Zagema et al. 2023). This large discrepancy is attributed to the net value of support, which is estimated as zero for non-concessional loans, highlighting the MDBs' reliance on such instruments. The discrepancy arises from the overestimation of the climate relevance of funding, with non-grant instruments being reported at face value rather than based on their financial benefit or grant-equivalent value (as required for official development assistance reporting). When converted to grant-equivalent value,[12] the contributions of loans and non-grant instruments from developed countries ranged from less than half (e.g., Austria, France, Japan, Spain, U.S., and MDBs) to between half and three-quarters (e.g., Canada, Germany, Italy, and Switzerland) of the reported amounts (Zagema et al. 2023).

7. Insufficient Domestic Resource Mobilization

Public finance is crucial for attracting the private investments necessary to cover the costs of the energy transition (UNFCCC 2023b) in both developing and developed countries. For developing countries, public finance is the principal source for financing long-term and high-cost infrastructure projects. However, insufficient affordable and long-term domestic public finance for large infrastructure works remains a key barrier (UNFCCC 2024), with significant implications for private sector engagement.

8. Insufficient Private-Sector Investments

While private finance accounts for 49% of climate finance in developed countries, economic constraints – such as currency issues, low returns, and high-risk assessments – limit investments in developing countries. Assets worth over USD 100 trillion (accessible to rated OECD countries) are largely unavailable to developing countries, where only 13 out of 145 least-developed and upper-middle-income countries exceed the investment-grade cut-off (IRENA 2023). Approaches used in advanced economies to mobilize private investment, such as blended finance, often fail to mobilize the necessary private capital in developing economies (Sweeney 2024). The Just Energy Transition Partnerships, for example, raise concerns about the actual disbursement of funds and the need for governments to finance through loans, which, even if concessional, are repaid with interest, thus imposing debt (Sweeney 2024). Other examples include the

---

11 For MDBs, average grant element percentages of bilateral finance based on OECD methodology were determined for concessional loans, while non-concessional loans were attributed a zero value for assistance (Zagema et al. 2023).

12 The loan's grant-equivalent value represents the calculated difference between a loan with favorable terms (like low interest) after considering repayments, grace periods, and other relevant factors, compared to a loan at standard market rates (Zagema et al., 2023).

solar transition project in Zambia, where most financing came from public investments and subsidies rather than private sector crowding-in (Kenny 2023).

9. Negative Impacts on Fuel-Based Economies and the Cost of the Energy Transition

Many developing countries depend heavily on fossil fuel revenues, which support public spending and foreign currency reserves. Low- and middle-income economies account for 31 out of the 40 top fossil fuel-based economies, with 13 of them being in "fragile and conflict-affected situations". Estimates of fossil fuel-generated rents from oil, coal, and gas for the 40 top fossil fuel-dependent economies amount to as much as 14.3%, on average, of GDP annually. International support, combined with urgent domestic fiscal and economic reforms, is of utmost importance to manage the impacts, particularly in countries that lack the capacity to address these impacts and where populations are already living in extreme poverty – e.g., Angola, Chad, Nigeria, and South Sudan (Jensen 2023).

Policies

While developed economies and China have mobilized domestic finance effectively (CPI 2023), many developing countries struggle with challenging domestic financing environments and policies for attracting the high levels of investment needed for cost-intensive clean energy infrastructure. For instance, in Africa, complex tax systems are not designed to mobilize clean energy investments, often failing to incentivize such investments and hindering tax revenue generation (UNFCCC 2024). Policy trade-offs, such as those related to privatization, must be carefully considered to avoid non-inclusive transitions. Practical cases in South Africa and Indonesia demonstrate how policy reforms that facilitate the privatization of public utilities face strong opposition from labor and union groups, raising socio-economic trade-off concerns related to inclusivity and a just energy transition (Sweeney 2024).

Solutions to Overcome Barriers

To effectively finance mitigation efforts and ensure a just energy transition, barriers must be addressed through coordinated actions on both policy and financial fronts.

Solutions to Address Economic and Financial Barriers

The support needed by developing countries should be reconsidered through the lens of equity and common but differentiated responsibilities and respective capabilities principles. Accelerating financial support from developed countries and other sources is identified as a critical enabler to enhance mitigation action in developing countries (IPCC 2022b).

1. Going Beyond the Insufficient New Collective Quantified Goal to Address the Actual Needs of Developing Countries

In 2009, developed countries pledged to provide USD 100 billion per year until 2020; however, this amount was not determined based on the quantified needs for addressing climate change in developing nations. The actual needs are estimated to be in the trillions, as previously discussed. Unfortunately, the New Collective Quantified Goal (NCQG) agreed upon at COP29 does not adequately address the needs of developing countries. All climate-related outflows from MDBs will be counted in the NCQG. The agreed target of at least USD 300 billion by 2035, when discounted to 2020 values and including contributions from developing countries through their MDB contributions, does not represent the required progress in supporting developing countries to implement their current Nationally Determined Contributions (NDCs) and increase their ambition to limit global warming to 1.5 °C. Moreover, the decision on the NCQG acknowledges the need for public and grant-based resources, as well as highly concessional loans, but lacks clear operationalization. The decision calls for all actors – public and private sources – to work together to scale up climate finance to developing countries to USD 1.3 trillion per year by 2035. This call primarily focuses on investment goals, which could impose significant debt burdens on developing countries. Unless grant-based and highly concessional climate finance is scaled up to meet the needs of developing countries, the achievement of the Paris Agreement goals will be jeopardized, potentially leading to failure.

Addressing the wide mitigation investment gap affecting all sectors in developing countries necessitates a significant increase in financial support that does not exacerbate debt distress. Financial support must increase in line with projected needs, which are estimated in the trillions, as evidenced by numerous references, including the Standing Committee on Finance (SCF 2024). There is also a need to scale up transparency regarding how climate finance is collected and distributed (Jensen 2023). To improve transparency in climate finance, it is necessary to report contributions based on climate relevance, particularly by using grant-equivalent value and employing a project-level approach, especially for large-scale, broad projects (Zagema et al. 2023).

2. Considering Equity and CBDR-RC Principles for Defining Financial Support

The principles of equity and CBDR-RC must be considered to redefine carbon space and address the disproportionate allocation of the mitigation burden. These principles also call for revising the underestimation of emission reduction targets set by advanced economies. Developed countries should honor their historical responsibility by providing increased financial support to developing countries, reflecting their true needs rather than the underestimation of current pledges (Zagema et al. 2023). The decision on the NCQG will be reviewed in 2030. This review would allow for an assessment of the situation in terms of NDCs implementation and the adequacy of the support provided to developing countries. It is hoped that such an assessment will lead to an increase in both the level of support and the quantum of the NCQG to a meaningful value with proper instruments, thus enabling the achievement of the Paris Agreement goals. On the international financing system front, a clear definition of what constitutes actual climate-specific contributions must be established. Furthermore, the international financial system must be reformed to enable developing countries to access affordable finance, particularly from MDBs (addressed in the next section).

3. Increasing MDBs and Multilateral Climate Fund Capital

Expanding the capital of MDBs will improve their ability to provide affordable finance and support climate action in developing countries. Reforming MDBs has gained significant traction as an essential component of addressing the financing gap. Proposed reforms to scale up and provide low-cost forms of finance include optimizing existing balance sheets, developing innovative tools such as portfolio guarantees and hybrid capital,[13] increasing capital through paid-in commitments from government shareholders, and enhancing private finance mobilization (Jacobs, Getzel, and Colenbrander 2024). The recent decision on the NCQG provided important guidance to international financial institutions, including MDBs, on how to adjust their operational models, channels, and instruments to be fit for purpose in addressing global climate change. The guidance includes the deployment of non-debt-inducing instruments, shifting the risk appetite in climate finance, simplifying access to finance, scaling up highly concessional finance, and increasing grant-based finance to Least Developed Countries (LDCs) and Small Island Developing States (SIDS).

4. Lowering the Cost of Capital and Addressing Currency Risk

Changes in financial systems are needed to address country-specific constraints, such as how credit ratings are assessed and assigned. This is a critical factor in reducing the high cost of capital and offering instruments that do not exacerbate debt distress vulnerability. In particular, reforms to internal risk-weighting rules and official development accounting rules are needed to allow the greater use of blended concessional guarantees (CPI 2023). Solutions to currency risk include lending in local currencies, with MDBs sharing the risks of currency mismatch through currency hedging facilities (CPI 2023). Modeling studies also suggest that credit guarantees can reduce risk premiums, improve credit ratings, and serve as a potential solution to de-risking and reducing the high cost of capital (Gautam, Purkayastha, and Widge 2023).

---

13 Hybrid capital is 'a type of financial instrument which is sold to investors to mobilize equity and associated leverage without diluting MDB shareholder rights' (Jacobs, Getzel, and Colenbrander 2024).

5. Addressing Debt

Financial systems and structures should consider the debt distress that characterizes many developing countries. Debt swaps have emerged as one of the innovative solutions gaining traction, where the borrowing country receives debt relief in exchange for a climate commitment, such as decarbonizing the economy and investing in climate-resilient infrastructure (Whiting 2024). Addressing debt distress to avoid the vicious cycle of debt and high cost of capital will also improve the business environment needed for private sector engagement.

6. Reconsidering the Role of Private Investment

Private investment is often touted as a key solution for bridging the financing gap, though its effectiveness is limited, especially in low-income and developing economies. The reliance on private investments can lead to increased debt burdens for governments, as they often need to secure loans to attract private capital. The macroeconomic constraints faced by many developing countries make it unrealistic to expect private investments alone to fill the financing gap. Instead, the root causes of the investment gap must be reconsidered within the broader economic context. One of the main reasons relates to the investment-grade ratings of countries; private investors can only invest in investment-grade countries, which prevents investment in non-investment-grade and unrated countries, as well as in small or unprofitable projects, leading to a shortage of investments in those countries (IRENA 2023). To unlock access to private investors controlling assets in the trillions (e.g., institutional investors like pension funds and insurance), risk–return profiles must fulfill investors' requirements. Risk–return profiles can be restructured through de-risking instruments such as risk guarantees, grants, subordinated debt, and junior equity, and by enhancing returns through providing "investors priority rights to cash flows generated" (IRENA 2023).

7. Considering Developing Countries' Needs and Circumstances in New Initiatives

For example, the New Global Financing Pact (Présidence de la République 2023) proposes an action plan to increase financing through four priority actions. The first action addresses solutions for the debt burden, citing "ways to secure a sufficient amount of concessional resources for least developed and most vulnerable countries", including renegotiations and restructuring, as well as requests targeting MDBs to develop a concessionality framework and a common definition for vulnerability, especially as it relates to the poorest countries. The second action defines new and innovative sources of finance, including development banks' delivery of concessional finance. The third action proposes carbon pricing and scaling-up investments in EMDEs based on partnerships. The fourth action relates to the role of MDBs and financial institutions, which includes expanding foreign exchange mitigation instruments to address currency risk, simplifying loan access, providing repayment flexibility, and integrating private sector investment policies into developing countries' national strategies. The Pact focuses on concessionality, not grant financing. Furthermore, carbon pricing has complex distributional impacts on the poor and on health, among other factors, which need to be assessed (Shang 2023). Studies show that carbon pricing, accompanied by universal cash transfers and targeted assistance, could protect those most likely to be affected (Shang 2023). In the context of developing countries already facing budgetary constraints for development, the availability of such assistance may not be guaranteed. Considering that concessional financing can still add to debt distress, carbon pricing will likely shift the added burden onto the poor. Additionally, the Pact does not call on historically responsible countries to increase their contributions, including to MDBs, reflecting an incomplete assessment of the causes of the finance gap. Finally, the Pact falls short of addressing the crux of the climate financing gap – calling on developed countries to increase their contributions.

Solutions to Address Challenges Related to Policies

1. Supportive Regulatory and Policy Frameworks

Supportive regulatory frameworks are needed for the deployment of new technologies. Standards and certification systems can stimulate innovation, drive economies of scale, and lower capital costs by reducing technology expenses (IRENA 2023). Creating domestic enabling environments through strengthened public financial policies and institutions, and domestic capital markets is considered key to increasing local investments (CPI 2023). Examples include incentives for electric vehicles, which played a principal role in increasing such investments in the United States, China, and Western Europe (2020–2021) (CPI 2023). Governments can also play an important role in providing clear policy signals, reducing projects' risk profiles, and increasing confidence for private sector investments by providing a long-term policy framework aligned with the characteristics of long-term investments in energy transition assets (IRENA 2023). In the case of developing countries, assessing the impacts of enabling policies on socio-economic development to ensure a just energy transition will require strengthened institutions and capacity building for performing such assessments.

2. Inclusivity and Social Impact Considerations in Policy Reforms

Policy reform to create an enabling business environment is a recurrent theme. For example, the New Global Financing Pact (Summit for a New Global Financing Pact 2023) suggests that developing countries integrate private sector enabling into national strategies. However, policy reforms to increase privatization could lead to unjust transitions. Examples from South Africa and Indonesia show that attempts to privatize public utilities have faced significant opposition from labor unions (Sweeney 2024). Ensuring that policy reforms are inclusive and considerate of social impacts is essential.

Conclusion

The pathways to achieving urgent mitigation targets and the potential to limit the temperature rise to 1.5 °C are known. While developing countries agreed to share the burden, respecting equity and CBDR-RC and under the condition of support (Article 9.1 of the Paris Agreement), the latter has thus far been inadequate, resulting in a large financing gap and the inability of developing countries to implement known mitigation pathways. Considering the debilitating financial and economic barriers facing developing countries is imperative to ensure that climate action and low-carbon transitions do not exacerbate already strained socio-economic realities.

Developed countries must strengthen their targets to accurately reflect their historical responsibility and avoid shifting additional burdens onto developing countries. Developing countries' NDCs will remain as targets only on paper, unless the required support is provided to implement these targets. Developed countries must live up to their commitments under the Paris Agreement and provide the necessary support. Unfortunately, the NCQG agreed upon at COP29 falls short of addressing the needs of developing countries. It was decided that the decision on NCQG will be reviewed in 2030. This will allow the assessment of the situation in terms of the implementation of NDCs, and the adequacy of the support provided to developing countries. It is hoped that such an assessment will lead to an increase in the support provided and the quantum of the NCQG to a meaningful value with proper instruments, which would allow the achievement of the Paris Agreement goals. Failure to provide necessary support will set the Paris Agreement on a path to failure.

References

Alcaraz, Olga, Manel Balfegó, Clàudia Cruanyes, Oliver Herrera, Cristián Retamal, Bàrbara Sureda, Katherine Tinoco, and Albert Turon. 2023. "Fair Carbon Budget for the European Union." The Group of Governance on Climate Change (GGCC) of the Universitat Politècnica de Catalunya (UPC). Accessed December 15, 2024. https://upcommons.upc.edu/bitstream/handle/2117/394675/EU%20Carbon%20Budget%20Final%20Document.pdf.

Bolson, Natanael, Pedro Prieto, and Tadeusz Patzek. 2022. "Capacity Factors for Electrical Power Generation from Renewable and Nonrenewable Sources." *Proceedings of the National Academy of Sciences* 119 (52): e2205429119. https://doi.org/10.1073/pnas.2205429119.

Climate Policy Initiative (CPI). 2023. *Global Landscape of Climate Finance 2023*. https://www.climatepolicyinitiative.org/publication/global-landscape-of-climate-finance-2023/

Evans, Simon, and Verner Viisainen. 2023. "Revealed: How Colonial Rule Radically Shifts Historical Responsibility for Climate Change." *Carbon Brief*, November 26. Accessed December 15, 2024. https://www.carbonbrief.org/revealed-how-colonial-rule-radically-shifts-historical-responsibility-for-climate-change/.

Gautam, Kushagra, Dhruba Purkayastha, and Vikram Widge. 2023. *Cost of Capital for Renewable Energy Investments in Developing Economies and the Need for a Global Credit Guarantee Facility*. Discussion

Paper. Climate Policy Initiative. Accessed December 15, 2024. https://www.climatepolicyinitiative.org/publication/cost-of-capital-for-renewable-energy-investments-in-developing-economies/

Hill, Katie, Chris Mitchell, Mills Schenck, Patrick Dupoux, and Warren Chetty. 2024. "More Money, Fewer Problems: Closing Africa's Climate Finance Gap." *Boston Consulting Group*. Accessed December 15, 2024. https://www.bcg.com/publications/2024/more-money-fewer-problems-closing-africas-climate-finance-gap.

Intergovernmental Panel on Climate Change (IPCC). 2022a. "Annex I: Glossary." In *Climate Change 2022: Mitigation of Climate Change. Contribution of Working Group III to the Sixth Assessment Report of the Intergovernmental Panel on Climate Change*, edited by P. R. Shukla, J. Skea, R. Slade, A. Al Khourdajie, R van Diemen, D. McCollum, M. Pathak, S. Some, P. Vyas, R. Fradera, M. Belkacemi, A. Hasija, G. Lisboa, S. Luz, and J. Malley. Cambridge, UK and New York, NY, USA: Cambridge University Press. https://doi.org/10.1017/9781009157926.020.

Intergovernmental Panel on Climate Change (IPCC). 2022b. "Summary for Policymakers." In *Climate Change 2022: Mitigation of Climate Change. Contribution of Working Group III to the Sixth Assessment Report of the Intergovernmental Panel on Climate Change*, edited by P. R. Shukla, J. Skea, A. Reisinger, R. Slade, R. Fradera, M. Pathak, A. Al Khourdajie, M. Belkacemi, R. van Diemen, A. Hasija, G. Lisboa, S. Luz, J. Malley, D. McCollum, S. Some, and P. Vyas. Cambridge, UK, and New York, NY, USA: Cambridge University Press. https://doi.org/10.1017/9781009157926.001.

Intergovernmental Panel on Climate Change (IPCC). 2023. *Climate Change 2023: Synthesis Report. Contribution of Working Groups I, II and III to the Sixth Assessment Report of the Intergovernmental Panel on Climate Change*. [Core Writing Team, H. Lee and J. Romero (eds.)] Geneva: IPCC. https://doi.org/10.59327/IPCC/AR6-9789291691647.

International Renewable Energy Agency (IRENA). 2023. *Low-cost finance for the energy transition*. Abu Dhabi: International Renewable Energy Agency.

Jacobs, Michael, Bianca Getzel, and Sarah Colenbrander. 2024. *International Development and Climate Finance: The New Agenda*. London: Overseas Development Institute (ODI).

Jensen, Lars. 2023. *Global Decarbonization in Fossil Fuel Export-Dependent Economies: Fiscal and Economic Transition Costs*. New York: United Nations Development Programme.

Kanitkar, Tejal, Akhil Mythri, and T. Jayaraman. 2024. "Equity Assessment of Global Mitigation Pathways in the IPCC Sixth Assessment Report." *Climate Policy* 24 (8): 1129–1148. https://doi.org/10.1080/14693062.2024.2319029.

Kenny, Charles. 2023. "The IFC and (De)Scaling Solar." *Center for Global Development*. Accessed October 26, 2024. https://www.cgdev.org/blog/ifc-and-descaling-solar.

Organisation for Economic Co-operation and Development (OECD). 2024. *Climate Finance Provided and Mobilised by Developed Countries in 2013–2022*. Climate Finance and the USD 100 Billion Goal. Paris: OECD Publishing. https://doi.org/10.1787/19150727-en.

Ritchie, Hannah. 2019. "Who Has Contributed Most to Global CO2 Emissions?" *Our World in Data*. Accessed December 15, 2024. https://ourworldindata.org/contributed-most-global-co2.

Ryan, Nicholas. 2021. *Holding Up Green Energy*. Working Paper 29154. National Bureau of Economic Research. https://doi.org/10.3386/w29154.

Shang, Baoping. 2023. "The Poverty and Distributional Impacts of Carbon Pricing: Channels and Policy Implications." *Review of Environmental Economics and Policy* 17 (1): Winter 2023.https://doi.org/10.1086/723899

Présidence de la République. 2023. "Chair's summary of discussions at the Summit on a New Global Financing Pact." *Summit for a New Global Financing Pact*. Accessed December 15, 2024. https://www.elysee.fr/admin/upload/default/0001/15/92948a175f53a5c4be735d284d4c7b9949442639.pdf

Sweeney, Sean. 2024. "The Fad Is Dead: Why 'Just Energy Transition Partnerships' Are Failing." *New Labor Forum* 33 (2): 95–102. https://doi.org/10.1177/10957960241241815.

United Nations. 2015. *Paris Agreement*. https://unfccc.int/sites/default/files/english_paris_agreement.pdf.

United Nations Conference on Trade and Development (UNCTAD). 2024. *A World of Debt: A Growing Burden to Global Prosperity*. Report prepared by the United Nations Global Crisis Response Group (UN GCRG) Technical Team. Geneva: UNCTAD.

United Nations Framework Convention on Climate Change (UNFCCC). 2023a. *Outcomes of the first global stocktake*. FCCC/PA/CMA/2023/L.17. United Nations Framework Convention on Climate Change. 13 December 2023. https://unfccc.int/documents/636608

United Nations Framework Convention on Climate Change (UNFCCC). 2023b. *Sharm el-Sheikh mitigation ambition and implementation work programme: Annual report by the secretariat*. FCCC/SB/2023/8. United Nations Framework Convention on Climate Change. 17 November 2023. http://unfccc.int/documents/631986

United Nations Framework Convention on Climate Change (UNFCCC). 2023c. *Compilation and synthesis of fifth biennial reports of Parties included in Annex I to the Convention: Report by the secretariat*. FCCC/SBI/2023/INF.7/Add.1. United Nations Framework Convention on Climate Change. 17 October 2023. https://unfccc.int/documents/632262

United Nations Framework Convention on Climate Change (UNFCCC). 2024. *Sharm el-Sheikh mitigation ambition and implementation work programme: Annual report by the secretariat*. FCCC/SB/2024/5. United Nations Framework Convention on Climate Change. 29 October 2024. https://unfccc.int/documents/641886

Standing Committee on Finance (SCF). 2024. *Second report on the determination of the needs of developing country Parties related to implementing the Convention and the Paris Agreement*. https://unfccc.int/documents/641873

Vigna, Leandro, and Johannes Friedrich. 2023. "9 Charts Explain Per Capita Greenhouse Gas Emissions by Country." *World Resources Institute*. Accessed October 26, 2024. https://www.wri.org/insights/charts-explain-per-capita-greenhouse-gas-emissions.

Whiting, Kate. 2024. "Climate Finance: What Are Debt-for-Nature Swaps and How Can They Help Countries?" *World Economic Forum*. Accessed October 26, 2024. https://www.weforum.org/agenda/2024/04/climate-finance-debt-for-nature-swaps/.

Zagema, Bertram, Jan Kowalzig, Lyndsay Walsh, Andrew Hattle, Christopher Roy, and Hans Peter Dejgaard. 2023. *Climate Finance Shadow Report 2023: Assessing the Delivery of the $100 Billion Commitment*. Oxfam International. https://oxfamilibrary.openrepository.com/bitstream/handle/10546/621500/bp-climate-finance-shadow-report-050623-en.pdf;jsessionid=02CFF8CFF6CDA7BF84C51EA0CE6B3A6C?sequence=19.

Sabrina Bachrach, with Nidhi Upadhyaya, Jorge Gastelumendi,
Juan José Guzmán Ayala, and Puninda Thind

Chapter 6
Financing the New Adaptation Economy

Abstract: The history of humankind tells a story of adaptation and resilience to changing political systems, conflicts, innovations, and even climatic changes. Nevertheless, the accelerating impacts of anthropogenic climate change are unprecedented and require society to adapt quickly and systematically with a strong focus on nature and those most vulnerable to climate change, often women and children.

The good news is that the solutions to finance adaptation and resilience are already there. The financial system is waking up to the transformational role it can play in creating the new adaptation economy that has climate-resilient communities, businesses, and ecosystems at its center. Modern technology, like AI and various innovative financial instruments, can mobilize adaptation finance needs at speed and scale. So why is the current state of adaptation and resilience finance still far below where it needs to be to create systemic resilience to the impacts of climate change?

This chapter looks into the barriers to financing climate adaptation and resilience and the immense potential and solutions that private finance can offer. While the quantitative analysis shows that the private sector currently contributes around 2% of adaptation and resilience finance flows, it does not capture the qualitative but significant mobilization of banks, investors, and insurers. There are immense political opportunities in the evolution of international financial architecture, and this mobilization presents a moment in time to get the financial system fit for purpose. This chapter assesses the environment and closes with a manifesto for the adaptation economy.

Keywords: Adaptation economy, Climate adaptation finance, Resilience investment, Adaptive capacity, Climate-resilient development, Institutional frameworks

Introduction

The future is becoming increasingly clear. The Intergovernmental Panel on Climate Change (IPCC) Assessment underscores the trajectory toward a world that is 1.5 °C warmer than pre-industrial levels by 2040. Such a scenario will disrupt nearly every facet of life (IPCC 2023). Adaptation serves as an uncomfortable reminder of our collective failure to act swiftly and decisively on mitigation. Adaptation is a secondary response to climate change; where mitigation falls short, communities need to turn to adaptation solutions to protect themselves from the locked-in consequences of climate change. As the climate rapidly changes, achieving decarbonization goals becomes even more critical, emphasizing the interdependence between mitigation and adaptation.

Adapting to climate change and building resilience does not signify giving up on the 1.5 °C goal. However, the locked-in impacts of climate change threaten the clean energy transition that is needed to deliver the Paris Agreement. Hydropower plants face reduced output due to droughts, solar panels overheating, and storms and hail damaging wind turbines. Despite this, the intricate relationship between adaptation, resilience, and mitigation remains largely absent from policy, planning, and transition strategies of financial institutions. A fundamental shift is required to recognize that building adaptation and resilience demands a comprehensive societal transformation – both now and in the future.

The earth has granted humanity a long grace period as we pushed its resilience to the brink. Today, the human, natural, and economic losses we face leave us no choice but to adapt and build resilience. The increasing frequency of extreme weather and slow-onset events resulting from climate change have prompted the financial system to awaken to this new reality. Public and private financial institutions worldwide are beginning to recognize that physical climate risks are also financial and systemic risks. Effectively managing these risks, mitigating losses, and seizing new opportunities presented by a changing climate will define economic success.

A study by S&P Global estimates that between 3.2% and 5.1% of global GDP could be lost annually by 2050, if we fail to adapt to climate change (Munday, Amiot, and Sifon-Arevalo 2023). For context, the global economy experienced a 3.4% GDP contraction during the COVID-19 pandemic in 2020 (Statista 2024). This underscores the urgency of making adaptation and resilience finance central to economic planning.

Against this backdrop, this chapter aims to define adaptation and resilience finance, arguing that current investment levels are insufficient. Although the importance of adaptation and resilience finance is widely recognized, these elements remain largely excluded from financial decision-making. The chapter challenges three prevailing narratives: (i) that the private sector is absent from adaptation and resilience efforts; (ii) that adaptation and resilience are not systemic issues; and (iii) that adaptation and resilience represent burdens rather than opportunities. By addressing these misperceptions, the chapter identifies actionable pathways to scale up adaptation and resilience finance and concludes with a vision for a future financial system that effectively mobilizes these critical resources.

Defining Adaptation and Resilience Finance

While no unified definition of adaptation and resilience finance exists, it can broadly be described as financial flows directed toward enhancing resilience and adaptation to climate change. Resilience encompasses the ability to anticipate, cope with, and recover from shocks (UK Government 2016), while adaptation involves reducing risks posed by climate change and, where possible, capitalizing on associated opportunities (Grantham Research Institute on Climate Change and the Environment 2021).

Frameworks such as the Climate Bonds Resilience Taxonomy Methodology (Climate Bonds Initiative 2024) are valuable tools for financial institutions to plan, track, and account for adaptation and resilience investments. Despite this, adaptation and resilience are not yet mainstreamed into financial decision-making processes. The billions of dollars needed for adaptation, particularly in Emerging Markets and Developing Economies (EMDEs), remain unmet.

One reason is the framing of adaptation and resilience finance as a failure. Too often, adaptation and resilience are dismissed as defeat, rather than embraced as necessary for a whole-of-society transformation. Mainstreaming adaptation and resilience into financial decisions and mobilizing the billions needed is an unavoidable opportunity (Global Adaptation and Resilience Investment Working Group 2024). Although every dollar invested in adaptation and resilience can yield an economic return of 12 dollars (Standard Chartered Bank n.d.), and such investments could add USD 7.1 trillion to the global economy (Verkooijen 2019), they are often associated with disasters and losses. By redirecting financial flows toward resilience-building for communities, businesses, and ecosystems, we can create a thriving, sustainable future.

However, adaptation and resilience are not perceived as opportunities. Decision-makers in public and private finance institutions often struggle to develop strategies that align their portfolios with resilience goals. These institutions may recognize the necessity of investing in adaptation and resilience, but they are often driven by a preventative approach, looking at the costs of flooded homes, burned forests, and lost lives. However, they still lack the knowledge to guide financial flows toward resilient communities, ecosystems, and businesses.

Adaptation and resilience are frequently relegated to Corporate Social Responsibility (CSR) initiatives, despite their macroeconomic significance. They require systemic integration into the planning and management frameworks of households, businesses, financial institutions, and governments. The critical question remains: How can we integrate adaptation and resilience into financial models that effectively price in their long-term benefits and mitigate projected losses?

Adaptation and Resilience: A Macroeconomic Necessity

A lack of investment in adaptation and resilience can compromise global economic power, development, and mitigation efforts – particularly for frontline communities, minorities, and women. For instance, if carbon sinks like the vast peatlands in Borneo ignite due to extended droughts or if Indigenous communities lose income because flooded cotton fields prevent them from producing and selling artisanal products, the need for adaptation becomes glaring. Similarly, water shortages preventing artificial intelligence (AI) data centers in Silicon Valley from cooling underscore that adaptation and resilience are not luxuries: they are macroeconomic necessities.

Narrative 1: The Private Sector and Adaptation Finance

Any comparison between climate change and past disruptions does not do justice to the unprecedented, global, and systemic threats climate change poses to nature, people, and the economy. Despite this, there is evidence to suggest that the private sector invests more in adaptation and resilience than the public sector – albeit without standardized metrics to track such investments. This lack of standards perpetuates the misconception that private finance for adaptation and resilience is nonexistent (CPI 2023a).

For example, when a smallholder farmer purchases drought-resistant seeds on credit, it is a private sector investment in adaptation. Smallholder farmers worldwide collectively invest approximately USD 68 billion annually in climate adaptation measures, dwarfing the USD 63 billion of tracked public adaptation finance in 2021–2022 (Hou Jones and Sorsby 2023; CPI 2023b).

Repeating the narrative of private sector inaction closes the door to existing and scalable solutions. Rather than blaming the private sector for inaction, it is more productive to explore how public–private collaboration can extend adaptation finance to underserved communities and nations. The private sector is leading on initiatives from setting standards to insuring climate hazards, exemplified by the following case studies:

Standards and Taxonomies

Standard Chartered Bank, KPMG, and the United Nations Office for Disaster Risk Reduction (UNDRR) released a "Guide for Adaptation and Resilience". Further studies from Standard Chartered Bank have shown that every dollar invested in adaptation and resilience can create USD 12 in return (Standard Chartered Bank, KPMG, and UNDRR 2024).

This guide, developed by a commercial bank, could set a precedent for global markets. Due to the absence of government standards, the financial industry has filled the gap. It will be important in the coming years to ensure that these are interoperable. Defining high-level principles can be useful to help align these standards and create a common understanding of adaptation and resilience finance for private as well as public financial institutions.

In addition, the Climate Bonds Initiative launched the Climate Bonds Resilience Taxonomy (CBRT) in September 2024 to provide a science-based, common framework for identifying credible climate adaptation and resilience (A&R) investments. The CBRT classifies both adapted and enabling investment – those that either increase an asset's own climate resilience or help other systems adapt and sets draft eligibility criteria aligned with high-level resilience goals. With over USD 4 trillion already mobilized through green, social, and sustainable bonds, this taxonomy aims to unlock further private sector investment into resilience by offering clear definitions, rigorous criteria, and guidance for financial institutions, governments, and investors. Importantly, the CBRT is designed to be interoperable and complementary with other market-based standards, supporting the development of national taxonomies and guiding fiscal incentives and disclosures. As sustainable finance evolves, such tools will be essential to ensuring the credibility, scalability, and impact of adaptation and resilience financing (Climate Bonds Initiative 2024).

Risk Analytics

Risk analytics are a foundational part of scaling private investment in adaptation, but their use is still limited. While platforms like the Resilient Planet Data Hub offer open access to physical climate risk data, more work is needed to make this kind of information actionable across financial systems. The lack of access to risk analytics limits transparency and creates barriers for investors. To change this, governments and financial institutions need to work together to improve access to physical climate risk data and to align standards, disclosures, and taxonomies that are both usable and interoperable. Done well, risk analytics can not only guide smarter investment decisions but also build confidence and bring more capital to where it is most needed (Resilient Planet Hub 2023).

Metrics

Metrics for adaptation and resilience are still evolving but are increasingly recognized as essential to unlock private capital. The UNEP FI Adaptation and Resilience Investors Collaborative has laid the groundwork for metrics that support investment decisions in developing countries. Building on this, new efforts emphasize the need for harmonized global frameworks and national taxonomies that define what qualifies as adaptation. This clarity enables investors to assess risks, track adaptation outcomes, and compare impact across regions and asset classes. To be effective, metrics must also capture co-benefits such as improved livelihoods or ecosystem services. Ensuring that metrics are integrated into disclosure policies and financial instruments can accelerate market confidence and drive investment at scale (Adaptation & Resilience Investors Collaborative 2024).

Financial Instruments

Over the past few years, a range of financial instruments has emerged, particularly in the areas of infrastructure and agricultural value chains – sectors that are highly vulnerable to climate change impacts. Blended finance instruments show significant promise as they have the potential to leverage private capital through de-risking mechanisms and catalytic public or philanthropic funding (Convergence 2024). Companies such as YAPU Solutions have focused on providing finance to frontline communities in EMDEs through inclusive financial institutions (YAPU Solutions n.d.).

Increasing access to finance remains a critical issue in the climate finance landscape, requiring attention at both the sovereign and community levels. A notable example is GAWA Capital's Kuali Fund, a EUR 300 million fund that raises capital from institutional investors using innovative blended finance structures to make smallholder farmers and businesses more resilient to climate change. The Kuali Fund invests in financial institutions that currently offer or plan to offer climate adaptation finance to vulnerable communities (COFIDES 2023).

Regarding infrastructure investment, the Insurance Development Forum, in collaboration with BlackRock, has developed a blueprint for infrastructure investments in emerging markets. This initiative aims to mobilize at least EUR 500 million in public and private investments (Insurance Development Forum 2024). However, it is crucial to acknowledge that today's infrastructure is often ill-equipped to address the locked-in impacts of climate change. Storms, flooding, and heat waves significantly reduce the longevity of infrastructure assets. Given that approximately USD 94 trillion will be required for global infrastructure investments by 2040 (Global Infrastructure Hub n. d.), it is essential to design and implement future projects in a climate-proof manner.

Infrastructure projects are frequently publicly funded and span long timelines. Nevertheless, private finance can be integrated through mechanisms such as thematic bonds or public–private insurance schemes that de-risk investments over extended periods, surpassing the traditional annual insurance coverage cycle (Atlantic Council Climate Resilience Center 2024).

Insurance

The Cambridge Institute for Sustainability Leadership (CISL) at the University of Cambridge has conducted an analysis on risk sharing for loss and damage. The report proposes an umbrella stop-loss mechanism to protect national economies above specified levels of GDP, with particular emphasis on the Vulnerable Twenty Group (V20) and Small Island Developing States (SIDS) (CISL 2023a).

Other insurance initiatives demonstrate how collaboration between governments and insurers can enhance community resilience. For example, Flood Re in the United Kingdom illustrates a successful partnership that protects private households from flooding (Flood Re n.d.).

These examples also explore untapped aspects of the climate crisis. The Atlantic Council's Climate Resilience Center developed a first-of-its-kind parametric insurance mechanism that covers lost income due to extreme heat. This program was piloted with 21,000 women working in India's informal economy, providing coverage for daily wages lost during heat waves (Dabrowski n.d.).

Additionally, Marsh McLennan is working on a standard for adaptation and resilience that encompasses client services in risk analytics, consulting, and resilience building. The company also suggests industry-wide standards for the insurance sector (Marsh McLennan, the Race to Resilience, the Adrienne Arsht-Rockefeller Foundation Resilience Center, and Oliver Wyman 2023).

Banking

YAPU Solutions, a leading technology provider, collaborates with microfinance institutions in Latin America and Sub-Saharan Africa to develop financial and nonfinancial products dedicated to supporting adaptation and resilience in rural communities. YAPU Solutions provides microfinance institutions with a tool that integrates physical climate risk data, adaptation, and resilience metrics directly into their credit evaluation systems. In collaboration with several of these institutions, YAPU has co-developed tailored financial products such as resilience loans, which enable smallholder farmers to access financing for targeted climate adaptation measures, including crop diversification and drip irrigation systems.

Further, Standard Chartered completed its first labeled adaptation finance transaction for a corporate client, supporting JinkoSolar in delivering storm- and sandstorm-resistant solar modules to sites in the U.S., UAE, and Saudi Arabia. The deal, facilitated through bank guarantees, demonstrates how climate-resilient infrastructure – such as solar modules designed to withstand extreme weather – can be treated as an investable asset class. This transaction operationalizes the bank's Guide for Adaptation and Resilience Finance and highlights the commercial and climate value of financing adaptation in vulnerable markets (Standard Chartered Bank 2025).

The UNEP Finance Initiative (UNEP FI) has also introduced the *Adaptation Target Setting Framework for Adaptation*. A group of 27 commercial bank members of the Principles for Responsible Banking Adaptation Working Group developed it to outline pathways for banks to set adaptation targets and create financial products tailored to their clients' adaptation and resilience needs (UNEP FI 2023).

Narrative 2: Systemic Necessity of Adaptation

In 2024, the economic costs of extreme weather events exceeded USD 2 trillion (Oxera 2024). Climate-related disasters damage infrastructure, disrupt supply chains, and reduce agricultural productivity. Disasters divert resources from essential services like education and poverty reduction. Investing in adaptation measures such as sustainable agriculture, water management, and resilient infrastructure not only mitigates these risks but also promotes economic stability. It can also enable quicker recovery from increasingly frequent climate shocks, preventing prolonged economic downturns.

This is essential not only for affected regions but also for the global economy. A resilient financial system can prevent localized banking crises from escalating into global financial disruptions. Even though financial institutions still face data asymmetries and uncertainties around how to best incorporate climate risk into their strategies and operations, high-level portfolio insights already show where adjusted financial products could improve their portfolio resilience.

Narrative 3: Adaptation and Resilience Are a Burden, Not an Opportunity

Investing in adaptation and resilience is not a burden; rather, it is an economically sound decision. For example, food and agriculture systems – already at the forefront of climate impacts – paint a clear picture. Smart water harvesting and drip irrigation systems are no longer optional but necessary for reliable harvests in the face of changing precipitation patterns and droughts.

The science is unequivocal: Early investment in adaptation and resilience yields triple dividends by avoiding future losses, generating economic returns, and delivering social and environmental benefits.

Avoiding Future Losses

During the pandemic, global inflation increased dramatically. Studies suggest that, similarly, climate change will drive inflation over the coming decade. Rising temperatures could drive food inflation up by 3.2 percentage points and overall inflation by 1.18 percentage points annually by 2035 (Kotz et al. 2024). Severe weather events such as hurricanes and wildfires, which are becoming increasingly frequent and intense due to climate change, disrupt supply chains by damaging infrastructure, reducing production capacity, and delaying goods transportation. These disruptions often lead to shortages and subsequently higher prices.

A temperature rise of 1.5 °C could reduce global working hours by 2.2% by 2030, costing the global economy USD 2.4 trillion (ILO 2019). To mitigate these effects, adapting work environments with solutions like natural air-conditioning via greening infrastructure can be highly effective. Nature-based infrastructure could meet around 50% of infrastructure needs by 2050, providing an opportunity to leapfrog traditional development paths (UNEP 2023).

Positive Economic Benefits

Research from the Global Center on Adaptation (GCA) shows that investing USD 1.8 trillion in adaptation and resilience measures could yield USD 7.1 trillion in economic benefits by 2030 (Verkooijen 2019). While this is a macroeconomic projection, microeconomic examples further illustrate the benefits of investing in adaptation and resilience strategies.

The return on investment (ROI) for climate-vulnerable enterprises should no longer be compared to historical performance. Instead, it must be assessed relative to the ROI of resilient comparables in a "new normal" defined by frequent and severe climate events. A resilience ROI spread is likely to grow as financial models increasingly account for the higher operational and capital expenses, as well as revenue risks, faced by vulnerable enterprises.

The adaptation technology innovation ecosystem is expanding rapidly, from wildfire detection systems to climate risk management tools and solutions for reducing extreme heat in buildings. Investing in nature-based solutions not only promotes climate adaptation but also advances biodiversity goals. Given the rising frequency of climate hazards, these solutions are increasingly in demand, creating immense opportunities for investors.

Social and Environmental Benefits

Adapting natural ecosystems and building resilience through nature-based solutions are vital for addressing the interconnected nature and climate crises. Nature-based solutions offer cost-effective and widely accessible approaches to climate adaptation. Estimates suggest that these solutions could save up to USD 104 billion in adaptation costs by 2030 and USD 393 billion by 2050 (IFRC and WWF 2022).

Private financial institutions have shown a growing interest in leveraging nature for climate adaptation, particularly in EMDEs, where favorable conditions for vegetation growth enable nature-based solutions like green corridors. For example, Medellín, Colombia, invested USD 16.3 million in green corridors to cool urban areas and improve water management. This initiative planted over 8,800 trees and 90,000 plant species, reducing temperatures by up to 2 °C in the surrounding areas. The project was funded through the city's participatory budget, allowing citizens to democratically decide on the allocation of funds (C40 Knowledge Hub 2019).

Food systems are also profoundly affected by climate change. Transforming these systems can protect livelihoods, restore biodiversity, and create equitable communities. Agroforestry solutions, for instance, reduce water inputs, improve soil health, and increase crop yields while enhancing farmers' incomes. Nature-based solutions can yield a range of benefits, including avoiding economic losses, job creation, cleaner air, carbon sequestration, and improved food security.

Promoting financial inclusion, particularly for women, is another critical aspect of adaptation and resilience financing. Empowering women with access to finance enhances community-wide resilience.

Actions Needed to Scale Up Adaptation Finance

According to the International Renewable Energy Agency (IRENA) (2022), 81% of renewables are cheaper than fossil fuels in developed economies and most EMDEs. This shift results from years of growing demand, the development of financial instruments, effective leadership, and policies that created an enabling environment for capital to flow into better alternatives. However, it should be emphasized that investors from developed countries continue to finance fossil fuels in EMDEs. Combined with national fossil fuel subsidies, this practice creates significant barriers to renewable energy in some markets. Consequently, it is crucial to design international financial architecture that provides EMDEs with access to highly concessional capital to support their transition to net-zero and climate-resilient development.

While the analogy of mitigation is only transferable in certain respects, it demonstrates that the right conditions can incentivize large-scale investments, particularly when paired with growing market demand. Nevertheless, many opportunities remain untapped to scale and accelerate investments in adaptation and resilience. This section of the chapter explores some of these opportunities and highlights specific existing solutions.

Increasing Access to Finance and Lowering the Cost of Capital in Developing Countries

The scale of climate change impacts exceeds what public finance can address alone. Blended finance mechanisms have shown that blended finance funds typically leverage USD 4 of commercial capital for each USD 1 of concessional finance (Convergence

2023). Public finance plays a crucial role in addressing the high cost of capital faced by developing countries.

For instance, Brazil, India, Indonesia, Mexico, and South Africa face borrowing costs of 10.6% for renewable energy projects, compared to only 4% in the European Union (CISL 2023b). This disparity, coupled with the undervaluation of growth potential in regions such as Sub-Saharan Africa, results in high perceived risks for capital markets. However, as governance and technologies improve and financial markets mature, the risk-return profile of investments in these regions is likely to become more favorable. It is imperative to address these barriers to ensure climate finance reaches the most vulnerable countries and communities.

Creating and Adopting Standards for Adaptation and Resilience

Establishing standards and taxonomies for adaptation and resilience finance is vital for scaling investments. Adaptation taxonomy categorizes economic activities based on sustainability criteria, enhancing transparency and reducing the risk of greenwashing. By providing standardized classifications, taxonomies help investors prioritize truly sustainable projects and foster global consistency in climate-resilient investments.

Beyond defining sustainable activities, taxonomies should assess how adaptation measures tangibly reduce risks to avoid maladaptation – where adaptation actions fail to address underlying physical risks. By boosting investor confidence and promoting sustainable practices, taxonomies play a key role in aligning financial flows with climate resilience and sustainable development goals.

Increasing Collaboration between the Public and Private Sectors

Discussions about the actions – and inactions – of both public and private sectors often lead to unproductive finger-pointing. This creates additional challenges without resolving existing ones. Instead, collaboration is a fundamental condition for scaling finance for adaptation and resilience.

The nascent adaptation economy requires a robust network and ecosystem to foster both the policy environment and financial instruments necessary for greater investments in adaptation and resilience.

The Atlantic Council's Climate Resilience Center, in partnership with the UN Climate Change High-Level Champions and key stakeholders, developed a "Call for Collaboration". The call mobilizes and scales private investments into adaptation and resilience. It has received support from several governments, private sector actors, and civil society organizations (Atlantic Council Climate Resilience Center 2023). Efforts like this can help identify more effective and collaborative ways forward, where governments can better provide critical climate information infrastructure, including data and guidance, while the private sector can offer finance and resources at scale.

The public sector can provide catalytic capital to attract private investments and develop an enabling environment. The private sector must complement these efforts by mobilizing capital, creating innovative financial instruments, and sharing expertise to improve resilience. Collaboration with policymakers helps address barriers and integrate climate risks into decision-making processes.

A Vision for 2040

As highlighted throughout this chapter, the conversations around financing adaptation and resilience are still hampered by misconceptions and a lack of foresight. This gap stems, in part, from the absence of a vision for a financial system that fully integrates adaptation and resilience into its decision-making processes.

Future systems must include context-specific financial instruments tailored to unique vulnerabilities. Grants can enhance resilience in highly exposed frontline communities, while commercial loans may suit large corporations pursuing adaptation and resilience measures.

Global adaptation efforts increasingly emphasize targeted support for frontline communities, especially in EMDEs). These communities can benefit from more targeted financing that enhances local solutions. Climate finance can bolster grassroots efforts as well as Micro, Small, and Medium Enterprises (MSMEs) through low-interest credits, subsidies, and grants to implement adaptation strategies. The new adaptation economy requires all stakeholders. Insurance companies are increasingly instrumental in adaptation efforts, providing critical climate-risk data and analytics to governments, businesses, and individuals. They can set industry standards, offering products and insights that help clients proactively manage climate risks. Publicly supported insurance mechanisms ensure equitable access for frontline communities and leverage blended finance instruments to attract private investments. Pension funds have adopted long-term strategies that incorporate physical climate risks, prioritizing investments in adaptation and resilience. Enhanced collaboration between banks and insurers can offer integrated credit and insurance packages, making supply chains more robust. Multilateral development banks and international financial institutions also play a vital role, from increasing access to finance in EMDEs to attracting private investments. Venture capital is emerging as a key driver of innovation in adaptation technology, particularly in EMDEs. Debt and equity investors increasingly recognize the dual benefits of adaptation investments – minimizing losses while creating growth opportunities. International and domestic policies incentivize financial institutions to help clients develop adaptation plans and access tailored financial tools.

Recognizing physical climate risks drives the private sector to address vulnerabilities proactively. Local governments are crucial in bolstering systemic resilience, particularly in highly exposed communities. Urban areas implement initiatives such as tree planting and cooling centers to mitigate extreme heat effects while simultaneously preserving ecosystems critical to resilience.

Recommendations for Achieving This Vision

To achieve this vision for 2040, working groups led by the Atlantic Council's Climate Resilience Center, with support from the UN Climate Change High-Level Champions, have proposed the following recommendations:

1. **Make countries' National Adaptation Plans (NAPs) investible and transparent**, including other adaptation communications and ensuring synergies with nationally determined contributions (NDCs).
2. **Support EMDEs' national and subnational governments** and their respective public and private finance institutions with technical assistance. This support can increase their adaptation and resilience capacities across ministries and enable collaboration with both domestic and international private sectors.
3. **Create high-level global guidance and harmonize standards, frameworks, and disclosures** for physical climate risks and adaptation. This allows public and private sectors to understand, manage, plan, and invest in adaptation and resilience at international, national (through NDCs and adaptation planning), and regional levels.
4. **Improve the availability of blended finance instruments** by increasing data transparency and accelerating, scaling, and harmonizing access to public and philanthropic capital. This can catalyze private investments across various providers for adaptation and resilience.
5. **Increase the availability of insurance products**, including parametric insurance, to support adaptation and resilience for countries, ecosystems, infrastructure, and people.
6. **Invest in locally led adaptation**, nature-based solutions, and ecosystem-based approaches that deliver adaptation benefits, along with emerging climate adaptation technologies.

References

Atlantic Council Climate Resilience Center. 2023. *Call for Collaboration: An Invitation to Governments to Mobilise Private Finance for Adaptation and Resilience*. Accessed April 15, 2025. https://onebillionresilient.org/cop28-call-for-collaboration/.

Atlantic Council Climate Resilience Center. 2024. *Six ways to scale private finance for climate adaptation*. Accessed April 15, 2025. https://onebillionresilient.org/private-finance-for-climate-adaptation/

Climate Bonds Initiative. 2024. *Climate Bonds Resilience Methodology*. Accessed April 15, 2025. https://www.climatebonds.net/files/documents/supporting-documents/Climate-Bonds_Resilience-Methodology_2024.pdf.

Climate Policy Initiative (CPI). 2023a. *State and Trends in Climate Adaptation Finance 2023*. https://www.climatepolicyinitiative.org/publication/state-and-trends-in-climate-adaptation-finance-2023/

Climate Policy Initiative (CPI). 2023b. *Global Landscape of Climate Finance 2023*. https://climatepolicyinitiative.org/publication/global-landscape-of-climate-finance-2023/

COFIDES. 2023. "The European Union approves a contribution of 17 million euros to the Kuali Impact Fund." February 6. Accessed September 26, 2024. https://www.cofides.es/en/noticias/notas-de-prensa/european-union-approves-contribution-17-million-euros-kuali-impact-fund

Convergence. 2023. *Blended Finance & Leveraging Concessionality*. February 21, 2023. Accessed April 15, 2025. https://www.convergence.finance/resource/blended-finance-and-leveraging-concessionality/view.

Convergence. 2024. *State of Blended Finance 2024*. https://www.convergence.finance/resource/state-of-blended-finance-2024/view

C40 Knowledge Hub. 2019. "Cities100: Medellín's Interconnected Green Corridors." October. Accessed September 26, 2024. https://www.c40knowledgehub.org/s/article/Cities100-Medellin-s-interconnected-green-corridors?language=en_US

Dabrowski, Jessica. n.d. "Fighting Extreme Heat with Parametric Insurance." *One Billion Resilient*. Accessed September 26, 2024. https://onebillionresilient.org/2023/03/07/fighting-extreme-heat-with-parametric-insurance/.

Flood Re. n.d. "Flood Re." Accessed September 26, 2024. https://www.floodre.co.uk/.

Grantham Research Institute on Climate Change and the Environment. 2021. "What Is Climate Change Adaptation?" *London School of Economics and Political Science (LSE)*, January 15. Accessed September 26, 2024. https://www.lse.ac.uk/granthaminstitute/explainers/what-is-climate-change-adaptation/.

Global Adaptation & Resilience Investment Working Group. 2024. *The Unavoidable Opportunity: Investing in the Growing Market for Climate Resilience Solutions*. Discussion paper. March 2024. https://img1.wsimg.com/blobby/go/66c2ce28-dc91-4dc1-a0e1-a47d9ecdc17d/downloads/GARI%202024.pdf?ver=1711122403467

Global Infrastructure Hub. n.d. "Global Infrastructure Outlook." Accessed September 26, 2024. https://outlook.gihub.org/.

Hou Jones, Xiaoting, and Nicola Sorsby. 2023. *The Unsung Giants of Climate and Nature Investment: Insights from an International Survey of Local Climate and Nature Action by Smallholder Forest and Farm Producers*. London: IIED. https://www.iied.org/21976iied.

Insurance Development Forum. 2024. "Insurance Development Forum Announces Plans to Facilitate Investments in Resilient Infrastructure in Developing Emerging Markets." April 10. Accessed September 26, 2024. https://www.insdevforum.org/press-release-insurance-development-forum-announces-plans-to-facilitate-investments-in-resilient-infrastructure-in-developing-emerging-markets/

The International Federation of Red Cross and Red Crescent Societies (IFRC), and the World Wide Fund for Nature (WWF). 2022. *Working with Nature to Protect People: How Nature-Based Solutions Reduce Climate Change and Weather-Related Disasters.*

International Labour Organization (ILO). 2019. "Increase in Heat Stress Predicted to Bring Productivity Loss Equivalent to 80 Million Full-Time Jobs." July 1. Accessed September 26, 2024. https://www.ilo.org/resource/news/increase-heat-stress-predicted-bring-productivity-loss-equivalent-to-80

Intergovernmental Panel on Climate Change (IPCC). 2023. *Climate Change 2023: Synthesis Report. Contribution of Working Groups I, II, and III to the Sixth Assessment Report of the Intergovernmental Panel on Climate Change.*

International Renewable Energy Agency (IRENA). 2022. *Renewable Power Generation Costs in 2021.* International Renewable Energy Agency, Abu Dhabi.

Kotz, Maximilian, Friderike Kuik, Eliza Lis, and Christiane Nickel. 2024. "Global Warming and Heat Extremes to Enhance Inflationary Pressures." *Communications Earth & Environment* 5: 116. https://doi.org/10.1038/s43247-023-01173-x

MarshMcLennan, the Race to Resilience, the Adrienne Arsht-Rockefeller Foundation Resilience Center, and Oliver Wyman. 2023. *Building a Climate Resilient Future: Five Priorities for the Global Insurance Industry.* https://www.marshmclennan.com/insights/publications/2023/december/building-a-climate-resilient-future.html

Munday, Paul, Marion Amiot, and Roberto Sifon-Arevalo. 2023. "Lost GDP: Potential Impacts of Physical Climate Risks." *S&P Global Ratings*, November 27. Accessed September 26, 2024. https://www.spglobal.com/_assets/documents/ratings/research/101590033.pdf.

Oxera. 2024. *The Economic Cost of Extreme Weather Events.* Prepared for the International Chamber of Commerce. November 7, 2024. https://iccwbo.org/wp-content/uploads/sites/3/2024/11/2024-ICC-Oxera-The-economic-cost-of-extreme-weather-events.pdf.

Resilient Planet Data Hub. 2023. "Resilient Planet Data Hub Secures New Agreements and Funding to Provide Open, Globally Consistent Climate Risk Data." *Resilient Planet Data*, June 1. Accessed September 26, 2024. https://resilient-planet-data.org/latest/Resilient-Planet-Hub-secures-new-agreements-and-funding-to-provide-open-globally-consistent-climate-risk-data.

Standard Chartered. *Standard Chartered Scales Finance for Resilient Infrastructure as Economic Cost of Extreme Weather Hits over $2 Trillion.* Press release, March 13, 2025. Accessed April 15, 2025.https://www.sc.com/en/press-release/standard-chartered-scales-finance-for-resilient-infrastructure-as-economic-cost-of-extreme-weather-hits-over-2-trillion/

Standard Chartered Bank. n.d. *The Adaptation Economy: The Case for Early Action on Climate Adaptation in Emerging Markets.* Accessed September 26, 2024. https://standardcharteredbank.turtl.co/story/the-adaptation-economy/page/1.

Standard Chartered Bank, KPMG, and the United Nations Office for Disaster Risk Reduction (UNDRR). 2024. *Guide for Adaptation and Resilience Finance.* London: Standard Chartered Bank. https://www.sc.com/en/adaptation-resilience-finance-guide/.

Statista. 2024. "Change in Global GDP Due to COVID-19 in 2020." Accessed September 26, 2024. https://www.statista.com/topics/6139/covid-19-impact-on-the-global-economy/.

UK Government. 2016. *What is Resilience?* May 2016. Accessed September 26, 2024. https://assets.publishing.service.gov.uk/media/57a08955ed915d3cfd0001c8/EoD_Topic_Guide_What_is_Resilience_May_2016.pdf.

Verkooijen, Patrick. 2019. "Adapting to Climate Change Could Add $7 Trillion to the Global Economy by 2030." *Global Center on Adaptation*, September 10. Accessed September 26, 2024. https://gca.org/adapting-to-climate-change-could-add-7-trillion-to-the-global-economy-by-2030/.

YAPU Solutions. n.d. "YAPU Solutions." Accessed September 26, 2024. https://www.yapu.solutions

United Nations Environment Programme (UNEP). 2023. *Nature-Based Infrastructure: How Natural Infrastructure Solutions Can Address Sustainable Development Challenges and the Triple Planetary Crisis*. Geneva: UNEP.

United Nations Environment Programme Finance Initiative (UNEP FI). 2023. *PRB Adaptation Target Setting Guidance*. Accessed September 26, 2024. https://www.unepfi.org/industries/banking/climate-adaptation-target-setting/

University of Cambridge Institute for Sustainability Leadership (CISL). 2023a. *Risk Sharing for Loss and Damage: Scaling Up Protection for the Global South*. Cambridge, UK: University of Cambridge Institute for Sustainability Leadership.

University of Cambridge Institute for Sustainability Leadership (CISL). 2023b. *Everything, Everywhere, All at Once: Achieving Climate, Nature, and Development Goals Together*. Cambridge: University of Cambridge Institute for Sustainability Leadership.

Razan Khalifa Al Mubarak and Simon Zadek

Chapter 7
Financing a Global Nature-Positive Economy

Abstract: Nature is the foundation of human well-being and economic prosperity, yet it is being degraded at an unprecedented rate. Forests, oceans, and biodiversity sustain life and regulate the climate, but global systems currently demand 1.6 Earths to maintain existing consumption levels. This overexploitation, stemming from economic undervaluation, marginalizes nature's stewards and accelerates climate change and inequality.

A transition to a nature-positive economy requires embedding the true value of nature into economic and financial systems, aligning public and private financial flows with biodiversity and climate goals, and securing the rights of Indigenous Peoples and local communities. International frameworks such as the Paris Agreement and the Kunming-Montreal Global Biodiversity Framework provide the foundation, but action remains grossly underfinanced and imbalanced – especially for the Global South.

Reforming global finance is central to reversing nature loss. This entails building a robust "nature finance operating system" with standardized data, natural capital accounting, and mandatory disclosures. Financial institutions, regulators, and governments must retool their mandates to integrate nature into decisions and prevent nature-destructive investments. This chapter presents practical insights into accelerating the flow of public and private capital toward nature-based solutions to advance climate action. It features a number of case studies and initiatives that aim at driving more capital "into" nature – conservation and restoration – but also "for" nature – shifting agriculture, fisheries, forestry, mining, and infrastructure – toward nature-positive outcomes. The chapter highlights lessons learned from these initiatives and case studies in order to unlock the current nature finance gap.

Keywords: Nature finance, Nature-positive economy, Bioeconomy, Biodiversity, Nature-based Solutions, Global Biodiversity Framework, Indigenous Peoples

Introduction

Nature has intrinsic value. It is our lifeline, providing the essential elements necessary for our existence: the air we breathe, the food we eat, the water we drink, and the landscapes that sustain us. The services it provides – including biodiversity, water,

Note: This chapter benefited from excellent research support provided by Puninda Thind.

and minerals – support every aspect of our technological society. In short, nature underpins every dimension of our lives.

Our forests and oceans act as the planet's lungs, regulating the climate, supporting the livelihoods of over a billion people, and absorbing 60% of global emissions. Nature is also the foundation of the global food system, valued at USD 8 trillion annually, which provides direct and indirect livelihoods for one in ten people worldwide (Furtado n.d.).

Protecting nature addresses poverty, enhances food security and human health, builds resilience against climate change, and creates jobs. Conversely, nature loss exacerbates inequalities within and between countries, as the world's poorest lose access to subsistence resources and nations become trapped in cycles of poverty.

The State of Nature

- Global biodiversity has declined by 70% since 1970, according to the World Wide Fund for Nature's *Living Planet Index* (WWF 2022).
- The world has lost 80% of its forests and continues to lose them at a rate of 375 km^2 per day.
- A garbage island, composed largely of plastics and spanning an area the size of India, Europe, and Mexico combined, floats in the Pacific Ocean.
- Every hour, 1,692 acres of productive dry land turn to desert.
- 83% of freshwater species have been lost in the past 50 years (The World Counts 2024).

Despite widespread awareness of nature's existential importance, humanity continues to exploit and degrade it at an unsustainable pace. Current global consumption levels require the equivalent of 1.6 Earths to sustain existing living standards (Dasgupta 2021). The Intergovernmental Science-Policy Platform on Biodiversity and Ecosystem Services (IPBES) has concluded: "Biodiversity is being lost, and nature's contributions to people are being degraded faster now than at any other point in human history" (IPBES 2022). Wildlife populations are declining at unprecedented rates, and humanity has crossed six of nine "safe and just" planetary boundaries (Bartels 2023).

This destruction stems not from mere negligence but from a history of exploitation, particularly since the Industrial Revolution. The exploitation of nature has often gone hand in hand with the marginalization of its stewards: Indigenous Peoples, local communities, and farmers. At a macro level, the undervaluation and overexploitation of natural resources have significantly contributed to global economic inequality, both within and between nations. Sustainable development requires recalibrating humanity's demand for nature's services to align with its capacity to supply them.

Nature is a critical ally in addressing the climate crisis. The degradation of ecosystems and biodiversity diminishes Earth's capacity to absorb greenhouse gases and regulate the climate, thereby exacerbating climate change. Conversely, climate change destabilizes ecosystems, creating feedback loops that worsen biodiversity loss. Science unequivocally shows that reversing biodiversity loss by 2030 is essential to avoiding the worst effects of climate change and building resilience to its impacts (Griscom et al. 2017).

The primary driver of biodiversity loss is land and sea use change, particularly for food production, compounded by the effects of climate change (UNEP 2023a). This includes the conversion of forests, peatlands, wetlands, and other habitats into agricultural and urban areas. Biodiversity loss reduces Earth's capacity for carbon sequestration, further fueling climate change. Addressing these crises requires coordinated action to mitigate climate change, while protecting and restoring nature.

Sharm El-Sheikh Adaptation Agenda

Nature offers the most cost-effective means to help vulnerable communities adapt to climate change. The Sharm El-Sheikh Adaptation Agenda (SAA) outlines 30 global adaptation targets by 2030 to build resilience for 4 billion people and transform five critical impact systems: food and agriculture, water and nature, coastal and ocean systems, human settlements, and infrastructure. Nature plays a central role in achieving these goals, as it reduces climate risks and enhances ecosystem and community resilience (UN Climate Change High-Level Champions 2022a).

Nature Must Count

Without embedding nature's true value into economic decision-making, the exploitation of the natural world will intensify with catastrophic consequences (NatureFinance 2023). A transformation to a nature-positive economy[1] is essential. This requires securing the rights and economic well-being of those who steward nature. As the *Dasgupta Review* argues, protecting both prosperity and the natural world demands a fundamental shift in how humanity thinks, acts, and measures economic success (Dasgupta 2021).

Traditional measures of GDP fail to account for the degradation of natural assets or broader aspects of well-being (Lewsey 2021; Stiglitz, Fitoussi, and Durand 2018). Decades ago, proposals such as the "Measure of Economic Welfare" sought to adjust GDP to include unpaid work, leisure time, and environmental damage (Moss 1973).

---

1 According to the Nature Positive Initiative (2023), "Nature Positive is a global societal goal defined as "Halt and reverse nature loss by 2030 on a 2020 baseline and achieve full recovery by 2050". To put this more simply, it means ensuring more nature in the world in 2030 than in 2020 and continuing recovery after that."

This inspired efforts to value "natural capital", but GDP remains the dominant measure of progress (Mohieldin and Zadek 2024).

The Kunming-Montreal Global Biodiversity Framework and the Paris Agreement have established multilateral goals for aligning public and private sector activities with nature and climate objectives. The Paris Agreement (Article 2.1 c) calls for financial flows to be consistent with climate goals, such as reducing greenhouse gas emissions and fostering climate-resilient development (UNFCCC 2015). Similarly, the Global Biodiversity Framework advocates aligning fiscal and financial flows with biodiversity goals, leveraging innovative financial mechanisms (Convention on Biological Diversity 2022a).

Transitioning to a nature-positive economy is a monumental task, intertwined with the shift to a zero-carbon economy. The global food system, valued at USD 7 trillion annually, generates an estimated USD 8 trillion in negative externalities, including environmental, climate, and public health costs (van Nieuwkoop 2019; UNEP 2023b).

Despite the urgent need for action, financing remains grossly inadequate. While an estimated USD 7 trillion annually supports nature-negative activities, less than USD 200 billion flows into nature conservation and restoration efforts, with private capital accounting for only 18% of this total (UNEP 2023b). Furthermore, the Global South, which holds the majority of biodiversity, receives only a fraction of global nature finance, despite its pivotal role in providing biodiversity-related services, such as carbon sequestration. 80% of global nature finance flows both originate from and are directed to advanced economies. With 60% of these countries in debt distress, their ability to invest in nature is severely constrained (Center for Global Commons 2023).

Making Nature Count

Markets have historically been the greatest source of damage to nature. It is the logic of finance, particularly private capital but also public finance, that shapes these markets as part of the global economy. Unless the global financial system incorporates nature into decision-making, it is unrealistic to expect businesses and the wider economy to do so (UNEP 2016). Ongoing efforts to reform the international financial architecture, notably through the Bridgetown Initiative, exemplify the progress that needs to be made.

Crucially, this involves more than mobilizing finance for nature conservation and restoration, although this mobilization is vital to achieving the "30 by 30" goal of conserving 30% of terrestrial and marine habitats by 2030 (Convention on Biological Diversity 2022b). There is a need to align the world's financial flows with nature-positive goals, as encapsulated by the Global Biodiversity Framework. The challenge is considerable, given the scale of global financial markets.

There is no simple blueprint for ensuring the alignment of global finance with nature-positive and equity goals, considering the following:

- The complexity of the global economy and its current toxic dependence on nature, which destroys business and market processes and outcomes.
- The challenges of pivoting a dynamic, short-term, profit-seeking financial community toward nature-positive investments, let alone those that deliver more equitable outcomes. This is due to the failure of our economic system to account for and properly value nature.
- The importance of finance, technological developments, and other real-economy advancements, as seen in the clean-tech revolution, which attracts more than USD 1 trillion in investment annually (IEA n.d.).
- The scale of public finance and its direct impacts, as well as its shaping influence on private financial flows.

Aligning global finance with nature and related equity goals requires a multifaceted approach, involving both carrots and sticks applied to actors across the financial ecosystem. Enforced policies and regulations must be a critical part of any meaningful solution. Such rules need to address issues ranging from eradicating nature crimes, which represent the third-largest source of illicit financial flows and a driver of nature destruction, to securing the rights of Indigenous Peoples, adequately protecting nature reserves, and encouraging citizens to act as consumers, savers, and voters to make nature count (Finance for Biodiversity Initiative 2022).

All of the above actions, and many more, will shape how finance counts nature. Yet, direct interventions in global finance can also make nature count, including:

- Pricing nature into financial decisions, especially investment decisions, which requires, at a minimum, the right data, accounting, and related standards.
- Developing regulatory standards and innovations in financial instruments and markets.
- Central banks and other governing bodies retooling their capabilities, applying nature to their existing instruments, and possibly reconsidering the adequacy of their mandates.
- Governments aligning procurement practices with nature-positive goals and repurposing subsidies that support nature-destructive business practices.
- Citizens, as savers and capital owners, becoming better informed and incentivized, as they must also act as consumers of final products and services.

Building a Nature Finance Operating System

Aligning global finance with nature-positive and equity goals requires a foundational "operating system", comprising the right data, accounting, standards, and governance.

This is essential for both private and public finance and is relevant for all financial flows, instruments, and governing arrangements.

There has been significant progress in developing the nature finance operating system, including:

- **Natural capital accounting**: Progress has been made toward harmonized approaches to natural capital accounting, such as the UN System of Environmental-Economic Accounting (SEEA), designed for sovereign and sub-sovereign systems, as well as entrepreneurial efforts in nature-financial accounting frameworks, like the LandBankingGroup and Intrinsic Exchange.
- **Disclosure standards**: The final disclosure recommendations of the Taskforce on Nature-related Financial Disclosures (TNFD) represent a major development, alongside the commitment by the International Sustainability Standards Board (ISSB) to integrate nature into its next iteration of guidance (IFRS 2024).
- **Biodata**: There is a surge in the origination and availability of biodata, driven by technological innovations, from eDNA to satellite monitoring, and increasingly sophisticated AI-driven analytical metrics such as the Biocomplexity Index and the Bio Intactness Index. Efforts are also underway to build open-source, public-access nature data platforms, such as the Nature-related Public Data Utility Platform (TNFD 2023).

While these developments are by no means sufficient to align global finance with nature-positive goals, the rapid maturation of these aspects of the operating system is essential. Although progress is ongoing, much more needs to be done to scale this operating system in a timely manner and to ensure it is applied widely and effectively, requiring both ambitious national and international action as well as effective governance.

Governing Nature Finance

Global finance lacks a single governing framework, with national and regional rules and institutions connected through international cooperation and voluntary standards, such as the G20, the Financial Stability Board, and the Bank for International Settlements, along with six major financial standards bodies like the International Organization of Securities Commissions (IOSCO).

Nature has become increasingly material to the governance of finance. There is growing recognition that the degradation of nature can have material investor-level, macroeconomic, macroprudential, and microprudential consequences. Notable developments include:

- **Disclosure**: National and regional developments are establishing mandatory nature-related disclosure requirements, notably in the European Community, EU member states like France, and China.
- **Financial stability**: The Network of Central Banks and Financial Supervisors for Greening the Financial System (NGFS) has recently concluded its Taskforce on Nature, which calls for all 120 members to consider nature-related risks (NGFS 2023).
- **Nature crimes**: Nature-linked crimes, representing the third-largest source of illicit financial flows, are increasingly subject to anti-money laundering developments (Finance for Biodiversity Initiative 2022).

Despite these positive developments, the narrow lens of material financial risk is likely insufficient to address the scale and speed of the nature and climate crises, as evidenced by recent global trends showing increased rates of deforestation and biodiversity loss (Ritchie 2024). What is needed is not simply more of the same, more quickly, but more ambitious shifts in governing arrangements to ensure that the regulation of nature's impacts and goals falls within the mandates of governing institutions. For example, the European Parliament's championing of mandatory, target-driven due diligence requirements on deforestation illustrates a potential direction for moving beyond financial risk, toward ensuring a transition to a nature-positive world. Such regulations can enable transparency across supply chains and ensure that financial institutions do not directly or indirectly fund or support deforestation linked to forest-risk commodities.

Driving Nature Finance Innovation

Accelerating nature-positive investments requires innovation in financial instruments, incentivized in part by regulations and leveraging the emergent operating system. The global financial system is diverse, encompassing massive sovereign debt markets, the critical market for publicly traded equities, extensive bank lending, and private equity, which, while smaller in scale, is essential for advancing the next generation of nature-positive businesses. Significant innovations in financial markets include:

- **Nature-linked sovereign financing**: System-critical sovereign debt markets are largely absent of effective consideration of nature risks and upside benefits. Nature-linked sovereign debt instruments have emerged to draw nature into these markets, including debt conversion mechanisms for nature (e.g., debt-for-nature swaps), alongside developments in the IMF's treatment of nature in its sustainable debt assessment framework, and making nature count in sovereign ratings (SSDH n.d.).

Addressing Debt Unsustainability and Investments in Nature

Emerging markets and developing economies (EMDEs), excluding China, account for an estimated 90% of the investment opportunity in protecting and restoring nature. At the same time, 60% of EMDEs are in debt distress, which limits their ability to increase public investment into nature (Center for Global Commons 2023). Comprehensively integrating nature into sovereign debt markets and scaling sustainability-linked sovereign financing instruments (such as debt conversion mechanisms for nature [Gabon, Belize, Ecuador] and sustainability-linked bonds [Uruguay, Chile] can help maintain a country's financial stability, while enhancing stewardship for future generations.

– **Nature credits**: Carbon credits, especially in voluntary markets, are significantly linked to nature-based carbon sequestration, and nature integrity is increasingly being built into these markets. Biodiversity credits of various kinds are also emerging as a significant financial instrument for channeling funds to restoration efforts and nature stewards, nudging behavior toward nature-positive business practices. These efforts are driven by the International Advisory Panel on Biodiversity Credits (International Advisory Panel on Biodiversity Credits n.d.).

One of the greatest challenges in shaping these innovations and related policy and regulatory developments is to ensure that they reinforce the rights and livelihood prospects of those who steward nature. Indigenous Peoples, in particular, while comprising about 5% of the world's population, are key to protecting 80% of the planet's biodiversity (Recio and Hestad 2022). Their values and holistic way of living with nature – centered on respect, care, reciprocity, and sustainability – show us the way forward but have historically been marginalized in modern economies. Likewise, nature-sensitized financial markets run the risk of excluding nature's stewards in their design, which could result in harm to these communities.

Direct Access Financing for Indigenous People-Led Nature Initiatives

Prioritizing traditional indigenous knowledge and stewardship practices is central to a nature-positive economy. Unfortunately, we are falling short of providing Indigenous Peoples with the financial support needed to safeguard their lands and waters. When the rights of Indigenous Peoples are recognized, secured, and protected, rates of deforestation tend to be lower, and carbon stocks tend to be higher than in forests managed by other actors. A recent study reveals that less than 1% of global climate finance has reached Indigenous Peoples and local communities in the Global South over the last ten years (Hatcher, Owen, and Yin 2021). Accelerating efforts like the Podong Indigenous Peoples Initiative, which aims to provide support for Indigenous-led programs aligned with climate and biodiversity goals, enhancing Indigenous Peoples' capacity to access and manage global funds, and supporting Indigenous communities in designing direct financing approaches for independent resource mobilization, is critical.

Public finance is also undergoing a significant pivot toward greater nature sensitivity, as highlighted and guided by major international initiatives such as UN BIOFIN. Multilateral development banks are increasingly embracing nature-related investments, such as the Asian Development Bank's newly launched Nature Finance Solutions Hub (Asian Development Bank 2024) and the nature-linked work of the Inter-American Development Bank (IDB, IDB Invest, and IDB Lab 2024).

Food Systems' Transformation

For instance, the majority of agricultural support from government subsidies benefits large producers and is linked to harmful environmental and health impacts. However, the global transition to a sustainable food and land-use system could alone provide USD 4.5 trillion a year in new business opportunities (UN Climate Change High-Level Champions 2022b). The number of material and credible national policy announcements focused on nature and land use doubled between 2022 and 2023 (Inevitable Policy Response 2024). Investors and companies worldwide risk being blindsided by ambition and the rapid pace of new policies if they fail to account for material, financial, nature-related, and climate-related risks.

A shift by governments away from subsidies and tax rebates for economic activities that deplete natural capital is lagging. Environmentally harmful subsidies increased by 55%, reaching USD 1.7 trillion from 2021 to 2022 (UNEP 2023b). Instead of providing environmentally harmful subsidies, better incentives could be introduced to incorporate nature-related risk management into public finance processes, including trade.

As the just energy transition has rapidly ascended the business agenda, the role of nature, land, and food in the climate transition remains undervalued in the financial system. The cross-cutting issue of equity also remains largely absent, despite growing, visible efforts to engage, involve, and empower Indigenous Peoples and local communities in the development of new nature-related financing instruments, such as biodiversity credits and nature-performance-linked debt.

Shaping a Global Nature-Positive Economy

Nature's future – and, ultimately, our continued presence on this planet – depends on progress in realizing the two interlinked goals of addressing climate challenges and pivoting the global economy toward an equitable, nature-positive state. Nature-based solutions have the potential to supply over one-third of cost-effective climate change mitigation needs by 2030 and contribute to adaptation goals, while supporting economies and future-proofing development priorities (Griscom et al. 2017).

For example:

– One estimate suggests that nature-based solutions could save USD 104 billion in adaptation costs by 2030 and USD 393 billion by 2050 (Griswold et al. 2023).
– Enhancing built infrastructure with plants, trees, or other alternatives could provide 50% of climate-resilient infrastructure needs by 2050 and save EMDEs at least USD 100 billion annually in climate change costs (Center for Global Commons 2023).

Such approaches need to be vigorously pursued, but they represent only one element in reshaping today's USD 105 trillion global economy. This shift will involve the development of many new businesses and sectors at the nexus of biodiversity and technology, collectively referred to as the "bioeconomy". This lens on nature includes growing sectors such as biofuels, biopharma, bioplastics, and, more broadly, bioengineering and manufacturing.

Already a USD 4 trillion annual economy, the bioeconomy is projected to grow rapidly, reaching as much as USD 30 trillion by one estimate (NatureFinance and GIB 2024). While this is encouraging, it is crucial to ensure that the bioeconomy develops in a way that delivers more equitable, nature-positive outcomes rather than simply exploiting biodiversity for profit. Financing – both in scale and form – will be a critical determinant of whether the surging bioeconomy will contribute to equity, nature, and climate goals (NatureFinance and The World Bioeconomy Forum 2024).

Advancing this ambitious agenda is closely connected to, but distinct from, our collective ambition to transition to a net-zero, climate-resilient economy. Success requires more systematic, nature-sensitive economic and industrial strategies, such as Brazil's Ecological Transformation Plan. Brazil has advanced this agenda as part of its G20 Presidency through a new workstream, the Global Initiative on the Bioeconomy, where a set of high-level principles has been agreed upon to inform policies and strategies for advancing a more equitable, sustainable bioeconomy (G20 2024). This agenda is being taken forward by Colombia, which has prioritized the bioeconomy in its role as President of COP16 of the Convention on Biological Diversity. It is expected that this agenda will be further advanced through the G20 during South Africa's Presidency in 2025.

The Path Forward

Making nature count in ways that deliver effective restoration and conservation – underpinned by a more equitable distribution of its bounty – is ultimately a policy choice. There is no shortage of knowledge, expertise, technology, and finance to accomplish this task; it simply needs to be deployed effectively. Similarly, markets are not inherently destructive to nature, just as they are not inherently emissions-intensive or unequal.

COP28 marked a pivotal moment in elevating the role of nature in global climate action. For instance, nature was placed at the heart of the Global Stocktake, with a strong call for zero deforestation by 2030 in the UAE Consensus. This initiative aligns with the Kunming-Montreal Global Biodiversity Framework (UNFCCC 2024). Over USD 2.7 billion was mobilized for projects targeting forest, ocean, and coastal ecosystems. Furthermore, the UAE Consensus – agreed upon by all parties – emphasized the importance of halting and reversing deforestation and forest degradation by 2030 (UN Climate Change High-Level Champions 2024).

Additionally, the COP28 Joint Statement on Climate, Nature, and People provides a crucial political signal to enable stronger synergies, integration, and alignment in the planning and implementation of national climate, biodiversity, and land restoration strategies (UNFCCC COP28 Presidency et al. 2024). Such initiatives can facilitate a whole-of-government approach, mainstreaming coherence, coordination, and efficient resource use across relevant ministries and departments. They also aim to scale up climate finance from all sources, ensuring that these strategies are ultimately investable.

These developments represent significant substantive progress and important signals of political will and momentum. However, unless these early steps transform into substantial leaps, their impact will remain limited. Achieving this phase-shift in action must occur under challenging conditions, with a fragile global economy and weakened international cooperation on multiple fronts.

Ambitious action on nature finance is neither guaranteed nor a panacea for addressing the changes required. Yet, despite troubling times, many foundational elements have been established in recent years. A range of market and policy developments offers a promising basis for progress. Most importantly, nature-rich countries now have a unique opportunity to leapfrog toward sustainable development by harnessing their biodiversity to shape a nature-positive bioeconomy.

References

Asian Development Bank. 2024. *Nature Solutions Finance Hub for Climate and the Environment*. Asian Development Bank. https://doi.org/10.22617/ARM240099-2.

Bartels, Meghan. 2023. "Humans Have Crossed 6 of 9 'Planetary Boundaries'." *Scientific American*, September 13, 2023. Accessed October 5, 2024. https://www.scientificamerican.com/article/humans-have-crossed-6-of-9-planetary-boundaries/.

Center for Global Commons. 2023. *Financing Nature: A Transformative Action Agenda*. Discussion paper, December 2023. Accessed October 5, 2024. https://cgc.ifi.u-tokyo.ac.jp/wp-content/uploads/2023/12/CGC_NatureFinanceReport_compressed.pdf.

Convention on Biological Diversity. 2022a. *Decision 15/4: Kunming-Montreal Global Biodiversity Framework*. Conference of the Parties to the Convention on Biological Diversity, Fifteenth Meeting (Part II), Montreal, Canada, December 7–19, 2022. https://www.cbd.int/doc/decisions/cop-15/cop-15-dec-04-en.pdf.

Convention on Biological Diversity. 2022b. "Target 3: Conserve 30% of Land, Waters and Seas." Secretariat of the Convention on Biological Diversity. Accessed October 1, 2024. https://www.cbd.int/gbf/targets/3.

Dasgupta, Partha. 2021. *The Economics of Biodiversity: The Dasgupta Review: Full Report*. London: HM Treasury. https://www.gov.uk/government/publications/final-report-the-economics-of-biodiversity-the-dasgupta-review.

Finance for Biodiversity Initiative. 2022. *Breaking the Environmental Crimes-Finance Connection*. https://www.naturefinance.net/wp-content/uploads/2022/08/BreakingEnvironmentalCrimesFinanceConnection.pdf.

Furtado, Marcelo. n.d. "Food Finance Nexus." *NatureFinance*. Accessed October 1, 2024. https://www.naturefinance.net/making-change/nature-markets/food-finance-nexus/.

G20. 2024. "G20 Reaches Consensus and Establishes High-Level Principles on Bioeconomy." September 11, 2024. Accessed Ocotber 5, 2024. https://g20.gov.br/en/news/g20-reaches-consensus-and-establishes-high-level-principles-on-bioeconomy.

Griscom, Bronson W., Justin Adams, Peter W. Ellis, Richard A. Houghton, Guy Lomax, Daniela A. Miteva, William H. Schlesinger, David Shoch, Juha V. Siikamäki, Pete Smith, Peter Woodbury, Chris Zganjar, Allen Blackman, João Campari, Richard T. Conant, Christopher Delgado, Patricia Elias, Trisha Gopalakrishna, Marisa R. Hamsik, Mario Herrero, Joseph Kiesecker, Emily Landis, Lars Laestadius, Sara M. Leavitt, Susan Minnemeyer, Stephen Polasky, Peter Potapov, Francis E. Putz, Jonathan Sanderman, Marcel Silvius, Eva Wollenberg, and Joseph Fargione. 2017. "Natural Climate Solutions." *Proceedings of the National Academy of Sciences* 114 (44): 11645–50. https://doi.org/10.1073/pnas.1710465114.

Griswold, Delilah, Emily Goodwin, Camila Donatti, and Chloe Pottinger Glass. 2023. *Nature-Based Solutions and the Global Goal on Adaptation: FEBA Issue Brief for UNFCCC COP27*. Friends of Ecosystem-based Adaptation (FEBA). https://iucn.org/sites/default/files/2022-11/feba-issue-brief-on-nbs-and-the-gga-for-cop27_0.pdf

Hatcher, Jeffrey, Michael Owen, and Daphne Yin. 2021. *Falling Short: Donor Funding for Indigenous Peoples and Local Communities to Secure Tenure Rights and Manage Forests in Tropical Countries (2011–2020)*. Norway: Rainforest Foundation.

International Advisory Panel on Biodiversity Credits. n.d. *Framework for High Integrity Biodiversity Credit Markets*. Accessed October 5, 2024. https://www.iapbiocredits.org/framework.

IDB, IDB Invest, and IDB Lab. 2024. *IDB Group Natural Capital and Biodiversity Mainstreaming Action Plan 2024-2025*. Inter-American Development Bank. https://doi.org/10.18235/0013120.

International Energy Agency (IEA). n.d. "Global Investment in Clean Energy Is on Course to Reach USD 1.8 Trillion in 2023 – Spotlight." *IEA*. Accessed October 5, 2024. https://www.iea.org/spotlights/global-investment-in-clean-energy-is-on-course-to-reach-usd-1-8-trillion-in-2023.

IFRS. 2024. "ISSB to Commence Research Projects about Risks and Opportunities Related to Nature and Human Capital." *IFRS*, April 23, 2024. Accessed October 1, 2024. https://www.ifrs.org/news-and-events/news/2024/04/issb-to-commence-research-projects-about-risks-and-opportunities-related-to-nature-and-human-capital/.

Inevitable Policy Response. 2024. Quarterly Forecast Tracker: Special Focus – Update of Global Land and Nature Policy Developments, Q3 2023 – Q1 2024. March 14, 2024. Accessed October 5, 2024. https://ipr.transitionmonitor.com/cms/wp-content/uploads/2024/03/2024-03-13-IPR-Land-Nature-QFT-final-layout.pdf.

Intergovernmental Science-Policy Platform on Biodiversity and Ecosystem Services (IPBES). 2022. "Media Release: IPBES Values Assessment – Decisions Based on Narrow Set of Market Values of Nature Underpin the Global Biodiversity Crisis." IPBES, July 10, 2022. Accessed October 1, 2024. https://www.ipbes.net/media_release/Values_Assessment_Published.

Lewsey, Fred. 2021. "Dasgupta Review: Nature's Value Must Be at the Heart of Economics." *University of Cambridge*, 2021. Accessed October 4, 2024. https://www.cam.ac.uk/stories/dasguptareview.

Mohieldin, Mahmoud, and Simon Zadek. 2024. "Beyond GDP: The Shift to New and Nature-Positive Measures of Progress Is Gaining Momentum." *World Economic Forum*, September 23, 2024. Accessed October 8, 2024. http://weforum.org/stories/2024/09/beyond-gdp-nature-positive-measures-progress-gaining-momentum/ .

Moss, Milton, ed. 1973. *The Measurement of Economic and Social Performance*. Studies in Income and Wealth, vol. 38. Conference on Research in Income and Wealth and Princeton University. New York: National Bureau of Economic Research; distributed by Columbia University Press.

NatureFinance and Getúlio Vargas Foundation for the G20 Initiative on Bioeconomy (GIB). 2024. *The Global Bioeconomy: Preliminary Stocktake of G20 Strategies and Practices – A Contribution to the Brazilian G20 Presidency's Global Initiative on Bioeconomy*. May 2024. Accessed October 4, 2024. https://www.naturefinance.net/resources-tools/global-bioeconomy-g20-stocktake/.

NatureFinance. 2023. *Making Nature Markets Work: Shaping a Global Nature Economy in the 21st Century*. August 2023. Accessed February 9, 2025. https://www.naturefinance.net/resources-tools/making-nature-markets-work/ .

NatureFinance and The World Bioeconomy Forum. 2024. *Financing a Sustainable Global Bioeconomy*. September 2024. Accessed February 9, 2025.https://www.naturefinance.net/wp-content/uploads/2024/08/FinancingASustainableGlobalBioeconomy-.pdf.

Nature Positive Initiative. 2023. *The Definition of Nature Positive*. November 27, 2023. Accessed October 1, 2024. https://www.naturepositive.org/app/uploads/2024/02/The-Definition-of-Nature-Positive.pdf

Network for Greening the Financial System (NGFS). 2023. *Nature-related Financial Risks: A Conceptual Framework to Guide Action by Central Banks and Supervisors*. September 2023. Accessed October 10, 2024. https://www.ngfs.net/system/files/import/ngfs/medias/documents/ngfs_conceptual-framework-on-nature-related-risks.pdf.

Recio, Eugenia, and Dina Hestad. 2022. "Indigenous Peoples: Defending an Environment for All." Policy Brief no. 36. International Institute for Sustainable Development (IISD). April 2022. Accessed October 5, 2024. https://www.iisd.org/system/files/2022-04/still-one-earth-Indigenous-Peoples.pdf

Ritchie, Hannah. 2024. "Deforestation and Forest Loss." *Our World in Data*. Accessed December 2, 2024. https://ourworldindata.org/deforestation.

Sustainable Sovereign Debt Hub (SSDH). n.d. *About the Sustainability-Linked Sovereign Debt Hub*. Accessed October 4, 2024. https://www.ssdh.net/about.

Stiglitz, Joseph E., Jean-Paul Fitoussi, and Martine Durand. 2018. *Beyond GDP: Measuring What Counts for Economic and Social Performance*. Paris: OECD Publishing. https://doi.org/10.1787/9789264307292-en.

The World Counts. 2024. "Environmental Degradation Facts." Accessed October 10, 2024. https://www.theworldcounts.com/stories/environmental-degradation-facts.

Taskforce on Nature-related Financial Disclosures (TNFD). 2023. "TNFD Publishes Scoping Study Exploring Global Nature-related Public Data Facility." Press release, August 1, 2023. https://tnfd.global/tnfd-publishes-scoping-study-data-facility/.

UN Climate Change High-Level Champions. 2022a. *Sharm-El-Sheikh Adaptation Agenda*. https://climatechampions.unfccc.int/wp-content/uploads/2022/11/SeS-Adaptation-Agenda_Complete-Report-COP27_FINAL-1.pdf.

UN Climate Change High-Level Champions. 2022b. *Assessing the Financial Impact of the Land Use Transition on the Food and Agriculture Sector*. September 2022. https://www.climatechampions.net/media/0fspjnvr/assessing-the-financial-impact-of-the-land-use-transition-on-the-food-and-agriculture-sector.pdf

UN Climate Change High-Level Champions. 2024. *Achievements at COP28*. Internal report.

United Nations Environment Programme (UNEP). 2016. *The Financial System We Need: Aligning the Financial System with Sustainable Development*. January 2016. https://doi.org/10.18356/599999aa-en.

United Nations Environment Programme (UNEP). 2023a. "Five Drivers of the Nature Crisis." September 5, 2023. Accessed October 10, 2024. https://www.unep.org/news-and-stories/story/five-drivers-nature-crisis.

United Nations Environment Programme (UNEP). 2023b. *State of Finance for Nature 2023: The Big Nature Turnaround – Repurposing $7 Trillion to Combat Nature Loss*. https://doi.org/10.59117/20.500.11822/44278.

United Nations Framework Convention on Climate Change (UNFCCC). 2015. *Paris Agreement*. https://unfccc.int/sites/default/files/resource/parisagreement_publication.pdf.

United Nations Framework Convention on Climate Change (UNFCCC). 2024. Outcomes of the Dubai Climate Change Conference – Advance Unedited Versions (AUVs) and List of Submissions from the Sessions in Dubai. https://unfccc.int/cop28/outcomes.

UNFCCC COP28 Presidency, UNFCCC COP30 Presidency, CBD COP15 Presidency, CBD COP16 Presidency, UNCCD COP15 Presidency, and Chairs of the Undersigned Partnerships, Initiatives and Coalitions. 2024. COP28 Joint Statement on Climate, Nature and People. Accessed October 10, 2024. https://www.cop28.com/en/joint-statementon-climate-nature.

van Nieuwkoop, Martien. 2019. "Do the Costs of the Global Food System Outweigh Its Monetary Value?" *World Bank Blogs*, June 17, 2019. Accessed October 10, 2024. https://blogs.worldbank.org/en/voices/do-costs-global-food-system-outweigh-its-monetary-value

WWF. 2022. *Living Planet Report 2022: Building a Nature-Positive Society*. Edited by Rosamunde Almond, Monique Grooten, Diego Juffe Bignoli, and Tanya Petersen. Gland, Switzerland: WWF. https://wwflpr.awsassets.panda.org/downloads/lpr_2022_full_report_1.pdf

Mohamed Nasr and Zaheer Fakir

Chapter 8
Financing Loss and Damage

Abstract: This chapter examines loss and damage as an independent element of climate action, distinct from mitigation and adaptation. It outlines how increasing climate-induced crises are exposing the limitations of traditional responses, particularly for nations least responsible for greenhouse gas emissions yet most vulnerable to its effects. The discussion traces the evolution of loss and damage within international climate negotiations and highlights the challenges of securing adequate, coherent financial support. Special focus is given to the establishment and operationalization of the Loss and Damage Fund, a pivotal step aimed at addressing both economic and noneconomic impacts while ensuring that support does not exacerbate developing countries' debt burdens. The chapter ultimately calls for enhanced global cooperation and innovative financial strategies to better meet the irreversible impacts of climate change.

Keywords: Loss and damage, Loss and damage fund, Adaptation limits, Climate justice, Climate negotiations, Financing mechanisms

Introduction

Climate-induced losses and damages affecting livelihoods, ecosystems, and infrastructure are undeniable realities in today's world. While mitigation and adaptation have long been recognized as the main pillars of international climate action, the recognition of loss and damage as a third, distinct pillar has faced resistance. Despite its official recognition in the Paris Agreement, loss and damage was often viewed, primarily by developed countries, as merely a subcomponent of adaptation. However, the ongoing rise in global temperatures, leading to an increase in the frequency of climate-induced disasters, coupled with the recognition of the limitations of adaptation efforts in averting, minimizing, and addressing these impacts, has underscored the need to address loss and damage as a standalone pillar of climate action.

The issue of loss and damage is intrinsically linked to climate justice, as developing countries are the most impacted due to their increasing vulnerability and limited resilience capacity, in particular those who face significant development and environmental challenges. Within the multilateral climate process, financing loss and damage has historically been a contentious subject. Several factors, including concerns about compensation and legal liability, have complicated international negotiations on this issue. Nonetheless, the reality remains that the scale of funding required to address losses and damages has not been met with sufficient, harmonized, and predictable financial flows.

The climate finance landscape addressing loss and damage has been fragmented, with funding typically deployed on an ad hoc basis in the aftermath of disasters. The absence of a single entity dedicated to mobilizing and deploying funds for loss and damage has undermined the effectiveness and coherence of existing funding arrangements. However, as a result of persistent calls from developing countries and the growing recognition of the scale of the challenge, a significant milestone was achieved in 2022 with the establishment of the Loss and Damage Fund at Sharm El-Sheikh COP27, which was operationalized in 2023 at UAE COP28. The Fund is designed to assist developing countries, particularly those most vulnerable to the adverse effects of climate change, in responding to the economic and noneconomic losses and damages associated with climate change, including extreme weather events and slow-onset events (UNFCCC 2023a).

This chapter begins by defining the scope of the term "loss and damage", followed by an overview of the realities of climate-induced losses and damages. It then provides a brief account of how international negotiations have addressed this issue. The chapter also explains the dynamics of establishing and operationalizing the Loss and Damage Fund, concluding with a discussion on the way forward to ensure the successful functioning of this crucial Fund.

What Is Loss and Damage?

The term "loss and damage" refers to the negative impacts of climate change that occur despite efforts at mitigation and adaptation. It encompasses the unavoidable and irreversible impacts of climate-induced crises (UNEP, n.d.). Both extreme weather events and slow-onset events[1] contribute to losses and damages (UNFCCC 2010).

Losses and damages from climate change are categorized into economic and noneconomic losses. Economic losses refer to the loss of resources, goods, and services that are traded in markets and, therefore, can be valued at market prices (UNFCCC 2013a). Examples include damages to physical infrastructure and agricultural productivity. Noneconomic losses, on the other hand, refer to losses that do not have a market value, as they are not traded in markets. These losses include the loss of lives, cultural heritage, local and indigenous knowledge, biodiversity, ecosystem services, and human displacement and mobility (UNFCCC 2013a). However, the distinction between

---

1 Examples of extreme weather events include droughts, heatwaves, tropical cyclones, and floods. In contrast, slow-onset events encompass sea-level rise increasing temperatures, ocean acidification, glacial retreat and related impacts, salinization, land and forest degradation, loss of biodiversity and desertification.

these two categories can be vague. For instance, while disruptions to natural ecosystems are classified as noneconomic losses, they can also lead to economic losses if the services provided by those ecosystems, such as food or livelihoods, are critical to the economy (UNFCCC 2010). For example, climate change is expected to significantly affect the tuna population in the tropical Pacific, which could have serious consequences for the small Pacific Island nations that rely on tuna fishing as a primary source of income. These nations could lose up to 17% of their government revenues as a result (Bell et al. 2021).

Climate-Induced Losses and Damages: Undisputed Realities

A long history of high GHG emissions has already altered the climate system, making certain climate change effects inevitable or irreversible (LSE Grantham Research Institute on Climate Change 2022). Given that the world is not meeting its mitigation commitments and that current climate policies are projected to lead to a temperature rise exceeding the Paris Agreement goal (UNEP 2023), losses and damages are becoming increasingly unavoidable. Risks and projected impacts are expected to rise with each increment of global warming, with impacts projected to be higher at 1.5 °C compared to current levels and even more severe at 2 °C. For instance, climate change contributed to the devastating floods in Pakistan in 2022, increasing rainfall by an estimated 50–75% (Otto et al. 2023).

Recent findings also indicate that the overall risk to human and natural systems will escalate to high or very high levels at lower degrees of warming than previously estimated. This is due to new insights into observed climate impacts, improved understanding of processes, and increased recognition of the limitations of adaptation actions and finance in addressing losses and damages (IPCC 2023). The limits to the capacity by which the world can adapt to climate change are reached either because there are "no adaptive actions possible to avoid intolerable risks", known as hard adaptation limits, or because "options are currently not available to avoid intolerable risks through adaptive action", known as soft adaptation limits. The latter can be due to financial, governance, institutional, and/or policy constraints (IPCC 2023). These factors also show that mitigation, adaptation, and loss and damage exist in a continuum. For instance, at less than 1.5 °C of global warming, terrestrial and aquatic ecosystems will increasingly encounter hard adaptation limits in their autonomous and evolutionary responses. Beyond 1.5 °C, some ecosystem-based adaptation strategies will no longer effectively benefit people (IPCC 2023). Small-scale farmers are already experiencing soft limits to adaptation in low-lying coastal areas, and hard adaptation limits have been reached for several ecosystems (IPCC 2023). In addition, climate change is increasingly causing human displacement due to factors such as extreme weather events, worsening resource scarcity, threats to food security, and conflict. Projections suggest that up to 1.2 billion people could be displaced globally by 2050 as a result of climate change and natural disasters[2] (IEP 2020). Slow-onset events leading to sea-level rise, storm surges, and decreased water availability and crop productivity are estimated to force 216 million people to become internal migrants by 2050 (Clement et al. 2021).

Climate-induced losses and damages are unequally distributed around the globe, marking the interdependence between human and ecosystem vulnerabilities (IPCC 2023). Regions and populations facing significant development challenges are highly vulnerable to climate-related crises and face considerable constraints in responding to these crises. The death rate from floods, droughts, and storms was 15 times higher in regions with high vulnerability compared to those with very low vulnerability between 2010 and 2020 (IPCC 2023). Climate-related losses and damages, along with increased reconstruction costs, have wiped out years of development gains in developing countries, deepening existing vulnerabilities.

All these factors place loss and damage as a third pillar of climate action, alongside mitigation and adaptation. Climate change has caused considerable monetary losses, with one analysis showing that extreme weather losses and damages attributed to climate change cost at least USD 2.86 trillion between 2000 and 2019, which can be disaggregated to USD 143 billion annually (Newman and Noy 2023). The future challenge is no less daunting. Estimates suggest that loss and damage, which exceed the scope of adaptation efforts, could cost developing countries between USD 290 billion and USD 580 billion by 2030, potentially rising to USD 1 trillion to USD 1.8 trillion by 2050 (Markandya and González-Eguino 2018).

Loss and Damage in Climate Negotiations: A Brief History

The 1972 Stockholm Conference on the Human Environment marks the first official step toward addressing the environment as a major issue (United Nations 1972). This was followed by the creation of the United Nations Environment Programme (UNEP) in the same year and later the creation of the Intergovernmental Panel on Climate Change (IPCC) in 1988 (IPCC n.d.; UNGA 1972). With the growing scientific consensus that human activities led to increased concentrations of GHGs in the atmosphere and mounting concerns about adverse effects on natural ecosystems and humankind, the

---

2 This projection includes displacement due to both natural disasters and armed conflicts. However, according to Figure 1.1 in the 2020 Ecological Threat Register, natural disasters would lead to approximately 1 billion people being displaced by 2050 (IEP 2020).

United Nations Framework Convention on Climate Change (UNFCCC) was drafted in 1991 (Bhandari et al. 2024). Concurrently, the island nation of Vanuatu made the first global call for support to address loss and damage resulting from the adverse impacts of climate change. This call, representing the Alliance of Small Island States (AOSIS), proposed establishing an insurance scheme to provide financial support to countries affected by sea-level rise. Under this plan, nations would contribute to the fund according to their proportionate share of global emissions and their percentage of the world's gross national product (Bhandari et al. 2024). The proposal was rejected, and the topic of loss and damage was excluded from the final text of the Framework Convention adopted in 1992[3] (United Nations 1992).

Following the devastating effects of Typhoon Haiyan on the Philippines, the loss and damage issue was officially recognized at COP19, which led to the creation of the Warsaw International Mechanism for Loss and Damage associated with Climate Change Impacts (Heinrich Böll Stiftung n.d.). The Mechanism was mandated with implementing approaches to address loss and damage through sharing knowledge, fostering dialogues and coordination among stakeholders, and addressing gaps in understanding of and expertise in approaches to address loss and damage (UNFCCC 2013b).

The milestone of having loss and damage as a third pillar of climate action occurred with the inclusion of Article 8 of the Paris Agreement, adopted in 2015. The Paris Agreement "recognizes the importance of averting, minimizing, and addressing loss and damage associated with the adverse effects of climate change, including extreme weather events and slow-onset events, and the role of sustainable development in reducing the risk of loss and damage" (UNFCCC 2015). Article 8 specifies areas of cooperation and facilitation to strengthen understanding, action, and support concerning loss and damage. It is important to highlight that the United Nations Office for Disaster Risk Reduction, through its Sendai Framework adopted in 2015, before the Paris Agreement, recognizes climate change as a key factor driving risk and contributing to the increased frequency, severity, and impact of various disasters. As such, it focuses more on resilience as a means to reduce climate-related disasters in the context of a disaster reduction approach.

---

3 The focus of the Convention was mainly on mitigation, with a limited focus on adaptation. This was reflected in the Kyoto Protocol, which focused on reducing emissions from developed countries under the principle of "common but differentiated responsibilities and respective capabilities" as they are the historical emitters (United Nations 1992; UNFCCC 1997). However, the main delivery on adaptation in the Kyoto Protocol was the creation of the Adaptation Fund, which was initially financed with a share of the proceeds from certified emissions reductions (CERs) issued in the context of the Protocol's Clean Development Mechanism (UNFCCC 2005). The Fund was a de facto solidarity fund to support adaptation action in developing countries. Later, the global climate agenda under the UNFCCC expanded by considering adaptation as another main pillar for climate action. The creation of the Nairobi Work Programme at COP11 acted as a vehicle to deliver on adaptation-related matters by supporting developing countries in improving their understanding of climate change impacts, vulnerabilities, and adaptation measures (UNFCCC 2005).

Despite the emergence of loss and damage as a third pillar of climate action and the repeated calls from developing countries grappling with the adverse effects of climate change, the issue of financing loss and damage remained sidelined. The controversy surrounding loss and damage finance largely stemmed from developed countries' concerns that offering compensation for climate-related losses could be interpreted as admitting legal liability. This, in turn, would open the door to large-scale compensation claims, particularly because developed nations are historically responsible for contributing to climate change. Consequently, even though the Paris Agreement does not mention finance in Article 8, developed countries managed to secure nonbinding language in the Paris Agreement such that Article 8 "does not involve or provide a basis for any liability or compensation" (UNFCCC 2015; UNFCCC 2022a). As a result, developed countries have relied on the humanitarian system to address climate change-related losses and damages while using the climate finance system to focus on the aversion and minimization components. This has been achieved by financing mitigation, adaptation, and resilience through institutions like the Green Climate Fund, the Adaptation Fund, and bilateral channels, along with funding from multilateral development banks (MDBs) under various development programs. Developed countries have mostly regarded addressing loss and damage as ex-ante adaptation that would minimize future losses and damages and have treated loss and damage as a part of adaptation (LSE Grantham Research Institute on Climate Change 2022). However, this overlooks the real scope of defining loss and damage, often called residual loss, which acknowledges that certain losses and damages are inevitable despite mitigation and adaptation efforts, particularly due to the limits of adaptation in averting, minimizing, and addressing loss and damage.

Toward the Establishment of the Loss and Damage Fund

The economic and noneconomic costs of losses and damages exceed the capacities of developing countries. The inherent problem is that these limited capacities interact with numerous limitations of the current financing landscape. Climate finance flowing to developing countries is largely insufficient, with current funding being 5–10 times below these countries' estimated annual needs (UNEP 2022). In the context of loss and damage, funding gaps are particularly evident in recovery, reconstruction, and social protection (UNFCCC 2023b). Even in the context of humanitarian assistance, which is only designed to address the immediate aftermath of a disaster, the humanitarian appeals related to extreme weather events were eight times higher in 2019–2021 compared to 2000–2022. However, the humanitarian system was able to meet only about 54% of these appeals on average, leaving an estimated funding gap of USD 28–33 billion (Carty and Walsh 2022).

Besides the insufficiency of resources, there are structural gaps within the financial system related to issues of eligibility and access to adequate, low-cost financing for vulnerable countries. For instance, the income classification of many Caribbean Small Island Developing States (SIDS) limits their access to concessional finance, neglecting the scale of the impacts of climate change they face. Similarly, many vulnerable countries, especially middle-income ones, are excluded from the eligibility scope of MDBs due to their income levels. Although SIDS and other countries are granted special-status access in these institutions, this access falls short of providing enough resources to address loss and damage (UNFCCC 2023b).

On top of these gaps, the climate finance landscape is predominantly characterized by the prevalence of lending instruments. Between 2016 and 2020, concessional and non-concessional loans made up 72% of public climate finance (for mitigation, adaptation, and cross-cutting initiatives), while grants contributed 26% of the funding (UNFCCC 2023b). Over 50% of the debt increase in vulnerable countries can be attributed to funding disaster recoveries (UNFCCC 2023b). This, combined with the increasing frequency of climate-related disasters and the growing needs of countries, heightens the risk of debt overhang and poses significant threats to debt sustainability. As a result, it further limits developing countries' ability to access financial markets to address these needs.

Substantial methodological and data gaps hinder the effective tagging and tracking of funding directed to losses and damages. The UNFCCC process has not produced a consensual and unified definition for loss and damage. Without a clear and agreed-upon definition, it has been difficult to separate finance flows related to loss and damage from other adaptation-related finance flows. These finance flows span several interconnected areas, such as macroeconomic and fiscal stability, disaster risk reduction and management, risk transfer and pooling, humanitarian aid, and national funds. Identifying finance flows associated with preparedness, early warning systems, insurance, emergency response, recovery, and reconstruction in the context of sudden-onset events and specific disasters can be done with some certainty. This is because multilateral and bilateral funders often have certain targets for earmarked funding windows, programs, and facilities for these categories, which are reported and monitored. In contrast, attributing finance flows from general adaptation funding to loss and damage is less certain due to the broad range of activities involved, including disaster preparedness and management, as well as addressing slow-onset events and impacts like sea-level rise, biodiversity loss, and glacier retreat, along with their compounded effects. Furthermore, finance flows toward loss and damage have not been systematically tagged, reported, or tracked through the UNFCCC's existing mechanisms or by institutions involved in funding arrangements addressing these issues. Bilateral and multilateral funders do not categorize their expenditures in loss and damage terms. This lack of specific tracking restricts the ability to generate, collect, and aggregate data and information that could provide more detailed insights into effective modalities for addressing loss and damage (UNFCCC 2023b).

The absence of a common body or mechanism to ensure the tracking, coordination, and coherence of the existing finance flows has limited the mobilization of effective resources to address loss and damage. All of these factors have highlighted that concurrent financial, governance, and institutional arrangements do not comprehensively address losses and damages, especially in vulnerable developing countries (IPCC 2023).

These developments created a collective, united position among developing countries and an acceptance among developed countries on the need to act quickly and respond collectively in support of those severely impacted. This was firmly supported by the United Nations Secretary-General, who called on developed countries and the international community to take climate-induced losses and damages seriously and respond with a sense of urgency and responsibility. With Pakistan's 2022 unprecedented floods, the increasing magnitude and frequency of cyclones and storms in the Caribbean and Pacific, and the growing number of displaced and forced migrants in Africa due to extended droughts and loss of livelihoods, it was the right time for the international community to respond at COP27 in Sharm El-Sheikh. The G77 and China, Africa, Least Developed Countries, and SIDS groups united their calls that the loss and damage agenda should go beyond the dialogue created a year before in Glasgow, and civil society requested a fair deal to reflect climate justice in Sharm El-Sheikh's outcomes.

The COP27 Presidency and the Establishment of the Loss and Damage Fund

The COP27 presidency sought to enact a landing deal for funding loss and damage, an effort supported by Chile and Germany, who facilitated consultations to ensure an agreement at COP27. These efforts included informal consultations with various stakeholders. The COP27 presidency adopted a multistep approach, starting with overcoming concerns around the liability and responsibility of developed countries by framing the discussions within the realm of solidarity and support. This framing allowed the creation of an agenda item to discuss funding loss and damage. However, the COP27 presidency recognized that creating an agenda item with the right framing was insufficient to respond to the calls of developing countries, civil society, and, more importantly, the impacted communities.

Challenges became evident during the final stretch of negotiations, particularly attempts to confine support to smaller groups or constituencies and redefine the beneficiaries based on geography or economic and development levels. This approach was not welcomed by developing countries collectively.

These negotiations culminated in a package deal at COP27 in Sharm El-Sheikh, which created a new fund for loss and damage. The Fund is designed to focus on addressing loss and damage by mobilizing new and additional resources. The deal acknowledges existing funding arrangements for loss and damage while recognizing their fragmentation and insufficiency (UNFCCC 2022b). It also emphasized that support provided through the new fund should reflect solidarity and not compensation. Furthermore, the decision underscored that this support should not increase the debt burden of developing nations and that additional funding for loss and damage should not divert resources designated for other areas of climate action, poverty reduction, or broader development priorities. The fund should also operate in a manner that ensures the holistic addressing of loss and damage throughout the lifespan of the climate-driven crisis. These clauses highlight the importance of coordination, coherence, and scaling up funding arrangements for loss and damage, including those outside the UNFCCC and the Paris Agreement (UNFCCC 2022b; UNFCCC 2023a).

Given the complexity of the task, the decision established a Transitional Committee with the mandate to provide recommendations on the operationalization of the new Fund. The committee's recommendations would cover institutional arrangements, modalities, structure, governance, and potential funding sources while ensuring coordination and complementarity with existing funding arrangements (UNFCCC 2022b). The work of the Committee throughout 2023 proved challenging for several reasons, including the definition of climate-related losses and damages, the inclusion of support for minimizing impacts, managing the scale of impacts and resources[4] needed, ensuring complementarity with existing mechanisms,[5] and positioning the new fund within the existing ecosystem.

Toward the Operationalization of the Loss and Damage Fund

At COP28 in the UAE, an agreement was reached to operationalize the new funding arrangements, including the Loss and Damage Fund, following the Transitional Committee's recommendations. COP28 welcomed contributions toward the new funding arrangements for loss and damage worth USD 792 million, including USD 661 million directed to the new fund (UNFCCC 2023a). However, as discussed in the previous section, the decision to operationalize the Loss and Damage Fund followed several meetings held to finalize its governing instruments.

---

4 For instance, the financing needs due to loss and damage will be different in the case of extreme weather events, which often require rapid payouts, compared to slow onset events, which necessitate financial protection for the most vulnerable (UNFCCC 2022a).
5 In particular the newly created ones such as the "Global Shield against Climate Risks" launched at COP27 between the V20 and the G7.

Discussions within the Committee aimed to define the Fund's roles in three key timeframes related to loss and damage: before the disaster, immediately after the disaster, and during reconstruction and recovery. It is necessary to consider loss and damage not only as disaster relief, rehabilitation, and recovery but also in the context of safe migration, resettlement, and long-term stability for rebuilding lives and livelihoods. This approach is particularly important as noneconomic losses and slow-onset events complicate the definition of what constitutes loss and damage. The governing instrument of the Fund, outlined by the Committee and approved at COP28, states that the Fund will provide support for a range of climate change-related challenges, such as climate-related emergencies, sea-level rise, displacement, migration, and insufficient climate information. It will also address the need for climate-resilient reconstruction, recovery, and mitigation of both economic and noneconomic losses, whether caused by extreme weather or slow-onset events (UNFCCC 2023a).

This structure recognizes three layers of loss and damage along the time horizon of climate-induced crises:

A. **Pre-Loss and Damage Phase**: Scientific research indicates increasing impacts of climate-induced crises in both magnitude and frequency. During this phase, additional resilience support is needed to mitigate and reduce losses in areas such as human lives, economic assets, and cultural heritage. This includes anticipatory measures like contingency funds and insurance. However, this approach is most feasible in regions with sufficient historical data to forecast climate impacts, making it less applicable in areas facing novel or unexpected climate events, such as the extreme weather events in Libya and Pakistan in 2021 and 2022, respectively.

B. **Concurrent and Immediate Aftermath of Climate Impacts**: A significant gap exists between the global response, which is often limited to temporary food and shelter from humanitarian agencies. There is a need for more comprehensive livelihood support, particularly for communities whose livelihoods have been disrupted, such as fishing villages affected by cyclones or typhoons. Loss and damage funding could help with relocation efforts or diversifying the skills of affected populations.

C. **Post-Event Phase (Building Back)**: Currently, the rebuilding phase is carried out through ad hoc measures, such as appeals and international conferences for reconstruction, as well as loans from MDBs and international financial institutions. These efforts aim to restore impacted areas and communities to their pre-crisis conditions, attempting to recover lost development gains.

The Transitional Committee also discussed access modalities and which financial instruments the Fund would employ. The governing instrument of the Fund established several access modalities, such as direct budget support; direct access via subnational, national, and regional entities; and international access through multilateral or bilateral entities. The Fund would also provide small grants for vulnerable communities and incorporate rapid disbursement modalities (UNFCCC 2023a). These modalities follow the work of accredited entities, which must meet fiduciary standards and other requirements to ensure effective and efficient delivery. The Committee recommended that existing accredited entities be automatically recognized without new accreditation processes, using the concept of "functional equivalency" to establish criteria for additional new entities.

The Fund will primarily offer grants and highly concessional loans to avoid adding to developing countries' debt burdens. However, the Fund's Board still needs to finalize the policies for providing these instruments, as well as decide on the criteria, such as climate impact indicators and debt sustainability, that will guide funding decisions. It remains undecided whether and how these criteria will vary based on the nature of the event or the stage of impact.

Given the scale of funding required and the limited available resources, it was agreed that a global approach to addressing loss and damage would use all available tools and mechanisms, ensuring they work in harmony and coordination. This approach will increase impact, avoid duplication, and deliver at scale and speed. The existing ecosystem includes initiatives such as the Global Shield, bilateral support from the United States and European Union countries, and insurance companies, among others. The Fund should ensure coherence and coordination with these arrangements while mobilizing new funding. Additionally, the Board has yet to discuss issues related to the Fund's capitalization and how to replenish its resources to meet the scale of the financial needs of developing countries.

A key consideration for the Fund's operationalization is whether the World Bank, identified as the potential host and trustee, can meet the global community's expectations as articulated in the COP28 decision. The conditions for the World Bank to host the Fund as a financial intermediary include (UNFCCC 2023a): consistency with the Fund's Governing Instrument, the guarantee of full autonomy for the Board, the application of the Fund's eligibility criteria over World Bank policies when necessary, direct access for all developing countries to the Fund's resources, the ability to receive contributions from various sources in line with due diligence, and that the Fund's assets and secretariat are provided with necessary immunities.

Conclusion

As the climate crisis intensifies, the need to address loss and damage has become undeniable, establishing it as the third pillar of climate action alongside mitigation and adaptation, particularly with the recognition that not all climate impacts can be mitigated or adapted to. This chapter has explored the critical need for a dedicated finance framework to support countries most vulnerable to such losses and damages despite contributing the least to the current crisis. This framework must be integrated into a broader, more holistic climate finance regime – one that addresses both immediate and long-term recovery needs, builds resilience, and fosters justice for those disproportionately affected.

The establishment of the Loss and Damage Fund marks a significant step forward in addressing the challenges of financing climate-induced losses and damages. The Fund represents more than a symbolic gesture; it reflects a long-overdue acknowledgment of the financial needs that developing countries face as they bear the brunt of climate impacts. With the operationalization of the Loss and Damage Fund, there is hope that this mechanism will provide a lifeline for communities struggling with both sudden-onset disasters, such as floods and hurricanes, and slow-onset events like sea-level rise and desertification. While the Fund will not address all the current and forthcoming challenges of developing countries, it signals that multilateralism works and is the only path forward to address global crises, placing humanity, compassion, and solidarity at the heart of solutions to existential threats.

References

Bell, Johann D., Inna Senina, Timothy Adams, Olivier Aumont, Beatriz Calmettes, Sangaalofa Clark, Morgane Dessert et al. 2021. "Pathways to Sustaining Tuna-Dependent Pacific Island Economies during Climate Change." *Nature Sustainability* 4: 900–910. https://doi.org/10.1038/s41893-021-00793-5.

Bhandari, Preety, Nate Warszawski, Deirdre Cogan, and Rhys Gerholdt. 2024. "What Is 'Loss and Damage' from Climate Change? 8 Key Questions, Answered." *World Resources Institute*, November 4. Accessed November 28, 2024. https://wri.org/insights/loss-damage-climate-change

Carty, Tracy, and Lyndsay Walsh. 2022. *Footing the Bill: Fair Finance for Loss and Damage in an Era of Escalating Climate Impacts*. Oxfam Briefing Paper, June. Oxfam. Accessed November 28, 2024. https://oxfamilibrary.openrepository.com/bitstream/handle/10546/621382/bp-fair-finance-loss-and-damage-070622-en.pdf.

Clement, Viviane, Kanta Kumari Rigaud, Alex de Sherbinin, Bryan Jones, Susana Adamo, Jacob Schewe, Nian Sadiq, and Elham Shabahat. 2021. *Groundswell Part 2: Acting on Internal Climate Migration*. Washington, DC: The World Bank.

Heinrich Böll Stiftung. n.d. "Spotlighting the finance gap – What differentiates finance for addressing loss and damage from other types of finance?" *Unpacking finance for Loss and Damage Dossier*. Accessed November 28, 2024. https://us.boell.org/en/unpacking-finance-loss-and-damage

Intergovernmental Panel on Climate Change (IPCC). 2023. *Climate Change 2023: Synthesis Report. Contribution of Working Groups I, II and III to the Sixth Assessment Report of the Intergovernmental Panel on Climate Change*. [Core Writing Team, H. Lee and J. Romero (eds.)] Geneva: IPCC. https://doi.org/10.59327/IPCC/AR6-9789291691647.

Intergovernmental Panel on Climate Change (IPCC). n.d. "History of the IPCC". Accessed November 28, 2024. https://www.ipcc.ch/about/history/

Institute for Economics & Peace (IEP). 2020. *Ecological Threat Register 2020 – Understanding Ecological Threat, Resilience and Peace*. Sydney. Accessed November 28, 2024. https://www.visionofhumanity.org/resources/

LSE Grantham Research Institute on Climate Change and the Environment. 2022. "What is Climate Change Loss and Damage?" *Grantham Research Institute Explainers*, October 28. Accessed November 28, 2024. https://www.lse.ac.uk/granthaminstitute/explainers/what-is-climate-change-loss-and-damage/.

Markandya, Anil, and Mikel González-Eguino. 2018. "Integrated Assessment for Identifying Climate Finance Needs for Loss and Damage: A Critical Review." In *Loss and Damage from Climate Change: Climate Risk Management, Policy and Governance*, edited by Reinhard Mechler, Lisa Bouwer, Thomas Schinko, Susanne Surminski, and Jurgen Linnerooth-Bayer, 241–257. Cham: Springer. https://doi.org/10.1007/978-3-319-72026-5_14.

Newman, Rebecca, and Ilan Noy. 2023. "The Global Costs of Extreme Weather That Are Attributable to Climate Change." *Nature Communications* 14: 6103. https://doi.org/10.1038/s41467-023-41888-1.

Otto, Friederike E. L., Mariam Zachariah, Fahad Saeed, Ayesha Siddiqi, Shahzad Kamil, Haris Mushtaq, T. Arulalan et al.. 2023. "Climate Change Increased Extreme Monsoon Rainfall, Flooding Highly Vulnerable Communities in Pakistan." *Environ. Res.: Climate* 2 (2): 25001. https://doi.org/10.1088/2752-5295/acbfd5

United Nations. 1972. *Report of the United Nations Conference on the Human Environment*. United Nations Conference on the Human Environment, Stockholm, Sweden, June 5–16, 1972. United Nations.

United Nations. 1992. *United Nations Framework Convention on Climate Change, with Annexes*. UNFCCC. Accessed November 28, 2024. https://unfccc.int/sites/default/files/convention_text_with_annexes_english_for_posting.pdf.

United Nations Environment Programme (UNEP). 2022. *Adaptation Gap Report 2022: Too Little, Too Slow – Climate Adaptation Failure Puts World at Risk. Nairobi.* https://www.unep.org/adaptation-gap-report-2022

United Nations Environment Programme (UNEP). 2023. *Emissions Gap Report 2023 – Temperatures Hit New Highs, Yet World Fails to Cut Emissions (Again). Nairobi.* https://doi.org/10.59117/20.500.11822/43922.

United Nations Environment Programme (UNEP). n.d. "About Loss and Damage." *Climate Action: Loss and Damage.* Accessed November 28, 2024. https://www.unep.org/topics/climate-action/loss-and-damage/about-loss-and-damage.

United Nations Framework Convention on Climate Change (UNFCCC). 1997. "Decision 1/CP.3:Adoption of the Kyoto Protocol to the United Nations Framework Convention on Climate Change." *Third Conference of the Parties* (COP3), Kyoto, Japan, December 1–11, 1997. UNFCCC. Accessed November 28, 2024. https://unfccc.int/resource/docs/cop3/07a01.pdf

United Nations Framework Convention on Climate Change (UNFCCC). 2005. *Report of the Conference of the Parties Serving as the Meeting of the Parties to the Kyoto Protocol on Its First Session, Held at Montreal from 28 November to 10 December 2005, Addendum Part Two: Action Taken by the Conference of the Parties Serving as the Meeting of the Parties to the Kyoto Protocol at Its First Session.* UNFCCC. Accessed November 28, 2024. https://unfccc.int/documents/4252

United Nations Framework Convention on Climate Change (UNFCCC). 2010. R*eport of the Conference of the Parties on Its Sixteenth Session, Held in Cancun from 29 November to 10 December 2010. Addendum. Part Two: Action Taken by the Conference of the Parties at Its Sixteenth Session.* Accessed November 28, 2024. https://unfccc.int/resource/docs/2010/cop16/eng/07a01.pdf.

United Nations Framework Convention on Climate Change (UNFCCC). 2013a. *Non-Economic Losses in the Context of the Work Programme on Loss and Damage.* Accessed November 28, 2024. https://unfccc.int/resource/docs/2013/tp/02.pdf.

United Nations Framework Convention on Climate Change (UNFCCC). 2013b. "Decision 2/CP.19: Warsaw International Mechanism for Loss and Damage associated with Climate Change Impacts." *Nineteenth Conference of the Parties (COP19)*, Warsaw, Poland, 11–23 November 2013. UNFCCC Accessed November 28, 2024. https://unfccc.int/documents/8106

United Nations Framework Convention on Climate Change (UNFCCC). 2015. "Decision 1/CP.21: Adoption of the Paris Agreement." *Twenty-first Conference of the Parties (COP21)*, Paris, France, November 30–December 15, 2015. UNFCCC. Accessed November 28, 2024. https://unfccc.int/resource/docs/2015/cop21/eng/10a01.pdf

United Nations Framework Convention on Climate Change (UNFCCC). 2022a. *Fifth Biennial Assessment and Overview of Climate Finance Flows*. Standing Committee on Finance, UNFCCC. Accessed November 28, 2024. https://unfccc.int/documents/619173

United Nations Framework Convention on Climate Change (UNFCCC). 2022b. "Decision 2/CP.27: Funding Arrangements for Responding to Loss and Damage Associated with the Adverse Effects of Climate Change, Including a Focus on Addressing Loss and Damage." *Twenty-seventh Conference of the Parties (COP27)*, Sharm El-Sheikh, Egypt, November 6–18, 2022. UNFCCC. Accessed November 28, 2024. https://unfccc.int/documents/626561

United Nations Framework Convention on Climate Change (UNFCCC). 2023a. "Decision 1/CP.28: Operationalization of the New Funding Arrangements, Including a Fund, for Responding to Loss and Damage Referred to in Paragraphs 2–3 of Decisions 2/CP.27 and 2/CMA.4." *Twenty-eighth Conference of the Parties (COP28)*, Dubai, United Arab Emirates, November 30– December 13, 2023. UNFCCC. Accessed November 28, 2024. https://unfccc.int/documents/637067

United Nations Framework Convention on Climate Change (UNFCCC). 2023b. *Synthesis Report on Existing Funding Arrangements and Innovative Sources Relevant to Addressing Loss and Damage Associated with the Adverse Effects of Climate Change.* Second meeting of the Transitional Committee. UNFCCC. May 25, 2023. https://unfccc.int/documents/628198

United Nations General Assembly (UNGA). 1972. "Resolution 2997 (XXVII): Institutional and Financial Arrangements for International Environmental Cooperation." *A/RES/2997 (XXVII)*, United Nations General Assembly, 27th session, December 15, 1972. United Nations. https://docs.un.org/en/a/res/2997(XXVII)

Part Three: **Means to Close the Climate Finance Gap**

Navid Hanif

Chapter 9
Domestic Resource Mobilization

Abstract: This chapter discusses the role of domestic resource mobilization as a major source of development and climate finance in developing and emerging economies. It highlights the magnitude of the climate finance gap and underscores the need to raise domestic resources through fiscal reforms, strategic public budgeting, and innovative taxation instruments like carbon pricing. The chapter also explores how central banks and financial regulators can play a catalytic role by aligning monetary policies and financial systems with sustainability objectives, highlighting their capacity to influence credit allocation, set green lending standards, and mitigate systemic risks. By embedding climate goals within national budgets and regulatory frameworks, and by fostering the development of local financial markets alongside public–private partnerships, countries can advance a just and effective climate transition. The chapter calls for coordination between national efforts and international cooperation to unlock scalable, equitable, and sustainable climate finance.

Keywords: Domestic resource mobilization, Fiscal policy, Climate funds, Monetary authorities, Carbon pricing, Public-private partnerships

Introduction

Climate change is occurring at an alarming pace, with far-reaching consequences for countries and communities. The need for urgent action is evident and has been repeatedly acknowledged in commitments made at global, regional, national, and local levels. Addressing climate change is not only imperative for basic human security but also presents significant opportunities to unlock new and improved forms of sustainable economic development. However, current efforts remain far below the necessary speed and scale.

One of the primary obstacles to tackling climate change is the growing financing gap. According to the Independent High-Level Expert Group on Climate Finance, an estimated USD 2.4 trillion per annum is required to meet the Paris Agreement and related development goals in emerging and developing countries (excluding China) by 2030 (Bhattacharya et al. 2024). Of this amount, USD 1.4 trillion per annum must be raised through domestic resource mobilization (Bhattacharya et al. 2024). To achieve

---

Note: The views expressed herein are those of the author and do not necessarily reflect the views of the United Nations.

this, countries must implement a combination of policies aimed at increasing domestic revenues and enhancing spending efficiency. Additionally, fiscal systems and regulatory policies must play a central role in incentivizing decarbonization and climate adaptation. Financing climate action will likely require a mix of instruments, including taxes, user fees, carbon markets, regulations, and subsidies, to ensure political feasibility, administrative practicality, and effectiveness.

Policies and incentives established by central banks and financial regulatory authorities will be crucial in driving climate action. These institutions can support governments and relevant stakeholders in creating new markets by directing credit to priority sectors, setting interest rate controls, shaping lending quotas for commercial banks, and promoting lending schemes for green projects (Davies and Palacin 2024).

However, national policies alone will not suffice to generate the necessary domestic resources. Supportive international economic and financial policies are critical in enabling countries to mobilize domestic financing. One key area requiring extensive international support is taxation. The United Nations General Assembly has recognized the need for fully inclusive and more effective international cooperation to ensure that countries can exercise their right to tax profits generated through commercial activities within their jurisdictions, including through digital platforms. The ongoing work on a United Nations Framework Convention on International Tax Cooperation aims to assist countries in raising domestic resources to finance the Sustainable Development Goals (SDGs), including climate action (UNGA 2023). Per its terms of reference, the Convention will include commitments, among others, to addressing tax-related illicit financial flows, tax avoidance and evasion, which deprive countries of essential resources, and to ensuring that approaches to international tax cooperation contribute to sustainable development.

This chapter examines fiscal policies and financing mechanisms for climate action, emphasizing the integration of climate objectives into national budgets and the strategic use of tools such as taxation, carbon pricing, subsidy reforms, and National Climate Funds (NCFs) to bridge capacity gaps and foster private-sector participation. It also highlights the critical role of monetary authorities and central banks in promoting green investments through regulatory frameworks, financial incentives, and macroprudential tools. The final section underscores the importance of harmonizing global regulations, strengthening local financial markets, and fostering public–private partnerships (PPPs) to scale up climate finance, address market inefficiencies, and mitigate risks for private investments, particularly in developing countries. The chapter concludes by advocating for enhanced international economic and financial cooperation to fully realize the potential of domestic resources in financing climate action.

Fiscal Policies

Countries facing high debt, high capital costs, and weak growth prospects should avoid relying solely on public spending to combat climate change. Public investment and subsidies for renewable energy entail significant fiscal costs (IMF 2023). Therefore, governments must employ a range of financial instruments and strategies, making climate action a strategic budgetary objective. Taxation should serve both as a revenue-generating mechanism and as an incentive to modify business and consumer behavior. These taxes help address market failures by internalizing the costs of over-production and overconsumption of natural resources. Carbon pricing should be integrated into a broader policy mix that includes feebates, green subsidies, and regulations (IMF 2023).

National Budgets

National budgets, funded through domestic taxes and levies, can play a crucial role in financing climate action, particularly for adaptation. Since most adaptation efforts involve making development investments more resilient to climate change, there is a compelling case for integrating adaptation spending into development budgets (Allan et al. 2019). Governments can also prioritize climate action within their budgets by creating dedicated revenue streams. However, this process faces challenges, including (i) the sectoral nature of budgeting, which fails to capture climate change's cross-cutting impact; (ii) the political economy of balancing short-term governance priorities with long-term returns; and (iii) the ambiguity surrounding the definition of adaptation (Duncan, Allan, and Nicholson 2016). Some studies argue that public financial management (PFM) systems do not effectively account for cross-sectoral issues like climate adaptation.

Despite these challenges, some governments have adopted innovative strategies to enhance budgetary resources for adaptation. These include: (i) establishing a central board with decision-making authority to oversee climate budgeting reforms; (ii) embedding climate budgeting within existing PFM processes; (iii) strengthening institutional capacity for innovation and adaptation; and (iv) aligning climate budget initiatives with political leadership priorities.

To support private-sector participation in climate adaptation, governments can offer fiscal incentives such as tax credits, subsidies, and carbon pricing measures with minimal fiscal burden. Evidence suggests that well-designed fiscal incentives can minimize their fiscal impact, while effectively promoting climate-friendly investments (IMF 2023).

Carbon Tax and Carbon Pricing

The Addis Ababa Action Agenda on financing for development advocates for carbon pricing as an innovative financing mechanism (United Nations 2015). The primary goal of carbon pricing is to implement the polluter-pays principle. Beyond encouraging emissions reduction, carbon pricing generates revenue and can be implemented through various policy instruments, including emissions trading systems and carbon taxes (United Nations, Inter-Agency Task Force on Financing for Sustainable Development 2024).

According to the 2024 *Financing for Sustainable Development Report*, global revenues from carbon taxes and emissions trading systems have increased nearly fivefold over the past decade, reaching a record USD 100 billion in 2022. These revenues can support decarbonization, strengthen government balance sheets, promote sustainable development, and finance a just transition. Achieving these outcomes requires effective budgetary mechanisms, such as annual budgeting frameworks and midterm expenditure frameworks that prioritize climate action.

Currently, approximately 25% of global greenhouse gas emissions are subject to a carbon tax or emissions trading system, with 73 such instruments in operation worldwide (United Nations, Inter-Agency Task Force on Financing for Sustainable Development 2024). Carbon taxation offers several advantages: (i) generating revenue, (ii) providing clear price signals for emissions reduction, (iii) allowing firms, flexibility in emissions reduction strategies, and (iv) explicitly communicating the cost of pollution. However, challenges include potential regressive impacts, political resistance, carbon leakage, and implementation difficulties, particularly in developing countries with limited administrative capacity. Emissions standards, on the other hand, provide greater regulatory control and are easier to monitor but limit market flexibility and may impose administrative burdens.

Effective carbon pricing must be tailored to national circumstances and policy objectives. Technical support should be provided to countries to facilitate the adoption and implementation of carbon pricing instruments. From a practical point of view, carbon taxation is an instrument that is relatively simple to administer, and it can take advantage of the existing fiscal infrastructure present in most countries. The United Nations Handbook on Carbon Taxation for Developing Countries (United Nations 2021) provides options for policy design and administration, responding to different needs and priorities of countries. It also provides a guide on how to increase the acceptability of carbon taxation and how to deal with potential interactions that a carbon tax may have with other existing laws and policy measures.

A major challenge remains the harmonization of carbon pricing across economies, as the lack of a unified approach contributes to carbon leakage and policy disputes, including debates over Carbon Border Adjustment Mechanism (Cosbey et al. 2019).

For carbon taxation and pricing to be effective, global agreement on standards and norms is essential. An UN-led agreement under the United Nations Framework

Convention on Climate Change (UNFCCC) should establish clear targets, such as a minimum carbon tax of USD 30 per ton of CO_2 by 2030, with incremental increases to USD 40 and USD 50 per ton in subsequent years (Ocampo 2022).

Alternatively, a differentiated pricing framework could be implemented, with minimum prices set at USD 10 per ton in developing countries and USD 40 per ton in developed countries in 2024, aiming to reduce global emissions by 10 gigatons by 2030. Under this scheme, the minimum price would increase every two years, reaching USD 50 per ton in developing countries and USD 100 per ton in developed countries by 2030 (Al Hussein and Khan 2023). Ensuring that revenues from this pricing scheme are effectively managed and reinvested into low-carbon development pathways will be crucial to its success.

A global carbon pricing framework under the UNFCCC could ensure inclusivity and effectiveness. Additionally, strengthening global tax cooperation on carbon taxes would enhance their implementation and acceptance worldwide.

Subsidy Reforms

The full economic and environmental costs of fossil fuel consumption are not internalized in determining fuel prices. Consequently, these prices do not reflect the true cost of burning carbon-based fuels. Such pricing, coupled with subsidies, exacerbates the situation. Global fossil fuel subsidies reached an estimated record of USD 7 trillion in 2022 amid significant energy price volatility, including USD 1.3 trillion in explicit subsidies (Black et al. 2023).

Subsidizing fossil fuels is a significant impediment to generating climate finance. Phasing out harmful subsidies is not only a crucial step toward implementing positive carbon pricing but also improves incentives to reduce emissions and environmental damage, while freeing up resources for climate-related investments.

Several countries have successfully removed explicit subsidies and introduced pricing measures to cover external costs. India, Morocco, Saudi Arabia, and Ukraine have phased out explicit subsidies and, in some cases, introduced carbon taxes; numerous countries also tax road transportation use (Black et al. 2023). However, many governments face difficulties in reforming subsidies due to potential social unrest resulting from price increases. There is no universal solution for subsidy reform, but the IMF (n.d.) recommends several measures: (i) a comprehensive energy sector reform plan with clear long-term objectives and impact analysis; (ii) transparent and extensive communication; (iii) a phased increase in prices; (iv) measures to protect vulnerable populations; and (v) institutional reforms to depoliticize energy pricing.

If fiscal space is available, particularly in developing countries, subsidies can be repurposed to promote investments in renewable energy and low-carbon technologies. Such fiscal incentives can stimulate firm investment in sustainable solutions (IMF 2023).

Climate Funds

Governments can establish dedicated funds to finance climate change initiatives, sourcing revenue from general taxation and levies on fossil fuels (Bhandary 2022). Many developing countries lack the capacity to implement comprehensive climate mitigation and adaptation policies. In such cases, National Climate Funds can bridge the capacity gap, enabling the formulation of specialized policy instruments. Additionally, NCFs can effectively address the distributional aspects of climate change.

Regarding capitalization and revenue sources, approximately 20% of implementing countries[1] generate funding for their climate initiatives through pollution taxes. For example, India imposes a tax on coal, Thailand levies petrol sales, and China applies taxes on Clean Development Mechanism transactions (Bhandary 2022).

NCFs have adopted various mechanisms for engaging the private sector. Some funds collaborate with financial institutions to enhance energy efficiency investment. For instance, India's Partial Risk Guarantee Fund for Energy Efficiency provides guarantees to financial institutions that issue loans to businesses, encouraging private-sector participation. Similarly, the Bangladesh Climate Change Resilience Fund supports farmers by subsidizing solar irrigation pump installation (Bhandary 2022).

Countries often employ a combination of NCFs and other financing mechanisms to support climate action. India's national climate strategy, for instance, consists of eight distinct missions backed by five dedicated funds (Bhandary 2022).

The choice between establishing National Climate Funds and utilizing the national budget for climate financing is not mutually exclusive. Both approaches offer advantages and disadvantages. While NCFs can be shielded from political budgetary constraints and allow for more technically driven investments, they may not fully integrate climate action within broader development frameworks that enhance societal resilience.

Although developing countries are expected to optimize public investment in adaptation and mitigation through improved domestic budget processes, development partners and international climate institutions must also provide support.

Monetary Authorities and Central Banks

Central banks and financial regulatory authorities play a crucial role in prioritizing climate finance and fostering new markets. These institutions can allocate credit to priority sectors, set interest rate controls, establish lending quotas for commercial banks, and develop schemes for green projects. Additionally, they can support public

---

[1] It is 20% of the 38 countries that have National climate funds out of the 142 countries, as examined by Bhandary (2022).

development institutions by purchasing climate-related securities and equities or applying differential discount rates to promote climate-aligned capital allocation (Davies and Palacin 2024).

Central banks possess a suite of policy tools to drive innovative climate financing. They can adjust monetary policy to incentivize climate-aligned lending, encourage financial institutions to integrate sustainability criteria, and strengthen disclosure requirements to ensure sustainability risks are adequately priced into financial instruments. For instance, Bangladesh mandates that commercial banks and nonbank financial institutions allocate 5% of their loan portfolios to green sectors, while the Reserve Bank of India includes loans to renewable energy companies in its priority sector lending program.

Financial regulatory authorities can also influence credit allocation by establishing credit ceilings for non-priority activities and imposing differential reserve requirements. Additional macroprudential tools include countercyclical capital buffers, higher risk weights for carbon-intensive sectors, and restrictions on exposure concentration to environmentally harmful assets (Davies and Palacin 2024).

Enhanced disclosure of sustainability risks ensures that capital is not misallocated to environmentally detrimental activities. Brazil, for example, enforces lending restrictions in environmentally sensitive areas. Central banks can also differentiate discount rates to promote sustainable lending practices or adjust reserve requirements based on the sustainability composition of a bank's loan portfolio. Furthermore, they can incentivize green lending by allowing sustainability-linked securities to qualify as part of commercial banks' legal reserves. Reducing the cost of capital for low-carbon projects can be achieved by issuing sustainability certificates, which could be exchanged for concessional loans (Davies and Palacin 2024).

Regulatory Policies

Financial Regulations and Incentives

Policies that require or incentivize private financial institutions to invest in green assets or disclose climate-related risks in their portfolios can mobilize private capital toward climate solutions. The laws and regulations related to climate finance must establish long-term targets that set the strategic direction for the country's efforts toward achieving its climate agenda and Nationally Determined Contributions targets. Long-term targets play a pivotal role in helping policymakers identify the adaptation and mitigation activities that are compatible with the country's development trajectory.

Regulatory frameworks designed to align financial flows with national, regional, or global objectives can do so effectively by shaping the roles of actors across the financial system, including pension funds and insurers. Similarly, sustainable finance policy must be viewed as part of a whole-of-government approach and a broader set of economic and financial policies. This comprehensive approach will help create enabling conditions for sustainable transformations. Countries may need to undergo a dynamic process of legislative reform, which requires conducting regular assessments of all regulations to ensure they meet their intended economic objectives efficiently and effectively. Additionally, policymakers need to design instruments that can accommodate changing circumstances, such as technological advances (United Nations, Inter-Agency Task Force on Financing for Sustainable Development 2024).

Sustainable finance policy reform has become a key consideration for financial policymakers, and it is no longer solely the concern of environmental ministries. This shift has led to a special focus on the interplay between sustainability and financial stability, exemplified by the development of climate transition plans. These plans serve as roadmaps to manage the risks and opportunities associated with the transformation to a net-zero future. The Network for Greening the Financial System (NGFS) has called for creating enabling conditions for transition plans by providing economy-wide incentives for their development and disclosure to broaden adoption and close the information gap.

It is also crucial that broader fiscal and regulatory policies are designed to create the right incentives for the real economy actors and the financial sector. Macroeconomic policies supportive of sustainable transformations, which create investment opportunities for sustainable finance at scale, are also critical for such transitions (United Nations, Inter-Agency Task Force on Financing for Sustainable Development 2024).

The growing regionalization of sustainable finance legislation reveals disparities and fragmentation across jurisdictions, underscoring the need for global interoperability. To address this fragmentation, concrete steps should be taken to harmonize and ensure the interoperability of regulations across jurisdictions to accelerate sustainable finance flows. For example, a global taxonomy could link all industry activities to a global framework, such as the Paris Agreement and the SDGs, helping regions coordinate their visions across regional taxonomies. The G20 Working Group on Sustainable Finance (SFWG) is developing actionable recommendations to promote such interoperability, including actions to promote consistent, comparable, and decision-useful information on sustainability risks, opportunities, and impacts.

Development of Local Financial Markets

Strengthening local financial institutions and markets can help facilitate access to finance for climate-related projects at the local level (United Nations, Inter-Agency Task Force on Financing for Sustainable Development 2024). Well-developed local financial markets can facilitate risk-sharing and improve the availability of long-term finance beyond the small number of large firms that can access global financial markets. Despite efforts to promote long-term finance in domestic markets and an increase in bank lending to the private sector over the past 20 years, financial and capital markets remain underdeveloped in terms of size, liquidity, and maturity in many developing countries. There are several reasons for this, but one key factor is that the development of local capital markets is inherently gradual, depending on the country's needs and context, including its size (United Nations, Inter-Agency Task Force on Financing for Sustainable Development 2024). Countries could also consider creating subregional capital markets if the national market size is too small to be viable.

A mature and well-developed banking sector that is transparent and provides timely data is an essential component of the effective functioning of these markets. Other contributing factors include market inefficiencies, a lack of local currency financing, institutional gaps, and macroeconomic volatility.

Long-term credit remains scarce for both sovereigns and corporations in developing countries, despite improvements in financial depth (United Nations, Inter-Agency Task Force on Financing for Sustainable Development 2024). This maturity mismatch between available finance and long-term needs for combatting climate change should be addressed through both local and global actions.

Policies that support the development of capital markets include strengthening institutional legal frameworks and fostering financial infrastructure. Many countries need external technical and financial support to build credible and dependable local capital markets. Technical support can be provided by international financial institutions in terms of building financial infrastructure and human resource development. Development partners should give special attention to supporting such initiatives, including through South–South cooperation, which also has the potential to assist local capital market development.

Public–Private Partnerships (PPPs)

Leveraging public funds to attract private investment can help scale up climate finance. Such de-risking can be crucial in sectors like renewable energy and public transport. While private-sector investors can provide a large share of financing, the public sector can underwrite more risks, take on equity or junior tranches, provide guarantees in credit announcements, and assist with project selection and assessment, capacity development, and diversification. The public sector may accept below-market returns in exchange for the risk it takes, aiming for positive climate outcomes (United Nations, Inter-Agency Task Force on Financing for Sustainable Development 2024). Crowd funding and community-based initiatives are also viable alternatives as small-scale funding mechanisms, which can be effective in developing and deploying local renewable energy projects or community-led adaptation efforts.

Conclusion

One of the main obstacles to achieving climate action at scale is the annual financing gap of USD 2.4 trillion. To overcome this gap, all possible means should be deployed, including domestic resource mobilization, which should contribute at least USD 1 trillion toward climate finance. Countries will need to use a broad range of fiscal, monetary, and regulatory measures to mobilize domestic resources. However, these efforts will not suffice without an enabling international economic and financial environment, as well as targeted development cooperation, to help countries realize their full potential in generating domestic resources. Some key areas for action include:

- Making climate finance a strategic objective of the national budget.
- Pursuing carbon taxation and carbon pricing tailored to meet domestic needs and circumstances.
- Phasing out harmful fossil fuel subsidies through well-designed policies and measures to minimize negative impacts on vulnerable populations.
- Establishing National Climate Funds with well-defined revenue streams to finance their activities.
- Engaging monetary authorities and central banks in prioritizing financing for climate action to create new markets and support national development finance institutions.
- Using financial regulations and incentives to align finance with climate action and sustainable development objectives.
- Undertaking policy, regulatory, and capacity-building measures to develop local financial markets.
- Leveraging public funds to attract private investment through well-designed public–private partnerships.

A broad range of measures – including legislative, fiscal, monetary, regulatory, administrative, and capacity building – will be required to realize the full potential of domestic resources to bridge the financing gap for climate action. These efforts should be fully supported through commensurate international measures to augment the efforts of developing countries, which are bearing the disproportionate cost of the climate crisis. The principle of common but differentiated responsibilities remains the bedrock of financing climate action.

References

Al Hussein, Zeid Ra'ad, and Farrukh Iqbal Khan. 2023. "The Case for a Global Carbon-Pricing Framework: An Agreement Is the Last, Best Hope for Averting Climate Disaster." *Foreign Affairs*, September 11, 2023. Accessed September 16, 2024. https://www.foreignaffairs.com/world/case-global-carbon-pricing-framework

Allan, Stephanie, Aditya V. Bahadur, Shivaranjani Venkatramani, and Vidya Soundarajan. 2019. *The Role of Domestic Budgets in Financing Climate Change Adaptation: A Background Paper for the Global Commission on Adaptation*. Global Center on Adaptation. Accessed September 16, 2024. https://gca.org/reports/the-role-of-domestic-budgets-in-financing-climate-change-adaptation/

Bhandary, Rishikesh Ram. 2022. "National Climate Funds: A New Dataset on National Financing Vehicles for Climate Change." *Climate Policy* 22 (3): 401–410. https://doi.org/10.1080/14693062.2022.2027223.

Bhattacharya, Amar, Vera Songwe, Emmanuel Soubeyran, and Nicholas Stern. 2024. *Raising Ambition and Accelerating Delivery of Climate Finance*. London: Grantham Research Institute on Climate Change and the Environment, London School of Economics and Political Science.

Black, Simon, Antung A. Liu, Ian W.H. Parry, and Nate Vernon-Lin. 2023. *IMF Fossil Fuel Subsidies Data: 2023 Update*. Working paper, International Monetary Fund, Washington, DC.

Cosbey, Aaron, Susanne Droege, Carolyn Fischer, and Clayton Munnings. 2019. "Developing Guidance for Implementing Border Carbon Adjustments: Lessons, Cautions, and Research Needs from the Literature." *Review of Environmental Economics and Policy* 13 (1): 3–22. https://www.journals.uchicago.edu/doi/full/10.1093/reep/rey020.

Davies, Stuart, and Jose Palacin. 2024. "Policy Brief: Innovative Financing Mechanisms and Solutions." United Nations Economist Network (UNEN). Accessed September 16, 2024. https://www.un.org/sites/un2.un.org/files/innovative_fincancing_14_march.pdf.

Duncan, Allan, Stephanie Allan, and Kit Nicholson. 2016. *In Depth: Key Lessons for Developing Climate Change Financing Frameworks*. May. Oxford Policy Management. Accessed September 16, 2024. https://www.opml.co.uk/publications/in-depth-lessons-developing-climate-change-financing-frameworks.

International Monetary Fund (IMF). 2023. *Fiscal Monitor: Climate Crossroads: Fiscal Policies in a Warming World*. October 10, 2023. Accessed September 16, 2024. https://www.imf.org/en/Publications/FM/Issues/2023/10/10/fiscal-monitor-october-2023.

International Monetary Fund. n.d. "Fossil Fuel Subsidies." September 16, 2024. https://www.imf.org/en/Topics/climate-change/energy-subsidies#A%20Plan%20for%20Reform.

Ocampo, José Antonio. 2022. "Time for a UN Agreement on Carbon Pricing." *OECD Development Matters*, April 20, 2022. Accessed September 16, 2024. https://oecd-development-matters.org/2022/04/20/time-for-a-un-agreement-on-carbon-pricing/.

United Nations. 2015. *Addis Ababa Action Agenda of the Third International Conference on Financing for Development*. New York: United Nations.

United Nations. 2021. *Handbook on Carbon Taxation for Developing Countries*. New York: United Nations.

United Nations General Assembly (UNGA). 2023. *Resolution Adopted by the General Assembly on 22 December 2023: 78/230. Promotion of Inclusive and Effective International Tax Cooperation at the United Nations.* 28 December 2023. Accessed September 16, 2024. https://documents.un.org/doc/undoc/gen/n23/431/97/pdf/n2343197.pdf.

United Nations, Inter-Agency Task Force on Financing for Sustainable Development. 2024. *Financing for Sustainable Development Report 2024: Financing for Development at a Crossroads*. New York: United Nations. Accessed September 16, 2024. https://developmentfinance.un.org/fsdr2024.

Martin Kessler

Chapter 10
Managing Debt Vulnerabilities to Allow for Climate Action

Abstract: The chapter examines how rising debt burdens, particularly from external debt, and tightening global financial conditions constrain climate action in developing countries. It tracks the international financing dynamics since the "fourth debt wave" during the 2010s and the subsequent challenges many low- and middle-income countries now face in terms of elevated debt levels, higher interest costs, and limited access to concessional and private finance. These pressures coincide with escalating climate risks, creating a vicious cycle where fiscal constraints hinder resilience investments, worsening climate vulnerability and debt sustainability. The chapter analyzes recent shifts in debt dynamics – driven by global shocks and rising U.S. interest rates – and their implications for sovereign liquidity and insolvency risks. It presents a stylized exercise, which illustrates that a large number of low- and lower-middle-income countries face refinancing risks in the next few years, which could turn into solvency risks if interest costs remain high and maturity shorten. A number of tools (debt-for-development swaps, or more generally, the efficient use of guarantees) can reduce risks for countries with infrequent but significant market access.

Keywords: External debt, Debt sustainability, Interest Costs, Climate resilience, Sovereign liquidity risk, Global financial conditions

Introduction

The linkages between debt tensions and climate change are increasingly clear. While only a few countries have defaulted as a direct result of natural disasters, rising physical and transition risks could lead to sovereign defaults in the future. These risks are already affecting credit ratings and will become even more evident as global temperatures continue to rise. In June 2023, Kenya, Colombia, France, and Germany commissioned a review on debt, climate, and nature, which warned of a "vicious cycle" of debt risks and climate damages. (The Expert Group on Debt, Nature & Climate 2024).

The concept of a vicious cycle links debt pressures with a reduced ability to invest in climate resilience. As a result, damages occur more frequently and with greater in-

---

Note: This chapter is an update of Albinet and Kessler (2022) and Albinet, Kessler, and Brancher (2023). It benefitted from excellent data analysis by Andrea Cavallini.

tensity, reducing economic growth and accelerating the risk of debt crises. This, in turn, weakens governments' ability to invest in resilience, leading to a compounding climate risk exposure. When financed by grants or concessional loans, resilience efforts can support medium-term growth and help break this negative cycle. These considerations, previously peripheral in debt management discussions, have now become central: the World Bank and the International Monetary Fund (IMF) recently revised their guidelines to incorporate climate change into debt sustainability assessments (IMF and World Bank 2018).

The methodology behind these assessments, however, remains a topic of debate. Some argue that incorporating climate investment needs into debt assessments renders a large share of developing countries effectively insolvent (Zucker-Marques, Gallagher, and Volz 2024). At the same time, the number of actual defaults and restructurings remains limited. A long history of research on sovereign defaults suggests that the decision to default depends on both domestic and international incentives, including the benefits and costs of corrective policies and the perceived value of future borrowing. (Sachs and Cohen 1982). While immediate debt relief provides fiscal space, it also comes with costly market exclusion. When climate change is factored in, such trade-offs become even starker: defaulting after a major catastrophe may be more appealing but risks reducing access to future external loans needed for climate adaptation and mitigation.

A long line of research has refined these insights (Ams et al. 2014, Willems and Zettelmeyer 2022), emphasizing the narrow margins of choice available to governments that highly value market access and future borrowing options. Defaulting can provide a "fresh start" only if it results in a significant reduction in external debt stock, which has not been the experience in recent restructuring cases (IMF 2023).

Even when governments wish to avoid reneging on financial obligations, they may face difficulties refinancing their debt. Illiquidity – the inability to roll over debt at sustainable interest rates – is particularly problematic when governments rely on private markets for financing (Calvo 1988, Cole and Kehoe 2000). While official borrowing can also present challenges, private markets, especially bond markets, tend to be more volatile and create significant redemption obligations. With a diversified creditor base and a shifting external environment, developing countries must manage both long-term insolvency risks and short-term rollover risks.

This chapter provides an updated overview of these challenges in the context of rising climate investment needs. It is structured into three parts: first, it examines the financing conditions that developing countries can expect in the near future and their impact on debt stock and service projections. The second section translates these dynamics into two categories of policy challenges: first, how debt service flows may trigger risk assessments from the IMF and the World Bank, and second, the constraints on fiscal space: high debt service reduces the amount available for investment. The conclusion explores possible debt management strategies for at-risk countries. While debt restructuring may be necessary in some cases, liability management and debt rescheduling should also be considered as part of a broader policy toolkit.

A Difficult Context: High Debt and High Interest Costs

This chapter focuses on the external public debt of developing countries. For low- and lower-middle-income countries, the 2010s marked a "fourth debt wave" (Kose et al. 2021): large investment needs were financed through debt, often public debt, against the backdrop of low interest rates. Between 2010 and 2019, the external public debt of low-income countries rose from 20% to 30% of GDP (see Figure 10.1), with a similar, albeit smaller, increase in middle-income countries. This period ended in 2020 when developing countries faced successive global shocks, including the COVID-19 pandemic (2020–21), the war in Ukraine, and rising global interest rates (2022–23). While COVID-19 was a worldwide crisis, the impact of the subsequent surge in food and energy prices varied, depending on countries' dependence on imports. Since then, external public debt has declined to 24% of GDP for low-income countries and about 16% for middle-income countries. Although these levels remain elevated compared to historical norms, a more concerning trend is the deterioration of debt terms.

The dynamics moving forward will depend on external financial conditions, which are likely to deteriorate. The interest rate on long-term (10-year) U.S. Treasury bonds increased in 2022–23, reaching 4.9% in October 2023, and has since remained at elevated levels throughout 2024 and early 2025. This rise has significantly increased the cost of rolling over debt for emerging markets, leading to the exclusion of frontier markets from bond markets. Consequently, these markets have turned into limited alternative financing sources, such as syndicated loans or credit-enhanced bonds. Official loans have also become more expensive, particularly non-concessional sources such as International Bank for Reconstruction and Development (IBRD) loans, which the World Bank provides to middle-income countries. In contrast, the International Development Association (IDA) – the World Bank arm that provides zero-interest loans to the poorest countries – does not pass through the global rise in interest rates, thereby partially shielding its borrowers from adverse global financial conditions.[1]

To evaluate debt management prospects, we analyze three scenarios that reflect possible paths for global financial conditions. In the baseline scenario, global interest rates decline gradually to their historical average, and exchange rates remain stable. The pessimistic scenario envisions a strong USD and persistently high interest rates that negatively affect financing conditions for all developing countries, particularly lower-rated ones. Conversely, the optimistic scenario assumes a rapid return to pre-2020 financial conditions. These assumptions are summarized in Figure 10.2, which

---

1 This is an assumption we will maintain for our projections, although somewhat conservative: countries eligible to those concessional conditions also obtain financing from other official sources: several other bilateral, plurilateral, and multilateral sources do adjust their lending rates. However, considering that interest rates are fixed at low rates for poor countries is a credible assumption.

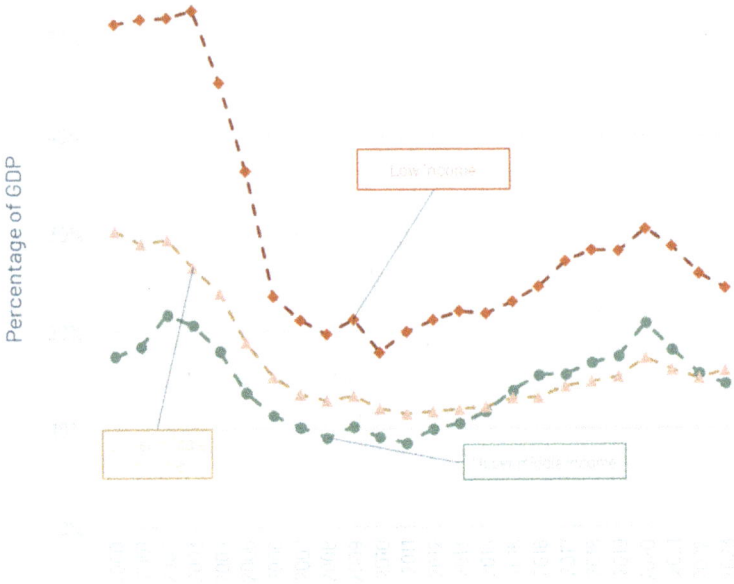

Figure 10.1: External public debt to GDP for developing countries.
Note: This covers all developing countries, with data available in both databases, excluding China and Ukraine. The variable used is the total stock of public and publicly guaranteed (PPG) debt.
Sources: IMF World Economic Outlook (October 2024) and World Bank International Debt Statistics (December 2024). Data was accessed on December 15, 2024.

compares financing conditions to nominal growth projections from the International Monetary Fund.

Global interest rate trends influence financing options from both official and private sources. The critical test for debt sustainability is whether interest rates remain below or exceed the growth rate of repayment capacity. As a proxy, we use the growth rate of gross domestic product (GDP), though our analysis will focus specifically on government revenues.[2] Figure 10.2 illustrates that financing terms vary by source: official lenders, including multilateral and bilateral creditors, generally offer more favorable terms, especially for low-income countries. However, nominal growth is expected to stagnate or decline in developing economies, remaining well below baseline private interest rates across all country groups. Consequently, on average, the growth rate of repayment capacity (GDP or public revenues) will barely exceed the growth rate of debt.

---

[2] In this note, we focus less on exports, another key indicator to assess external sustainability. One reason is that while projections of real exports exist, nominal exports depend on future commodity prices, where off-the-shelf forecasts are hard to find.

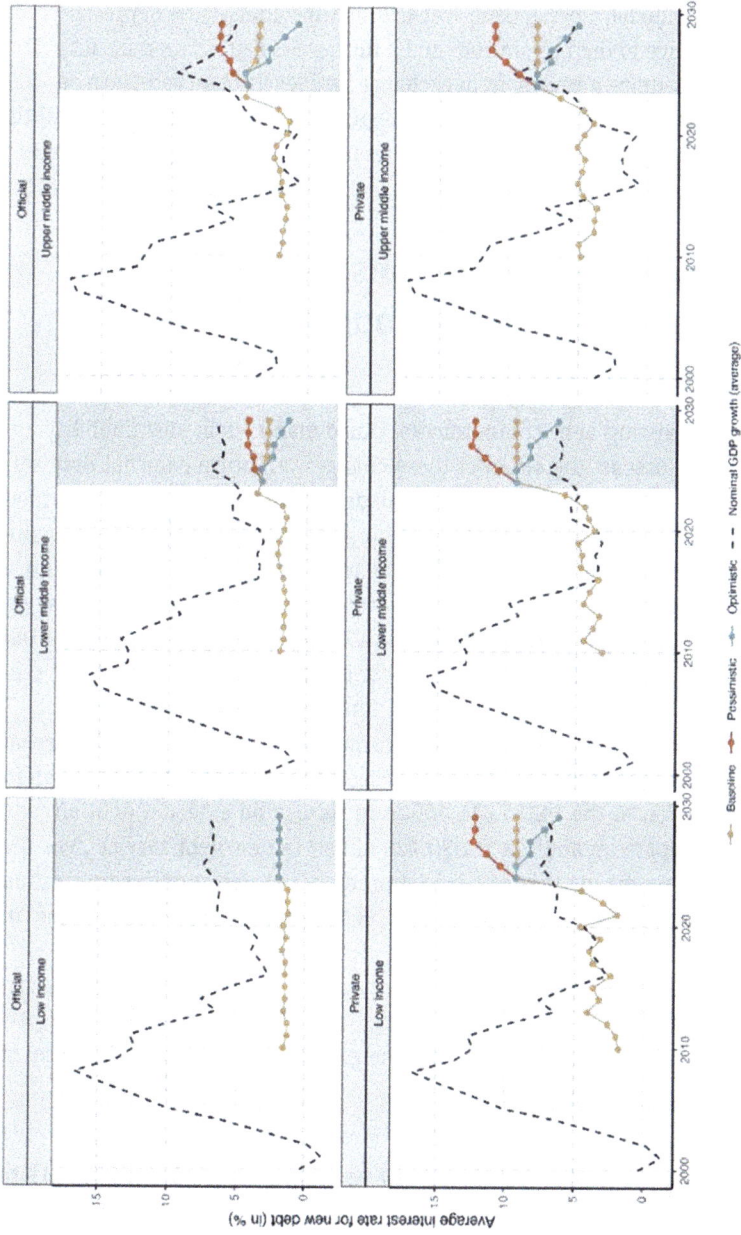

Figure 10.2: Average nominal interest rates by income group and scenario.

Note: See technical appendix for the details of each scenario.

Source: World Bank's International Debt Statistics (2024) for historical average, authors for projections, IMF World Economic Outlook (October 2024) for USD nominal growth rates. Data was accessed in December 2024.

Additionally, we model a pessimistic scenario that includes a 10% depreciation of local currencies, relative to the USD, in 2025 and a further 5% depreciation in 2026.[3] The optimistic scenario assumes a reversion to exchange rate levels observed between 2015 and 2019. As of early 2025, financial conditions align more closely with the pessimistic scenario; however, they may improve as policy rates normalize in advanced economies.

Difficult Financing Options Constraining Policymakers in Developing Countries

We use our model to forecast future debt, drawing on IMF forecasts to complement information about existing debt commitments. Our dynamic debt sustainability approach allows us to forecast the effect of these changes on future external debt service. It takes the IMF's projections of primary balances and GDP growth (as presented in the *World Economic Outlook* of October 2024) as given, which determine the evolution of public debt. On average, these projections tend to be optimistic about future growth and primary balances. Assumptions regarding financing conditions from external sources are derived from the World Bank's *International Debt Statistics* (IDS) database,[4] which documents existing external debt commitments. We then make reasonable assumptions about the funding of future financing needs.

As a result, our model provides not only information about the existing external debt burden, derived from the IDS, but also a projected debt burden. This is shown in Figure 10.3. In addition to the USD 1,644 billion in service on external debt already contracted, we anticipate an additional USD 428 billion of new debt service over the 2025–2029 period. This means that our model predicts 26% more debt service than would be expected from a purely static debt service approach, as presented in the IDS.[5]

Our exercise enables us to simulate debt dynamics for 103 countries,[6] providing a comprehensive view of future risks. Our findings reveal that debt service, as a percentage of revenues, has increased for all income groups, particularly in the wake of

---

3 This can be interpreted as a "Trump-effect", with sharp appreciation of the USD and extended high interest rates. These can be considered as conservative: since the IMF forecasts were published in October 2024, the USD appreciated by about 5% against a basket of currencies, before the imposition of tariffs. A 5% further depreciation in 2025, and 5% in 2026 does not seem farfetched.

4 With IDS 2024, covering 2023 as its last year.

5 More details on the mechanics of the model are in the appendix.

6 Out of 120 countries in IDS. We remove countries for a variety of reasons: lack of data in the WEO or IDS, data points that we could not explain and attributed to errors, as well as countries where the situation is to complex and uncertain to fit in this analysis, such as conflict-affected countries (Russia, Ukraine, Yemen, etc.). We also exclude China.

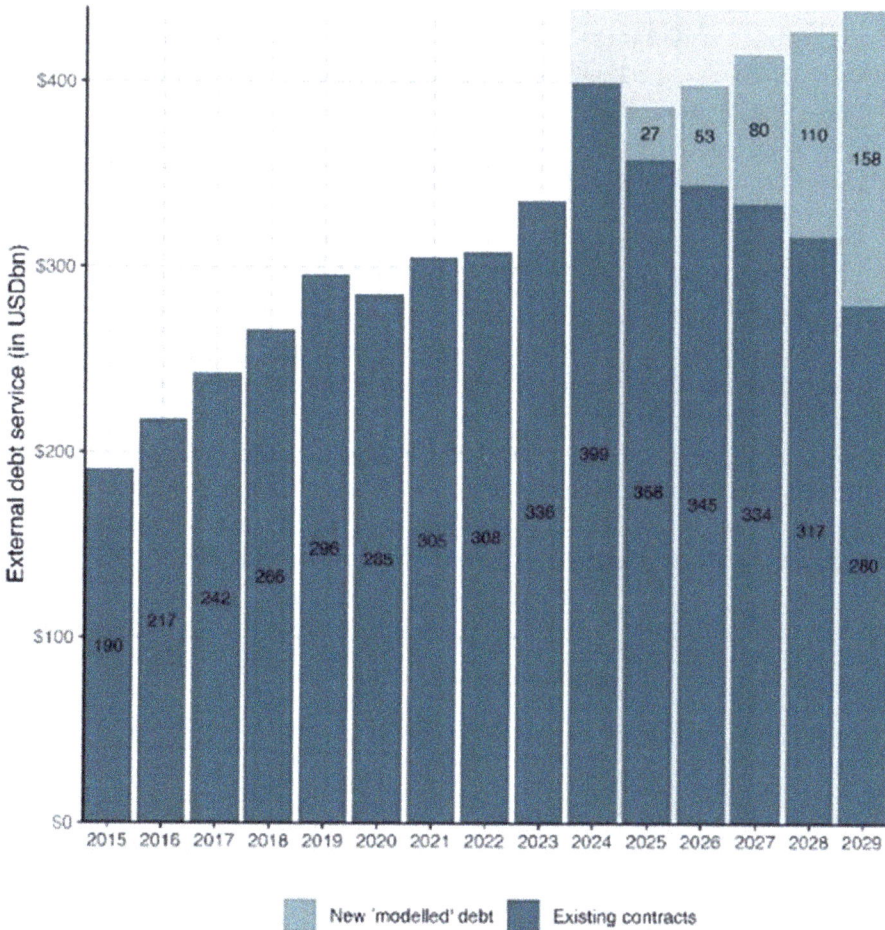

Figure 10.3: Debt service from existing contracts and projected by our model under the baseline. Source: World Bank International Debt Statistics (2024) for historical average and "existing" series, authors for "modeled" debt.

the COVID-19 crisis. It is important to note that, in the future, different income groups will experience varying trends.

Under the baseline scenario, debt service in the median low-income country (LIC) is expected to peak in 2026, with 14.8% of revenues allocated to external debt service, up from 14.5% in 2023. It will then decline slowly until 2029 (Figure 10.4). Even with this projected decline, resources allocated to external debt service will remain above historical levels. Under the pessimistic scenario, low-income countries would experience a dramatic increase in external debt service to revenues, driven by currency depreciation, reaching a median of 17.5%.

Lower-middle-income countries (LMICs) also face rapidly climbing external debt service, with a significant rise in 2024, to 15% of government revenues. This sudden "debt service wall" is particularly noteworthy, amounting to an increase of five percentage points in government revenues. Despite this, no new defaults occurred in LMICs in 2024 due to a variety of factors, such as the use of the global financial safety net, reliance on domestic markets, and the use of reserves. Several countries also employed liability management operations (LMOs) to reduce liquidity risks.

Under the baseline scenario, these depleted buffers are unlikely to be replenished, and the tension will persist, with external debt service remaining at 15% of revenues for the median LMIC. The situation is more severe under the pessimistic scenario, where a combination of interest rate and exchange rate shocks would make market borrowing significantly more expensive, pushing debt service to nearly 19% of government revenues. Only the optimistic scenario would allow these countries to rebuild their buffers, with debt service returning to pre-2020 levels by 2029.

Finally, upper-middle-income countries have been able to smooth their repayment profiles and would face relatively low and stable debt service through 2029, although the pessimistic scenario could present significant challenges.

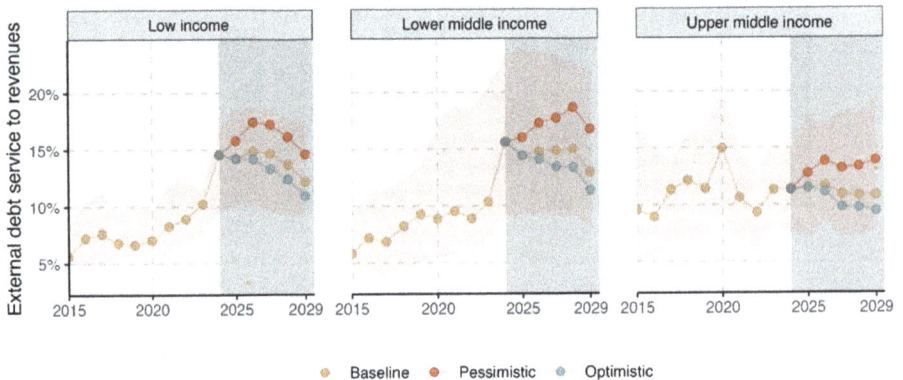

Figure 10.4: External debt service dynamics.
Source: Author's calculations.
Note: The shaded area is the interquartile range for the baseline scenario. In other words, under baseline, 75% of LMICs have a debt service-to-revenue ratio between 7.5% and 22.5% in 2023.

Beyond the median, a subset of countries faces acute difficulties. The shaded area represents the interquartile range, meaning that a quarter of the countries are above these levels. This group includes 11 out of 45 LMICs in our sample, which will experience debt service exceeding 23% of their revenues between 2024 and 2027. A minority of LICs are also affected, with five out of more than 20 countries surpassing 18% of revenues.

It is important to note that the mechanics of our scenarios exclude roll-over tensions: financing is provided at any interest rate. While this is an unrealistic assumption, it is useful for our analysis. In reality, market access becomes constrained when spreads increase and can even be completely closed. However, this assumption allows us to track the dynamics of external public debt and understand the conditions under which an explosive path would materialize.

The composition of debt in low-income and upper-middle-income countries provides some protection against rising interest rates in the U.S., but for different reasons. Low-income countries may experience a slight improvement in dynamics after 2023 under our baseline scenario, as their debt refinancing strategy relies more on official sources of finance (Figure 10.4). These lenders provide loans, whose costs are less dependent on global interest rate fluctuations. Rising rates are painful for UMICs, but their refinancing needs are less concentrated in 2025–2026. UMICs are also more dependent on domestic debt.

Furthermore, our pessimistic scenario incorporates "spreads": rates rise faster for countries with lower credit ratings, which explains why the deterioration is most pronounced for LMICs. So-called "frontier markets", which are relatively new issuers of sovereign bonds in hard currency, are the most affected in a liquidity crisis. These countries do experience the transmission of U.S. interest rates to their borrowing costs, but, in addition, their investor base is thinner than that of emerging markets with a longer history of borrowing from bond investors.

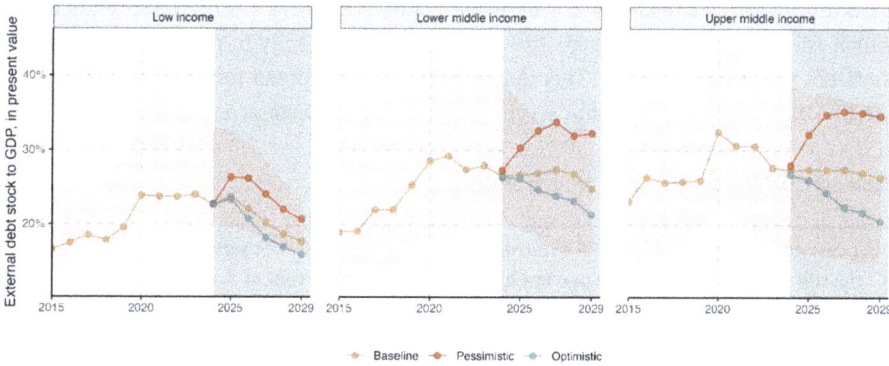

Figure 10.5: External debt-to-GDP ratios, in present value terms.
Source: Author's calculations based on World Bank's International Debt Statistics (2024) and IMF World Economic Outlook (October 2024) data.

After an explosive path from 2015 to 2021, we expect debt stocks to stabilize under the baseline scenario (Figure 10.5), although significant downside risks remain if the pessimistic scenario materializes. As debt stocks rise, the risk of debt overhang becomes a possibility, where no feasible adjustment path can restore sustainability, leaving debt restructuring as the only option. The dynamics of this variable depend primarily on future primary balances and the "r-g" factor, which is the difference between the interest rate and GDP growth. In general, the IMF, on whose projections we rely for fiscal deficits, is optimistic, meaning that actual dynamics are likely to be worse. While the baseline scenario would stabilize debt levels, a shock to exchange rates and interest rates, as included in our pessimistic scenario, would lead to large and likely unsustainable increases in debt for a significant share of developing countries. Median public external debt-to-GDP ratios would peak at 33% for LMICs and 35% for UMICs.

Countries at Risk of Breaching Prudential Thresholds

The IMF and World Bank's Debt Sustainability Framework for Low-Income Countries (LIC-DSF) suggest indicative thresholds for sustainability risks. We will use these indicators to determine whether a country is in a "risky zone" and whether the risk arises from flow considerations (similar to liquidity concerns) or stock considerations (akin to solvency concerns). While imperfect, these indicators are practically relevant, as the IMF and World Bank use them to assess a country's ability to undertake debt restructuring to restore sustainability, the level of concessionality in World Bank loans, and the determination of debt limit policies. Table 10.1 reproduces the IMF/World Bank indicators. Thresholds are determined by a country's "Composite Indicator", which combines variables predictive of a country's capacity to repay, also known as its "Debt Carrying Capacity". This indicator is only computed for countries subject to the LIC-DSF, so we set the debt-carrying capacity of IBRD countries to "strong".

Table 10.1: IMF/World Bank's debt carrying capacity.

Debt carrying capacity (CI classification)	PV of PPG external debt in percent of		PPG external debt service in percent of	
	GDP	Exports	Exports	Revenue
Weak	30	140	10	14
Medium	40	180	15	18
Strong	55	240	21	23

Note: PPG is public and publicly-guaranteed debt; PV is present value, and CI is the composite indicator that denotes level at which debt is deemed risky for each indicator.
Source: IMF and World Bank (2018).

In this brief note, we focus on a single indicator for each type of risk. A country is considered to be at risk of a solvency crisis if it crosses one of its thresholds for debt at present value over GDP. We define liquidity risk as occurring when the flow indicator – debt service to revenues – crosses the threshold. Due to the lack of a reliable forecast for future nominal exports, we do not use indicators that rely on exports.

The results are striking, as shown in Figure 10.6: stock-level risks, in present value terms, peaked during the COVID-19 crisis, with 23 countries breaching the thresholds. However, these risks are stagnating and are expected to decline, according to current forecasts. In contrast, flow risks are projected to increase until 2025, particularly for LMICs, with a total of 33 countries expected to be at risk by 2025.

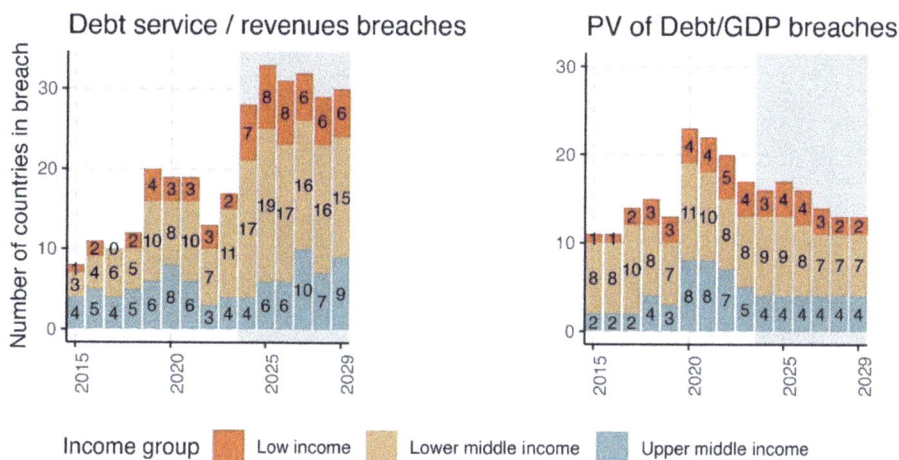

Figure 10.6: Comparing breaches under liquidity and solvency indicators (Baseline scenario). Source: Author's calculations.

When aggregated, significant amounts of debt service are at risk, making the problem – primarily one of liquidity – a systemic issue. Total debt service payments across all income groups exceed USD 92 billion per year (Figure 10.7). This amount remains stable from 2024 to 2028, peaking in 2029 to a total of USD 97 billion. Of the USD 92 billion annually, slightly less than half is owed to private creditors, while about 20% is owed to bilateral creditors. Multilateral debt, which holds senior status, is particularly difficult to restructure and accounts for a substantial portion of debt service, potentially exacerbating the problem.

Large debt service obligations signal the potential for a liquidity crisis, but one that would only materialize if rolling over debt became impossible. This is precisely what we are witnessing. Most IDA countries have been entirely excluded from bond markets since March 2022, while other private lenders have only partially filled the gap (Properzi 2023). In 2023, except for Uzbekistan, IDA and blend countries did not issue any new external sovereign bonds. As advanced economies began lowering their policy rates in 2024, markets reopened, with six LMICs issuing a total of about USD 9 billion. While assessing the size of loans by private lenders is more difficult, it seems clear that only a portion of the USD 23 billion expected to refinance private

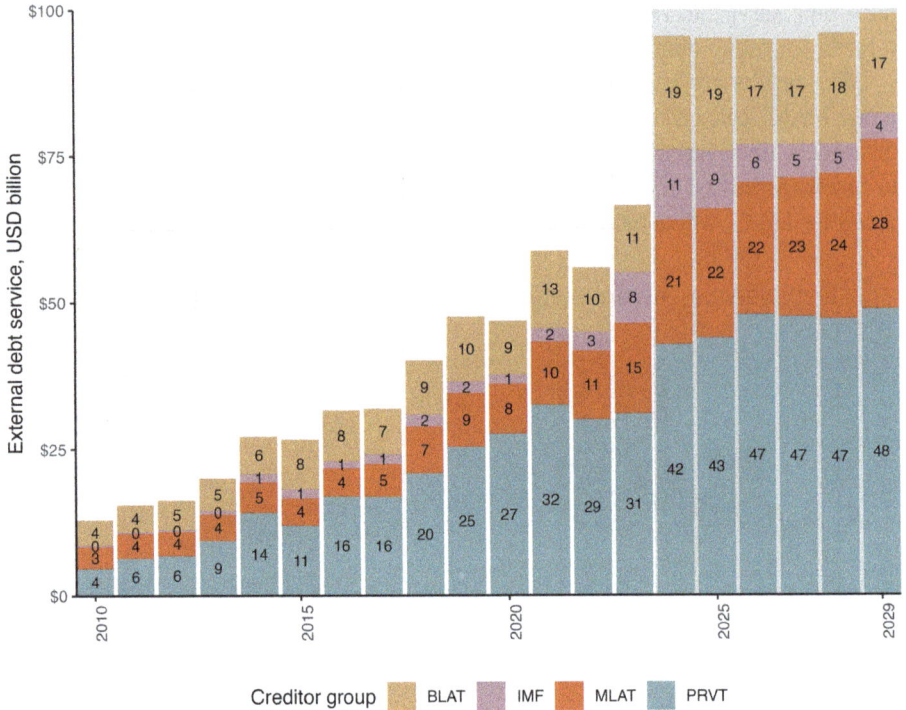

Figure 10.7: Debt service at risk under the baseline.
Note: BLAT = Bilateral, MLAT = Multilateral, PRVT = Private.
Source: Author's calculations

debt has been issued. In 2023, private lenders were net takers of liquidity from poor countries, and this trend is likely to have continued in 2024, albeit to a lesser extent. Meanwhile, China, which was a major provider of net positive flows in the 2010s, has turned negative in 35 IDA countries by 2021 and worsened to 43 countries by 2023.

Conclusion

Managing large debt service obligations will require concerted action by governments, bilateral partners, and international financial institutions. In some cases, debt restructuring is necessary. However, the length of the process, the insufficient quantum of debt relief provided, and the value that governments place on future market access all limit the appeal of this option.

Reducing immediate liquidity tensions through liability management operations is a key component. Debt-for-climate or debt-for-nature swaps combine such operations with commitments to climate or nature protection (Albinet, Chekir, and Kessler

2024). Although these mechanisms place significant demands on countries' authorities in terms of guarantees and administrative burdens, they can help alleviate immediate pressures. While their mechanics are often complex, they essentially aim to alleviate liquidity pressures by buying back expensive bonds or loans with new sources of financing. This enables countries with limited market access to reduce debt service and simultaneously commit to climate and biodiversity objectives.

However, under current global conditions, it is unlikely that a purely voluntary approach will be sufficient. Additional support from international institutions is likely to be necessary. The Bridge proposal (Diwan, Kessler, and Songwe 2024; Diwan et al. 2024) aims to create the necessary coordination and commitments from each actor, including the private sector. The IMF and the World Bank have also proposed managing liquidity tensions through a three-pronged approach. All of these refinancing strategies must be anchored in a climate investment perspective, which can improve medium-term growth prospects.

This chapter has sought to demonstrate that, under current conditions, especially if deterioration occurs, debt management must prioritize external liquidity pressures. Climate investment will be constrained by reduced new flows and the high cost of external finance. However, proactive management of debt obligations can create fiscal space for additional investments.

Appendix 1: List of Countries Included in the Analysis

We consider 103 countries in our analysis. We excluded (i) China because its size would overwhelm any aggregate figures, and its dynamics are different from all other developing countries; (ii) a number of countries in conflicts where projections are too uncertain and (iii) Countries with no or limited data in IDS/WEO.

Table A.10.1: List of countries.

Income group	Lending category		
	IDA	**Blend**	**IBRD**
Low income	Burkina Faso, Burundi, Central African Republic, Chad, Congo Dem. Rep., Ethiopia, Gambia, The Guinea-Bissau, Liberia, Madagascar, Malawi, Mali, Mozambique, Niger, Rwanda, Sierra Leone, Togo, Uganda		

Table A.10.1 (continued)

Income group	Lending category		
	IDA	**Blend**	**IBRD**
Lower middle income	Bangladesh, Benin, Bhutan, Cambodia, Comoros, Côte d'Ivoire, Djibouti, Ghana, Guinea, Haiti, Honduras, Kyrgyz Republic, Lao PDR, Lesotho, Mauritania, Myanmar, Nepal, Nicaragua, São Tomé and Príncipe, Senegal, Solomon Islands, Tajikistan, Tanzania, Vanuatu, Zambia	Cabo Verde, Cameroon, Congo Rep., Kenya, Nigeria, Pakistan, Papua New Guinea, Uzbekistan, Zimbabwe	Algeria, Angola, Bolivia, Egypt Arab Rep., Eswatini, India, Jordan, Mongolia, Morocco, Philippines, Tunisia, Vietnam
Upper middle income	Maldives, Tonga	Dominica, Fiji, Grenada, St. Lucia, St. Vincent and the Grenadines	Albania, Argentina, Armenia, Azerbaijan, Belarus, Belize, Bosnia and Herzegovina, Botswana, Brazil, Bulgaria, Colombia, Costa Rica, Dominican Republic, Ecuador, El Salvador, Gabon, Georgia, Guatemala, Indonesia, Jamaica, Kazakhstan, Mauritius, Mexico, Moldova, Montenegro, North Macedonia, Paraguay, Peru, Serbia, South Africa, Thailand, Türkiye

Table A.10.2: Private lending remaining after a shock.

Rating	Lending category		
	IDA	**Blend**	**IBRD**
Baa			100%
Ba	66%	66%	100%
B	33%	33%	50%
C	10%	10%	10%
No rating	10%	10%	10%

Appendix 2: Debt Sustainability Assumptions

The external debt sustainability analysis aims to assess the evolution of external public debt service in developing economies. In this regard, it relies mainly on two databases: (i) external debt service, as published by the World Bank in its International Debt Statistics database (October 2024), and (ii) the International Monetary Fund's World Economic Outlook (October 2024) for macroeconomic data.

We also use:
- IMF BoP and African Regional Economic Outlook for reserves
- Existing DSA list for assessments of Debt Carrying Capacity
- WDI for a number of macroeconomic series

Financing assumptions:
Each year, countries need to issue new debt to refinance their external needs. Those are the sum of: (1) External debt service due and (2) primary deficit financed externally.

We assume that (1) is fully refinanced externally, and (2) is financed partly externally and partly from domestic sources.

The share of primary deficit financed externally is equal to the share of external debt, in general government debt (comparing WEO public debt with IDS external debt). When the primary balance is in surplus, the surplus is affected by the same sources.

The same procedure applies to each of the three sources: multilateral, bilateral, and private.

Financial conditions:
The terms of these new debt instruments are defined as follows:
- We use conditions for new loans in 2015–2019 as our "reference rate", for each source, official (r_o) and private (r_p). We then apply the following procedure:
  - We compute a "spread" between r_o, r_p and the U.S. interest rate. Future interest rates are equal to the U.S. interest rates between 2024 and 2029.
  - U.S. interest rates are projected to revert to 3% nominal linearly (1% real + 2% inflation), following the IMF (2023).
- We "protect" IDA-eligible countries from the spread by assuming that the official rates they borrowed during 2015–19 apply in 2024–29.
- This describes the "baseline". The two other scenarios add some assumptions.

Scenarios:
1. **Pessimistic:**
   a. *Exchange rates:* 10% depreciation in 2025 and an additional 5% depreciation in 2026.
   b. *Interest rates:* + 100 bps in 2025 + 300 bps, from 2027 to 2029.
   c. *Spreads:* We shock private interest rates by increasing the spreads (as determined by Moody's rating) by + 1000 bps, from 2025 to 2027.
2. **Optimistic:**
   a. *Exchange rates:* appreciation of + 500 bps in 2025 and 2026.
   b. *Interest rates:* − 100 bps in 2026 and 2027.
   c. *Spreads:* no shock.

Additional Notes:
- Given the net flows of multilateral, bilateral, and private external debt accumulated over a given period, we compute the share of fiscal deficit that will be covered by each type of debt. If the accumulated net flows of all debt types are zero, then the shares for all types are assumed to be 1/3.
- We compute a per-country exchange rate index over time. This index tracks a basket of currencies, whose weights are given by the PPG debt currency composition in the last year before the simulation starts.

References

Albinet, Charles, and Martin Kessler. 2022. "The Coming Debt Crisis: Monitoring Liquidity and Solvency Risks." Working Paper 1, November. Finance for Development Lab. https://findevlab.org/wp-content/uploads/2022/12/FDL_CAMK_DebtService.pdf.

Albinet, Charles, Martin Kessler, and Marco Brancher. 2023. "Mapping External Debt Vulnerabilities – An Update." November. Finance for Development Lab. https://findevlab.org/wp-content/uploads/2023/12/FDL_Debt-distress-update_final20231204.pdf.

Albinet, Charles, Hamouda Chekir, and Martin Kessler. 2024. *Debt-to-Sustainability Swaps (D2S): A Practical Framework.* Finance for Development Lab, Policy Note 16. https://findevlab.org/wp-content/uploads/2024/07/FDL_Policy-Note_D2S_June-2024.pdf

Ams, Julianne et al. 2014. "The Fund's lending framework and sovereign debt – preliminary considerations." IMF Staff Report. May 2014.

Calvo, Guillermo A. 1988. "Servicing the Public Debt: The Role of Expectations." *American Economic Review* 78 (4): 647–61.

Cole, Harold L., and Timothy J. Kehoe. 2000. "Self-Fulfilling Debt Crises." *The Review of Economic Studies* 67 (1): 91–116. http://www.jstor.org/stable/2567030.

Diwan, Ishac, Martin Kessler, and Vera Songwe. 2024. "A Bridge to Climate Action: A Tripartite Deal for Times of Illiquidity." Policy Note 14. Finance for Development Lab, January. https://findevlab.org/wp-content/uploads/2024/01/FDL_A_Bridge_to_Climate_Action_final.pdf

Diwan, Ishac, Martin Guzman, Martin Kessler, Vera Songwe, and Joseph E. Stiglitz. 2024. "An Updated Bridge Proposal: Towards a Solution to the Current Sovereign Debt Crises and to Restore Growth."

Policy Note 1. Finance for Development Lab, July. https://findevlab.org/wp-content/uploads/2024/07/
    FDL-and-IPD_Policy-Note_An-Updated-Bridge-Proposal-Towards-A-Solution-to-the-Sovereign-Debt-
    Crises-And-To-Restore-Growth_-July24_FINAL.pdf
International Monetary Fund (IMF) and the World Bank. 2018. "Guidance Note on the Bank-Fund Debt
    Sustainability Framework for Low-Income Countries", Policy paper. https://www.imf.org/en/Publica
    tions/Policy-Papers/Issues/2018/02/14/pp122617guidance-note-on-lic-dsf
International Monetary Fund (IMF). 2023. "The Natural Rate of Interest: Drivers and Implications for
    Policy." *In World Economic Outlook, April 2023*, chap. 2. Washington, DC: International Monetary Fund.
International Monetary Fund (IMF). 2024. *World Economic Outlook, October 2024: Policy Pivot, Rising Threats.*
    Washington, DC: International Monetary Fund.
International Monetary Fund (IMF) and the World Bank. 2024. "Supplement to 2018 Guidance Note on the
    Bank-Fund Debt Sustainability Framework for Low Incomes Countries". Policy Papers.
    August 5, 2024.
Kose, M. Ayhan, Peter Nagle, Franziska Ohnsorge, and Naotaka Sugawara. 2021. *Global Waves of Debt:
    Causes and Consequences*. Washington, DC: World Bank.
Properzi, Emanuele. 2023. "Closing the Spigots: The Rise and Collapse of Bond Markets for Developing
    Countries". *Finance for Development Lab*. October 31, 2023. Accessed January 10, 2025.
    https://findevlab.org/closing-the-spigots-the-rise-and-collapse-of-bond-markets-for-developing-
    countries/
Sachs, Jeffrey, and Daniel Cohen. 1982. "LDC Borrowing with Default Risk." NBER Working Paper No. 925.
    Cambridge, MA: National Bureau of Economic Research. https://doi.org/10.3386/w0925.
The Expert Group on Debt, Nature & Climate. 2024. *Interim Report of the Expert Review on Debt, Nature &
    Climate: Tackling the Vicious Circle*. Accessed January 10, 2025. https://d1leqfwiwfltz5.cloudfront.net/
    documents/Tackling_the_Vicious_Circle.pdf.
World Bank International Debt Statistics. 2024. Data Sources and Methodology. December 2024.
    https://www.worldbank.org/en/programs/debt-statistics/ids
Willems, Tim, and Jeromin Zettelmeyer. 2022. "Sovereign Debt Sustainability and Central Bank Credibility."
    Annual Review of Financial Economics 14: 75–93. https://doi.org/10.1146/annurev-financial-112921-
    110812.
Zucker-Marques, Marina, Kevin P. Gallagher, and Ulrich Volz, with Shamshad Akhtar, Maria Fernanda
    Espinosa, Jörg Haas, Patrick Njoroge, and Bogolo Kenewendo. 2024. *Defaulting on Development and
    Climate: Debt Sustainability and the Race for the 2030 Agenda and Paris Agreement*. Boston, London,
    Berlin: Boston University Global Development Policy Center; Centre for Sustainable Finance, SOAS,
    University of London; Heinrich Böll Foundation.

Jean-Paul Adam, Justin Mundy, and Arend Kulenkampff

Chapter 11
Connecting the Virtuous Circle: From Debt-for-Development Swaps to Sustainability-Linked Sovereign Finance

Abstract: The world faces a financing crisis, with a USD 4 trillion annual shortfall for the Sustainable Development Goals (SDGs) and an imminent debt crisis, especially in developing countries. These countries depend on donor-driven finance or debt relief, which has been inadequate. The chapter calls for a comprehensive approach to the debt crisis that reduces the debt burden, frees up fiscal space, and boosts investment. This approach should also enhance climate resilience and natural capital preservation through National Determined Contributions, Biodiversity Strategy Action Plans, and National Adaptation Plans. Debt swaps are a key instrument to free up resources for these priorities. The chapter further recommends using debt restructuring instruments and increased deployment of sustainability-linked bonds, use-of-proceeds bonds, and debt swaps. Key performance indicators (KPIs) aligned with SDGs and climate goals should also be used for sustainability-linked financing. Increased deployment and harmonization of credit enhancement instruments are essential. Debt swaps can effectively provide an entry point to deliver finance instruments, aligned with SDGs and climate resilience, improving access and pricing for investments. As conditions for accessing predictable and affordable finance may further worsen for emerging and developing economies (EMDEs) in an unfavorable global environment, the use of such instruments becomes even more pivotal.

Keywords: Sustainability-linked finance, Sovereign debt, Sustainable Development Goals, Debt swaps, Debt restructuring, Emerging and developing economies

Introduction

As the world faces an acute shortage of financing for achieving the Sustainable Development Goals (SDGs), estimated at USD 4 trillion annually (United Nations 2024, *2–3*), it is simultaneously grappling with an intensifying debt crisis concentrated in the developing world. The rise in this gap has corresponded with increased vulnerability to external shocks, including the increased cost of climate change, as well as a burgeoning youth population in the developing world and the relatively slow rate at which financing has accompanied these changes. At the end of 2023, 37 out of 69 low-income countries, the majority in Africa, were assessed to be at high risk or in debt distress

(IMF and World Bank 2024). This scenario has made those developing countries, with limited ownership of the tools for investment in the SDGs and climate resilience, either dependent on donor-driven finance, which is in short supply, or on debt relief, which the G20 Common Framework has had limited success in delivering (Hill and Martin 2024).

Against this backdrop, there is an urgent need for a comprehensive approach to tackling the impending debt crisis that reduces the debt burden, frees up fiscal space, and increases investment in the SDGs. Moreover, such an approach must support countries' resilience to climate change and natural capital depletion by providing a coherent framework for reducing risk. This framework should cover the implementation of countries' Nationally Determined Contributions (NDCs) under the Paris Agreement to address climate change, their Biodiversity Strategy Action Plans, and National Adaptation Plans under the Kunming-Montreal Global Biodiversity Framework (GBF).

Achieving this objective will require the deployment of the full range of innovative debt reprofiling and restructuring instruments that have emerged in recent years, including sustainability-linked bonds and loans (SLBs and SLLs, respectively), use-of-proceeds bonds (UoP bonds), and debt swaps, along with appropriately designed blended finance solutions. Debt swaps (also known as debt conversions) are unique, in that they combine elements of both sustainability-linked bonds and use-of-proceeds bonds, plus the critical ingredient of credit enhancement to free up resources that can be channeled into conservation funding and climate resilience.

The building blocks of these approaches include the systematic use of KPIs that track progress against SDGs, climate goals, and other sustainability targets (see Figure 11.1 for examples). When packaged together with enhanced reporting protocols and incentive mechanisms, they create the feature set of sustainability-linked financing instruments, which encompass debt swaps, SLBs, and SLLs. The KPIs, anchored within national plans, are a signal to markets of both the issuer's credibility of commitment to the targets as well as the long-term economic value of these investments. The performance-based incentive mechanisms include coupon ratchets – i.e., step-ups in coupon interest rates when targets are missed, and vice versa – or other performance-based changes in contractual terms, as well as credit enhancements in the form of credit guarantees, credit insurance, and collateralization mechanisms. Credit enhancement can be viewed as a concession to the issuer for voluntarily embedding sustainability commitments into binding financial contracts, which contrasts with traditional development finance approaches of creditor-imposed conditionality.

Whereas debt swaps, and to a lesser extent, SLBs and SLLs, have been successfully deployed by several countries in the past 5 years, their implementation has generally been ad hoc and piecemeal, addressing only segments of a much larger debt problem. Furthermore, these instruments swaps, SLBs/SLLs, and UoP bonds – are often framed as substitutes or competitors. This perspective has hindered their broader application and scalability, as each instrument, on its own, is insufficient to achieve the dual objectives of creating fiscal space and safeguarding debt sustainability.

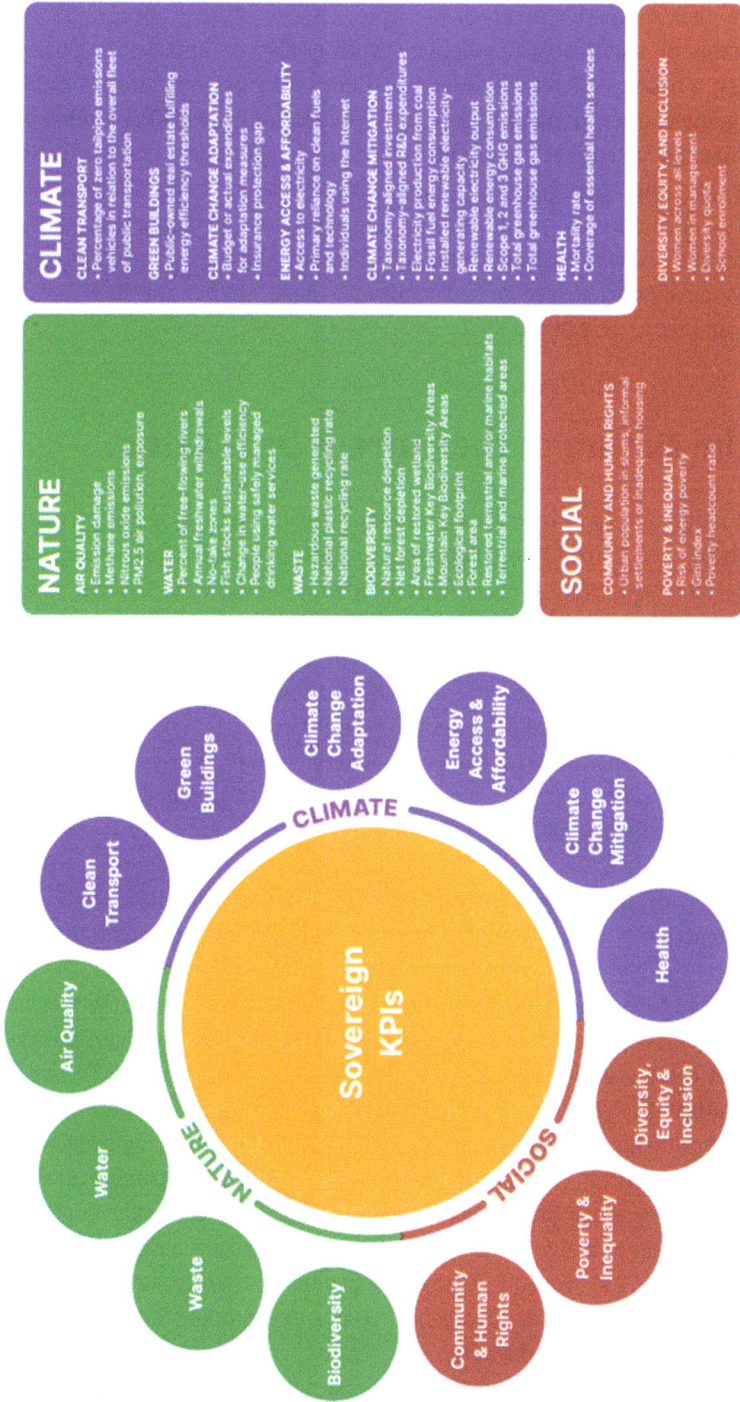

Figure 11.1: Examples of key performance indicators for biodiversity and climate resilience.
Source: ICMA, as featured in Sustainable Sovereign Debt Hub (SSDH) 2025.

We propose that swaps be incorporated into a more holistic, programmatic framework, capable of accommodating diverse types of climate and nature finance instruments. Such a framework should integrate these solutions with broader public financial management operations and objectives. Importantly, the KPIs embedded within these financial instruments should extend to the planning and budgeting stages, ensuring that funding and spending align with targets and commitments. Debt swaps play a critical role in this programmatic approach, complementing other sustainability-linked and conventional instruments. They remain one of the most effective mechanisms for aligning sovereign financing with the attainment of the SDGs, climate resilience, and nature conservation.

Framing the Nature of the Current Debt Crisis

The global debt landscape has undergone profound transformations in recent years, primarily driven by the COVID-19 pandemic and its cascading economic impacts. Efforts to address the health crisis and mitigate economic downturns resulted in unprecedented increases in government spending worldwide, causing global debt levels to surge. Emergency funding for healthcare, economic stimulus packages, and social support measures prompted countries to increase borrowing. Together with rising global interest rates, this led to inflated debt-to-GDP ratios, higher borrowing costs, and mounting debt-servicing burdens. These challenges were further exacerbated by increased import costs, particularly for energy and food, which strained the financial capacities of many nations, especially those in emerging markets and developing economies (EMDEs).

The rising levels of debt raise concerns not only about the overall amounts but also about the structure of debts, the alignment of maturities with potential flows, currency risks, and the types of payments required, such as bullet payments. The historic levels of debt-to-GDP ratios across various regions underscore the gravity of the debt sustainability crisis, necessitating concerted efforts and innovative financial strategies to foster economic resilience and stability.

While debt ratios have climbed, an even greater concern is the diversion of resources, away from investments in the SDGs and toward meeting debt-servicing obligations. For example, in Africa, debt service costs have surpassed healthcare expenditures since 2020 – precisely at a time when fiscal space was most needed. Concurrently, education spending, as a proportion of budgets, has declined, with debt-service costs escalating to an all-time high. Figure 11.2 shows how debt service payments are increasingly consuming a larger share of African countries' budgets, diverting expenditures away from critical investments in healthcare and education.

There is a significant risk of experiencing a "lost decade", during which investment in critical development drivers may stall. Limited additional financing from con-

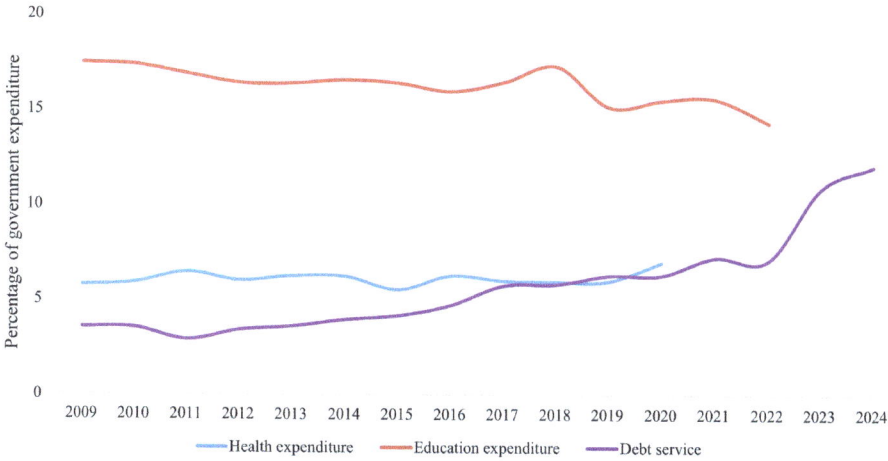

Figure 11.2: Debt service payments and African budgets.
Source: United Nations Office of the Special Adviser on Africa [UNOSAA] (2024).

cessional sources, including grants and loans, is compounded by the high cost of accessing international capital markets. This elevated cost of capital is driven by inflation-targeting policies in developed markets and exacerbated by the already substantial impact of the so-called "Africa premium" – the higher cost of investing in Africa, relative to other regions, as shown in Figure 11.3.

The premium on the cost of capital in EMDEs reflects both real and perceived risks and vulnerabilities in these markets. As climate and nature-related risks materialize and investors become more attuned to the macro-fiscal effects of climate change and environmental degradation, risk premiums are likely to rise further. In practice, this results in less capital flowing to regions that most urgently require investment. Notably, Africa receives the least private sector-mobilized climate finance, accounting for only 14% of total flows – nearly three times less than the next lowest region, Southeast Asia.

While large-scale mobilization of additional financing resources – primarily as grants and concessional financing – is necessary, it will not be sufficient to sustain long-term progress without also crowding in private finance. The availability of additional financing is unevenly distributed across the developing world. According to data from the Global SDG Database, gross receipts of mobilized private finance by developing countries have faced challenges across all three major developing regions. Only Latin America and the Caribbean (LAC) have returned to pre-pandemic levels of investment, while Africa, which had the lowest mobilization capacity prior to the pandemic, has experienced the fastest and most pronounced reduction in these flows. Figure 11.4 illustrates the mobilization of private sector finance, on an experimental basis, across the three major developing regions: Africa, LAC, and Asia.

10Y Bond Yield (%)

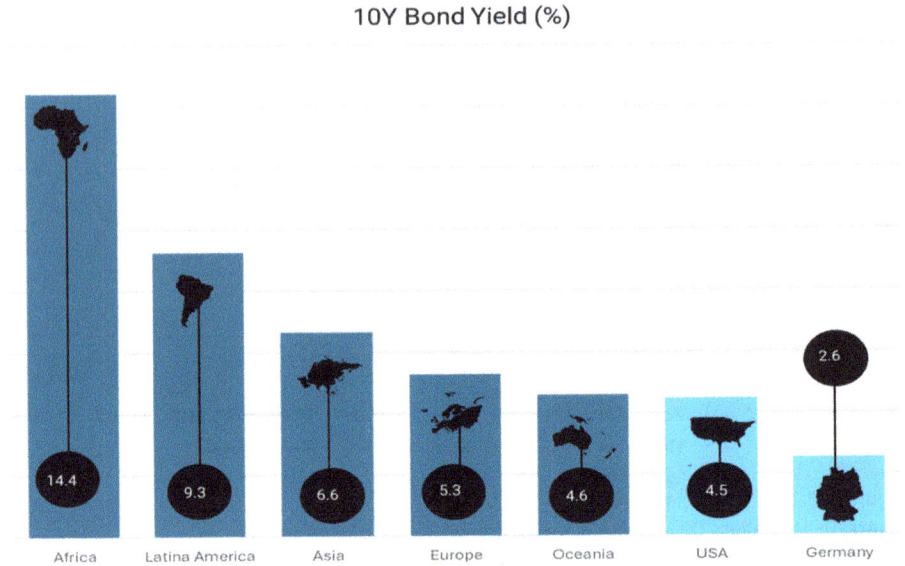

Figure 11.3: The high cost of access to international capital markets for emerging economies, emphasizing the "Africa premium".
Source: UNOSAA (2024, 25).

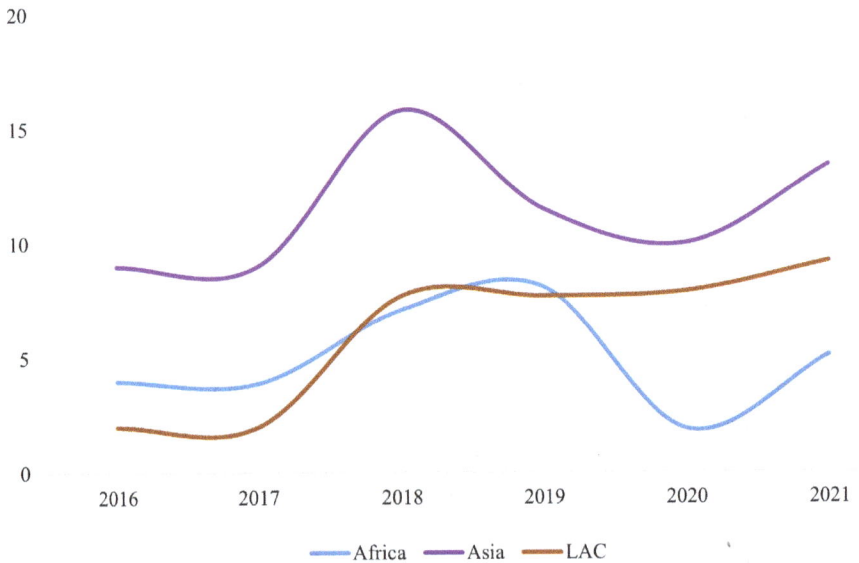

Figure 11.4: Mobilized private finance on an experimental basis in the three major developing regions – Africa, Latin America and the Caribbean, and Asia (in USD billion).
Source: Authors based on the Global SDG Database – UNDESA (2024).

The Role of Debt Swaps in Tackling the Unfolding Sovereign Debt Crisis

The mounting sovereign debt crisis has coincided with a wave of innovation in sovereign financing models that incorporate environmental, social, and governance (ESG) considerations, while simultaneously addressing debt sustainability issues. This trend arguably began with the debt-for-nature swap arranged between Seychelles and The Nature Conservancy (TNC) in 2015[1] and gained momentum with the Belize debt-for-nature conversion in 2022. Although debt swaps date back to the 1980s, this latest wave stands out for leveraging credit enhancements in debt financing to buy back outstanding commercial debt at a discount, with the savings from swapping expensive for cheaper debt channeled into long-term conservation funding. In contrast, bilateral or multilateral debt swaps of earlier decades involved a smaller subset of official creditors and relied on write-downs to generate fiscal savings. Whereas past transactions primarily channeled these savings into nature conservation, this new wave applies debt swaps to broader Sustainable Development Goals.

The landmark Belize transaction was, in effect, a sustainability-linked debt restructuring. This deal involved buying back a portion of the country's commercial foreign debt at a discount, followed by the issuance of new "blue bonds" facilitated by TNC. The bonds were structured to fund marine conservation projects, and, thanks to credit insurance provided by the Development Finance Corporation (DFC) of the U.S. Government, they were issued on highly favorable terms at a time when Belize had lost access to the international bond market (DFC 2021). The transaction generated approximately USD 180 million for marine protection and management, with Belize committing to increase the percentage of the ocean under protection from 15.9% to 30% (The Nature Conservancy 2022). At the same time, the restructuring allowed Belize to reduce its public debt stock by USD 189 million and its debt service bill by USD 200 million, directly benefiting its fiscal health, while channeling funds into ocean conservation.

The Belize transaction provided proof of concept for commercial debt-for-nature conversions in Barbados, Ecuador, and Gabon. It incorporated several innovative sustainability-linking features, including a conservation trust fund, project and policy KPIs, and use-of-proceeds provisions in the blue bonds. Subsequent transactions were variations on these themes, with each iteration introducing or optimizing features of the original design. For instance, in the Barbados transaction in 2022, domestic creditors were also involved, alongside international creditors, in exchanging existing debt, while credit enhancement was provided by both a development bank – the Inter-American Development Bank (IDB) – and a conservation organization, The Nature Conservancy (IDB 2022).

---

1 See The Commonwealth Case Study 2020.

The unique value proposition of debt swaps, such as those executed by Belize and Barbados, lies in their potential to mobilize private capital for sustainability objectives on superior terms for the sovereign borrower, especially during times of financial market turmoil.

Guarantees and other credit enhancement solutions are embedded in the financing leg of the transactions, lowering the perceived credit risk of the issuance and, by extension, the cost of borrowing. This makes them more attractive to risk-averse investors who might otherwise avoid the credit risk of lower-rated or distressed sovereigns. For instance, Belize secured a 17-notch improvement on the instrument rating of its blue bonds over its sovereign standalone rating, from Caa3 to Aa2. This enabled access to a more diversified pool of debt investors, replacing yield-hungry and flighty emerging market debt investors with patient, long-term capital and sustainability-oriented funds. Hence, debt swaps can be instrumental for countries with limited or constrained market access, particularly during times of high global interest rates. By extending maturities on debts coming due during credit down cycles, debt swaps can help vulnerable sovereigns navigate periods of tight liquidity when other conventional liability management operations are unavailable, thereby possibly avoiding default.

While not a substitute for debt relief, debt swaps can be pivotal in helping countries with heavy debt burdens achieve fiscal sustainability. This involves aligning financial obligations with current economic capacity, strengthening the sovereign's solvency position and "ability to pay". Furthermore, swaps can support prudent debt management and fiscal planning by safeguarding funding flows to critical development investments, bolstering the credibility of commitments, policy effectiveness, and predictability – key considerations in assessing a sovereign's "willingness" to pay. By laying the groundwork for performance-based financing – such as inter-agency coordinating committees and KPI management information systems – debt swaps can unlock complementary funding from analogous instruments such as sustainability-linked loans (SLLs) and bonds (SLBs) or access to multilateral financing facilities like the International Monetary Fund's Resilience and Sustainability Trust (RST). This was the case for Barbados, which became the first country to access the RST, immediately following its debt swap.

Debt Swaps and Their Limitations

Despite their demonstrated success in providing financial relief and channeling funding to SDGs, debt swaps are no silver bullet for resolving sovereign liquidity or solvency problems. The complexity of these deals entails high transaction costs and lengthy structuring times, which can render them financially inefficient in contexts where the outstanding debt being swapped is not trading at a meaningful discount. The *World Bank Framework on Debt for Development Swaps* outlines several constraints inherent to these instruments (World Bank 2024). Limited interest savings, as evidenced in the cases of Gabon and Barbados, undermine the claim that debt swaps necessarily provide meaningful debt relief, although they have helped reprofile these countries' debt repayments.

The supply of credit enhancement by multilateral development banks (MDBs), Development finance institutions (DFIs), and multilateral climate funds (MCFs) remains constrained and subject to high fees and onerous conditions. For example, credit rating agencies often require guarantees to cover the entirety of the principal amount being guaranteed, representing full credit "substitution" rather than mere credit "enhancement". Additionally, stakeholders have raised transparency concerns regarding the terms of sovereign lending arrangements and the allocation of funds to conservation projects (Fresnillo 2023). A shallow pipeline of deals, following the initial surge in 2022–2023, underscores these challenges, which coincide with a global credit cycle downturn, leading to smaller discounts on bond repurchases in secondary markets – critical for the financial efficiency of swaps.

A counterargument holds that debt swaps remain an effective mechanism for securing long-term funding for sustainable development without adding to the debt stock. The high upfront transaction costs must also be weighed against the lifetime savings generated by these transactions. Moreover, many issues observed in the first series of deals are being addressed and improved in subsequent models. Lessons learned are being documented in manuals and standards prepared by organizations such as The Nature Conservancy (2024) and the Task Force on Sustainability-Linked Sovereign Financing for Nature and Climate, established at COP28[2] (Climate Champions 2023). This initiative, driven by the Sustainability-linked Sovereign Debt Hub (SSDH), TNC, and the UN Climate Change High-Level Champions, also seeks to tackle supply-side constraints hindering credit enhancement.

Finally, debt swaps must be integrated into a programmatic approach, combining multiple conventional, thematic (use-of-proceeds), and sustainability-linked sovereign financing solutions. These include sustainability-linked bonds and loans, discussed in the following section.

---

2 This initiative brings together a group of MDBs, other DFIs, Multilateral Climate Funds (MCFs) and international organizations, to promote increased effectiveness, efficiency, affordability, accessibility and scalability of credit enhancements to support sustainability-linked sovereign financing for nature and climate.

SLBs, SLLs, and Other Sustainability-Linked Instruments

SLBs and SLLs are financial instruments that tie the financial characteristics of the bond or loan to the issuer's achievement of specific sustainability outcomes. Specifically, they incorporate KPIs to track progress against predefined Sustainability Performance Targets (SPTs), which must be ambitious and aligned with "strategic national development plans or policies", per the *International Capital Market Association's Sustainable Bond Principles* (ICMA 2024). Unlike debt swaps, these instruments do not designate how proceeds are used, allowing issuers to employ them in liability management operations, such as repaying or buying back other debt obligations. Instead, sustainability-linked instruments embed reporting protocols and financial incentives to promote action toward sustainability targets. Unlike use-of-proceeds instruments, SLBs and SLLs can cover policy actions, in addition to program and project funding.

For EMDEs, SLBs offer significant mobilization potential by providing access to international capital markets, beyond traditional grants and concessional finance. This access is crucial for diversifying funding sources and tapping into the growing ESG investor base, enabling countries to leverage additional financial resources to achieve sustainability goals, accelerate economic development, and reduce dependency on unpredictable aid flows.

Uruguay and Chile illustrate how SLBs can be effectively utilized in EMDEs.[3] Uruguay's issuance of an SLB in 2022, aimed at funding sustainable forestry and renewable energy projects, demonstrated how these bonds can support key economic sectors, critical for sustainable development. The country followed up in 2023 with its debut issuance of a sovereign SLL. Similarly, Chile has issued SLBs focused on energy transition and social inclusivity, showcasing the versatility of these instruments in addressing diverse developmental challenges, while enhancing their profiles in global markets.

Issuing SLBs and SLLs is not without challenges. These include the additional burden of reporting on sustainability criteria and limited evidence of a "greenium" – a premium or superior pricing terms at issuance, driven by higher demand from sustainability-oriented investors. However, in both Uruguay and Chile, issuance was grounded in domestic budgeting strategies, ensuring that the instruments advanced established goals, while adding enhanced reporting and financial incentives.

On the investor side, the coupon ratchet feature presents several challenges in valuation and risk management, as well as ambiguity regarding accounting and capital treatment. Additionally, reputational risks – stemming from perceptions that in-

---

3 Discussions of these issuances and opportunities on how these experiences can be further leveraged for future issuances are available from the Sustainability-Linked Sovereign Debt Hub (SSDH) (2023a) and Stewart and Caputo Silva (2022).

vestors could benefit financially from a coupon step-up (the "rooting for failure" problem) – persist. These issues are gradually being addressed, but achieving scale with these instruments will require concerted and sustained efforts.

Scaling Debt Swaps, SLBs/SLLs, and Other Sustainability-Linked Debt Instruments

To issue debt swaps, sustainability-linked bonds, sustainability-linked loans, and other sustainability-linked debt instruments at scale in EMDEs, improvements in key aspects of the enabling environment are essential. Five non-exhaustive pathways to achieve this scaling include:

1. **Credit enhancement**: Establishing guarantees, insurance, and collateralization mechanisms to reduce perceived credit risk, and thereby "crowd in" private capital, amplifying the impact of public funds.
2. **Standardization**: Creating common principles and best practices for target setting, KPI selection and calibration, pricing, and structuring of these instruments. Such efforts build trust and reduce transaction costs.
3. **Capacity building**: Strengthening the institutional and technological capabilities of issuers to handle the additional data management workload for compiling and reporting KPIs. This should include safeguards for full transparency, traceability, and data integrity upon which performance tracking depends.
4. **Policy and regulations**: Developing a policy and regulatory environment that enables sustainability-linked securities. At a minimum, regulations should avoid unnecessarily inhibiting or discouraging issuance or purchase of such instruments, and instead actively encourage them.
5. **Political will**: Harnessing political leadership to address coordination failures and collective action problems associated with issuing these instruments, while maintaining consistent pressure to ensure accountability in data compilation and investor reporting.

Of these pathways, credit enhancement is likely the most catalytic. However, the availability of guarantees and credit insurance solutions is currently limited, representing less than 2% of MDBs' portfolios (Kulenkampff and Orozco 2024). This constraint stems, in part, from institutional rules that incentivize both borrowers and MDBs to favor loans. For instance, MDBs often treat guarantees as loans, in terms of provisioning and pricing. Both guarantees and loans consume an equal portion of a country's lending envelope, despite guarantees being contingent instruments with much lower call rates compared to loan default rates (Humphrey 2022).

Addressing these credit enhancement bottlenecks on the MDBs' side will require time. In the interim, innovative solutions are needed to catalyze sustainability-linked sovereign financing transactions and enhance their appeal to a broader investor base. For example:

- International philanthropies and development donors could fund the "step-downs" in SLBs/SLLs, compensating issuers for achieving performance targets, while leaving the coupon rate faced by investors unchanged. This approach mitigates investor concerns about coupon ratchets and reputational risks associated with "rooting for failure".
- MDBs and DFIs could bundle guarantees with SLBs and SLLs in a structure that addresses supply-side barriers, as proposed by Kulenkampff and Orozco (2024) and illustrated in Figure 11.5.

This proposal envisions stripping the SLB of its coupon ratchet, while retaining it in an accompanying SLL. The SLB-SLL bundle would share identical targets, KPIs, and terms, ensuring that performances are measured consistently. The SLB could then be priced and managed like a standard bond, while retaining the performance-tracking and incentive mechanisms of the SLL.

By applying step-up/step-down features only to the loan provided by the MDB, the issuer cannot exploit a loophole by buying back the loan early to avoid a step-up – a common issue with SLBs. Moreover, since MDBs hold preferred creditor status, bond issuers are less likely to default on penalties. Additionally, monitoring loan servicing could eliminate the need for an external second-opinion provider, thereby reducing issuance costs and mitigating vendor risks associated with third-party involvement.

Standardization, the second scaling pathway listed above, will be crucial for transforming sustainability-linked instruments from niche offerings into mainstream financial products. Principles and best practices for SLBs and SLLs have been developed by organizations such as the International Capital Market Association (ICMA). Additionally, entities like The Nature Conservancy and the Task Force on Sustainability-Linked Sovereign Financing for Nature and Climate have issued specific principles and guidelines for swaps. Meanwhile, accounting standards for SLBs and SLLs are being clarified, particularly in addressing the complex valuation and accounting treatment of the "embedded option" within coupon ratchets. Despite these advancements, further harmonization is needed to address concerns raised by market participants, particularly regarding the definition and development KPIs.

To ensure investor and creditor confidence in the performance-tracking mechanisms, integral to sustainability-linked products, the integrity and reliability of underlying data must be beyond reproach. Indeed, robust data is the foundation of sustainability-linked finance (see Figure 11.6). Any evidence of inaccuracies or manipulation in the underlying data or reporting pipelines can undermine demand for specific instruments – or worse, erode confidence in the entire asset class. Significant data gaps and technological capacity constraints currently hinder progress and contribute to the reluctance of some treasury debt management offices (DMOs) to adopt sustainability-linked instruments.[4]

Plugging these gaps will require capacity building and policy and regulatory reforms – the third and fourth scaling pathways, respectively. Governments must ensure the availability of adequate expertise and infrastructure to monitor, report, and evaluate based on established KPIs. This includes training personnel, upgrading technology, and developing robust monitoring frameworks to capture the required data accurately and promptly. Institutional barriers to issuance must also be addressed. For instance, some countries have budgetary laws prohibiting the use of coupon ratchets, necessitating legal reforms or policy adjustments.

On the "back end" of sustainability-linked instruments, governments often lack the IT infrastructure or skilled personnel to implement certain KPIs, such as those requiring geospatial imaging or machine learning expertise – both of which were integral to Uruguay's forest cover KPI for its sustainability-linked bond. Upgrades in financial management information systems (FMIS) and data management capabilities may be required to accommodate the workflows of more complex KPIs. Robust governance frameworks must also be instituted to guarantee the reliable supply of transparent data for the entire lifespan of the bond or loan. Institutional reforms, supported by sustained political will, are essential for achieving these objectives.

Building and Sustaining Political Buy-In for Sustainability-Linked Finance

The final scaling pathway – political will – is arguably the most critical and challenging. Sustainability-linked financing often involves significant upfront and ongoing costs, including infrastructure upgrades, fees for additional participants (e.g., second-opinion providers), and the political capital required to coordinate ministries and stakeholders. Overcoming the principal–agent problem between finance ministries (principals) and implementing line ministries (agents) is crucial. Finance ministries may hesitate to assume the risk of a coupon step-up or reputational damage if line ministries fail to deliver on KPIs. Furthermore, DMOs may not perceive sustainability targets as part of their core mandate, which typically focuses on optimizing debt management strategies and minimizing costs and risks.

To ensure the success of sustainability-linked finance, sustained political support and effective monitoring mechanisms are imperative. Aligning incentives between stakeholders is also essential. The following mechanisms can help address these challenges:

---

4 A summary of some of this additional burden is usefully provided in Sustainability-Linked Sovereign Debt Hub (2023b).

1. Aligning targets and KPIs with international commitments
2. Incorporating financial materiality assessments
3. Extending targets and KPIs from financing to spending

Together, these mechanisms confer increased accountability and ownership over performance to Ministries of Finance, while achieving a goal firmly anchored in and legitimized by domestic processes. These mechanisms complement other technical remedies incorporated into transaction design, such as force majeure clauses that reduce the likelihood of failed targets due to exogenous factors, including natural catastrophes or conflicts, and mitigating the potential political risks of step-ups.

Adopting existing national commitments and policy priorities can also enhance political buy-in. Sustainability-linked instruments can serve as the "scaffolding" for delivering finance effectively to priority needs already defined by countries through international processes, such as the SDGs and the Paris Agreement, which hold varying degrees of domestic political support. In this context, issuers can effectively "download" targets from strategic development, climate, and nature goals, including their Paris Agreement NDCs and Kunming-Montreal Global Biodiversity Framework National Biodiversity Strategic Action Plans (NBSAPs). Embedding these policy targets into sustainability-linked financing structures strengthens commitment credibility as they become enshrined in legal contracts, often under foreign jurisdictions (as is typical for bonds issued in international markets). This arrangement also introduces a degree of market discipline through financial market performance monitoring.

Simultaneously, the fact that the SPTs and KPIs are selected by issuers, rather than imposed by creditors, enhances their legitimacy in the eyes of governments. Traditionally, debt instruments have been associated with stringent creditor-imposed conditions, often misaligned with a debtor country's most pressing needs. This misalignment can result in inefficient resource allocation, diverting funds from areas of significant strategic impact. By allowing debtor countries to establish KPIs aligned with their NDCs, NAPs, and SDG frameworks, these nations can prioritize projects that reflect their developmental and environmental commitments. Furthermore, sustainability-linked finance can enhance the credibility and efficacy of policy commitments and international agreements. The integration of these targets and KPIs into public financial management reinforces their role in fiscal governance.

A further mechanism to enhance the political appeal of sustainability-linked financing models for Ministries of Finance involves demonstrating the financial materiality of the selected targets and KPIs. When these metrics closely align with the issuer's credit rating and debt sustainability profile, achieving the targets can lead to improved credit risk metrics and public debt dynamics. Consequently, DMOs can justify the additional reporting workload and operational expense associated with sustainability-linked finance by aligning these efforts with the core debt management mandate. Moreover, performance-based instruments signal to markets and credit rating agencies the seriousness of plans to address financially material – and therefore credit-relevant – sustainability risks. This credibility is reinforced by robust performance tracking and reporting protocols. The market and credit rating agencies, in turn, should acknowledge the "uplift" provided by adopting a KPI-linking framework, both in terms of quantitative macro-fiscal effects and qualitative assessments of policy effectiveness and predictability.

The relationship between financially material KPIs and debt sustainability analysis (DSA) is particularly significant. The DSA plays a pivotal role in determining sovereign access to financial markets and credit facilities at international financial institutions, particularly the International Monetary Fund. Many governments in EMDEs lack the capacity to undertake their own DSAs and depend on support from development partners. By integrating sustainability KPIs and their macro-fiscal impacts into the DSA, governments can demonstrate how resilience-enhancing measures and expenditures bolster long-term solvency. This counters the excessive focus on debt stocks, which often overlooks the importance of investment flows in achieving universal access to energy, healthcare, education, and other economic development enablers. Linking KPI frameworks to sustainability objectives strengthens the case for long-term debt sustainability and credibility.

Although integrating KPIs into sovereign credit rating models and DSAs is unlikely to yield immediate cost reductions, it strengthens the case for credit enhancement in sustainability-linked transactions. Credit guarantee and insurance providers can gain confidence in underwriting instruments targeting sustainability outcomes and enhancing the obligor's "ability to pay". Credit enhancement can provide immediate financial benefits, securing political buy-in and facilitating investment in capacity-building systems and data infrastructure, essential for such instruments.

Another key mechanism to address the principal–agent problem in sustainability-linked transactions is performance-based budgeting. Instead of relying solely on use-of-proceeds provisions, programmatic spending can align with sustainability targets by embedding the same KPIs into expenditure budgeting and tracking frameworks. This alignment ensures accountability both internally and externally. Internally, KPIs offer a metric-based tool for evaluating the progress and impact of funded projects. Aligning KPIs with project pipelines and sustainable budgeting practices ensures that fiscal allocations reflect the priorities outlined in the KPIs. This approach embeds sustainability into financial planning, guaranteeing funding for projects meeting KPI criteria and promoting transparency. It also allows for strategic adjustments to improve outcomes. Externally, integrating KPIs addresses concerns about greenwashing. Defining precise, measurable indicators of success that are publicly reported and audited enables creditors and investors to verify that funds genuinely contribute to green and sustainable projects, enhancing trust and credibility in the financial instruments issued.

Robust KPI data architecture and reporting pipelines are prerequisites for financing and for ensuring buy-in across policy applications, such as performance-based budgeting and sustainability-linked budgeting, thereby improving overall effectiveness.

Some examples of KPIs related to biodiversity and nature are provided in Figure 11.5, while Figure 11.6 illustrates a proposed conceptual framework for using KPIs. This framework covers the process from identifying robust data to aligning with country-specific contexts, setting targets, and implementing them.

A. Single Provider Scenario

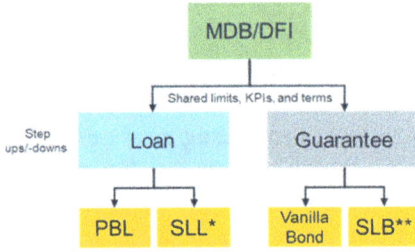

B. Risk-Sharing Scenario

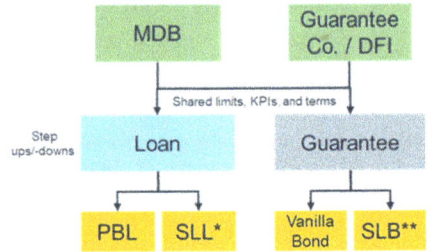

Figure 11.5: Stylized scenarios for packaging loans and guarantees.
Note: *Sustainability-linked loan (SLL) – Sustainability-linked bond (SLB)
Source: Kulenkampff and Orozco (2024).

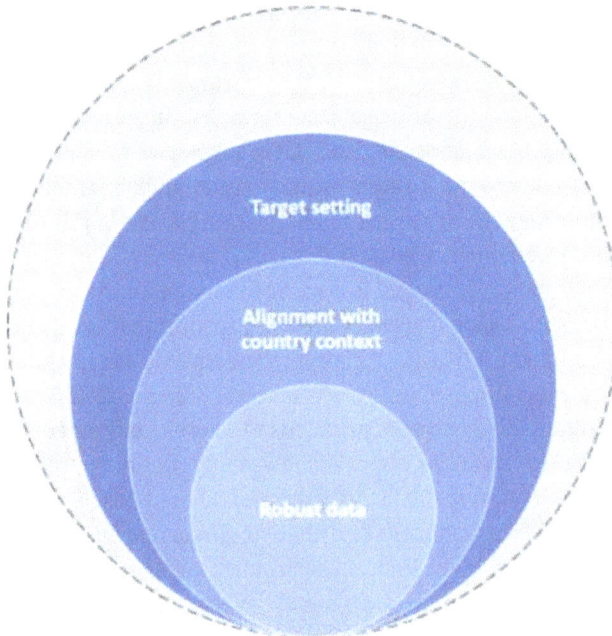

Figure 11.6: Conceptual framework for use of KPIs in sustainability-linked bonds.
Source: Flugge, Mok, and Stewart (2021).

Conclusion

EMDEs face unprecedented fiscal constraints, precisely when growth- and resilience-enhancing investments in the SDGs, climate adaptation, and nature conservation are most urgent. Debt swaps offer an important avenue to free up resources for development, while promoting debt sustainability. While not ideal for sovereigns facing extreme debt distress, they can help countries smooth their debt profile, weather credit cycle downturn, and reallocate savings toward priority investments.

Debt swaps should not be viewed as piecemeal solutions for narrow policy goals, such as expanding protected ocean areas. Instead, they must form part of a broader toolkit that includes sustainability-linked bonds and loans. This approach relies on credit enhancement as a key enabler, particularly in developing countries, to mobilize substantial private capital for the SDGs. Ultimately, this toolkit should be anchored in performance-based principles of public financial management that maximize local ownership and ensure flexibility and accountability.

References

The Commonwealth. 2020. "Case Study: Innovative Financing – Debt for Conservation Swap, Seychelles' Conservation and Climate Adaptation Trust and the Blue Bonds Plan, Seychelles". November 28. Accessed October 5, 2024. https://thecommonwealth.org/case-study/case-study-innovative-financing-debt-conservation-swap-seychelles-conservation-and

Climate Champions. 2023. "Joint Declaration and Task Force on Credit Enhancement for Sustainability-Linked Sovereign Financing." December 4, 2023. Accessed October 5, 2024. https://www.climatechampions.net/media/bldjbtzz/joint-declaration-and-task-force-on-credit-enhancement-for-sustainability-linked-sovereign-financingpdf.pdf

U.S International Development Finance Corporation (DFC). 2021. "DFC Provides $610 Million in Political Risk Insurance for Innovative Debt Conversion in Support of Marine Conservation in Belize." Media release. November 5, 2021. https://www.dfc.gov/media/press-releases/dfc-provides-610-million-political-risk-insurance-innovative-debt-conversion

Flugge, Mark L., Rachel C. K. Mok, and Fiona E. Stewart. 2021. Striking the Right Note: Key Performance Indicators for Sovereign Sustainability-Linked Bonds. Washington, DC: World Bank Group.

Fresnillo, Iolanda. 2023. *Miracle or Mirage: Are debt swaps really a silver bullet?* European Network on Debt and Development (EURODAD). https://assets.nationbuilder.com/eurodad/pages/3225/attachments/original/1701693052/debt-swaps-report-final-dec04.pdf?1701693052

Hill, Matthew, and Eric Martin. 2024. "Why the G20 Common Framework for Debt Relief Is Not Helping Poor Countries." *Bloomberg*, April 4. Accessed October 5, 2024. https://www.bloomberg.com/news/articles/2024-04-04/why-g20-common-framework-for-debt-relief-isn-t-helping-poor-nations.

Kulenkampff, Arend, and Dileimy Orozco. 2024. *From Conditionality to Commitment: A Sustainability-Linked Approach to Financing the Green Transition*. T20 Policy Brief. https://www.t20brasil.org/media/documentos/arquivos/TF03_ST_02_From_Conditionality66e199f6765ab.pdf

Humphrey, Chris. 2022. "Chapter 1: Follow the Money-The financial Machinery of MDBs", in *Financing the Future: Multilateral Development Banks in the Changing World Order of the 21st Century*. Oxford University Press.

The International Capital Market Association (ICMA). 2024. *Sustainability-Linked Bond Principles: Voluntary Process Guidelines*. https://www.icmagroup.org/assets/documents/Sustainable-finance/2024-updates/Sustainability-Linked-Bond-Principles-June-2024.pdf

Inter-American Development Bank (IDB). 2022. "Barbados Places Climate Financing Firmly on Agenda with IDB, Nature Conservancy Support." News release. September 21, 2022. https://www.iadb.org/en/news/barbados-places-climate-financing-firmly-agenda-idb-nature-conservancy-support

International Monetary Fund (IMF). 2022. *IMF Executive Board Approves US$113 Million under the Extended Fund Facility and US$189 Million under the Resilience and Sustainability Facility for Barbados*. Press Release No. 22/417, December 7, 2022. https://www.imf.org/en/News/Articles/2022/12/07/pr22417-barbados-imf-executive-board-approves-usd113m-under-eff-and-usd189m-under-rsf.

Stewart, Fiona, and Anderson Caputo Silva. 2022. "Stepping out of the comfort zone: What's next for sustainability-linked financing?" *World Bank Blogs*, December 14. Accessed October 5, 2024. https://blogs.worldbank.org/en/psd/stepping-out-comfort-zone-whats-next-sustainability-linked-financing

Sustainable Sovereign Debt Hub (SSDH). 2023a. "Data and governance requirements of sovereign sustainability-linked bonds." October 25. Accessed October 5, 2024. https://www.ssdh.net/news/data-and-governance-requirements-of-sustainability-linked-bonds

Sustainable Sovereign Debt Hub (SSDH). 2023b. "A sober assessment of the sovereign sustainability-linked bond value proposition". October 25. Accessed October 5, 2024. https://www.ssdh.net/news/a-sober-assessment-of-the-sovereign-sustainability-linked-bond-value-proposition

Sustainable Sovereign Debt Hub (SSDH). 2025. *Nature as a Shock Absorber: A Financial Materiality Assessment of Forestry-linked Sovereign Indicators in Ghana*. February 26, 2025. https://www.naturefinance.net/wp-content/uploads/2025/02/NatureAsAShockAbsorber-4.pdf.

The Nature Conservancy (TNC). 2022. *Case Study: Belize Blue Bonds for Ocean Conservation*. https://www.nature.org/content/dam/tnc/nature/en/documents/TNC-Belize-Debt-Conversion-Case-Study.pdf

The Nature Conservancy (TNC). 2024. *Nature Bonds Project Toolkit: A proven approach to leveraging debt refinancing and technical assistance for effective, durable conservation and climate action*. May 2024. Accessed October 5, 2024. https://www.nature.org/content/dam/tnc/nature/en/documents/nature-bonds-toolkit-v1-english.pdf

United Nations, Inter-agency Task Force on Financing for Development. 2024. *Financing for Sustainable Development Report 2024: Financing for Development at a Crossroads*. New York: United Nations.

United Nations Department for Economic and Social Affairs (UNDESA). 2024. *Global SDG Database*. Accessed October 5, 2024. https://unstats.un.org/sdgs/metadata

United Nations Office of the Special Adviser on Africa (UNOSAA). 2024. *Unpacking Africa's Debt: Towards a Lasting and Durable Solution*. https://www.un.org/osaa/content/unpacking-debt-africa-towards-lasting-and-durable-solution

World Bank. 2024. *Debt for Development Swaps: An Approach Framework*. Washington, D.C.: World Bank Group. http://documents.worldbank.org/curated/en/099080524122596875.

Avinash Persaud

Chapter 12
De-risking Macro-finance and Unblocking the Green Transition in Emerging Economies

Abstract: While a handful of developed countries are responsible for the majority of historical greenhouse gas emissions, a significant share of future emissions is projected to come from a few large middle-income countries such as India, Mexico, Brazil, Indonesia, and South Africa. Left unchecked, these emissions will exhaust the planet's remaining carbon budget – the amount of greenhouse gases that can still be emitted while keeping the climate within safe limits. There is now no viable path to climate stability without a rapid green transition in these and similar middle-income countries – one that outpaces what domestic savings alone can support. International capital flows will be essential. Renewable energy systems require significant upfront investment but generate long-term revenue in local currency. While much of this transition is now commercially viable in developed economies, financial flows to the Global South remain insufficient. The high cost of capital in developing countries remains a key barrier to the climate transition. A major contributor to this is the high cost of hedging foreign exchange (FX) risk associated with foreign investment in green projects. This chapter argues that this cost, however, can be significantly reduced by disaggregating FX risk into its underlying components and allocating them to entities better equipped to manage them. In the long run, the majority of this risk stems from local inflation, which can be best managed by domestic firms through inflation-indexed pricing. The remaining risk is more efficiently absorbed by AAA-rated multilateral development banks, which can provide counter-cyclical liquidity and pass it on to investors or projects at a lower cost of capital. Taken together, this policy approach has the potential to unlock capital flows and finance the green transition at the pace and scale that climate goals demand.

Note: This chapter is an updated version of the concept paper the author presented at the G20 Climate Task Force meeting in Belém in July 2024. Several individuals who were critical of the rollout of the pilot in Brazil made invaluable contributions to that paper and should be considered "co-conspirators". Most notably, these include Rogerio Ceron, Secretary of the National Treasury in the Ministry of Finance in Brazil, and Anderson Caputo Silva, Division Chief of the Connectivity, Markets, and Finance Division of the Inter-American Development Bank (IDB), along with members of his team – in particular, Sector Lead Orlando De Souza Lima and Senior Consultant Rafael Cavazzoni Lima. The ideas presented in this paper were developed in 2017 and are inspired by practical experience in three earlier pieces: Persaud (2023), Wolf (2023), and Silva and Gragnani (2017). The continued development of this idea at the Inter-American Development Bank (IDB) would not have been possible without the encouragement of Ilan Goldfajn, IDB President, and the financial support of the UK Government.

Keywords: Foreign exchange risk, Cost of capital, Currency hedging, Renewable energy, Real exchange rate, Emerging markets

Introduction

The planet has a finite budget for the stock of greenhouse gases it can accommodate before the probability of exceeding critical temperature thresholds rises above 50%. These thresholds represent major tipping points for the climate. Since the onset of the Industrial Revolution, much of this budget has been depleted, primarily due to the burning of coal and oil. Industrialization, economic development, and the accumulation of greenhouse gas emissions have historically been closely linked. Currently, approximately 85% of this budget has been used (Evans 2021). Industrialized economies, including the former Soviet Union, account for 70% of the current stock of emissions, representing over 50% of the planetary carbon budget[1] (Our World in Data, n.d.).

Partly in response to global warming, pollution concerns, and shifting industrial activity, as well as changes in consumer spending patterns associated with high-income levels, greenhouse gas emissions from wealthy nations have stabilized. However, per capita emissions in these countries remain inconsistent with the planetary carbon budget (Ritchie 2021). This stabilization is being offset by rising emissions in developing nations, where industrialization, population growth, and increasing per capita energy consumption drive higher greenhouse gas outputs. Over one billion people in developing countries lack adequate energy access (Min et al. 2024). While developed countries maintain the highest per capita emissions, over 63% of new greenhouse gas emissions originate from developing nations (Busch 2015). Moreover, emerging markets and developing economies (EMDEs) accounted for more than 80% of the increase in global energy demand in 2024 (IEA 2025).

There is no viable pathway to remaining below critical climate tipping points without accelerating investments in the green transformation of emerging economies. According to the Independent High-Level Expert Group on Climate Finance, the cost of these investments in climate mitigation and adaptation exceeds USD 1.9 trillion per year, excluding China (Songwe, Stern, and Bhattacharya 2022). Even under the most optimistic projections for domestic capital mobilization, foreign investors must contribute over USD 1 trillion annually in climate finance. However, this capital is not flowing southward at the necessary scale.

A key obstacle is the high cost of capital in developing countries, which both reflects and perpetuates economic constraints. Green energy projects typically have low

---

1 North America and Europe have contributed 70.8% of cumulative CO_2 emissions emitted between 1750 and 2021. Note that this measures CO_2 emissions from fossil fuels and industry only (Our World in Data n.d.).

operating costs but require significant upfront investment. Developing countries, by definition, face capital shortages, with investment needs far exceeding domestic savings. Even in large middle-income emerging markets, the cost of capital for renewable energy projects is two to three times higher than in developed markets and China, according to IEA (2024). In other regions of the developing world, the disparity is even greater. Despite the availability of abundant solar and wind resources, proven technologies, and standardized contracts, scalable green projects that are commercially viable in developed markets remain unviable in many developing countries. Attempting to accelerate decarbonization through trade and investment restrictions without first lowering the cost of capital would impose an undue economic burden on the very countries that need to act faster and more aggressively than wealthier nations, despite their lower historical contributions to climate change.

This chapter first highlights the substantial climate investments required in developing countries and the inadequacy of current foreign direct investment (FDI) and aid flows. It emphasizes the urgent need for structural reforms to mobilize international capital. The chapter then examines the high cost of capital in developing countries, arguing that this issue is driven primarily by macroeconomic risks, such as sovereign credit ratings and currency volatility, which deter renewable energy investments. The discussion underscores the importance of addressing both micro-level project risks and systemic macroeconomic risks to effectively reduce capital costs.

A key focus of this chapter is currency risk. The lack of deep hedging markets and prohibitively high hedging costs deter foreign investors. Drawing on prior research, the chapter identifies a significant ex-post foreign exchange (FX) risk premium in emerging markets, particularly during periods of global financial stress. This finding suggests structural inefficiencies in the pricing of currency risks. The chapter proposes several approaches to reducing hedging costs, including focusing on real exchange rates rather than more volatile nominal exchange rates, leveraging multilateral development banks (MDBs) for countercyclical support, and segmenting manageable risks. The chapter concludes by advocating for integrated platforms that involve governments, MDBs, regulators, and financial markets to address systemic risks, enhance credibility, and scale up private investment in renewable energy in developing countries.

Addressing Currency Risk to Unlock Sustainable Investment in Developing Economies

The cost of capital is the minimum rate of return projects must offer to attract investors, serving in part as compensation for risks and investors' aversion to them. Previous efforts to reduce the cost of capital have focused on mitigating project-specific risks, such as contract, technological, and regulatory risks, to make investors more comfortable holding these risks. However, despite these efforts, the cost of capital remains high, and capital flow to developing countries is low. Recent trends indicate that capital is flowing in the opposite direction. The movement of capital from developed countries, where it is abundant and inexpensive, to developing countries, where it is costly and scarce, is obstructed not only by the micro risks mentioned but also by systemic or macro-risks and uncertainties related to currency, sovereign credit, and political factors. These macro-risks significantly increase the overall risk of any project for foreign investors. Most macro-risks contribute to and manifest in currency volatility. As currency markets are often the most liquid, they also serve as effective vehicles for hedging these macro-risks.[2]

Unlike extractive commodity projects, renewable energy projects predominantly generate local currency revenues. International investors need to convert this local currency revenue into their own currency, exposing them to exchange rate risk. Not all investors hedge against this risk, but the scale of investment required necessitates attracting not only emerging market specialists willing to remain unhedged but also mainstream institutional investors who typically hedge such risks. These investors prefer to transfer FX risk to banks in exchange for a currency-hedged return, meaning a return denominated in their own currency. However, the cost of hedging – often exceeding double digits annually – lowers the currency-hedged return to levels that fail to attract global investors (Persaud 2023).

If these hedging costs accurately reflected the actual risk of currency depreciation, there would be little recourse other than attempting to boost returns, which would ultimately be borne by consumers in developing countries. However, this is not the case for the largest emerging economies. A study published by Climate Policy Initiative examined five of the largest emerging markets (Brazil, India, Indonesia, Mexico, and South Africa) over the past 20 years, analyzing 5-year FX hedge costs against actual currency depreciation. The study found that hedging costs exceeded currency depreciation 53% of the time, with an average excess of 2.7% per year[3] (Persaud 2023). The study utilized 5-year forward exchange rates, the longest period for which consistent data was available across these countries. The results would likely be even more pronounced for longer-term forward contracts. This "ex-post risk premium" rises to an average of 4.7% per year and is positive 74% of the time during 5-year periods that began with above-average hedging costs – essentially, during visibly stressed market conditions (Persaud 2023). Consequently, reducing the ex-post risk

---

2 Some believe that currency risk cannot be so critical if countries with fixed exchange rates also suffer from a dearth of financial flows. But currency risk, like broader macro-risk, is not simply eliminated by having a fixed or managed exchange rate regime. It transitions from the risk of currency fluctuations to the risk and uncertainty that the currency regime proves unsustainable at some point in the future and breaks in an adverse and likely dramatic way. This may be considered to be "devaluation risk".

3 This is the average across 372, 5-year hedges, in the exercise cited above.

premium during these periods could substantially increase currency-protected returns, thereby unlocking capital flows without requiring additional public subsidies.

To achieve this, the reasons behind the large ex-post risk premium must be addressed. In cases where no natural or intrinsic offsets exist for a given risk, risk holders must allocate capital as a buffer. A critical factor driving the high ex-post risk premium in FX hedging costs is the lack of natural offsets among traditional hedge providers. Emerging economies do not issue international reserve currencies and therefore experience the international financial cycle with greater amplitude. During periods of global financial distress, when liquidity contracts and risk appetite declines, their currencies depreciate, even in the absence of local economic changes. Governments in these economies often respond to potential inflationary pressures by tightening fiscal and monetary policies, exacerbating economic downturns. In contrast, developed countries, particularly those issuing international reserve currencies, possess greater capacity to act countercyclically, mitigating the effects of global shocks and expediting recovery.

This divergence was evident in the aftermath of the COVID-19 pandemic. Developed countries expanded monetary policy more aggressively than developing countries could, ultimately tightening policy sooner, which placed pressure on some emerging market currencies. International banks recognize these divergent risks but struggle to absorb them due to their own exposure to financial cycles. Their capital is finite, their liquidity is short-term, and their other risks correlate with economic fluctuations. As a result, when pricing emerging market currency hedges, banks incorporate buffers for additional volatility, greater procyclicality, and highly concentrated and uncertain risks. Regulatory requirements further compel them to do so.[4]

Given this dynamic, reducing the cost banks charge for hedging requires lowering the size, maturity, and cyclicality of the risks banks are asked to hedge by project promoters or investors. The recently announced "ECO Invest Brasil", developed by the Brazilian government with support from the Inter-American Development Bank (IDB), aims to achieve this by integrating strong sector regulation, stable macro-policy frameworks, and the countercyclical lending capacity of MDBs into a national platform (Government of Brazil n.d.). Here, we propose a more standardized approach that can be implemented regionally or globally, building on the FX Liquidity Facility component of ECO Invest Brasil – a platform designed for sustainability projects spanning renewable energy, resilient infrastructure, and nature-positive businesses.[5]

---

4 Insurance and bank regulations often have non-risk-based geography-based capital requirements, like the requirement on European insurers to set aside twice as much capital for risks in non-OECD countries, or four times as much for blended finance transactions compared with risks in OECD countries. We thank Amelie de Montchalin for pointing this out to us.
5 This concept aligns with strategies outlined in a 2017 internal World Bank paper by Anderson Caputo Silva and José Antonio Gragnani, titled Foreign Currency Hedge for Infrastructure Markets: Proposed Approaches Based on FX Liquidity Facility.

To reduce the size, maturity, and cyclicality of hedging requirements, we deconstruct FX risk in two ways: first, by distinguishing nominal exchange rate depreciation from real (inflation-adjusted) exchange rate depreciation; and second, by isolating extreme plunges in the real exchange rate, leaving only more modest, short-term, and symmetrical cycles. When working with sustainability projects that operate under robust regulatory frameworks allowing for long-term cost recovery and price adjustments over time, as in Brazil, the risk being hedged shifts from substantial nominal exchange rate depreciation to the more negligible real exchange rate trend. Furthermore, in countries with stable macroeconomic frameworks – such as Brazil, which has an inflation-targeting independent central bank and a government adhering to fiscal rules – the real exchange rate follows cycles around a stable long-term trend.

Due to their high credit ratings, MDBs in general, and the IDB in particular under ECO Invest Brasil, can provide countercyclical and long-term lending. In this program, a prearranged commitment by the IDB to lend dollars at market exchange rates but at the MDB's typically lower interest rate and longer maturity during periods of market stress reduces banks' exposure to short-term, asymmetric, and procyclical risks, allowing them to offer substantially cheaper hedging. Analysis suggests that in major middle-income countries with sound regulation and stable macroeconomic policies, the real exchange rate typically reverts to its mean within 2–3 years following a steep depreciation. Historical evidence supports this claim; for example, Brazil experienced a sharp devaluation in January 1999, yet within 2 years, the real exchange rate had nearly recovered its previous losses. Thus, projects can feasibly repay MDBs over 5 years through a combination of price adjustments aligned with inflation and the real exchange rate's natural mean reversion.

By segmenting FX risks into real exchange rate components and isolating non-stressed conditions, we can significantly reduce the scale, maturity, and procyclicality of the exchange rate risk banks must hedge. This, in turn, reduces hedging costs. Without such a framework, total risk remains unmanageable for banks, resulting in minimal hedging activity and limited market liquidity. However, by allocating risk where it is best managed and making residual risks more manageable, financial activity and liquidity will increase substantially. The certainty provided by this approach benefits investors, projects, and banks, lowering the cost of capital without subsidies. Furthermore, MDBs, as envisioned in ECO Invest Brasil, could lend directly to government-sponsored entities that then on-lend to eco-projects, thereby assuming government risk rather than project risk.

The Climate Finance Background

In the introduction, we explained that the planet's carbon budget is now 85% (Evans 2021). Developed countries continue to have the highest emissions per capita; however, over 63% of new greenhouse gas emissions originate from developing countries, and EMDEs accounted for more than 80% of the increase in global energy demand in 2024 (Busch 2015; IEA 2Q25).There are only three viable pathways to remain below critical climate tipping points: (1) substantial degrowth in the developed world, which, despite having some adherents, lacks significant political support; (2) keeping the energy poor in poverty, which has even less support; or (3) a massive shift in how new energy demand in the developing world is generated. Since degrowth lacks political backing and shifting future energy demand is easier than decarbonizing existing energy generation, the latter strategy warrants the most attention. This approach not only offers a promising growth path for developing countries but also presents an unprecedented challenge requiring significant effort and commitment from those who have contributed the least to climate change.

The Domestic Investment Gap

According to the Independent High-Level Expert Group on Climate Finance of COP Presidencies 26, 27, and 28, developing countries (excluding China) need approximately USD 1.9 trillion annually for the green transformation, with a significant portion allocated to shifting towards renewable energy generation and use (Songwe, Stern, and Bhattacharya 2022). This analysis focuses on the developing world excluding China, because China is unique: it is the world's largest emitter in total, though middle-ranking in per capita emissions. Moreover, China benefits from a large pool of domestic savings, a low cost of capital, and 5-year plans that guide investment. Currently, China is installing more renewable energy capacity per year than all other countries combined.

Developed country officials often argue for greater mobilization of domestic sources in developing countries, such as through developing savings and investment institutions and deepening financial markets. While more local currency financing is important, the gap between the required investment and local savings capacity is greater than often acknowledged. Even without a significant energy transition, developing countries are already capital-short. The estimated USD 2.4 trillion per year required for climate investments – comprising USD 1.9 trillion for the green transformation and approximately USD 0.5 trillion for adaptation and climate loss and damage (Songwe, Stern, and Bhattacharya 2022) – represents a significant proportion of current domestic savings. This is before considering competing demands for housing, healthcare, and education. Furthermore, the USD 2.4 trillion estimate is likely too low, given rising adaptation costs and damages from insufficient mitigation efforts. Given the urgency and scale of the investment needed, domestic savings alone cannot suffice; FDI must fill the gap. If it does not, the transition is not happening quickly enough.

Even under the most optimistic assumptions regarding domestic capital mobilization, nearly USD 1 trillion in cross-border investment per year will be required

(Bhattacharya et al. 2022). This poses a major challenge. At present, cross-border private investment in emerging markets remains low, particularly outside of China, India, Mexico, and Brazil – and even in these countries, flows are inadequate. In 2023, total FDI to all developing countries amounted to just USD 841 billion, with the majority directed toward Asia, primarily China and India. South America received only USD 150 billion, while sub-Saharan Africa received just USD 36 billion (UNCTAD 2024). Simultaneously, developing country governments face significant constraints on external borrowing due in part to the fiscal burdens of climate-related loss and damage. Official development assistance (ODA) from developed countries is estimated by the Organisation for Economic Co-operation and Development to be approximately USD 212 billion per year in 2024 (OECD 2025), falling far short of the required climate finance. Incremental reforms will not suffice; structural changes are necessary.

Cost of Capital: The Obstacle to Private Investment Flows

According to the International Renewable Energy Agency (2022), since 2015, the cost of generating electricity from intermittent renewable sources such as solar and wind has been lower than fossil fuels. However, these technologies require significant upfront capital. The need for battery storage to ensure renewables can replace rather than merely supplement fossil fuels further intensifies their capital requirements. In countries where capital is abundant and inexpensive, the long-term economic benefits of renewables, combined with supportive policies such as taxes and subsidies, have driven private investment. In developed countries, private investors finance approximately 81% of renewable energy investments (CPI 2023). This is not the case in developing countries, where capital is scarce, subsidies are limited, and the high cost of attracting foreign investment renders even standard renewable energy projects unprofitable. Currently, less than 14% of renewable energy investments in developing countries are privately financed (CPI 2023).

The cost of capital determines the minimum rate of return required to attract investment. Data from comparable solar projects worldwide indicate that while required equity returns in Europe and the United States range from 7% to 9%, in India and Brazil they range from 17% to 22% per annum. This disparity makes similar projects financially unfeasible in many developing markets (see Table 12.1). Without a concerted effort to reduce the cost of capital, the green transformation cannot occur at the necessary scale and pace. Attempting to force this transition through tariffs, developed-country carbon taxes, or investment restrictions on nongreen activities, without addressing the cost of capital, risks reducing already insufficient investment flows to developing countries. This would impose a development penalty on poorer nations that contributed little to climate change.

To date, efforts to lower the cost of capital have primarily focused on reducing project-specific or "micro" risks, such as legal, contractual, technological, and regulatory uncertainties. Considerable resources have been devoted to mitigating these risks through standardized contracts, regulatory frameworks, technical assistance, technology guarantees, and dispute resolution mechanisms via international arbitration or courts. The World Bank's Multilateral Investment Guarantee Agency (MIGA), among others, plays a critical role in these efforts. While important, these initiatives have not sufficiently lowered the cost of capital or spurred significant cross-border investment flows. Notably, required equity returns for renewable energy projects in developing countries are closely correlated with systemic or macroeconomic factors, such as credit and currency risks (see Table 12.1). Addressing these broader risks is essential for unlocking the necessary scale of investment.

Table 12.1: Return expectations from solar projects in emerging economies.

Country	S&P rating	Required return from solar project (%)
Germany	AAA	7%
United States	AA+	9%
United Arab Emirates	AA	10%
Saudi Arabia	A–	12%
Chile	A	12%
Morocco	BBB–	15%
India	BBB–	17%
Algeria	B	18%
Oman	BB–	20%
Peru	BBB	21%
Costa Rica	B	21%
Namibia	BB–	22%
Ghana	B–	22%
Brazil	BB–	22%
Nigeria	B+	22%
Bolivia	B+	24%
Tanzania	B	24%
Egypt	B	28%
Zambia	CCC–	38%
Argentina	CCC+	52%

Source: CPI (2023).

Currency and country credit risks act as a floor for the overall risks of a project. Credit rating agencies adhere to the rule that a project's credit rating cannot typically exceed the credit rating of the country in which it operates. Sovereign guarantees are only as reliable as the sovereign's credit, and the more project guarantees there are, the more stressed the sovereign credit becomes. Given that development officials focus on project and sector regulatory risks to explain the high cost of capital, the close correlation between investors' required equity returns for similar renewable energy projects and macro-sovereign credit ratings is noteworthy, as shown in Table 12.1.

Another way of looking at this is to compare the weighted cost of capital (averaging between debt and equity) across projects with the government cost of borrowing. The government's cost of borrowing is a good representation of countrywide or macro-risks, so subtracting the government's borrowing costs from the total project-weighted cost of capital leaves an approximation of the cost of micro risks (see Table 12.2). While these are approximations and deductions, they provide compelling evidence that macro-risk factors deserve as much attention as micro-risk factors – yet project de-risking and micro-risk factors often dominate the discussion. Both must be considered.

Table 12.2: Comparative project, sector, and micro risks in developed and industrializing developing countries.

Country category	(1) Weighted cost of capital (source CPI)	(2) Government cost of borrowing	(3) Project/ sector risk (1)–(2)
Developed countries (represented by the European Union as a sample group)	4.0%	−0.3%	4.3%
Industrializing developing countries – sample average	10.6%	7.7%	2.9%
Sample breakdown			
Brazil	13.1%	9.7%	3.4%
India	9.9%	6.3%	3.8%
Indonesia	10.1%	6.2%	3.7%
Mexico	9.7%	6.8%	2.9%
South Africa	10.0%	9.3%	0.7%

Notes Weighted cost of capital. The figures shown are based on 2021 annual data.
Source: IEA Cost of Capital Observatory (n.d.) and TradingEconomics (n.d.a). Data was last accessed in June 2023.

The Cost of Hedging FX and Macro-risks

A significant proportion of FDI in developing countries is in export businesses, including fossil fuels, largely because the costs and revenues are denominated in USD (or another liquid foreign currency), which eliminates local currency risk. However, when investors fund renewable energy projects in developing countries, the underlying revenue is paid by local consumers in local currency. Over the long term, it often makes sense for foreign investors to assume the currency risk, forgo hedging costs, and, from time to time, benefit from high local currency interest rates (one of the oldest empirical findings in financial markets is the "forward rate bias"). However, the largest pool of investors consists of non-emerging market specialists who are unwilling to take on trading exposures they do not feel they have expertise in. Moreover, fair-market accounting and regulatory rules often mean that institutional investors, such as insurance and pension funds, cannot focus solely on the long term but must also factor in short-term risks. Consequently, overseas investors generally avoid unhedged exposure to local currency risk. To attract USD 1 trillion in investment annually, it is these "cross-over" or mainstream investors who need to be offered returns in their currency or the option to hedge their exposure to FX risk, not the dedicated emerging market funds, which hold only a small fraction of assets in portfolio investments in developed countries.

Many countries lack deep, long-term, forward foreign exchange markets. In these countries, Currency Exchange Funds (TCX), initially established by MDBs and DFIs, do an excellent job of synthetically replicating the FX market for small investments. However, the countries whose accelerated green transformation will have a planetary impact are sizable middle-income nations with forward, swap, and derivative markets, though these markets do not extend far into the future. The problem we are addressing is not the absence of markets. Indeed, because there are few alternative ways to hedge long-term macro-risks in these countries, FX hedging markets often serve as the vehicle for hedging macro-risks that likely have an indirect FX impact, not just direct currency risk. For instance, markets often express rising political and default risks through downward pressure on currencies. However, when foreign investors or local promoters use these markets to hedge local currency revenues into foreign currency returns, the hedging costs are so high that they make the investments unattractive to foreign investors or the size of the required local currency return becomes too high for the project to be viable.

The Structural Nature of the Ex-post FX Risk Premium

If these FX hedging costs largely reflect actual risks, there is little that can be done. However, a background study for this paper (Persaud 2023) on five of the largest emerging economies, spanning the past 20 years and comparing the costs of taking out 5-year FX hedges and the actual exchange rate outcomes 5 years later, revealed that across 372 5-year hedges, the average hedge cost was 2.7% points per year more than the actual FX depreciation. This is an average, and the premium can be negative, occurring 47% of the time. The ex-post premium rises to an average of 4.7% points per year and is negative only 26% of the time if the hedge is taken out during the downward or more stressed half of the international financial cycle (see Table 12.3).[6] These numbers are consistent with other measures of the emerging market risk premium (Gbohoui, Ouedraogo, and Some 2023). If we could reduce this large ex-post risk premium, particularly during periods of market stress, and increase currency-hedged returns by anywhere from 2.7% to 4.7%, we could unlock the flow of finance without distortion or subsidy.

The no-subsidy potential of this route is significant because it makes this solution more scalable than any other approach so far. If the only way to secure private financing is through blending it with grants, it is unlikely that we will have enough grants to reach USD 1.9 trillion per year in financing. Moreover, while there will always be a role for blended finance for necessary projects that the private sector would not otherwise finance, a blended finance process would need to be carefully managed to ensure a minimal risk of public grants being wasted or perceived as wasted. The presence of a large, systematic ex-post risk premium – essentially the appearance of market participants leaving money on the table – suggests this is not a

Table 12.3: Annual ex-post excess risk premium for hedging over the last 25 years and when hedging costs exceed the trailing 3-year average, using spot versus 5-year forwards, 5 years prior.

Country	Average ex-post risk premium for all periods (annual percent)	Average ex-post risk premium when hedging costs are greater than the 3-year moving average (annual percent)
Brazil	4.71%	5.31%
India	1.95%	3.68%
Indonesia	3.18%	5.07%
Mexico	1.54%	4.33%
South Africa	2.2%	3.89%
Group Average	2.72%	4.65%

Notes: Figures for India are calculated using the 10-year bond spread as there is a longer data series. For all other countries, calculations use spot FX versus 5-year forward rates, 5 years before.
Source: Persaud (2023).

---

6 A contemporary measure of the downward part of the financial cycle when global liquidity is in retreat is when current FX hedging costs rise above a 3- or 5-year trailing average. The period of the trailing average should be about the length of the typical cycle.

missing market issue (which would provide an incentive for the market to emerge) but more likely a structural issue preventing the achievement of the much smaller ex-post risk premia seen in developed markets.

A market structure issue typically arises when there is a mismatch in the ability of market participants to absorb the risks they hold. The less capable they are of ab-sorbing the risk naturally, the more they must build additional risk premiums into their pricing to offset it, which in turn pushes demand away. There are several intan-gible factors often cited as structural justifications for high FX hedging costs. These factors are difficult to quantify or refute as explanations for a high risk premium, in-cluding poor information, institutional credibility, market shallowness, and the rule of law (Gbohoui, Ouedraogo, and Some 2023). A strong, quantifiable candidate for the structural issue is the extra volatility and procyclicality of emerging market curren-cies – risks that banks with short-term liquidity cannot easily absorb or cheaply offset. In this context, "procyclicality" refers to the tendency for risks to rise and fall in tan-dem with the economic cycle, making it challenging for entities subject to cyclical risks, such as commercial banks, to spread and diversify those risks.

Emerging economies do not issue international reserve currencies, so they experi-ence greater volatility in line with the international financial cycle. In times of global distress, when global liquidity and risk appetite retreat – perhaps due to rising inter-est rates in developed markets – these economies' currencies come under downward pressure, even if their local fundamentals remain unchanged (Kumar and Persaud 2001). Governments in these countries are then pressured to respond to the poten-tially inflationary effects of currency depreciation or to defend weakening currencies by tightening fiscal and monetary policies, thus deepening a crisis that likely origi-nated abroad. The resulting economic slowdown, exacerbated by more restrictive pol-icies, could lead to increased unemployment, heightened credit and political risks, and the rapid localization of risks that began overseas.[7] This stands in stark contrast to developed countries, which can act countercyclically, implement quantitative eas-ing, and temporarily run significant fiscal deficits to absorb the economic impact and generate quicker recoveries from external shocks.

There is substantial empirical evidence showing the ebb and flow of global liquid-ity and investor risk appetite on emerging market risk premia (Kumar and Persaud 2003), and this pattern of divergence in policy responses was most recently observed in the aftermath of the COVID-19 pandemic. Indeed, the rapid recovery of developed countries – those able to respond countercyclically with monetary and fiscal policies to the COVID-induced economic slowdown – led to such swift recoveries and early

---

7 Reflective of the nexus between the economic cycle and political pressure, there was a spike of nine coups and several coups attempts in Africa since 2020, in the wake of rising interest rates, debt, and drought (Vines 2024).

returns to normal interest rates that it complicated the policy environment for developing countries with less countercyclical capacity and slower recoveries.

International banks face short-term, cyclical liquidity, expensive capital, and highly cyclical risks. When pricing emerging market currency hedges, they must factor in buffers to account for this added medium-term volatility and cyclicality. Their regulators require them to do so, and the capital requirements for exposures to low-rated borrowers further amplify the costs for banks to offer these hedges (Griffith-Jones and Persaud 2008). Life insurers and pension funds, with their long-term liabilities, may be better equipped to absorb this short-term volatility and cyclicality, but their regulators often require additional capital for long-term investments in developing countries due to their geography and country credit ratings (Persaud 2015).

Within this market structure, the cost of hedging can only be reduced if we can mitigate the size, maturity, and cyclicality of the risks that banks are asked to hedge. "ECO Invest Brasil" is an effort to address this challenge by combining effective sector regulation, a stable macro-policy framework, and the ability of MDBs to lend counter-cyclically on a country platform to support climate and nature-positive investments, including renewable energy projects, sustainable infrastructure, and nature-positive businesses. Building on this recently announced program, particularly the Long-Term FX Liquidity Facility component, we propose a more standardized version of this approach that can be extended to other countries, MDBs, and projects.

Reducing Hedging Costs by Reducing the Size, Cyclicality, and Asymmetry of What We Ask the Banks to Hedge

From Nominal to Real Exchange Rates

In the long term, inflation differentials are a significant driver of exchange rate depreciation worldwide. Nominal exchange rates typically fall far more than real[8] (inflation-adjusted) exchange rates. For example, the Brazilian Real has depreciated by over 40% in nominal terms against a basket of trading partner currencies since the January 1999 devaluation. However, the real exchange rate has fallen by less than 5% (see Figure 12.1), implying that approximately 90% of the Real's weakness can be attributed to inflation differentials. By partnering with approved green projects that are well-regulated and where regulation allows for cost recovery and the adjustment of local prices over time with local inflation, we can reduce the substantial nominal exchange rate risk to the more modest real exchange rate risk, requiring far less to be hedged.

---

8 This is why purchasing power parity is used to estimate long-term exchange rates.

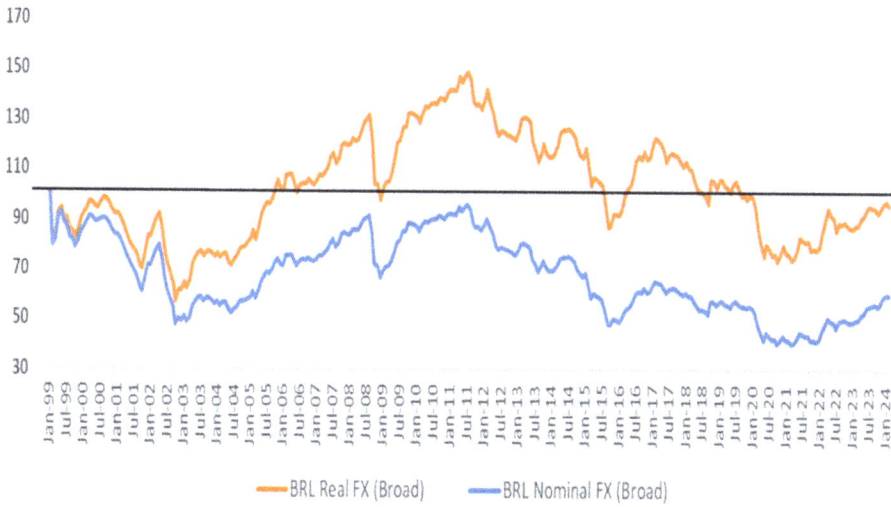

Figure 12.1: Real and nominal exchange rates for the Brazilian Real.
Source: Author's calculation based on exchange rate and inflation data from TradingEconomics (n.d.b).
Data was last accessed in June 2023.

From Long-Term Downtrends to Symmetrical Cycles Around a Stable Trend

In countries with stable macroeconomic frameworks, such as Brazil's inflation-targeting, independent central bank and fiscal-rule-following government, the real exchange rate follows broad cycles around a stable long-term trend. For example, since just before the Brazilian Real's devaluation in January 1999, the nominal effective exchange rate has never returned to that level, but the real exchange rate returned close to its pre-devaluation level eighteen months later and has spent 50% of the last 24 years above that level (see Figure 12.1). This same pattern can be observed in large emerging market economies with growing emissions and stable macro-policy frameworks, such as central bank independence and fiscal rules.

Removing Sharp Plunges in the Down Cycle to Leave Moderate Short-Term Cycles in Calmer Markets

The remaining risks can be reduced further by breaking them down into two parts. First, there are the periods when the real exchange rate plunges below its mean and returns during times of international distress, following a "V" pattern beneath the trend. When we remove these plunges and recoveries, what remains comprises symmetrical short-term cycles above and below stable trends during calmer periods.

MDBs can commit to providing a predetermined amount of foreign currency liquidity during periods when the real exchange rate falls below its stable trend, at rates close to the MDBs' borrowing rate, and over the long term against project revenues. Projects can repay these loans as the real exchange rate recovers, and their prices and revenues rise in line with inflation. In Brazil, we observe five plunges in the real exchange rate, each close to 10%, when the exchange rate is at or below its mean. Each plunge was followed by a recovery within 1–3 years (see Figure 12.1), well within the payback period for a 5- to 7-year loan in foreign currency. The observation that steep plunges in the real exchange rate are followed by recoveries is consistent with the earlier analysis in Persaud 2023, which found a high average – and mostly positive – ex-post FX risk premium during the financial and economic "down cycle".

Using "Stops" and "Limits" to Market Exposures and Separate the Plunges from the Symmetrical Part of the Risk

We can use "stops" and "limits" to market exposures to separate the plunges from the symmetrical part of the risk. Projects can hedge the symmetrical component cheaply with local financial institutions and markets or even self-insure. This is possible because, having stripped out the long downward trend from inflation differentials, stabilized the real exchange rate with a stable macroeconomic framework, and removed the sharp plunges during the down cycle, the remaining downside risk is short-term, moderate, symmetrical, and far easier for commercial banks to absorb or lay off.

MDBs may, but do not need to, lend directly to projects. As envisaged in "ECO Invest Brasil", they could lend directly to a government-guaranteed structure that on-lends to eco-projects, thereby taking on government risk rather than project risk.

Conclusion

We can substantially reduce hedging costs by unpacking risk into components that are best managed elsewhere, significantly reducing the cost of capital for renewable energy projects in emerging markets. By having projects and regulations manage inflation risks, governments manage macro-risks and stabilize the real exchange rate, and MDBs play their natural countercyclical and long-term lending roles during times of international distress, we can reduce hedging costs without subsidies. This would enable us to scale up inward investment flows to the levels needed. Bringing together critical players – sustainability projects, sector regulators, Ministries of Finance, central banks, and MDBs – on one platform or linked platforms, adds credibility, liquidity, and reassurance for investors. This proposal will help unblock the flow of foreign and local investment into the green transformation of emerging economies, increase the liquidity of local financial markets, and, importantly, reinforce and reward the benefits of sound sector regulation and stable macro-frameworks.

References

Bhattacharya, Amar, Meagan Dooley, Homi Kharas, and Charlotte Taylor. 2022. *Financing a Big Investment Push in Emerging Markets and Developing Economies for Sustainable, Resilient, and Inclusive Recovery and Growth*. London: Grantham Research Institute on Climate Change and the Environment, London School of Economics and Political Science, and Washington, DC: Brookings Institution.

Busch, Jonah. 2015. "Climate Change and Development in Three Charts." *Center for Global Development*, August 18. Accessed October 28, 2024. https://www.cgdev.org/blog/climate-change-and-development-three-charts.

Climate Policy Initiative (CPI). 2023. *Global Landscape of Climate Finance 2023*.November 2023. https://www.climatepolicyinitiative.org/publication/global-landscape-of-climate-finance-2023/

Evans, Simon. 2021. "Analysis: Which Countries Are Historically Responsible for Climate Change?" *Carbon Brief*, October 5. Accessed October 28, 2024. https://www.carbonbrief.org/analysis-which-countries-are-historically-responsible-for-climate-change/.

Gbohoui, William, Rasmané Ouedraogo, and Yirbehogre Modeste Some. 2023. *Sub-Saharan Africa's Risk Perception Premium: In the Search of Missing Factors*. IMF Working Paper No. 23/130. Washington, D.C.: International Monetary Fund.

Griffith-Jones, Stephany, and Avinash Persaud. 2008. "The Pro-Cyclical Impact of Basel II on Emerging Markets and Its Political Economy." In *Capital Market Liberalization and Development*, edited by José Antonio Ocampo and Joseph E. Stiglitz. Oxford: Oxford University Press. https://doi.org/10.1093/ac prof:oso/9780199230587.003.0010.

Government of Brazil. n.d. "Eco Invest Brasil." Accessed October 28, 2024. https://www.gov.br/tesourona cional/en/sustainable-finance/eco-invest-brasil

International Energy Agency (IEA). n.d. *Cost of Capital Observatory*. November Accessed June 30, 2023. https://www.iea.org/reports/cost-of-capital-observatory/tools-and-analysis#abstract

International Energy Agency (IEA). 2024. *Reducing the Cost of Capital: Strategies to Unlock Clean Energy Investment in Emerging and Developing Economies*. https://www.iea.org/reports/reducing-the-cost-of-capital.

International Energy Agency (IEA). 2025. "Growth in Global Energy Demand Surged in 2024 to Almost Twice Its Recent Average." *IEA*, March 24, 2025. Accessed April 1, 2025. https://www.iea.org/news/growth-in-global-energy-demand-surged-in-2024-to-almost-twice-its-recent-average.

International Renewable Energy Agency (IRENA). 2022. *Renewable Power Generation Costs in 2021*. Abu Dhabi: International Renewable Energy Agency.

Kumar, Manmohan S., and Avinash Persaud. 2003. "Pure Contagion and Investors' Shifting Risk Appetite: Analytical Issues and Empirical Evidence." *International Finance 5(3)*:401–406. https://doi.org/10.1111/1468-2362.00102

Kumar, Manmohan S., and Avinash Persaud. 2001. *Pure Contagion and Investors' Shifting Risk Appetite*. IMF Working Paper No. 2001/134. Washington, D.C.: International Monetary Fund.

Min, Brian, Zachary P. O'Keeffe, Babatunde Abidoye, Kwawu Mensan Gaba, Trevor Monroe, Benjamin P. Stewart, Kimberly Baugh, and Bruno Sánchez-Andrade Nuño. 2024. "Lost in the Dark: A Survey of Energy Poverty from Space." *Joule* 8 (7): 1982–98. https://doi.org/10.1016/j.joule.2024.05.001

Organisation for Economic Co-operation and Development (OECD). 2025. *Preliminary Official Development Assistance Levels in 2024: Detailed Summary Note*. Paris, April 16, 2025. Accessed April 30, 2025. https://one.oecd.org/document/DCD(2025)6/en/pdf.

Our World in Data. n.d. *Cumulative CO₂ Emissions*. Last updated November 21, 2024. Accessed March 5, 2025, 2024. https://ourworldindata.org/grapher/cumulative-co-emissions.

Persaud, Avinash D. 2015. "Reinventing Financial Regulation." In *Reinventing Financial Regulation*, 1–6. Berkeley, CA: Apress. https://doi.org/10.1007/978-1-4302-4558-2_1.

Persaud, Avinash. 2023. *Unblocking the Green Transformation in Developing Countries with a Partial Foreign Exchange Guarantee*. Climate Policy Initiative. Accessed October 28, 2024. https://www.climatepolicyi nitiative.org/wp-content/uploads/2023/06/An-FX-Guarantee-Mechanism-for-the-Green-Transformation-in-Developing-Countries.pdf.

Ritchie, Hannah. 2021. "Many Countries Have Decoupled Economic Growth from CO₂ Emissions, Even If We Take Offshored Production into Account." *Our World in Data*. December 1. Accessed October 28, 2024. https://ourworldindata.org/co2-gdp-decoupling.

Silva, Caputo, and José Antonio Gragnani. 2017. "Foreign Currency Hedge for Infrastructure Markets: Proposed Approaches Based on FX Liquidity Facility." *World Bank internal paper*. Washington, DC: World Bank.

Songwe, Vera, Nicholas Stern, and Amar Bhattacharya. 2022. *Finance for Climate Action: Scaling Up Investment for Climate and Development*. London: Grantham Research Institute on Climate Change and the Environment, London School of Economics and Political Science.

Trading Economics. n.d.a. *Government Bond Yields*. Accessed June 30, 2023. https://tradingeconomics.com/bonds.

Trading Economics. n.d. *Brazil Currency*. Accessed June 30, 2023. https://tradingeconomics.com/brazil/currency.

United Nations Conference on Trade and Development (UNCTAD). 2024. *Investment Trends and Prospects in the Digital Economy*. Accessed October 28, 2024. https://unctad.org/system/files/official-document/dia eiainf2024d1_en.pdf.

Vines, Alex. 2024. "Understanding Africa's Coups." *Georgetown Journal of International Affairs*, April 13, 2024. Accessed April 30, 2025. https://gjia.georgetown.edu/2024/04/13/understanding-africas-coups/.

Wolf, Martin. 2023. "The Green Transition Will Not Happen Without Financing for Developing Countries." *Financial Times*, June 30. Accessed October 28, 2024. https://www.ft.com/content/770aadbb-1583-40ae-b072-9ef44c27cc15

Stephen Hammer

Chapter 13
Multilateral Development Banks Support for Climate Action: A Story of Evolution, Rather than Revolution

Abstract: With an annual funding gap of USD 4 trillion, on average, whether for climate action or the Sustainable Development Goals (SDGs), we know that public funds alone will not be sufficient. There is an urgent need to provide a massive boost from multilateral channels and private investment in developing countries. Multilateral development banks (MDBs) have the unique ability to mobilize private capital, at scale, in emerging and frontier markets – well beyond the two-digit billion dollars. Even more important than the direct financial assistance provided by MDBs is how this assistance is used to catalyze, mobilize, and crowd in both public and private sources of funds for development. In this chapter, the discussion is centered on the catalytic role of MDBs in mobilizing climate finance. It provides sound recommendations for MDB reforms, including but not limited to devoting more attention to the provision of global public goods, and especially to climate action, improving MDBs' leverage of private finance through innovative ways of de-risking private investments in developing countries, and more concessional financing for middle-income countries, in support of climate change mitigation programs.

Keywords: Multilateral development banks, Paris alignment, CAF review, Concessional finance, Climate action, Adaptation and resilience

Introduction

With the window narrowing for action, sufficient to limit global warming to 1.5 °C above pre-industrial levels, the clamor for increased investment in mitigation and adaptation activities grows louder. Within the global climate policy community, multilateral development banks (MDBs) are viewed by both countries and financial experts as central to efforts aimed at increasing finance flows to developing nations.

Although originally created to rebuild states, foster economic growth, and finance poverty alleviation efforts, the mandate of MDBs has broadened over the years to include – and in some cases, prioritize – financing mitigation and adaptation measures worldwide.

This shift began after the 15th Conference of the Parties (COP15) in Copenhagen, where developed countries committed to providing increased support for climate action in developing nations, pledging to reach no less than USD 100 billion per year by 2020. Pressured by their boards of governors – largely composed of representatives from developed countries funding the USD 100 billion commitment – seven MDBs[1] agreed on common methodological approaches to track adaptation and mitigation support within 2 years (MDBs 2012a; MDBs 2012b).

Given the MDBs' critical role in the climate finance landscape, this chapter first provides an overview of how these institutions have established climate finance targets and aligned their operations with the Paris Agreement, with varying goals, based on sectoral needs and country priorities. Despite the evolution of MDBs' role in climate finance and technical support, critiques from advocacy groups, governments, and forums such as the G20 highlight gaps in their climate performance. These critiques often urge MDBs to expand their climate efforts by redefining their missions, improving operational practices, and increasing their capacity to address global climate challenges more effectively. The chapter concludes by recognizing the MDBs' progress in evolving their climate action role, while emphasizing the need for transformative measures, including shifts in funding priorities, stricter alignment criteria, and greater focus on adaptation and resilience to meet global climate targets.

Multilateral Development Banks, Global Climate Finance, and Paris Alignment

By 2015, when the Paris Agreement was reached, most of these MDBs had established formal targets regarding the proportion of their overall development support allocated to climate action as a co-benefit. These goals varied across banks[2], some adopted absolute numerical targets, while others set minimum percentage thresholds of total lending. These variations reflected differences in the types of sectoral lending provided. For instance, climate-related lending was more likely in countries with significant energy or agricultural portfolios, and less likely in cases where support focused on education or other fiscal matters.

Targets also partially reflected the varying levels of client interest in climate-related lending, as countries or firms prioritized other development needs, alongside climate action. Notably, these targets did not always align with the actual needs of

---

1 These are: African Development Bank (AfDB), Asian Development Bank (ADB), European Bank for Reconstruction and Development (EBRD), European Investment Bank (EIB), Inter-American Development Bank (IDB), International Finance Corporation (IFC) and the World Bank (WB).
2 For example, the EBRD set its first climate finance target to ensure that 40% of its annual investments would be climate-related by 2020, while the World Bank pledged that 28% of its total investments would deliver climate co-benefits by the end of 2020. The ADB's target was based on the total volume of support, committing to double climate financing from its own resources to USD 6 billion annually by 2020.

countries, as the required funding levels often exceeded the total resources available to support a country in any given year.

Since 2011, when the first joint MDB report tracking collective finance levels was published, MDB project-level financial support for low- and middle-income countries has more than doubled, increasing from USD 27.0 billion in 2011 to USD 60.9 billion in 2022, as illustrated in Table 13.1.[3]

Table 13.1: MDB support for climate action in developing countries (in USD billions).

	2011	2012	2013	2014	2015	2016	2017	2018	2019	2020	2021	2022
ADB	3.2	3.3	3.3	2.9	2.9	4.4	5.2	4	7.1	5.3	4.8	7.1
AfDB	1.6	2.2	1.2	1.9	1.4	1.1	2.3	3.3	3.6	2.1	2.4	3.7
AIIB										1.1	2.7	2.3
CEB												0.3
EBRD	3.7	3.1	3.5	4.1	3.2	3.5	4.6	3.8	3.9	2.3	4.8	4.3
EIB	5.6	3.7	5.2	5.2	5.1	4.3	5.5	5.7	3.6	3.2	3.4	4.2
IDBG	2.2	1.9	1.2	2.5	1.7	2.7	4.3	5	4.4	2.5	4.8	5.9
IsDB									0.5	0.3	0.7	1.1
NDB												0.5
WBG	10.7	12.7	9.4	11.8	10.7	11.5	13.2	21.3	18.4	21.3	28	31.7
	27.0	26.9	23.8	28.4	25.0	27.5	35.1	43.1	41.5	38.1	51.6	60.9

Note: Figures do not include investments unlocked as a result of financing provided by MDBs.
Sources: MDBs (2016) and MDBs (2023a).

There are several factors driving these increases in climate finance. First, four additional MDBs are now tracking and reporting their climate finance data. Second, both public and private clients of MDBs are increasingly focused on addressing climate-related needs and meeting policy commitments. This shift reflects the growing severity of droughts, heat waves, and extreme weather events that governments must manage. Countries are also striving to fulfill various national or subnational climate strategies, including their Nationally Determined Contributions (NDCs) submitted to the United Nations Framework Convention on Climate Change (UNFCCC), as part of their Paris Agreement commitments, as well as other regional obligations.

Many international institutions have also expanded their climate-related technical support since the Paris Agreement, including the NDC Partnership, the United Nations Development Programme (UNDP), the United Nations Environment Programme (UNEP), and the C40 Cities network. This support has generated additional momentum for climate action at both sovereign and sub-sovereign levels.

---

3 Several of the MDBs also support climate-related investments in high-income economies. In 2022, this amounted to an additional USD 38.8 billion in support, most of which was provided by the European Investment Bank (USD 32.9 billion) (MDBs 2023a).

Despite this broader landscape of support, MDBs deserve significant credit for the growth in climate-related lending. This progress is attributed to several factors, including heightened management attention to climate priorities, training programs that enhance staff capacity to design climate-aware projects, and a range of improved engagement strategies and analytical tools aimed at raising client awareness of the multiple benefits of climate-related investments (See Table 13.2 for some examples).

Table 13.2: Examples of MDB initiatives to support climate action.

World Bank *Country Climate and Development Reports (CCDRs)*	CCDRs are core diagnostics, designed to help countries prioritize investments, policy changes, and institutional reforms, which reduce greenhouse gas (GHG) emissions and/or enhance climate resilience, while supporting broader development goals (e.g., poverty alleviation, trade enhancement, and job creation for specific populations).
World Bank *Climate Support Facility*	A multi-donor trust fund that supports the development of countries' long-term climate strategies, promotes ambition in countries' NDCs, and integrates mitigation and adaptation measures into World Bank projects and country development plans using a whole-of-economy approach.
Inter-American Development Bank *NDC Invest*	An integrated effort to help countries design long-term climate strategies with mid-century climate goals and pathways, develop aligned NDCs, and translate short- and medium-term NDC strategies into investment and financing plans.
African Development Bank *Africa NDC Hub*	Supports long-term climate strategy development project financing, capacity building, technology development and transfer, and coordinates NDC support activities across the continent.
Asian Development Bank *Just Transition Support Platform*	A technical assistance platform aimed at helping clients plan, implement, and finance just transition efforts to manage the negative impacts – and leverage potential benefits – of transitioning away from fossil-intensive economic activities.
Multiple MDBs *Joint MDB Long-Term Strategy Program*	A technical assistance platform hosted by the World Bank to improve coordination among MDBs in supporting countries to formulate, operationalize, and finance long-term climate strategies, including net-zero emissions and climate-resilient development.

Source: ADB (2022), AfDB (n.d.), World Bank (n.d.a), and World Bank (2024).

In 2018, MDBs took an additional step by committing to jointly develop common principles that would facilitate assessments of the "alignment" of their project-level financing support with the goals of the Paris Agreement (World Bank Group 2018). The rationale for this initiative was to establish a metric that conveyed the overall climate value of a project, rather than merely tracking the costs of climate-related projects.

The MDBs also jointly identified project types as either "universally [Paris] aligned" or "universally non-aligned". Since then, each MDB has developed guidance, training, and toolkits for staff to fully operationalize these principles. This includes setting deadlines, by which 100% of their new project support would be considered aligned with the Paris Agreement. Table 13.3 summarizes the most recent climate strategies announced by each MDB, along with their respective target dates for achieving Paris Alignment.

Table 13.3: Timeline of the Paris Alignment commitment status of all MDBs.

MDB	Latest climate strategy/policy adopted	Paris alignment commitments, with dates
ADB	July 2018 (Strategy 2030)	Alignment of sovereign operations by July 1, 2023; 85% of non-sovereign operations by that same date. Full alignment by July 1, 2025.
AfDB	Climate change and Green growth framework: Long-term strategy (2021–2030) and Action plan (2021–2025)	Full Paris Alignment by 2025; currently rolling out the implementation plan.
Asian Infrastructure Investment Bank (AIIB)	Corporate strategy (2021–2030): Financing infrastructure for tomorrow	Full alignment by mid-2023.
Council of Europe Development Bank (CEB)	CEB strategy 2020–2022. Development plan with key policy goals.	Paris Alignment roadmap was approved by the CEB Administrative Council on November 18, 2022. The objective was to align direct lending by the end of 2022, with final methodologies applied starting in January 2023.
EBRD	July 2020. Green economy transition approach (2021–2025)	Application to new operations started in 2021; Full alignment of activities from January 1, 2023.
EIB	November 2020. EIBG Climate bank roadmap (CBR) and Updated EIB climate strategy covering all six building blocks, including alignment to 1.5 °C goal.	As of the 2019 Board decision, all financing was to be Paris-aligned by the end of 2020. New projects have been aligned since 2021, with a Paris Alignment framework for counterparts applied, starting January 2022. A progress review is planned for the CBR 2023 midterm review.
IDB	Climate change action plan 2021–2025	All new IDB Group operations aligned with Paris Agreement goals by January 2023, integrating Paris Alignment into IDB, IDB Lab, and IDB Invest.

Table 13.3 (continued)

MDB	Latest climate strategy/policy adopted	Paris alignment commitments, with dates
Islamic Development Bank (IsDB)	Action plan for operationalization of the Paris Alignment (2022–2023)	Fully aligning sovereign operations by the end of 2023.
New Development Bank (NDB)	NDB's general strategy for 2022–2026	New operations will align with the Paris Agreement goals by the end of the strategy cycle (2022–2026).
World Bank Group (WBG)	WBG Climate change action plan (2021–2025)	World Bank alignment for new financing flows, effective July 1, 2023. IFC and MIGA operations are 85% aligned, as of July 1, 2023, and will achieve 100% alignment by July 1, 2025.

Source: MDBs (2023b).

Unlike the easier-to-track metric of climate finance levels, it is still too early to assess the impact of Paris-aligned projects on individual countries' emission trajectories or resilience needs. This is partly because guidelines developed by each MDB provide staff with significant latitude in determining what constitutes progress toward a country's Paris goals.

For instance, the EBRD guidelines require that projects demonstrate "consistency with long-term low-carbon development" and result in a "low likelihood of carbon lock-in . . . [if] economically preferable, lower-carbon options could replace it" (EBRD 2024, 6). What constitutes "consistency" may vary between countries, as teams attempt to account for the substantial differences in the enabling environment across their client base.

Global Critique and Push for Increased Climate Financing Support from MDBs

Despite significant growth in climate finance and technical support, critiques of MDB efforts persist. Advocacy groups and governments worldwide have called on MDBs to do more, both individually and collectively.

Some of the greatest pressure comes from the G20. Other influential groups, such as the Independent High-Level Expert Group on Climate Finance (Songwe, Stern, and Bhattacharya 2022) and the Bridgetown Initiative (Prime Minister's Office, Government of Barbados 2023), championed by Barbados Prime Minister Mia Mottley, have also gained traction among MDB board members, advocacy groups, and developing-country governments.

The critique of the banks' climate performance centered on three key areas:

- The need to rethink the core mission of MDBs, given how much the world has changed since their creation.
- The need to reform operational practices to maximize their impact and reflect the changing circumstances of their clients.
- The need to scale up operations so MDBs can expand what they do well.

Mission

The call for MDBs to broaden their core mission – moving beyond their traditional focus on poverty alleviation and development to address global public goods like climate change – has existed for decades but has gained urgency in recent years. Lord Nicholas Stern recently argued that these goals are deeply interconnected. He noted that failing to address climate change undermines progress on poverty alleviation and shared prosperity, as the poor are disproportionately vulnerable to climate impacts and face greater challenges to recovery. (Dissanayake 2023).

The World Bank has responded by updating its mission statement to read: "To end extreme poverty and boost shared prosperity on a livable planet." It has also introduced new concessional financing resources to address climate change and other global public goods.

Nevertheless, some critics argue that the scale of support for global public goods[4] at the World Bank and similar institutions remains insufficient, given the global needs. They suggest that instead of relying on concessional funds to incentivize the disbursement of existing funding pools, entirely new financing structures are needed, with different goals, terms, and eligibility requirements (Khanna and Healy 2023).

Operational Changes

Proposals for reforming MDBs include both long-standing critiques and new concerns arising from climate change-related challenges. Long-standing criticisms focus on the speed of project approval and fund disbursement, particularly during emergency response situations (e.g., following climate-related monsoons or droughts) and in regular lending operations. Reforming this has proven difficult due to safeguards proto-

---

4 Prior to the recent change, the mission statement of the World Bank was "To end extreme poverty and promote shared prosperity." For more information about the new mission and strategy, see Development Committee (Joint Ministerial Committee of the Boards of Governors of the Bank and the Fund on the Transfer of Real Resources to Developing Countries) (2023).

cols that ensure the environmental, social, and fiduciary integrity of projects (DeSeve 2020). However, the Green Climate Fund's simplified approval process offers a potential model for MDB reforms (GCF 2022).

Advocates and governments have also emphasized the importance of country-owned and country-led "platforms" to improve coordination, collaboration, and co-financing of projects prioritized by sovereign governments. Governments often raise concerns about increased transaction costs caused by the lack of coordination among MDBs, while MDBs point to institutional constraints. For example, multi-year framework agreements between MDBs and a country's Ministry of Finance outline lending priorities, making rapid adjustments difficult.

Despite these challenges, platform-based collaboration is not new. For over a decade, the Climate Investment Funds' country "investment plans" have facilitated joint MDB engagement in climate-related projects. More recently, the Just Energy Transition Partnerships (JETPs) and Country Forest Packages have followed a similar model. In April 2024, MDBs announced plans to explore the development of country platforms to enhance coordination, focusing on how these platforms could be adapted to specific countries or contexts and whether they might prompt procedural changes within individual banks (MDBs 2024). Coordination could include co-financing individual projects or enabling environment reforms to support projects financed by other institutions.

In the same April announcement, MDBs launched the Collaborative Co-Financing Portal, hosted by the World Bank. This portal enables MDBs and bilateral financing institutions to securely share co-financing opportunities across their portfolios (Collaborative Co-Financing Portal n.d.). It remains unclear whether all project opportunities will be shared or whether the portal will be accessible to private financiers.

The lending instruments MDBs use to support climate action have also faced increased scrutiny, particularly as many developing countries experience debt distress. Recent data from MDBs (see Figure 13.1 below) reveals that most climate-related financial support involves debt, with grants comprising just 10% of total support (MDBs 2023a). Although grant levels have grown – from 3.8% of total MDB climate support in 2016 to 5.2% in 2018 – they remain far lower than debt-based financing. This reliance on lending reflects the MDB model, which dates back to the World Bank's founding in 1944. The Bank's primary concessional facility, the International Development Association (IDA), was not established until 1960. As concessional facilities depend on periodic replenishments, the availability of grants will continue to depend on donor contributions every 3–5 years.

Within their toolkit of debt instruments, the Banks face criticism for their reliance on senior debt structures, which prioritize loan repayments to the MDBs over other creditors. While this approach helps MDBs maintain the highest possible credit ratings and offer clients support at the lowest cost, it can also crowd out private capital. Recent data indicates that private deals supported by MDBs utilized senior debt structures nearly four times more often than subordinated roles (IDB Invest 2023).

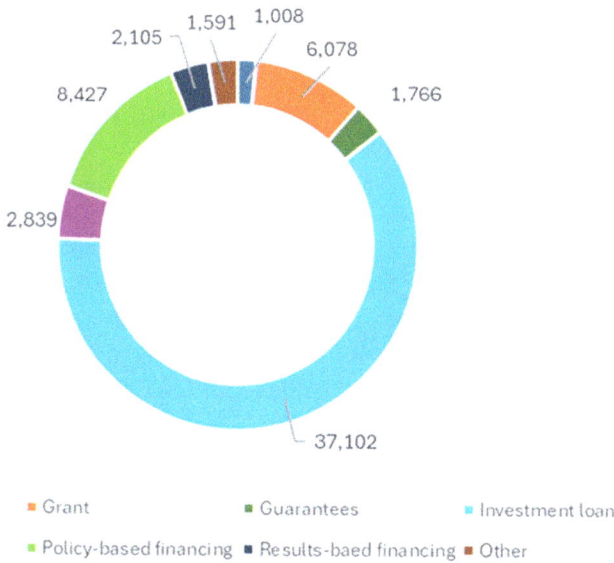

Figure 13.1: MDB climate finance by type of instruments in low- and middle-income countries (in millions of USD).
Source: MDBs (2023a).

A similar issue arises with the use of guarantees to de-risk projects and attract private capital. Since the adoption of the *Addis Ababa Action Agenda on Financing for Development* in 2015, MDBs have been encouraged to increase their use of guarantees to maximize private capital in projects. However, progress has been slow. In 2021, guarantees accounted for only 3% (by volume) of the private finance deals they supported.

In February 2024, the World Bank announced an overhaul of its guarantee business to expand private capital mobilization for climate initiatives. The reforms aim to triple annual guarantee issuance (across all sectors, not just climate) by 2030 (World Bank Group 2024). Changes include consolidating all guarantee operations under a single entity, increasing transparency around guarantee offerings, and streamlining the application and review process to reduce burdens on both public and private sector clients.

Two additional operating reforms could allow MDBs to expand their overall lending capacity. The first involves revising their capital adequacy framework practices to enable higher risk tolerance, thereby increasing lending levels. The second is a shift to an "originate-to-share" model, where MDBs transfer later-stage, performing investments to private investors. This approach could create additional capacity for new loans.

In 2020, under Italy's G20 presidency, a review of MDBs' capital adequacy frameworks was commissioned. Capital adequacy refers to an institution's ability to meet its financial obligations to bondholders if borrowers fail to repay loans. To ensure this, MDBs maintain financial reserves, determined by shareholder policies or governing documents. They may also consider rating agency evaluations to safeguard their high credit ratings.

The CAF review concluded that MDBs were overly cautious in maintaining asset reserves, partly due to their preferred creditor status, which reduces the likelihood of debtor defaults. The review also noted that MDBs have access to 'callable capital' from shareholders that has yet to be drawn upon. If other reforms are implemented, MDBs could collectively unlock hundreds of billions of dollars in additional lending capacity for clients (Boosting MDBs' Investing Capacity 2022).

Following the CAF review's release, the World Bank agreed in spring 2023 to reduce its equity-to-loan ratio from 20% to 19%, freeing up an additional USD 5 billion in annual lending capacity for IBRD clients, or USD 50 billion over the next decade (World Bank Group 2023a). In early 2024, MDBs jointly agreed to continue implementing and reporting on CAF recommendations, part of a broader package expected to generate an additional USD 30–40 billion in annual lending capacity (MDBs 2024).

The bundling and sale of performing loan portfolios is a common practice among private banks but would be a new strategy for MDBs to leverage private capital and free up lending capacity. Regional development banks may face challenges with the "originate-to-share" strategy, as loan performance in their regions may be highly correlated, with shared vulnerabilities to climate impacts or broader economic trends. This could dampen investor interest in such portfolios (Gregory 2023).

There may also be hesitancy among potential purchasers due to a lack of data on debtor performance. To build investor confidence, the G20 has recommended the expanded use of the Global Emerging Markets Risk Database (GEMs), which pools credit risk information from private and sub-sovereign lending in emerging markets. The database now covers default and recovery data across twenty-five different MDBs and development finance institutions (DFIs) operating in emerging market countries (GEMS 2024). Access to this information can help investors make more informed decisions if MDBs or other DFIs seek to sell off portions of their portfolios to private investors.

One strategy focused on providing relief to clients is the promotion of Climate Resilient Debt Clauses (CRDCs), allowing governments to suspend payments to MDBs, immediately following natural disasters. This allows governments to free up funds for disaster response that would otherwise be used for debt repayment. The Inter-American Development Bank pioneered this strategy in 2021, enabling governments to request a postponement of principal payments after triggering qualifying events. The Bahamas and Barbados have already exercised these clauses, following hurricanes (IDB 2023). The model was expanded by the World Bank in 2023 to allow the deferral of both principal and interest payments (World Bank Group 2023b).

Bigger Banks = More Lending?

MDBs have widely accepted the recommendation that donors increase their capital, allowing for a larger scale of lending support to clients. The banks can leverage this paid-in capital by issuing new bonds and using the new funds to expand their lending capacity. For instance, in 2018, shareholders in the World Bank injected USD 13 billion in paid-in capital, boosting the Bank's lending ability by approximately USD 41 billion annually, through 2030 (Kenny and Morris 2021).

"General" capital increases, such as the one provided to the World Bank in 2018, are unrestricted in terms of the types of lending they support. This has led some advocates to push for a "green" capital increase, where funds would be specifically allocated for climate- and nature-related investments. The Center for Global Development has proposed a USD 32 billion green capital increase at the World Bank, which could lead to an additional USD 100 billion in climate lending capacity by 2030 (Kenny and Morris 2021). However, donor interest in such a green increase has been limited, with conversations instead focusing on operational reforms to maximize lending within the existing capital framework.

An alternative approach being explored involves using the International Monetary Fund's (IMF) Special Drawing Rights (SDRs) as hybrid capital, which MDBs could leverage to mobilize additional resources. The African and Inter-American Development Banks (AfDB) and IDB) are pursuing this proposal, although the IMF's board has not yet determined whether it meets their criteria for the use of SDRs (IDB 2024).

More of the Same or an Even Greater Commitment?

The story of MDBs' engagement on climate is one of evolution, with incremental changes resulting in a greater focus on climate action that delivers both local and global value. Despite rhetoric suggesting a revolution, MDB governing boards seem hesitant to act too quickly or drastically. What can be done?

The COVID-19 crisis demonstrated that developed country governments were willing to expand multilateral support for poorer nations (OECD 2022), but this level of support has not been matched by MDB boards, particularly regarding green capital increases.

IMF SDRs could provide significant new resources for MDBs' climate action, but this requires both IMF board approval and action by the governments eligible to receive SDRs to ensure funds are directed toward climate initiatives in the Global South.

Discussions surrounding the green capital increase often overlook the potential drawbacks of expanding MDB lending capacity for countries already deep in debt distress. Therefore, any progress on debt relief or reform is closely linked to whether additional MDB resources lead to more effective climate support.

Regarding MDB spending, the push for Paris Alignment reframes the focus on outcomes rather than inputs. However, MDBs' alignment decisions are heavily influenced by the ambitions and policies of the governments they support. If commitments in NDCs and other national strategies fall short of Paris Agreement targets (UNFCCC 2023), MDB projects may inadvertently lock in higher-than-expected emissions for decades. Moving toward temperature-based alignment criteria – where projects are evaluated on their contribution to limiting global warming to 1.5 °C – may be the next necessary step. While challenging (Marsh 2024), MDBs have previously been innovators in new methods and could be pushed to make further advancements.

A more straightforward solution is for MDBs to reduce their financing of fossil fuel projects. Although MDB support for such projects has declined in recent years (Neunuebel et al. 2023), it still totals billions of dollars annually. MDBs could set firm deadlines for ceasing support for fossil fuel projects, similar to the prohibitions in place for coal projects. Although politically difficult, this approach has been partially embraced by the European Investment Bank, which expanded its list of nonaligned projects to exclude specific types of ineligible projects. Other MDBs could adopt similar targets with gradual deadlines, such as by 2035 or 2040, to give clients time to plan for a shift in their energy transition strategies.

Addressing more aggressive adaptation and resilience targets is a tougher challenge. While all MDBs have committed to increasing their adaptation support, achieving parity with mitigation remains elusive, particularly for projects involving private capital. To attract private investment, projects must generally have shorter timeframes and cash flow potential (Choi, Jang, and Laxton 2023).

In many respects, MDBs have been leaders in enhancing their climate action efforts, pioneering methods, setting targets, and building capacity to engage systematically on climate issues. Despite this progress, the scrutiny of these banks often surpasses the attention given to domestic spending or bilateral aid. MDBs were specifically created to address the world's most difficult development challenges, and given the urgency of the climate crisis, their leadership in this space remains crucial.

References

African Development Bank (AfDB). n.d. "Africa NDC Hub." Accessed October 22, 2024. https://www.afdb.org/en/topics-and-sectors/initiatives-partnerships/africa-ndc-hub.

Asian Development Bank (ADB). 2022. "ADB Launches Just Transition Support Platform." News release, November 14, 2022. Accessed October 22, 2024. https://www.adb.org/news/adb-launches-just-transition-support-platform.

Boosting MDBs' investing capacity. 2022. *An Independent Review of Multilateral Development Banks' Capital Adequacy Frameworks*. https://www.dt.mef.gov.it/export/sites/sitodt/modules/documenti_it/news/news/CAF-Review-Report.pdf

Choi, Esther Sekyoung, Eunkyung Jang, and Valerie Laxton. 2023. "What It Takes to Attract Private Investment to Climate Adaptation." *Climate Champions*, May 16. Accessed October 22, 2024.

https://climatechampions.unfccc.int/what-it-takes-to-attract-private-investment-to-climate-adaptation/.

Collaborative Co-Financing Portal. n.d. "Collaborative Co-Financing Portal for the Public Sector." Accessed October 2022, 2024. https://www.cofinancing.org/#/ebiz/cofinancelogin

DeSeve, G. Edward. 2020. "The Agile Journey at the World Bank." *National Academy of Public Administration*, June 22. Accessed October 22, 2024. https://napawash.org/grand-challenges-blog/the-8220-agile-journey-8221-at-the-world-bank.

Development Committee (Joint Ministerial Committee of the Boards of Governors of the Bank and the Fund on the Transfer of Real Resources to Developing Countries). 2023. *Ending Poverty on a Livable Planet: Report to Governors on World Bank Evolution*. DC2023-0004, September 28, 2023. https://www.devcommittee.org/content/dam/sites/devcommittee/doc/documents/2023/Final%20Updated%20Evolution%20Paper%20DC2023-0003.pdf.

Dissanayake, Ranil. 2023. "You Can't Have It Both Ways: Why the MDB System Cannot Deliver Both Development and Global Public Goods Well." *Center for Global Development*, July 26. Accessed October 22, 2024. https://www.cgdev.org/blog/you-cant-have-it-both-ways-why-mdb-system-cannot-deliver-both-development-and-global-public.

European Bank for Reconstruction and Development (EBRD). 2024. *Methodology to determine the Paris Agreement alignment of EBRD investments*. https://www.ebrd.com/paris-agreement-methodology.pdf

Global Emerging Markets Risk Database (GEMs). 2024. "GEMs FAQs. Updated April 5, 2024". Accessed October 22, 2024. https://www.gemsriskdatabase.org/wp-content/uploads/2024/04/FAQs-April-2024.pdf

Green Climate Fund (GCF). 2022. "GCF in Brief: Simplified Approval Process." May 31. Accessed October 22, 2024. https://www.greenclimate.fund/document/gcf-brief-simplified-approval-process#:~:text=To%20simplify%20and%20streamline%20the,from%20project%20conception%20to%20implementation.

Gregory, Neil. 2023. "Taking Stock of MDB and DFI Innovations Mobilizing Private Capital for Development". Center for Global Development. Policy Paper 290, April 2023. https://www.cgdev.org/sites/default/files/taking-stock-mdb-and-dfi-innovations-mobilizing-private-capital-development.pdf

Inter-American Development Bank (IDB). 2021. *Special Bulletin: NDC Invest – Supporting Transformational Climate Policy and Finance in Latin America and the Caribbean*. https://doi.org/10.18235/0003416.

Inter-American Development Bank (IDB). 2023. "IDB President Urges MDBs to Work Together to Use More Efficient, Innovative Financial Instruments to Scale Climate Finance". June 27. Accessed October 22, 2024. https://www.iadb.org/en/news/idb-president-urges-mdbs-work-together-use-more-efficient-innovative-financial-instruments

Inter-American Development Bank (IDB). 2024. "Special Drawing Rights (SDRs) and Hybrid Capital". May 15. Accessed October 22, 2024. https://www.iadb.org/en/news/sdrs-and-hybrid-capital

IDB Invest. 2023. *DFI Working Group on Blended Concessional Finance for Private Sector Projects (2023)*. April 24, 2023. https://idbinvest.org/en/publications/dfi-working-group-blended-concessional-finance-private-sector-projects-2023.

Kenny, Charles, and Scott Morris. 2021. "A Climate-Dedicated Capital Increase at the World Bank and IFC." *Center for Global Development*, March. https://www.cgdev.org/sites/default/files/Kenny-Morris%20Note-ClimateCapitalIncreaseWorldBankIFC.pdf.

Khanna, Rohit, and Claire Healy. 2023. "Proposal for a Global Public Goods Financing Facility at the World Bank." *Center for Global Development*, August 10. Accessed October 22, 2024. https://mdbreformaccelerator.cgdev.org/proposal-for-a-global-public-goodsfinancing-facility-at-the-world-bank/.

Marsh, Alistair. 2024. "How One of the Most Revered Climate Groups Descended Into Chaos." *Bloomberg*. May 29. Accessed October 22, 2024. https://www.bloomberg.com/news/articles/2024-05-29/inside-the-sbti-scope-3-scandal-how-the-group-is-rethinking-carbon-offsets.

Multilateral Development Banks(MDBs). 2012a. *Joint MDB Report on Adaptation Finance 2011*. African Development Bank, Asian Development Bank, European Bank for Reconstruction and Development,

European Investment Bank, Inter-American Development Bank, World Bank, and International Finance Corporation. December. https://www.ebrd.com/sites/Satellite?c=Content&cid=1395238569604&d=&pagename=EBRD%2FContent%2FDownloadDocument.

Multilateral Development Banks(MDBs). 2012b. *Joint MDB Report on Mitigation Finance 2011*. African Development Bank, Asian Development Bank, European Bank for Reconstruction and Development, European Investment Bank, Inter-American Development Bank, World Bank, and International Finance Corporation. December. https://www.ebrd.com/sites/Satellite?c=Content&cid=1395238569473&d=&pagename=EBRD%2FContent%2FDownloadDocument.

Multilateral Development Banks(MDBs). 2016. *2016 Joint Report on Multilateral Development Banks Climate Finance*. African Development Bank, Asian Development Bank, Asian Infrastructure Investment Bank, Council of Europe Development Bank, European Bank for Reconstruction and Development, European Investment Bank, Inter-American Development Bank Group, Islamic Development Bank, New Development Bank, and World Bank Group. https://www.ebrd.com/2016-joint-report-on-mdbs-climate-finance.pdf

Multilateral Development Banks(MDBs). 2023a. *2022 Joint Report on Multilateral Development Banks Climate Finance*. African Development Bank, Asian Development Bank, Asian Infrastructure Investment Bank, Council of Europe Development Bank, European Bank for Reconstruction and Development, European Investment Bank, Inter-American Development Bank Group, Islamic Development Bank, New Development Bank, and World Bank Group. https://thedocs.worldbank.org/en/doc/3258e1d4c1e84fd961b79fe54e7df85c-0020012023/original/2023-0128-MDB-Report-2022-NEW.pdf

Multilateral Development Banks(MDBs). 2023b. "Joint MDB Presentation on Paris Alignment". Conference presentation, COP28, December 8. Accessed October 22, 2024. https://www.eib.org/attachments/press/05-12-2023-joint-mdb-paris-alignment-presentation.pdf

Multilateral Development Banks (MDBs). 2024. "Viewpoint Note: MDBs Working as a System for Impact and Scale." April 20, 2024. Washington, DC. https://www.iadb.org/document.cfm?id=EZIDB0000577-986313001-135.

Neunuebel, Carolyn, Joe Thwaites, Valerie Laxton, and Natalia Alayza. 2023. "The Good, the Bad and the Urgent: MDB Climate Finance in 2022." *World Resources Institute*, December 1. Accessed October 22, 2024. https://www.wri.org/insights/mdb-climate-finance-joint-report-2022#:~:text=Oil%20Change%20International%20(OCI)%20analysis,fuel%20finance%20targeted%20energy%20access.

Organisation for Economic Co-operation and Development (OECD). 2022. "COVID-19 assistance to developing countries lifts foreign aid in 2021 – OECD". Press Release, April 12, 2022. Accessed October 22, 2024. https://www.oecd.org/en/about/news/press-releases/2022/04/covid-19-assistance-to-developing-countries-lifts-foreign-aid-in-2021-oecd-.html

Prime Minister's Office, Government of Barbados. 2023. "Urgent and Decisive Action to Reform the International Financial Architecture". Consultation Document. May 2023. Accessed October 22, 2024. https://pmo.gov.bb/wp-content/uploads/2022/10/The-2022-Bridgetown-Initiative.pdf.

Songwe, Vera, Nicholas Stern, and Amar Bhattacharya. 2022. *Finance for Climate Action: Scaling Up Investment for Climate and Development*. London: Grantham Research Institute on Climate Change and the Environment, London School of Economics and Political Science.

United Nations Framework Convention on Climate Change (UNFCCC). 2023. "New Analysis of National Climate Plans: Insufficient Progress Made, COP28 Must Set Stage for Immediate Action." Press Release, November 14, 2023. Accessed October 22, 2024. https://unfccc.int/news/new-analysis-of-national-climate-plans-insufficient-progress-made-cop28-must-set-stage-for-immediat

World Bank. n.d.a Country Climate and Development Reports (CCDRs). Accessed October 22, 2024. https://www.worldbank.org/en/publication/country-climate-development-reports.

World Bank. n.d.b "Climate Support Facility." Accessed March 19, 2025. https://ppp.worldbank.org/library/climate-support-facility.

World Bank. 2024. *Joint Multilateral Development Banks Long-Term Strategy Program (LTS-P)*. November 13, 2024. Accessed March 19, 2025. https://thedocs.worldbank.org/en/doc/5ede0588723ff3bdb3a4 d1e319f18fc5-0320052024/original/Primer-MDB-LTS-Program-Web.pdf.

World Bank Group. 2018. "Multilateral Development Banks (MDBs) Announced a Joint Framework for Aligning Their Activities with the Goals of the Paris Agreement." Press release, December 3. Accessed October 22, 2024. https://www.worldbank.org/en/news/press-release/2018/12/03/multilateral-development-banks-mdbs-announced-a-joint-framework-for-aligning-their-activities-with-the-goals-of-the-paris-agreement.

World Bank Group. 2023a. "Spring Meetings 2023: Toward a New Era." April 20. Accessed October 22, 2024. https://www.worldbank.org/en/news/feature/2023/04/16/toward-a-new-era.

World Bank Group. 2023b. "World Bank Extends New Lifeline for Countries Hit by Natural Disasters." December 1. Accessed October 22, 2024. https://www.worldbank.org/en/news/factsheet/2023/12/01/world-bank-extends-new-lifeline-for-countries-hit-by-natural-disasters.

World Bank Group. 2024. "World Bank Group Prepares Major Overhaul to Guarantee Business." Press Release, February 28, 2024. Accessed October 22, 2024. https://www.worldbank.org/en/news/press-release/2024/02/27/world-bank-group-prepares-major-overhaul-to-guarantee-business.

Adriana Erthal Abdenur

Chapter 14
The Role of Multilateral Development Banks in Climate Adaptation

Abstract: What has been the role of multilateral development banks (MDBs) in financing climate adaptation? What role should they play? This chapter highlights the mismatch between global financial architecture and the realities of climate vulnerability. While MDBs have increased their climate commitments, adaptation remains underfunded and often sidelined in favor of mitigation. In addition, current adaptation lending risks deepen the debt accumulated by developing countries. The chapter argues for a rethinking of MDB mandates to prioritize concessional, just, and locally responsive adaptation finance.

The chapter calls for MDBs to strengthen their analytical and planning capacity for adaptation, moving beyond infrastructure to support social resilience, technology transfer, local innovation, and capacity-building, including in rural and marginalized communities. Strategic use of grants, concessional loans, and debt relief, alongside innovative mechanisms like resilience bonds and climate insurance, can enhance the scale and accessibility of adaptation finance when public goods are prioritized. Crucially, locally led solutions and inclusive governance should guide MDB efforts, ensuring community priorities shape design, implementation, and monitoring. MDBs can also support integrated planning and help mainstream adaptation into national development strategies. Ultimately, enabling developing countries to transform their economies towards low-carbon development and to embed adaptation into a countercyclical, demand-driven approach will allow MDBs to play a transformative role in advancing climate resilience.

Keywords: Multilateral development banks, Adaptation finance gap, Concessional finance, Climate-resilient development, Global financial architecture, Local innovation

Introduction

Beginning in April 2024, heavy rains struck the state of Rio Grande do Sul in southern Brazil. The unusually high and prolonged rainfall, intensified by the El Niño phenomenon and climate change, swelled the state's rivers, many of which originate in mountainous terrain and flow down the slopes into the Guaíba, a hybrid lake-and-river system flanking the state capital, Porto Alegre. Due to Rio Grande do Sul's unique topography, this rainfall did not easily drain into the Atlantic Ocean. Additionally, land use patterns, including human settlements and agriculture, exacerbated the situation. As a result, the disaster was severe, with flooding and landslides directly impacting an estimated 417 municipalities and displacing more than 442,000 people. The catastrophe was also unusually prolonged, as it took weeks for the floodwaters to recede.

Beyond the tragic loss of life and widespread displacement, the damage to infrastructure, agriculture, and industry was so extensive that the economic impact of the floods reached well beyond the region itself. Given that Rio Grande do Sul is one of Brazil's economically strongest states, the floods became a national concern, extending beyond humanitarian considerations.

As the disaster unfolded, it became clear that, like other vulnerable areas in developing countries, the region urgently needs climate adaptation measures to address extreme weather events, sea-level rise, and shifting precipitation patterns. The floods in Rio Grande do Sul were not an isolated incident. The year 2024 saw record-breaking global temperatures and numerous extreme weather events, including wildfires, droughts, and heat waves. Additionally, severe flooding occurred in Indonesia, Kenya, China, and the Middle East within the first half of the year alone. The year 2025 has also brought its share of climate disasters, including major flooding in Nigeria and wildfires in the United States. This aligns with the conclusion of the Intergovernmental Panel on Climate Change (IPCC) in 2023: "It is unequivocal that human influence has warmed the atmosphere, ocean, and land" (IPCC 2023).

The increasing frequency of climate-related disasters underscores the fact that mitigation alone is insufficient (IPCC 2023). Adaptation is equally urgent – not only to safeguard existing development gains but also to prevent future losses and protect vulnerable communities. Housing, agrifood systems, infrastructure, water resources, and industries are all susceptible to climate shocks and require adaptive strategies. While low-income countries are particularly vulnerable, the case of Rio Grande do Sul demonstrates that middle-income nations are also at risk.

The need for climate adaptation has been acknowledged for decades. Within multilateral climate governance, adaptation has been on the agenda for 30 years (UNFCCC 2019). Since the inception of the international climate regime, notable progress has been made. An Adaptation Fund was established at COP7,[1] and in 2010, the Adaptation Committee was created as the principal body under the United Nations Framework Convention on Climate Change (UNFCCC) to comprehensively address adaptation.[2] More recently, COP27 launched the Sharm el-Sheikh Adaptation Agenda[3] to enhance the resilience of vulnerable communities to climate change.[3]

---

[1] The Adaptation Fund finances projects and programs that help vulnerable communities in developing countries adapt to climate change. More information can be found here: https://www.adaptation-fund.org/.
[2] The Adaptation Committee was created to promote the implementation of enhanced action on adaptation in a coherent manner under the UNFCCC and its Paris Agreement (UNFCCC n.d.).
[3] The Sharm el-Sheikh Adaptation Agenda highlights 30 global adaptation outcome targets by 2030 that are urgently needed to increase the Race to Resilience goal of building the resilience of 4 billion

Despite these milestones, adaptation continues to receive significantly less attention than mitigation in public policy formulation, legislation, and international decision-making. The gap in adaptation finance has continued to widen. According to the 2023 Adaptation Gap Report, the scale of adaptation financing needs is now between 10 times and 18 times greater than international public adaptation funding, which is already 50% higher than previous estimates (UNEP 2023). This gap is now estimated to be between USD 94 billion and USD 366 billion per year (UNEP 2023, 23).

Beyond the climate regime, the global economic context has not been conducive to expanded climate finance. The New Collective Quantified Goal (NCQG) of USD 300 billion per year, agreed upon at COP29 in Baku, represents only a fraction of the USD1.3 trillion requested by developing countries. Furthermore, despite the 2025 goal of doubling adaptation finance, the topic did not feature prominently in discussions leading up to the final decision in Baku (Watson et al. 2024). In 2021, UN Secretary-General António Guterres emphasized the need for at least 50% of total climate finance to be allocated to resilience-building and adaptation (UNFCCC 2021). However, the NCQG document issued in Baku only makes a vague reference to "achieving a balance between mitigation and adaptation" (UNFCCC 2024).

Despite mounting evidence of the accelerating climate crisis, the architecture of international climate cooperation remains fragile. Developing countries continue to call for more equitable financing, access to green technologies, and structural reform of the global financial system to support their climate goals. Forums like the UNFCCC, G20, and the COP process have helped elevate these issues, but progress has been slow and uneven. Meanwhile, the scale of climate-linked disasters – from mega fires and floods to food system collapse – continues to rise, exposing a widening gap between the promises of global climate governance and the lived reality in the Global South.

Compounding these systemic challenges is the resurgence of geopolitical polarization and nationalist politics, which have weakened the multilateral institutions tasked with addressing shared threats. Efforts to reform the Bretton Woods institutions, unlock loss and damage financing, or implement global taxation mechanisms have been met with resistance, often from countries with the greatest historical responsibility for emissions. As a result, many climate-vulnerable countries are being forced to pursue adaptation under conditions of fiscal austerity and mounting debt, even as their exposure to climate shocks deepens.

The return of Donald Trump to the presidency of the United States in 2025 has created new obstacles to global climate governance. Within weeks of taking office, Trump officially withdrew the United States from the Paris Agreement once again – undermining a core pillar of international climate cooperation and sending shock-

---

people to accelerate transformation across five impact systems (UN Climate Change High-Level Champions n.d.).

waves through already-delicate negotiations. In addition to rolling back domestic climate regulations, his administration has openly opposed references to climate finance in multilateral forums and blocked consensus on joint communiqués at the G20 and other platforms. Sharp reductions in U.S. contributions to international climate funds have further signaled Washington's retreat from global responsibility.

This reversal has serious implications for developing countries, including on the adaptation front. The Trump administration has continued its combative stance toward multilateral development banks, opposing capital increases and blocking governance reforms that would give greater voice to emerging economies. U.S. resistance has stalled efforts to operationalize new loss and damage mechanisms and slowed momentum behind proposals for debt relief tied to climate resilience. For many countries in the Global South, especially Small Island Developing States (SIDS) and climate-vulnerable regions in Africa, Asia, and Latin America, this means less access to concessional finance and a growing risk of being locked into cycles of underinvestment and disaster recovery. Without a coherent and supportive global financial framework, adaptation goals under the Paris Agreement risk becoming unreachable.

At the same time, fiscal constraints in most developing countries have been exacerbated by overlapping crises – a trend often reinforced by the austerity measures prescribed by traditional international financial institutions, particularly the Bretton Woods organizations. Dozens of countries remain deeply burdened by sovereign debt and are unable to mobilize domestic resources to address their most pressing challenges. Many also struggle to raise external funding due to high capital costs and perceived investment risks. As a result, more than 3.3 billion people live in countries where debt service outpaces spending on education and healthcare (United Nations n.d.). These financial constraints also limit their ability to implement climate adaptation measures.

As Summers and Singh (2024) put it, "rising interest rates and bond and loan repayments meant that nearly USD 200 billion flowed out of developing countries to private creditors in 2023, completely dwarfing the increased financing from the international financial institutions. "Billions to trillions" the catchphrase for the World Bank's plan to mobilize private-sector money for development, has become "millions in, billions out". The adaptation gap must be understood not only within the context of local, national, and regional needs but also in light of the deeply regressive nature of the current international financial system.

Over the past few years, Official Development Assistance (ODA) flows have become increasingly precarious. While they initially appeared to grow, much of the increase was driven by donor countries reallocating funds toward refugee-related expenditures within their own borders (Staur 2023). Today, ODA is not only stagnating but openly retracting, as many high-income countries divert public resources to defense and military budgets in response to heightened geopolitical tensions. This shift signals a worrying deprioritization of long-term development cooperation and climate action. Meanwhile, vague promises about "unlocking private finance" – including through MDBs – have not materialized into meaningful increases in concessional or accessible financing for developing countries. The last issuance of Special Drawing Rights (SDRs) by the International Monetary Fund (IMF), in response to the COVID-19 pandemic, disproportionately benefited wealthy nations with the capacity to create their own liquidity: nearly 60% of the allocation went to high-income countries (Eichengreen 2021), leaving many low-income economies with limited support in the face of cascading climate and development challenges.

Inadequate adaptation financing has enormous implications – not only for those directly affected by fatalities, injuries, trauma, and loss of infrastructure, but also for global economic stability. Failure to adapt dramatically increases the need for resources to address climate-related losses and damages. At the current pace of climate action, even greater losses are expected in the future. Conversely, investing in adaptation can significantly reduce climate-related costs. For example, the Global Commission on Adaptation has estimated that providing just 24-h warning before a storm or heatwave can reduce resulting damage by 30% (Global Commission on Adaptation 2019). The gap in adaptation financing foreshadows even greater needs in the future as climate emergencies intensify.

The Role of Multilateral Development Banks

MDBs can and should play a key role in climate adaptation – both by incorporating adaptation into their operations and by channeling greater and more effective resources toward it. Additionally, MDBs must integrate adaptation financing into broader institutional reform efforts.

While MDBs are not the only potential sources of climate financing for developing countries, they remain a critical channel. Other potential sources include domestic resource mobilization, progressive taxation, national and public development banks, solidarity levies, global climate funds, and direct bilateral flows. As of 2019, MDBs collectively managed nearly USD 2 trillion in assets worldwide: USD 695 billion in global MDBs, USD 1.2 trillion in regional development banks (RDBs), and USD 76 billion in subregional development banks (SRDBs) (Ray 2019). These institutions can play a crucial role in developing innovative financial instruments – such as climate risk insurance, green bonds, and blended finance – that help mitigate climate-related risks and make adaptation financing more accessible.

MDBs can also provide technical and financial support to developing countries as they implement their National Adaptation Plans (NAPs) and related policies, including at the subnational level. Regional and subregional MDBs can fund cross-border adaptation initiatives that individual states may struggle to finance alone. These capabilities are especially relevant for boosting climate resilience across the Global South.

Over the past decade, MDBs have increased their engagement with climate change. Initially, this engagement focused on integrating climate metrics into bank operations and establishing financing targets. In 2022, MDBs allocated approximately USD 66 billion to climate finance – an increase of 24% compared to the previous year (Neunuebel et al. 2023). The proportion directed to low- and middle-income countries also grew by 20%, from USD 50.7 billion in 2021 to USD 60.7 billion in 2022. However, inflationary pressures make it difficult to determine whether this increase reflects real gains (Neunuebel et al. 2023).

Beyond increasing the volume of climate financing, MDBs have also deepened their political and strategic engagement. In 2017, several large MDBs committed to aligning their operations with the Paris Agreement by July 1, 2023. This process has included developing methodological principles for assessing different categories of climate-related operations.

MDBs also play a role in adaptation financing through their growing engagement with country platforms designed to build pipelines of investable projects. In theory, these platforms can help direct financial flows from developed to developing countries, supporting both national development priorities and international climate goals. However, concerns remain about whether MDBs are equipped to integrate the "just transition" dimension into their platforms. The concept of justice can create tensions within MDBs, given their historical focus on economic efficiency, which often overlooks equity and fairness in resource allocation. Additionally, while MDBs aim to reduce poverty and promote inclusive growth, their mandates prioritize economic considerations, restricting their ability to engage in political issues – even though justice is crucial for effective poverty reduction and sustainable development (Steadman et al. 2024; Neunuebel et al. 2023).

Collaboration across MDBs is also increasingly relevant to adaptation financing. On April 20, 2024, leaders of 10 MDBs announced joint steps to work more effectively as a system, aiming to enhance the scale and impact of their efforts (IDB 2024). Among their commitments is the expansion of lending capacity by an additional USD 300–400 billion over the next decade. They also pledged to continue aligning operations with the Paris Agreement and to develop a unified approach to measuring climate adaptation and mitigation outcomes.

At COP29 in Baku, the 10 largest MDBs projected that by 2030, their collective annual climate financing for low- and middle-income countries will reach USD 120 billion, including USD 42 billion specifically for adaptation. Additionally, they committed to mobilizing USD 65 billion from the private sector for developing countries. These commitments mark an important step forward, but whether MDBs will fully implement them – and whether they will be sufficient to close the adaptation financing gap – remains to be seen, especially in light of recent political changes.

Since Trump's reelection on a climate denial platform, the legacy multilateral institutions have visibly stifled their climate ambitions. Both the World Bank and IMF have trodden a fine line during the 2025 Spring Meetings – pulling back from bold climate commitments and prioritizing traditional mandates. The U.S. Treasury has explicitly labeled climate and social initiatives as "mission creep", urging the Bretton Woods institutions to re-center on macroeconomic stability and even expand finance for fossil fuels and nuclear energy. Without an assertive U.S. or commitment on adaptation grants or loss and damage funding, support for climate adaptation in vulnerable countries tends to wither.

The consequences for developing nations could be profound. With MDBs sidelining climate action and rich nations increasingly rerouting funds toward military budgets, the already-scarce climate adaptation finance may evaporate. This retrenchment further constrains low-income countries' ability to build resilience, forcing them into cycles of humanitarian aid (itself also in retreat) and reconstruction rather than sustainable development. If this trend continues, it may render key climate commitments under the Paris Agreement hollow, deepening global inequities and leaving the most climate-impacted nations insufficiently equipped to cope with escalating environmental risks.

The Adaptation Attention Gap

Despite the growing urgency of climate adaptation, mitigation continues to dominate the climate portfolios of MDBs. In 2022, adaptation financing accounted for only 37% of total MDB climate funds (IDB 2024). This proportion has remained relatively unchanged, even though more than 70 countries have issued or are developing NAPs (UNEP 2022).

Additionally, definitions of adaptation and related accounting methods vary widely across MDBs. Due to resistance from wealthier nations, there is no universally agreed-upon definition of climate finance. Consequently, the term encompasses a broad range of parameters and practices, often conflated with related concepts such as sustainable finance, green finance, and low-carbon finance. In some MDBs, adaptation appears as a secondary consideration within mitigation projects, rather than as a distinct category deserving of dedicated analysis, planning, and monitoring.

Several factors explain why MDBs – and other actors – have historically prioritized mitigation over adaptation. First, mitigation has been a central focus of multilateral climate negotiations since the inception of the climate regime. While adaptation has also been on the agenda, it remains less understood and harder to quantify compared to mitigation. Unlike mitigation, which involves measurable emissions reductions, adaptation requires localized, long-term interventions that are often difficult to assess in immediate and tangible terms, leading to reduced political and public attention.

Second, wealthier nations, which wield significant influence over MDBs, tend to favor initiatives that provide direct benefits to them. Over the past 5 years, this preference has manifested in a discourse emphasizing "global public goods" and "global challenges" – often at the expense of addressing localized climate adaptation needs. Mitigation is perceived as a universal necessity; for instance, reducing a gigaton of carbon dioxide emissions has the same global impact regardless of where it occurs. By contrast, adaptation measures are highly context specific. Coastal cities may require sea barriers and floodable parks, while mountainous regions might prioritize landslide risk reduction and reforestation. Despite the localized nature of adaptation, inadequate measures can have broader consequences, such as disruptions to global supply chains and regional water shortages due to altered precipitation patterns and glacier melt.

More broadly, the prioritization of mitigation stems from the lack of adequate representation of developing nations in key decision-making spaces within the international financial system. Institutions such as the World Bank and the International Monetary Fund (IMF) remain dominated by wealthier nations, despite frequent rhetoric about "country-led development". This imbalance mutes the climate-related demands of developing countries, particularly those concerning adaptation.

Third, within the current financing landscape, mitigation is more attractive to private investors than adaptation. While renewable energy markets have matured, creating profit-driven opportunities for mitigation investments, adaptation projects often present unclear financial returns and this ambiguity discourages private investors. MDBs, increasingly focused on leveraging private capital rather than mobilizing grants and concessional resources, consequently, favor mitigation as the more financially viable path.

Private capital is not a reliable foundation for adaptation financing. While mitigation initiatives frequently generate direct economic gains through emissions reductions and energy efficiency improvements, adaptation investments tend to involve long-term commitments with uncertain or indirect returns. Large-scale adaptation projects, such as coastal defenses, drought-resistant agriculture, and flood mitigation infrastructure, require substantial upfront costs, ongoing maintenance, and technical expertise, making them less attractive to profit-seeking investors. Additionally, adaptation efforts often face policy and regulatory challenges, including unclear land tenure laws, bureaucratic inefficiencies, and legal uncertainties that hinder project implementation in many rural communities.

Although there are some instances where private sector involvement in adaptation may be viable – such as when businesses seek to mitigate risks from climate-related disruptions or respond to shareholder pressures – these cases remain exceptions rather than the norm. The 2023 Adaptation Gap Report highlights that while private-sector adaptation efforts exist in sectors such as water, energy, and agriculture, they remain difficult to track and are largely fragmented (UNEP 2023).

Public sector financing alone is insufficient to meet the vast and growing climate adaptation needs. Traditional climate finance mechanisms have struggled to attract private sector investment in climate-resilient projects due to high perceived risks, long payback periods, and uncertain financial returns. However, innovative financing mechanisms could play a complementary role in scaling up adaptation funding. These include repurposing existing financial instruments, developing new tools, and introducing hybrid mechanisms – particularly in nature-based finance.

Several financial instruments have been used to support priorities outlined in NAPs, including debt instruments, financial risk instruments, and catastrophe bonds. For example, the Caribbean Catastrophe Risk Insurance Facility (CCRIF) provides financial instruments to assist Caribbean and Central American nations in managing climate-related financial risks, particularly those associated with extreme weather events such as hurricanes. By issuing catastrophe bonds, the CCRIF enables countries to access rapid payouts in the aftermath of disasters, ensuring they can meet emergency adaptation needs without destabilizing national budgets. Such mechanisms align with NAP priorities by enabling swift responses to climate impacts and supporting critical adaptation measures such as rebuilding infrastructure and enhancing disaster preparedness.

Dedicated funds sourced from both governments and the private sector for results-based adaptation could also disburse funds to countries that meet set thresholds for adaptation in specific areas. Emerging areas, such as payments for ecosystem services, could be leveraged to finance certain types of adaptation.

The use of innovative financing instruments in climate adaptation and development presents new opportunities to address the immense funding gaps faced by developing countries. During its presidency of the G20, for instance, Brazil began working on a new model for financing standing forests. The Tropical Forest Forever Facility (TFFF) will use an investment fund to compensate developing countries with tropical forests for their conservation (G20 Brasil 2024). In addition to boosting mitigation, this represents a solution for adaptation: forests provide vital ecosystem services, such as regulating water cycles, preventing soil erosion, and mitigating floods and droughts. By conserving forests, the TFFF aims to protect these natural systems, which in turn reduces the vulnerability of communities to climate impacts, such as extreme weather events or disruptions to water supply. Additionally, tropical forests are home to a wide range of species, and maintaining biodiversity can improve ecosystem resilience. Diverse ecosystems are better able to withstand and recover from climate shocks, so protecting these forests through instruments like TFFF helps preserve the resilience of both human and ecological systems to changing conditions.

It is critical that innovative financial instruments for climate adaptation are designed and implemented in a way that reinforces, rather than undermines, the capacity of the state and its ability to design and enforce effective public policies. If the focus is solely on mobilizing private capital and creating atomized solutions that operate outside the state's framework, there is a risk of exacerbating existing governance challenges and creating a fragmented landscape of climate action. This could ultimately lead to a situation in which the state loses control over key decisions related to climate resilience and development, potentially undermining the long-term sustainability of adaptation efforts.

Beyond the Numbers

It is not enough to address the gap in adaptation but also its accessibility and quality. The type of financing offered and the conditions imposed can have repercussions for the entire economy of a country.

MDBs have traditionally played a dominant role in financing and guiding development and climate adaptation in developing countries. This can lead to a cyclical dependency, where countries rely on MDBs for financial resources, technical expertise, and policy guidance, rather than taking full ownership of their own adaptation and development processes. To break this cycle, MDBs should shift from being the primary drivers to enablers of sustainable development and climate action, supporting countries in developing their own financing mechanisms and building local capacity.

In the context of climate adaptation finance, this means MDBs should focus on empowering countries to finance their own adaptation efforts. They can do so by helping countries access diverse sources of climate finance (such as private capital and climate risk insurance), strengthening domestic financial institutions, and fostering policies that align with local priorities.

Thus far, adaptation is being financed primarily through debt. The Global Center on Adaptation estimates that, both globally and in Africa, the proportion of adaptation financing carried out through debt increased from 70% of flows in 2019–2020 to 80% in 2021–2022 (Global Center on Adaptation 2023). Given the extent of the sovereign debt crisis, this tends to aggravate indebtedness rather than create space for more adaptation capacity.

Even when concessional adaptation financing is available, many developing countries and vulnerable communities face hurdles in accessing these resources, due to factors such as limited financial resources, weak institutional capacity, and inadequate regulatory frameworks. Small Island Developing States (SIDS), Least Developed Countries, and rural communities – particularly vulnerable to climate impacts – struggle to access finance from traditional sources such as banks and international development institutions.

More broadly, we need to consider different types of adaptation. In many circumstances, adaptation is intertwined with humanitarian aid. This happens because, in the absence of a more precautionary approach, political momentum for adaptation tends to surge after major disasters. Yet, in humanitarian settings, additional challenges to adaptation arise, such as destroyed infrastructure, displacement and migration, and scarcities in health, food, and energy. Attention and resources tend to focus on these acute crises rather than on long-term adaptation measures.

Outside of acute humanitarian settings, adaptation initiatives can be based on a more long-term perspective. Some adaptation projects often require the construction or improvement of infrastructure, such as flood barriers, stormwater drainage systems, and resilient buildings. These projects create jobs and income in construction, engineering, and related sectors. Thus, there is a need to better understand how adaptation can contribute to sustainable development. However, the link is not automatic and therefore cannot be taken for granted. In some instances, certain approaches to adaptation may pose additional challenges for sustainable development or exacerbate existing societal challenges. Further research is needed on the conditions under which adaptation contributes to the fight against hunger, poverty, and inequality – or, more broadly, to the entire gamut of SDGs.

Some adaptation initiatives may fall under the category of transformative adaptation. The UNFCCC has defined transformative adaptation as "actions aiming at adapting to climate change resulting in significant changes in structure or function that go beyond adjusting existing practices" (UNFCCC 2023). Atomized, incremental adaptation initiatives are often necessary – and, under certain circumstances, may add up to transformative adaptation, especially if designed within the context of longer-term planning. But a precautionary approach requires moving beyond a strictly project-based focus and considering how, and to what extent, adaptation initiatives can contribute to the structural transformation of a country's or territory's economy. In other words, whenever possible, adaptation should be designed beyond just reducing the risk of climate-related damages and linked to ways to improve well-being and dignity in the long term, whether through healthcare, infrastructure, education, or improved livelihoods.

Some areas in which there may be overlaps between adaptation and development include:

– Sustainable management of natural resources, such as forests, wetlands, and coastal areas. Jobs and income can be created in ecosystem restoration, forestry, water management, and biodiversity conservation.
– Transitioning to renewable energy sources and improving energy efficiency are key components of climate adaptation. If carried out in a just and inclusive manner, this shift can create jobs in renewable energy industries like solar energy, wind energy, and hydroelectric power, as well as in energy-efficient construction and retrofitting. It can also boost public infrastructure.
– Climate-resilient agricultural practices, such as drought-resistant crops and improved irrigation techniques, can enhance food security and create employment opportunities in farming, agribusiness, and agricultural research. This is especially important in regions where youth have limited employment opportunities.
– Investing in disaster risk reduction measures, early warning systems, and emergency response capabilities can save lives and livelihoods in the face of climate-related disasters. Jobs are created in disaster preparedness, emergency response, and community resilience building.

- Climate adaptation efforts can enhance the resilience of tourism destinations and recreational areas, thereby supporting tourism-related businesses and creating jobs in hospitality, recreation, and ecotourism.
- Developing and deploying innovative technologies for climate adaptation, such as climate-resilient infrastructure, early warning systems, and weather forecasting tools, can spur technological innovation and create employment in the technology sector. This requires consideration of local development – or co-development – of green technologies, not just their transfer.
- Climate adaptation can play a crucial role in eradicating hunger and boosting food security by addressing the challenges posed by climate change to agricultural productivity and food systems. Key strategies include resilient agricultural practices such as conservation agriculture, agroforestry, crop diversification, and integrated pest management; developing and disseminating climate-resilient crop varieties that are tolerant to heat, drought, and waterlogging; and improving water management practices, such as rainwater harvesting, small-scale irrigation, and water-efficient irrigation techniques. These can be combined with social protection measures such as targeted cash transfers, food assistance, and labor inclusion initiatives.

Looking Ahead

There are several areas in which MDBs can work, whether alone or collectively, to improve the scale, access, effectiveness, and justness of adaptation financing. The first step is to dedicate analysis, research, and planning to this sub-area of climate finance, rather than treating it as an afterthought. Like mitigation, adaptation requires conceptual work in defining parameters, criteria, and methodologies.

Second, MDBs are well-equipped to strategically direct grants and concessional loans, as well as promote debt relief and forgiveness. In the current scenario, SDRs issuances to developing countries are necessary to increase liquidity, but longer-term solutions must also be designed as part of the reform of the international financial system. These efforts should include greater transparency and stakeholder engagement. Innovative finance mechanisms, such as green bonds, climate insurance, resilience bonds, and public–private partnerships, may offer new opportunities for mobilizing funding for climate adaptation, provided they offer flexible and affordable financing options for adaptation projects.

The role of MDBs in climate adaptation should extend beyond mobilizing finance. There is also need for greater engagement on technology and capacity-building support for different types of adaptation. Rural areas require adaptation funding and support tailored to their specific needs, especially in terms of boosting food and energy sovereignty and enhancing resilience in indigenous, traditional, and local communities. In some instances, adaptation involves planned relocation, which must always respect human rights, such as through consultation and free, informed, and prior consent.

Whether in urban or rural areas, social participation is essential to the design, implementation, and monitoring of adaptation initiatives. While the failure to adapt has consequences that reach beyond the local level, the design of solutions must be locally focused. Top-down decisions about adaptation can do more harm than good. In contrast, community-based approaches to climate adaptation empower local communities to identify their own adaptation priorities, mobilize resources, and implement solutions tailored to their needs and circumstances. Furthermore, adaptation initiatives that engage local communities through participatory planning processes, community-based adaptation projects, and citizen-led initiatives (such as community gardens and tree planting campaigns) are more sustainable in the long term. By involving communities as partners in the adaptation process, MDBs can build resilience, enhance social cohesion, and promote sustainable development from the ground up.

MDBs can also help developing countries with integrated planning by offering technical expertise, project management support, and access to procurement and contracting mechanisms. They can assist countries in incorporating climate considerations into land-use planning, transportation infrastructure, and building design, thereby creating more resilient and sustainable cities and communities. Additionally, they can support climate risk assessments, vulnerability studies, and sectoral planning processes to mainstream adaptation into development policies and plans.

MDBs, whether acting alone or collaboratively, should explore how governance reforms can enhance the effectiveness of climate finance and action. Strengthening the voice of developing countries and improving climate adaptation financing can only be achieved through structural reforms.

These topics are under intensifying debate as part of the Baku to Belém Finance Roadmap. Expectations for COP30 center heavily on scaling and structuring adaptation finance. With adaptation placed at the core of the agenda, the conference is expected to formalize global indicators for tracking adaptation progress, such as climate vulnerability reductions, resilience-building measures, and local community engagement. These indicators can help ensure greater accountability, comparability, and transparency in how adaptation finance is allocated and assessed.

COP30 is also expected to advance the implementation of the pledge to double adaptation finance by 2025 (first made at COP26) and push for deeper reforms in the international financial architecture. These reforms – such as increasing the concessionality of MDB financing, restructuring debt for climate-vulnerable countries, and expanding the issuance and redistribution of SDRs – can help unlock more predictable, accessible, and equitable climate finance flows for the Global South. By linking clear metrics with structural reform, COP30 has the potential to shift adaptation finance from a fragmented, underfunded afterthought to a core pillar of climate action. The Brazilian Presidency of COP30 has also launched a Circle of Finance Ministers, a high-level platform that can strengthen political commitment and align economic governance with climate resilience goals, including on adaptation finance in developing countries.

However, without a renewed commitment by developed countries to the global climate agenda – particularly to adaptation finance – rather little can ultimately be accomplished in the adaptation agenda at any scale. The effectiveness of any effort by MDBs hinges on the political will and financial contributions of their largest shareholders, who are overwhelmingly from the Global North. While domestic resource mobilization is often cited as a solution, especially in the context of increasing tax revenues or leveraging local capital markets, it can only go so far – particularly in countries facing high debt burdens, limited fiscal space, and competing development priorities. In many cases, it cannot go far at all. If wealthy nations continue to deprioritize climate and development cooperation, redirecting public funds toward military spending or narrowing multilateral mandates, MDBs will remain constrained in both ambition and delivery. The gap between rhetoric and resourcing will widen, leaving vulnerable countries exposed to escalating climate risks without adequate financial buffers or planning support. Reversing this trend will require not only more resources but also a genuine recommitment to multilateralism, solidarity, and global equity.

References

Eichengreen, Barry. 2021. "This SDR Allocation Must Be Different." *The Project Syndicate*, September 10, 2021. Accessed November 27, 2024. https://www.project-syndicate.org/commentary/how-to-get-new-imf-sdrs-to-poor-countries-by-barry-eichengreen-2021-09.

G20 Brasil. 2024. "Brasil Creates Fund for Tropical Forest Preservation." *G20*, October 14, 2024. Accessed November 27, 2024. https://g20.gov.br/en/news/brasil-creates-a-billion-dollar-fund-for-tropical-forest-preservation.

Global Center on Adaptation. 2023. *State and Trends in Adaptation Report 2023*. Rotterdam and Abidjan. https://gca.org/wp-content/uploads/2024/04/STA23_web-version.pdf

Global Commission on Adaptation. 2019. *Adapt Now: A Global Call for Leadership on Climate Resilience*. Global Center on Adaptation: Rotterdam, The Netherlands

Inter-American Development Bank (IDB). 2024. "Multilateral Development Banks Deepen Collaboration to Deliver as a System." *Inter-American Development Bank*, April 20, 2024. Accessed November 27, 2024. https://www.iadb.org/en/news/multilateral-development-banks-deepen-collaboration-deliver-system.

Intergovernmental Panel on Climate Change (IPCC). 2023. *Summary for Policymakers. In Climate Change 2023: Synthesis Report. Contribution of Working Groups I, II and III to the Sixth Assessment Report of the Intergovernmental Panel on Climate Change*, edited by Core Writing Team, H. Lee, and J. Romero, 1–34. Geneva, Switzerland: IPCC. https://doi.org/10.59327/IPCC/AR6-9789291691647.001.

Neunuebel, Carolyn, Joe Thwaites, Valerie Laxton, and Natalia Alayza. 2023. "The Good, the Bad and the Urgent: MDB Climate Finance in 2022." *World Resources Institute*, December 1, 2023. Accessed November 27, 2024. https://www.wri.org/insights/mdb-climate-finance-joint-report-2022.

Ray, Rebecca. 2019. "Who Controls Multilateral Development Finance?" *GEGI Working Paper 026*, Global Development Policy Center, March 2019. Accessed November 27, 2024. https://www.bu.edu/gdp/files/2019/04/GEGI-WP-R-Ray-2019-Power-Weights.pdf

Staur, Carsten. 2023. "The Elephant in the Room: In-Donor Refugee Costs." *OECD Development Matters*, May 11, 2023. Accessed November 27, 2024. https://oecd-development-matters.org/2023/05/11/the-elephant-in-the-room-in-donor-refugee-costs.

Steadman, Shandelle, Sarah Colenbrander, Nick Simpson, Alastair McKechnie, and Megan Cole. 2024. "Putting the 'Just' in Just Energy Transition Partnerships: What Role for the Multilateral Development Banks?" *ODI Working Paper*, March 2024. London: ODI. https://media.odi.org/documents/Putting_the_just_in_Just_Energy_Transition_Partnerships-what_role_for_the_MDBs.pdf

Summers, Lawrence H., and N.K. Singh. 2024. "The World Is Still on Fire." *Project Syndicate*, April 15, 2024. Accessed November 27, 2024. .https://www.project-syndicate.org/commentary/imf-world-bank-spring-meetings-need-to-get-four-things-right-by-lawrence-h-summers-and-n-k-singh-2024-04.

United Nations. n.d.. "Early Warnings for All". Accessed November 27, 2024. https://www.un.org/en/climatechange/early-warnings-for-all

UN Climate Change High-Level Champions. n.d. "Sharm El-Sheikh Adaptation Agenda." Accessed April 25, 2025. https://www.climatechampions.net/frameworks/sharm-el-sheikh-adaptation-agenda/.

United Nations Environment Programme (UNEP). 2022. "A New Era for National Adaptation Plans?" *United Nations Environment Programme – Global Adaptation Network*, October 20, 2022. Accessed November 27, 2024. https://www.unep.org/gan/news/blogpost/new-era-national-adaptation-plans.

United Nations Environment Programme (UNEP). 2023. *Adaptation Gap Report 2023: Underfinanced. Underprepared. Inadequate Investment and Planning on Climate Adaptation Leaves World Exposed.* Nairobi: United Nations Environment Programme. https://doi.org/10.59117/20.500.11822/43796.

United Nations Framework Convention on Climate Change (UNFCCC). n.d. "Adaptation Committee." Accessed April 25, 2025. https://unfccc.int/Adaptation-Committee.

United Nations Framework Convention on Climate Change (UNFCCC). 2019. *25 Years of Adaptation under the UNFCCC: Report by the Adaptation Committee*. Bonn, Germany: United Nations Framework Convention on Climate Change.

United Nations Framework Convention on Climate Change (UNFCCC). 2021. "António Guterres: 50% of All Climate Finance Needed for Adaptation." *UNFCCC*. January 25, 2021. Accessed November 27, 2024. https://unfccc.int/news/antonio-guterres-50-of-all-climate-finance-needed-for-adaptation.

United Nations Framework Convention on Climate Change (UNFCCC). 2023. "Concepts, Approaches and Examples of Transformational Adaptation – IPCC Presentation at the Fifth Workshop of the Work Programme on the Global Goal on Adaptation." *Intergovernmental Panel on Climate Change (IPCC)*, March 20, 2023. Accessed November 27, 2024. https://unfccc.int/documents/627408

United Nations Framework Convention on Climate Change (UNFCCC). 2024. "Draft decision -/CMA.6: New collective quantified goal on climate finance" Conference of the Parties serving as the meeting of the Parties to the Paris Agreement Sixth session, Baku, Azerbaijan, 11–22 November 2024. UNFCCC. Accessed November 27, 2024. https://unfccc.int/sites/default/files/resource/cma2024_L22_adv.pdf

Watson, Charlene, Elizabeth Tan, Laetitia Pettinotti, and Sarah Colenbrander. 2024. "Did COP29 End with a Good New Collective Quantified Goal Decision?" *ODI Global*. November 24, 2024. Accessed November 27, 2024. https://odi.org/en/insights/did-cop29-end-with-a-good-new-collective-quantified-goal-decision/.

Mohamed Farid Saleh
Chapter 15
Voluntary Carbon Markets: Promise or Peril in Global Climate Action

Abstract: Voluntary Carbon Markets (VCMs) have emerged as critical instruments in mobilizing private sector finance for climate mitigation. Yet, they remain fraught with challenges related to perceived lack of market integrity, transparency, and regulatory oversight. This chapter critically examines the evolving landscape of VCMs through the lens of Article 6 of the Paris Agreement, delineating the mechanisms of Articles 6.2, 6.4, and 6.8 and their implications for voluntary markets. The analysis identifies key structural weaknesses in the current global VCM architecture, such as the absence of standardized credit classifications, inconsistent regulatory treatment, and insufficient alignment between financial and environmental integrity objectives.

In response to these systemic issues, the chapter highlights global and regional initiatives aimed at enhancing the credibility and effectiveness of VCMs, including the efforts of the International Organization of Securities Commissions (IOSCO), the Integrity Council for Voluntary Carbon Markets (IC-VCM), and the Voluntary Carbon Market Integrity Initiative (VCMI). The chapter's core contribution lies in its case study of Egypt's regulatory leadership, where Egypt's Financial Regulatory Authority (FRA) has developed a comprehensive, multilayered framework for a regulated VCM. This framework includes the legal classification of carbon credits as financial instruments, the establishment of oversight bodies, validation and verification protocols, registry governance, and the introduction of formal accounting treatments. Egypt's experience offers a replicable model for both emerging and developed economies seeking to harness VCMs in a transparent and accountable manner.

By integrating regulatory innovation, stakeholder coordination, and alignment with international standards, the chapter demonstrates how well-governed VCMs can contribute meaningfully to national and global climate targets, particularly in the context of developing countries.

Keywords: Voluntary carbon markets, Article 6 of the Paris Agreement, Carbon credits, Climate finance, Financial and environmental integrity, Financial regulatory frameworks, Global climate governance.

Introduction

Human activities, primarily through greenhouse gas (GHG) emissions, have undeniably contributed to global warming, resulting in a global surface temperature increase of 1.1 °C above pre-industrial levels (1850–1900), between 2011 and 2020. GHG emissions continue to rise, driven by unequal historical and ongoing contributions associated with unsustainable energy practices, land use and land-use changes, and varying lifestyles and consumption patterns across regions, countries, and individuals (IPCC 2023).

Despite global efforts in mitigation and adaptation, including progress in policies, laws, and sectoral implementation, the trajectory of global GHG emissions remains concerning. Projections based on Nationally Determined Contributions (NDCs) for 2030 indicate that limiting warming to below 1.5 °C is unlikely, and maintaining the temperature below the 2 °C target is becoming increasingly challenging. While mitigation efforts have expanded recently, significant gaps persist between current emissions pathways and those required to meet climate targets. Similarly, adaptation initiatives have demonstrated measurable benefits across regions and sectors but remain insufficient. Adaptation gaps are expected to widen at the current pace of implementation, with many ecosystems already encountering both hard and soft limits. Financial flows for adaptation, particularly in developing countries, remain inadequate, significantly hindering the implementation of essential measures (IPCC 2023). To combat climate change and address biodiversity loss, global investments must rise to USD 400 billion annually by 2030, increasing to USD 480–580 billion annually by 2035, with a substantial portion directed toward emerging markets and developing economies (Bhattacharya et al. 2024).

Bridging the global financing gap requires innovative and collaborative solutions, with Article 6 of the Paris Agreement offering a key framework to facilitate this effort (Soezer 2022). By leveraging both market and nonmarket mechanisms, Article 6 aims to mobilize financial resources while fostering international collaboration. These mechanisms are designed to enhance global cooperation in tackling climate change, creating opportunities for countries to work together through market-driven solutions and alternative approaches.

This chapter provides a comprehensive exploration of carbon markets. It begins by examining international cooperation, focusing on Article 6 of the Paris Agreement and its application to carbon markets, offering an overview of the foundational principles guiding international carbon trading. It then explores emerging trends and dynamics in the global voluntary carbon markets (VCMs), highlighting key developments shaping these markets worldwide. The chapter further examines the challenges facing VCMs and how addressing these challenges impacts market effectiveness. The discussion then shifts to "United for Progress: Alliances Tackling VCM Challenges", which explores collaborative efforts to overcome barriers. Additionally, the chapter analyzes Egypt's regional carbon frontier, focusing on the Financial Regulatory Authority's (FRA) path to a regulated VCM. Finally, the chapter concludes by summarizing key insights and looking ahead to the future of carbon markets.

Unlocking Cooperation: Understanding Article 6 of the Paris Agreement and Its Application to Carbon Markets

Article 6 of the Paris Agreement provides a critical framework for international cooperation, enabling countries to achieve their climate goals through both market-based and nonmarket-based approaches. As part of their commitments under the Paris Agreement, signatory countries prepare, communicate, and maintain updated NDCs, which include targets for reducing GHG emissions. Instruments under Article 6 are expected to play a role in compliance strategies as countries work toward their climate targets. To achieve these targets, countries can utilize various mechanisms, with Article 6.2 offering guidance for accounting and reporting on voluntary market-based cooperation and Article 6.4 introducing a centralized, yet flexible carbon crediting mechanism (IOSCO 2024).

Article 6.2 provides a framework for countries to cooperate on achieving their climate targets by transferring Internationally Transferred Mitigation Outcomes (ITMOs). These ITMOs, essentially carbon credits (CCs), can be exchanged between countries to help meet NDCs. Countries that exceed their GHG reduction targets can generate ITMOs and trade them, in return for investments, capacity building, or technology access, while buyer countries use these credits to address shortfalls in their targets. One key avenue for trading ITMOs is compliance carbon markets (CCMs), which utilize regulated mechanisms such as emissions trading systems (ETSs) and sector-specific frameworks like the Carbon Offsetting and Reduction Scheme for International Aviation (CORSIA). These markets allow entities to fulfill binding commitments under national or international obligations using verified and accountable carbon credits, thereby linking the flexibility of Article 6.2 with the structured operations of CCMs.

Article 6.4 establishes a centralized, UN-supervised carbon market, allowing countries and private entities to generate and trade ITMOs. A significant milestone was achieved at COP29 when delegates finalized the rules governing its operation, marking a historic moment in international climate cooperation. Unlike Article 6.2, which facilitates bilateral or multilateral emissions trading between countries, Article 6.4 provides a standardized framework to ensure transparency and environmental integrity. The framework includes the development of methodologies for emission reduction projects, the registration of activities, the accreditation of third-party verification bodies, and the management of the Article 6.4 Registry. The UN's Article 6.4 Supervisory Body, established in 2022, oversees these mechanisms, ensuring the integrity of GHG reduction methodologies (UNFCCC n.d.).

While Article 6.4 does not explicitly regulate voluntary carbon markets, its application to VCMs largely depends on the host country's regulatory approach. Host governments may choose to implement specific regulations on how Article 6.4 rules intersect with VCMs. For example, countries may require VCM projects to obtain government approval, authorization, or non-objection/notification at various stages of project development. Additionally, governments may define the scope of activities permissible under a VCM program or establish minimum standards for social and environmental safeguards, as well as benefit-sharing mechanisms. These decisions allow countries to tailor the integration of Article 6.4 with VCMs to align with national priorities and objectives (Granziera, Hamrick, and Verdieck 2023).

In addition to market-based mechanisms, Article 6.8 provides a framework for supporting mitigation efforts through financial or technical assistance, without trading carbon credits. This mechanism facilitates collaboration by offering a centralized platform where countries and stakeholders can list planned mitigation projects and identify areas needing support, particularly for nations preferring a nonmarket approach.

To fully understand the scope and potential of these mechanisms, it is essential to explore the distinct types of carbon markets, namely CCMs and VCMs. Both markets have grown rapidly since the adoption of the Paris Agreement in 2015. In CCMs, tradeable carbon credits are used to fulfill obligations or binding commitments, such as national targets under the Paris Agreement, sector-specific requirements like CORSIA, or compliance mechanisms such as ETSs and carbon taxes. In contrast, VCMs involve the voluntary use of carbon credits, primarily by companies aiming to contribute to GHG mitigation efforts voluntarily (Wetterberg, Ellis, and Schneider 2024). Table 15.1 summarizes various market types, mechanisms, and products, along with domestic and international examples of their usage.

Table 15.1: Overview of the different market types, mechanisms, and types of products issued.

Type mechanisms		Issued product	Use examples
Compliance carbon markets (CCMs)			
Cap-and-trade mechanism		Carbon emission allowances	Compliance with domestic markets: – EU ETS – UK ETS – Western Climate Initiative
Baseline and credit mechanism	Carbon intensity	Emission performance credits (or certificates)/ carbon intensity credits (or certificates)	Compliance with domestic markets: – China National ETS – California Low Carbon Fuel Standard (LCFS) – Alberta TIER system – Australia Safeguard Mechanism
	Carbon reduction/ removal	Carbon credits	Compliance offset programs: – California Compliance Offset Program – China Certified Emission Reduction Schemes (CCER) – CORSIA

Table 15.1 (continued)

Type mechanisms		Issued product	Use examples
Voluntary carbon markets (VCMs)			
Baseline and credit mechanism	Carbon reduction/ removal	Carbon credits	Voluntary domestic markets: – China Certified Emission Reductions (CCER) – Australian Carbon Credit Unit Scheme (ACCU) – UAE AirCarbon Exchange (ACX) – KSA Regional Voluntary Carbon Market Company (RVCMC)
Regulated voluntary carbon markets (VCMs) – Egypt			
Baseline and credit mechanism	Carbon reduction/ removal	Carbon credits	A regulated framework developed by the Financial Regulatory Authority (FRA) for the issuance and trading of CCs on a platform managed by the Egyptian Exchange (EGX)

Source: The table is based on information from Voluntary Carbon Markets – IOSCO (2024), but has been edited and summarized by the author for clarity and conciseness.

Building on the above, most VCMs lack oversight from governments or financial regulators, rendering them unregulated. However, the Egyptian model, spearheaded by the Financial Regulatory Authority (FRA), distinguishes itself by providing a robust and flexible regulatory framework. This approach effectively addresses perceived gaps in existing VCMs and establishes a benchmark for regulated VCMs. The following section delves deeper into the intricacies of VCMs, examining their mechanisms, challenges, and contributions to global climate mitigation efforts.

Emerging Trends and Dynamics in Global VCMs

The VCM experienced significant growth, from its inception in the early 2000s through 2021, as shown in Figure 15.1. In 2021, carbon credits issuances peaked at 362 megatons of carbon dioxide (CO_2)-equivalent. However, this figure declined over the next 2 years, falling to 308 megatons of CO_2-equivalent by 2023. Similarly, the volume of carbon credits utilized to offset environmental impacts reached a high of 183 megatons of CO_2-equivalent in 2022, before decreasing to 174 megatons in 2023 (UNCTAD 2024).

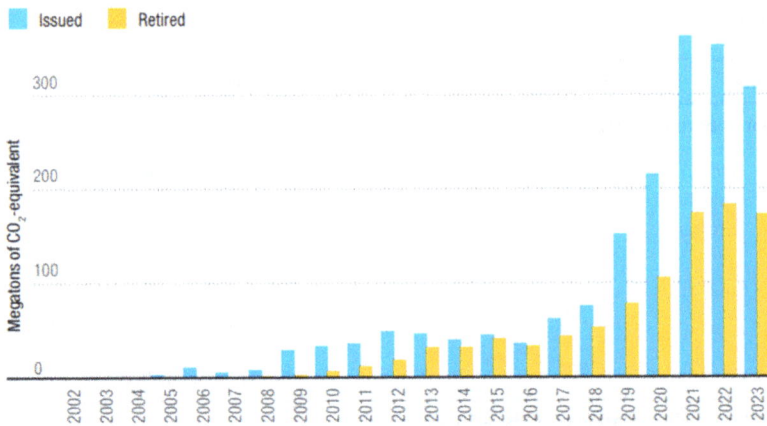

Figure 15.1: Growth in VCMs (2022–2023).
Note: The figure is based on data in the voluntary carbon market (VCM) dashboard of climate focus.
Source: UNCTAD (2024).

The decline in demand for CCs in 2023 was partially attributed to claims of corporate greenwashing and concerns about the authenticity of carbon credits. Consequently, both demand and prices for these credits fell. The value of carbon credits relies heavily on buyers' trust in the underlying projects, which is contingent upon the credibility and rigor of certification standards (UNCTAD 2024). These results underscore the critical need for a regulatory framework to enhance the credibility of VCMs and foster investor trust.

Challenges Facing VCMs

VCMs face significant challenges, with integrity and regulatory oversight emerging as critical issues that limit their credibility and effectiveness. These challenges manifest in various forms, including concerns over the quality of CCs and the prevalence of greenwashing practices. A closer examination of these risks highlights the factors undermining the market's potential.

Financial and Environmental Integrity

Carbon markets face two primary risks: financial integrity and environmental integrity. Financial sector regulators often prioritize financial integrity, focusing on transparency, accountability, and fraud prevention. However, environmental integrity is not equally addressed by environmental regulators. For instance, ensuring environmental integrity in VCMs requires that carbon credits represent real, measurable, and additional emission reductions or removals. A project claiming to mitigate deforestation must demonstrate that the forest was genuinely at risk and that the project directly contributed to its preservation.

CCs risk being overstated or misrepresented, undermining market credibility. Ensuring financial integrity alone is insufficient to guarantee environmental integrity, as financial oversight focuses on transactional transparency rather than the actual environmental impact. For example, a carbon credit transaction may be financially sound and free of fraud, but if the underlying project fails to deliver genuine emission reductions or causes unintended harm to local ecosystems or communities, the market's environmental integrity is compromised. Beyond the market itself, such shortcomings could undermine trust in carbon credit mechanisms, discouraging participation from investors and policymakers. Additionally, these issues may have broader social and economic consequences, potentially affecting local livelihoods, land rights, and biodiversity conservation efforts, which are often integral to sustainable development goals.

This disconnect highlights the need for robust environmental oversight, including rigorous monitoring, reporting, and verification (MRV) systems, to ensure that carbon credits achieve their intended climate benefits. Without such safeguards, VCMs risk becoming a tool for greenwashing rather than a meaningful driver of climate action. Balancing these two aspects is crucial for the overall success and credibility of carbon markets. Reports suggest that certain carbon-credit-generating activities may overstate their mitigation impacts, particularly within VCMs. Furthermore, the voluntary use of carbon credits could lead to misleading claims about buyers' climate performance (Trouwloon et al. 2023). While integrity risks may emerge at various stages of the value chain, VCMs currently fall outside the regulatory remit of most financial authorities, including those in the European Union and the United Kingdom (KPMG n.d.).

Lack of Domestic and International Consistency and Cooperation

The International Organization of Securities Commissions (IOSCO) (2024) report highlights additional challenges arising from the lack of domestic and international consistency and cooperation. It emphasizes fostering collaboration as a key best practice. However, the absence of globally aligned, transparent, and interoperable rules for emissions reduction calculation and verification processes across jurisdictions presents a major obstacle to VCM development. To support their growth, regulators and relevant authorities are encouraged to pursue both domestic (among national authorities) and international consistency. Where appropriate, they should also engage with peer regulators when shaping regulatory frameworks for carbon credits.

Furthermore, leveraging cross-border enforcement mechanisms is suggested as a means to enhance oversight and market development. Recent progress at COP29 regarding the establishment of a governance structure for the UN-supervised global carbon market is expected to introduce rigorous MRV requirements. These standards aim to reduce fraud, misreporting, and greenwashing in carbon credit projects, mitigating risks and fostering global coordination that could extend to national levels.

Absence of Regulatory Classification for CCs

According to IOSCO (2024), the lack of a clear legal and regulatory classification for carbon credits presents a significant challenge. One issue is the identification of the relevant regulatory body. If classified as financial instruments, carbon credits would fall under the jurisdiction of capital market regulators. If categorized as commodities, they would be overseen by commodity market regulators. Regulatory treatment varies across jurisdictions, with derivatives on carbon credits often regulated as commodity derivatives, while the credits themselves may be classified as financial or commodity instruments. IOSCO underscores the importance of clarifying the legal status of carbon credits, as such clarity is essential for the effective development and operation of VCMs.

Establishing clear regulatory frameworks by financial authorities is crucial to ensuring consistency and integrity within carbon markets. Such guidance can help eliminate uncertainties, build confidence among participants, and encourage greater market engagement.

United for Progress: Alliances Tackling VCM Challenges

Efforts to mitigate the above challenges in VCMs are gaining momentum through recent global and regional initiatives. A major development at COP29 was the approval of Article 6.4 of the Paris Agreement, which established standards for the global carbon market. While the full impact of these standards remains to be seen, they have the potential to accelerate climate action by increasing demand for carbon credit projects and channeling financial support to developing countries. By enhancing the credibility of carbon credits and reducing market risks, these standards could build investor confidence, stimulate demand, and create new revenue streams within the carbon market. If successfully mobilized, these financial flows could support sustainability initiatives, particularly in developing countries, where climate finance is limited. Climate negotiators estimate that these standards could reduce the annual cost of implementing national climate plans by approximately USD 250 billion, marking a significant step in improving the integrity of carbon markets worldwide (UNFCCC 2024).

Additionally, the United States released the Principles for Responsible Participation in VCMs, providing voluntary guidelines for market participants and outlining federal engagement with VCMs (The White House 2024). However, the long-term impact of this initiative remains uncertain, as political shifts could influence its implementation.

Other notable initiatives include the Integrity Council for Voluntary Carbon Markets (IC-VCM), which introduced its Core Carbon Principles and Assessment Framework in 2023, with a review planned for 2025 (ICVCM n.d.). Similarly, the Voluntary Carbon Market Integrity Initiative (VCMI) supports businesses in integrating carbon credits into credible net-zero strategies. On a regional level, the Africa Carbon Markets Initiative (ACMI), launched at COP27, aims to expand Africa's VCMs, enhancing the continent's role in global carbon reduction efforts.

Building on these global and regional efforts, Egypt has taken significant strides in developing its own regulated VCM framework, providing valuable insights into aligning national priorities with regional dynamics.

Egypt's Regional Carbon Frontier: FRA's Path to a Regulated VCM

The FRA has emerged as a pioneer in the African carbon market, aligning its efforts with Egypt's vision to become a regional platform for carbon credits, as announced at COP27. Egypt adopts a comprehensive approach that extends beyond regulatory oversight, focusing on infrastructure development, alignment with global standards, and fostering collaboration among public and private stakeholders.

Carbon Credits Classification: The Foundational Step

The FRA addressed uncertainties surrounding the CCs through amendments to the capital market executive regulations, defining CCs as financial instruments. This change, formalized by the Prime Minister's Decree No. 4664/2022, provided the foundational legal certainty required for a robust carbon market. This regulatory intervention established a transparent and structured environment for market participants, allowing CCs to be bought, sold, and traded like any other financial asset.

Statutorily Enforced Coordination: The Role of the Carbon Credit Regulatory Committee (CCRC)

In January 2023, the FRA enacted these amendments and formed the CCRC through Decree No. 57/2023. This committee comprises key stakeholders, including representatives from the Ministry of Environment, private sector experts, and the Egyptian Exchange (EGX). Its central mission is to ensure that Egypt's carbon market operates with transparency, integrity, and adherence to global standards.

The committee's responsibilities focus on several key areas:

- **Defining criteria for validation and verification bodies (VVBs):** The committee sets rigorous standards for VVBs, ensuring compliance with globally recognized frameworks such as the International Organization for Standardization (ISO) accreditation and methodologies from Verra, Gold Standard, and the GCC.
- **Establishing guidelines for CC integrity:** By incorporating the Integrity Council for the Voluntary Carbon Market (ICVCM) and the Core Carbon Principles (CCP), these guidelines ensure the credibility, traceability, and verifiability of CCs traded on the platform.
- **Authorizing voluntary carbon registries:** The committee approves registries that meet international standards – such as those endorsed by the International Carbon Reduction and Offset Alliance (ICROA) and the International Emissions Trading Association (IETA) – to enhance quality control and global acceptance of Egypt's carbon credits.

Through these mandates, the committee plays a crucial role in strengthening governance and integrating Egypt's carbon market into the global trading ecosystem.

Supporting Local VVBs: A Step Toward Market Inclusivity

A major challenge for developing countries in the carbon market is the high cost associated with VVBs, particularly for smaller developers. VVBs ensure the credibility of carbon reduction claims made by project developers; however, the validation and verification process is often poorly understood and perceived as an unrecognized service. Additionally, the absence of a formal registry for VVB approval has hindered market stability.

To address these challenges, the FRA implemented reforms to adapt global best practices to the local context, making validation and verification services more accessible and affordable. In August 2023, the FRA issued Decree No. 163/2023, establishing detailed requirements for VVBs. The regulation mandated accreditation through internationally recognized ISO standards such as ISO 14065 and ISO 17029 while specifying qualifications for VVB personnel. These measures ensure that the carbon market is governed by skilled professionals, enhancing credibility and operational integrity.

Further strengthening the market, the FRA collaborated with the Egyptian Accreditation Council (EGAC) to issue ISO certifications related to validation and verification, reducing accreditation costs and enabling local firms to participate in the carbon market. Additionally, the FRA adopted accreditation models from global carbon registries such as Verra and Gold Standard,[1] tailoring their requirements to suit the local platform. As a result, three VVBs – two local and one international – have been approved, with additional applications under review.

Enhancing Infrastructure: Carbon Registries in Focus

To reinforce its role as a regional CC hub, the FRA recognized the importance of robust registry systems and IT governance. In February 2024, Decree No. 30/2024 established detailed requirements for voluntary carbon registries, ensuring alignment with global standards set by ICROA. The decree mandated that approved registries conduct an annual review of at least 40% of total validation and verification operations for registered carbon reduction projects, exceeding the global ISO standard of 20%.

This regulation attracted international interest, leading to the FRA's final approval of BioCarbon Registry and EcoRegistry, with another registry, Economy of Love, under review. The FRA's technical team conducted due diligence to ensure compliance with the decree's requirements, facilitating these registries' entry into the platform.

Enhancing Market Transparency: Listing and Trading CCs

In March 2024, the FRA issued Decree No. 31/2024, establishing clear rules for listing and delisting voluntary CCs on the EGX trading platform. The decree outlined procedures for registering carbon reduction projects and set standard requirements for listing credits, ensuring publicly accessible project details such as location, developer, and associated registry.

To enhance transparency, the decree also mandated reporting obligations for issuers, ensuring market participants have access to timely and accurate information. Additionally, the FRA introduced forward contract listing and trading rules for carbon credits, providing market participants with risk-mitigation tools, rarely available in other carbon markets.

---

1 More information about Gold Standard can be found here: https://globalgoals.goldstandard.org/standards/109_V1.0_PAR_Validation-Verification-Body-Requirements.pdfand for Verra: https://verra.org/validation-verification/#accreditation

Official Accounting Treatment for CCs: Setting a Global Benchmark

In March 2024, the FRA addressed carbon credit accounting complexities through a decree based on best international practices and consultations with auditing firms. This framework distinguishes whether CCs should be classified as intangible assets or financial instruments based on the nature of their transaction. The guidelines specify:
1. When CCs are issued to a project developer and used for offsetting, they are treated as intangible assets. If sold, they are treated as financial instruments.
2. When CCs are issued to a third party different from the project developer, they are treated as financial instruments.
3. When CCs are purchased for carbon neutrality, they are treated as intangible assets.
4. When CCs are purchased for trading, they are treated as financial instruments.

These classifications provide clarity for market participants, enhancing compliance with international financial reporting standards. Figure 15.2 summarizes the challenges faced by VCMs and the FRA's proposed regulatory solutions.

Furthermore, the regulatory framework governs the entire life cycle of carbon credit issuance and trading for projects approved by the CCRC. It ensures effective coordination among relevant governmental stakeholders, while integrating input from the private sector. Figure 15.3 outlines the key regulations governing each stage of carbon credit issuance.

Launching the First Regulated VCM Trades

The culmination of Egypt's extensive regulatory reforms occurred on August 13, 2024, with the launch of its first regulated VCM. The inaugural trades featured three key transactions: ISIS Food Industries acquired 500 voluntary carbon certificates from the Egyptian Bio-Agriculture Association (EBDA), DALTEX purchased 1,500 certificates from VNV Advisory, and SCB Environmental Markets completed a transaction through CI Capital Securities Trading. Figures 15.4 and 15.5 illustrate the currently listed carbon credits, detailing the types of projects and their geographical distribution, which reflect the regional characteristics of the market. Furthermore, Figure 15.6 illustrates the currently listed carbon credits based on the applicable standard. It is also worth noting that Economy of Love (EoL), an Egyptian registry, is globally recognized in the agricultural sector.

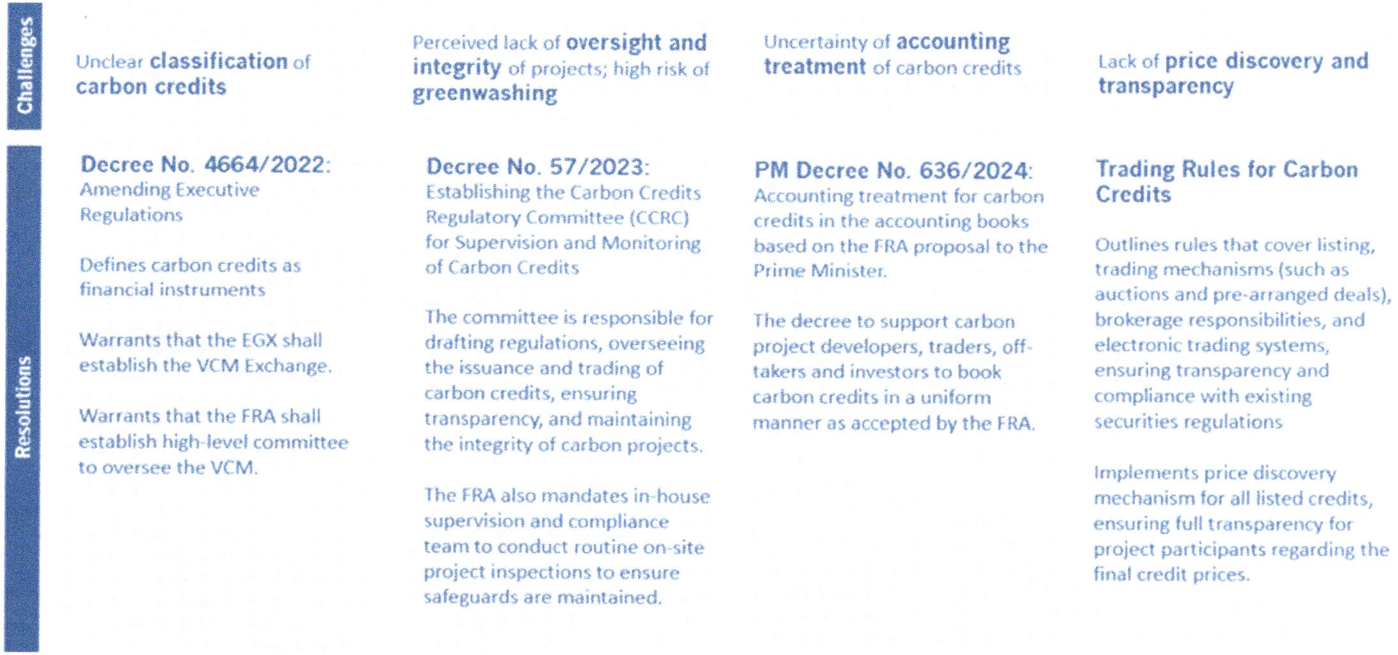

Challenges	Unclear classification of carbon credits	Perceived lack of oversight and integrity of projects; high risk of greenwashing	Uncertainty of accounting treatment of carbon credits	Lack of price discovery and transparency
Resolutions	**Decree No. 4664/2022:** Amending Executive Regulations Defines carbon credits as financial instruments Warrants that the EGX shall establish the VCM Exchange. Warrants that the FRA shall establish high-level committee to oversee the VCM.	**Decree No. 57/2023:** Establishing the Carbon Credits Regulatory Committee (CCRC) for Supervision and Monitoring of Carbon Credits The committee is responsible for drafting regulations, overseeing the issuance and trading of carbon credits, ensuring transparency, and maintaining the integrity of carbon projects. The FRA also mandates in-house supervision and compliance team to conduct routine on-site project inspections to ensure safeguards are maintained.	**PM Decree No. 636/2024:** Accounting treatment for carbon credits in the accounting books based on the FRA proposal to the Prime Minister. The decree to support carbon project developers, traders, off-takers and investors to book carbon credits in a uniform manner as accepted by the FRA.	**Trading Rules for Carbon Credits** Outlines rules that cover listing, trading mechanisms (such as auctions and pre-arranged deals), brokerage responsibilities, and electronic trading systems, ensuring transparency and compliance with existing securities regulations Implements price discovery mechanism for all listed credits, ensuring full transparency for project participants regarding the final credit prices.

Figure 15.2: VCMs' perceived challenges and the proposed regulatory solutions.
Source: The Author.

	Registries Approval	Validation and Verification	Project & CCs Listing	Credit Trading
Decree	**Relevant Party** Registry Operators **Relevant Decree** Decree No. 30/2024: Requirements for Approving Voluntary Carbon Registries **Description** Outlines governance requirements, particularly IT governance and cybersecurity measures, to ensure the integrity of carbon registries and issued carbon credits.	**Relevant Party** VVB's **Relevant Decree** Decree No. 163/2023: Requirements for approving VVBs **Description** Pertains to the regulations for international and local VVBs and requires VVBs to meet international best practices, including accreditation on ISO-14065, ISO-17029.	**Relevant Party** Project Developers **Relevant Decree** Decree No. 31/2024: Listing, Delisting & Disclosure Rules of Projects & Credits **Description** Establishes rules for registering carbon reduction projects in the FRA's database, allowing the trading of carbon credits. It also covers the listing of forward contracts for voluntary carbon credits and required disclosure.	**Relevant Party** Trading and Settlement Venues Brokerage Companies **Relevant Decree** Decree No. 1732/2024 on licensing requirements for brokerage companies FRA's Approval of Trading & Settlement Rules (EGX & Tasweyat) **Description** Establishes the different auction mechanisms for the trading of carbon credits, and the settlement and custody accounts for those trades. It permits bilateral trades and the trading of forward contracts
Challenge Addressed	Perceived lack of trust and understanding of registries' modus operandi to avoid double counting	Lack of ongoing and consistent regulatory oversight	Perceived lack of trust and transparency of the underlying projects against which carbon credits are issued	Perceived lack of traceability, trust and transparency in carbon credit trading & pricing, leading to inefficiencies in market participation by other players like insurance companies

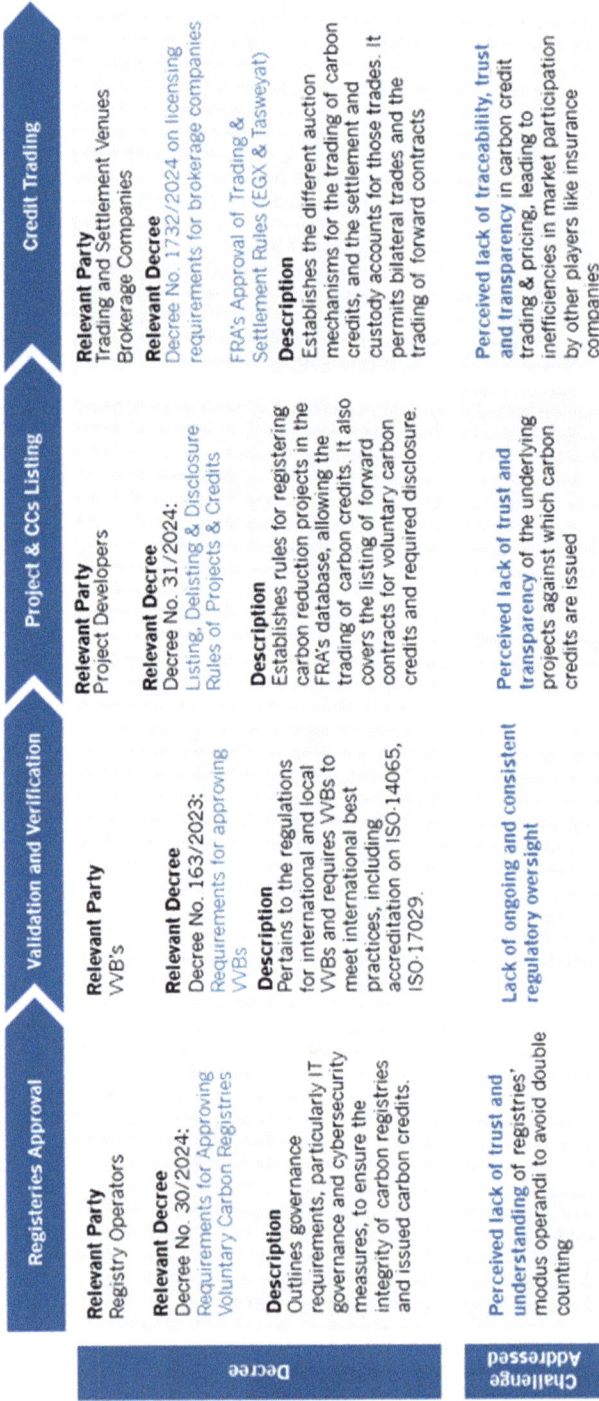

Figure 15.3: Regulatory framework addressing the main challenges of VCMs across all stages of carbon development, issuance, and trading.
Source: The Author.

Carbon Credits By Country

By Country	
Bangladesh	60,000
Nepal	18,414
India	38,000
Egypt	30,775
Oman	-
Total	**147,189**

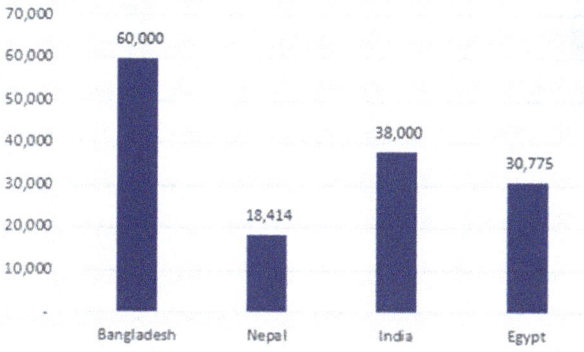

Figure 15.4: Listed projects by country.
Source: FRA CPR database (https://Climateprojectsregistry.org).

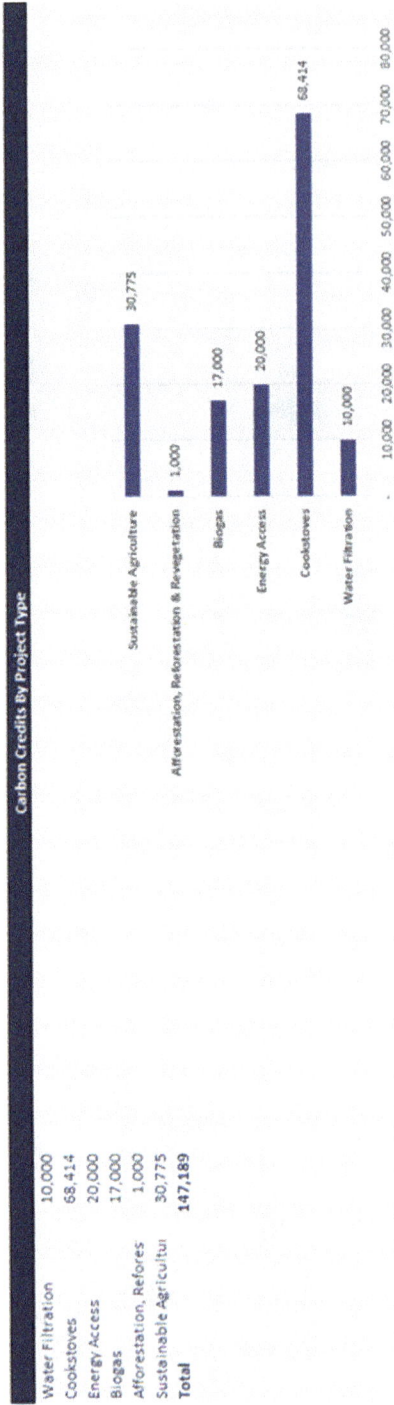

Water Filtration	10,000
Cookstoves	68,414
Energy Access	20,000
Biogas	17,000
Afforestation, Refores	1,000
Sustainable Agricultur	30,775
Total	**147,189**

Carbon Credits By Project Type

Sustainable Agriculture — 30,775
Afforestation, Reforestation & Revegetation — 1,000
Biogas — 17,000
Energy Access — 20,000
Cookstoves — 68,414
Water Filtration — 10,000

10,000 20,000 30,000 40,000 50,000 60,000 70,000 80,000

Figure 15.5: Listed projects by project type.
Source: FRA CPR database (https://Climateprojectsregistry.org).

Carbon Credits By Standard	
By Standard	
Gold Standard	97,000
Verra	19,414
EOL	30,775
Total	**147,189**

Chart Title

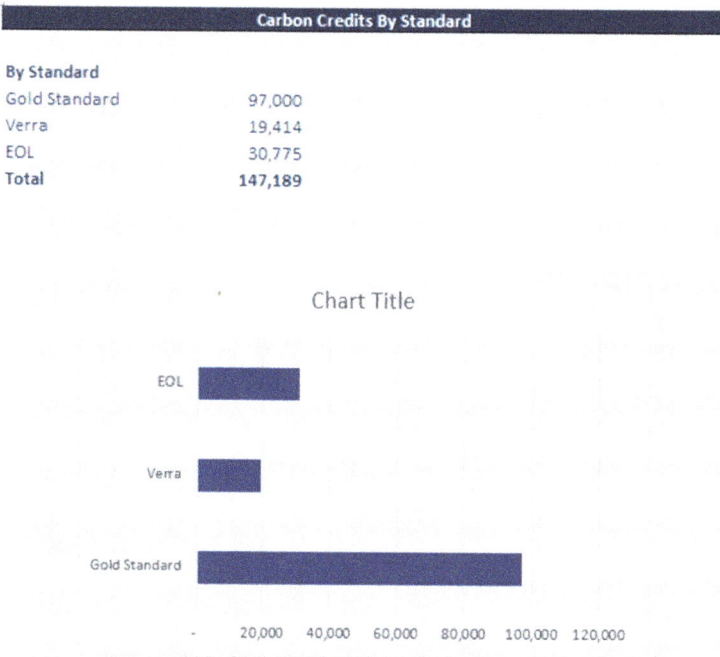

Figure 15.6: Listed projects by standard.
Source: FRA CPR database (https://Climateprojectsregistry.org).

Conclusion

Regulated VCMs play a crucial role in global climate action by mobilizing private finance for emissions reductions and sustainable development. However, challenges such as integrity concerns, transparency issues, and the absence of standardized regulations have raised significant questions about their effectiveness in addressing the urgent demands of climate finance. The Egyptian model provides a concrete solution by establishing a robust regulatory framework that mitigates these challenges. By prioritizing market governance, local accreditation, and alignment with global best practices, Egypt has strengthened the integrity and reliability of its VCM. This approach demonstrates how a structured and well-regulated framework can enhance market viability and ensure a meaningful contribution to climate action.

References

Bhattacharya, Amar, Vera Songwe, Eléonore Soubeyran, and Nicholas Stern. 2024. *Raising Ambition and Accelerating Delivery of Climate Finance*. London: Grantham Research Institute on Climate Change and the Environment, London School of Economics and Political Science.

Granziera, Beatriz, Kelley Hamrick, and John Verdieck. 2023. *Article 6 Explainer: Questions and Answers about the COP Decisions on Carbon Markets and What They Mean for NDCs, Nature, and the Voluntary Carbon Markets*. The Nature Conservancy. https://www.nature.org/content/dam/tnc/nature/en/documents/TNC_Article_6_Explainer.pdf

Integrity Council for the Voluntary Carbon Market (ICVCM). n.d. *Core carbon principles*. Accessed February 28, 2025. https://icvcm.org/core-carbon-principles/

Intergovernmental Panel on Climate Change (IPCC). 2023. *Climate change 2023: Synthesis report. Summary for policymakers*. IPCC. https://www.ipcc.ch/report/ar6/syr/downloads/report/IPCC_AR6_SYR_SPM.pdf

International Organization of Securities Commissions (IOSCO). 2024. *Voluntary Carbon Markets*. November. https://www.iosco.org/library/pubdocs/pdf/IOSCOPD774.pdf

KPMG. n.d. *Integrity issues in the voluntary carbon markets*. Accessed November 25, 2024. https://kpmg.com/xx/en/our-insights/regulatory-insights/integrity-issues-in-the-voluntary-carbon-markets.html

Soezer, Alexandra. 2022. "What Is Article 6 of the Paris Agreement, and Why Is It Important?" *United Nations Development Programme (UNDP)*, November 9. Accessed November 28, 2024. https://www.undp.org/energy/blog/what-article-6-paris-agreement-and-why-it-important.

Wetterberg, Klas, Jane Ellis, and Lambert Schneider. 2024. *The Interplay between Voluntary and Compliance Carbon Markets: Implications for Environmental Integrity*. OECD Environment Working Papers, no. 244. Paris: OECD Publishing. https://doi.org/10.1787/500198e1-en.

The White House. 2024. *Voluntary Carbon Markets Joint Policy Statement and Principles*. May. https://www.whitehouse.gov/wp-content/uploads/2024/05/VCM-Joint-Policy-Statement-and-Principles.pdf

Trouwloon, Danick, Charlotte Streck, Thiago Chagas, and Glenpherd Martinus. 2023. "Understanding the Use of Carbon Credits by Companies: A Review of the Defining Elements of Corporate Climate Claims." *Global Challenges* 7 (4) https://doi.org/10.1002/gch2.202200158.

United Nations Conference on Trade and Development (UNCTAD). 2024. *The least developed countries report 2024: Overview*. https://unctad.org/system/files/official-document/ldc2024overview_en.pdf

United Nations Framework Convention on Climate Change (UNFCCC). n.d. *Article 6.4 Supervisory Body*. United Nations Framework Convention on Climate Change. Accessed February 28, 2025. https://unfccc.int/process-and-meetings/bodies/constituted-bodies/article-64-supervisory-body.

United Nations Framework Convention on Climate Change (UNFCCC). 2024. *COP29 Agrees International Carbon Market Standards*. November 12. Accessed February 28, 2025. https://unfccc.int/news/cop29-agrees-international-carbon-market-standards

Dina Zayed
Chapter 16
Shaken or Stirred? Mobilizing Philanthropy for Climate Finance

Abstract: The world faces an inflection point and a moment for accountability on how far we have galvanized multi-stakeholder networks to meet the urgency and the scale of the climate crisis. Faced with an ever-daunting climate finance gap, flexible and risk-tolerant philanthropic capital has a clear, powerful role to play in transforming economies and supporting new models of social and political governance. This chapter examines the contours of this philanthropic role in addressing the climate finance conundrum. It argues that the power of philanthropic interventions lies in the multiplicity of approaches and that philanthropy is far from a monolith. Philanthropy has a unique ability and agency to work across private, public, and civil society spaces. What this indicates is a capacity to shape agendas and shift conversations. But to date, the realities of philanthropic funding disbursed reveal that far more needs to be done, and calls for a greater philanthropic footprint in addressing the climate crisis need to be tempered with a realistic and honest assessment of where philanthropy currently stands. However, there are many reasons for optimism, and the growth of philanthropic appetite and engagement with climate change is likely a trend that is here to stay. Policy observers must be clear that philanthropy is unlikely and should not be expected to substitute for public finance shortfalls, especially without an institutional reckoning with histories of philanthropic engagement and the relationships of power those create. We must also be mindful that the greatest strength the sector has to offer does not rest in its financial capital alone; philanthropy is most effective when it can mobilize others, build new centers of power, nurture advocacy pathways, experiment with different theories of impact, champion numerous perspectives over longer periods, and crowd in additional finance. When organized effectively and equitably, philanthropy is a force to be reckoned with.

Keywords: Philanthropy, Climate justice, Network governance, Impact investment, Civil society engagement, Climate resilience, Global South

Note: The author wishes to express immense gratitude and acknowledge the contributions, advice, and time of Faten Aggad, Maria Netto, Alice de Moraes Amorim Vogas, Charlene Watson, Jess Ayers, Iskander Erzini Vernoit, Andrés Mogro, Yamide Dagnet, Heather McGray, Michael Hugman, Clara Daré, Juliana Tinoco, Jessica Brown, Joshua Amponsem, Nathan Méténier, and Marilyn Waite for their thoughtful engagement with the research and writing of this chapter.

Introduction

Philanthropic mobilization around climate change has grown significantly in recent years. With unique expertise and flexible capital, philanthropies are well-positioned to address the scale and urgency of the climate crisis. As demonstrated at the inaugural COP28 Business and Philanthropy Climate Forum, catalytic partnerships can firmly position philanthropy at the center of international climate action. As a few recent examples show, philanthropies are already playing a crucial role. For example, in response to the United Nations Secretary-General's call to action on extreme heat, a coalition of philanthropies committed an initial USD 50 million to support resilience in regions most vulnerable to the impacts of climate change (Reifsteck 2024). Additionally, a USD 1 billion gift from the Doerr family, announced in 2022, is already beginning to show impact at the Stanford Doerr School of Sustainability (Esmaeili et al. 2024). Similarly, the USD 1 billion commitment from the Rockefeller Foundation to advance climate solutions over the next 5 years follows the 2020 Global Climate Action Summit, where 39 foundations pledged USD 6 billion for climate solutions by 2025 (Kempner 2023).

Amid the growing international climate finance gap, these and other developments suggest that philanthropy has a critical role to play in unlocking climate finance flows. This chapter seeks to examine the contours of that role, arguing that while philanthropy is an important player in the climate finance landscape, the reality is that there are multiple actors and various strategies involved. We must engage with a diversity of philanthropic tactics from a range of organizations working at different scales to fully understand the scope of philanthropy's role and its vast potential. Drawing on interviews with key leaders in the philanthropic community and the author's own experience in the field, this chapter will explore different forms of philanthropic interventions and offer a basic typology of the approaches being adopted. The goal is to help practitioners interested in collaborating with philanthropies to better diagnose the types of interventions that can be leveraged for effective partnerships. Furthermore, the chapter will put philanthropic grant-making into perspective, both in relation to the scale of the climate finance gap and within the broader context of institutional histories that have shaped attitudes toward philanthropy.

Philanthropic capital is uniquely positioned to take on high risks, explore innovative technologies and approaches, and operate in regions most vulnerable to climate change that are often beyond the reach of traditional financing. Philanthropy's distinct vantage point allows it to incubate ideas and catalyze scalable solutions. In the words of the European Climate Foundation's Laurence Tubiana and Sequoia Foundation's Christie Ulman, philanthropic resources – including "funding, but also courage, patience, and agility" – can elevate political ambition, galvanize institutional willpower, and mobilize action (Tubiana and Ulman 2022). Over the past decade, the philanthropic community, along with the broader civil society networks they support and are embedded in, has grown both in number and diversity, gaining agility in the process. Many significant climate policy victories, such as the negotiation of the historic Loss and Damage Fund, the U.S. Inflation Reduction Act, and the European Union's Fit for 55, have been supported, shaped, and in some cases enabled by philanthropic engagement (Reifsteck 2024).

From this context, this chapter proposes that while philanthropy can play a significant role in contributing to the climate finance conundrum, its greatest strength lies not in the sector's financial capital alone, which, as will be discussed in section "Context: Philanthropy in Perspective", remains untapped and unevenly allocated. Philanthropy possesses network capital and the ability to shape and influence agendas, making the sector a crucial part of the puzzle. There is a clear reason for optimism, as the growth and expansion of philanthropic giving toward climate action is a trend that is likely to continue. However, policy observers must be clear that philanthropy is unlikely to – and should not be expected to – substitute for public finance shortfalls, particularly without an institutional reckoning of the histories of philanthropic engagement and the power dynamics these relationships create, which will be addressed in section "Context: Philanthropy in Perspective" of this chapter.

Philanthropy has a unique capacity and agency to operate across private, public, and civil society spaces.[1] This indicates the potential to shape agendas and shift conversations. As section "Tackling the Elephant: Philanthropic Approaches and Tactics" will further discuss, flexible grant money may be most effective when it can help generate the enabling conditions for policy change, unlock political will, and build human and infrastructure capacity, creating the foundations for money, ideas, and people to flow.

In this critical decade of action, it will take a myriad of approaches to push the needle on the dial, and philanthropy undeniably has a role to play. However, ideas and approaches must be iteratively tested and reflectively studied, as changing the realities and inequities surrounding climate finance flows will require more than merely stirring the same old pot. Therefore, those with strong expectations of the power of philanthropy must engage with the current state of philanthropic giving and pay attention to the historical lessons learned from this powerful sector, which will be revisited later in this chapter.

---

[1] Borrowing from the environmental governance scholarship, agents are often described and situated across the "state, market, or civil society" lines but philanthropy does not fit neatly into any of these spheres, and as Betsill et al. (2022) show, it is often difficult to disentangle the public from private in understanding environmental philanthropy. This fluid identity also shapes philanthropy's rare perch.

Context: Philanthropy in Perspective

As other contributions to this series have clearly articulated, the international climate finance gap remains strikingly wide, and it is critical to first assess philanthropic capital against the broader annual global public and private sector finance bill of over USD 600 billion (Gosnell and Tsai 2021). Despite significant progress, the greatest total climate financial flows in a single year reached USD 850–940 billion, according to the Climate Policy Initiative in 2021, and USD 1.31 trillion in the BCG-Rockefeller Foundation tally in 2020 (Naran et al. 2022; Rockefeller Foundation and Boston Consulting Group 2022). These figures are far from the USD 4.3 trillion per annum needed by 2030 to avoid the worst effects of climate change (Naran et al. 2022). To meet the Paris Agreement's goals, donors need to double their climate finance delivery by 2025, compared to 2019, including more than doubling finance for climate resilience (Songwe, Stern, and Bhattacharya 2022). With the disappointing outcome of the negotiations over a New Collective Quantified Goal in Baku at COP29, the issue of inefficient, inequitable, and inadequate global climate finance flows was brought even further to the surface. In this context, philanthropies are faced with a pressing need for more ambitious action, and there must be mechanisms in place to raise expectations that philanthropy has a role in credibly and consistently mobilizing finance toward renewed global targets. However, they must do so in a manner that does not undermine the primary responsibilities or reduce the accountability of major global emitters.

Yet, the reality of funding mobilized toward climate action from philanthropic sources reveals that much work remains to be done. Calls for a greater philanthropic footprint in addressing the climate crisis must be tempered by a realistic and honest assessment of where philanthropy currently stands. However, there are clear reasons for optimism. ClimateWorks Foundation reports that while total philanthropic giving reached an estimated USD 885 billion in 2023, the growth in climate giving from foundations and individuals outpaced overall growth, with an estimated USD 9.3 billion to USD 15.8 billion mobilized for climate mitigation – a 20% increase from the previous year (Esmaeili et al. 2024). This compares to an overall total of USD 811 billion in 2022, with roughly USD 7.8 billion to USD 12.8 billion directed to climate mitigation (Desanlis et al. 2023). More critically, in 2023, foundation funding reached a record USD 4.8 billion – nearly triple the USD 1.7 billion committed in 2019 (Esmaeili et al. 2024).

This funding picture also reveals a large degree of variation across issues and regions. For example, clean electricity was identified in 2022 as the largest category of foundation spending, with a notable new push to reduce emissions of super pollutants and support efforts to decarbonize transportation and industry. In contrast, there has been some important movement around adaptation and resilience – such as the launch of the Adaptation and Resilience Funder Collaborative (ARC), which brought together more than 50 philanthropic organizations – preliminary data on adaptation spending and its potential are still limited. The philanthropic sector faces a long journey ahead to raise its ambition for resilience funding.[2] A year after a group of leading philanthropic funders pledged to accelerate adaptation funding, a report released in November 2024 showed that more than 40 of the largest foundations working in this space had committed over USD 600 million to adaptation and resilience activities in 2023. These same funders are on track to provide between USD 650 million and USD 700 million in funding in 2024 (Roeyer et al. 2024). This survey, however, does not offer details on how adaptation and resilience spending were categorized or clarify the distinction between adaptation and mitigation spending. It remains unclear whether the self-reported figure of USD 600 million is additional or embedded within the overall climate funding trends tracked by ClimateWorks. Nevertheless, the figure suggests that support for resilience and adaptation is currently below where it needs to be and that philanthropic funders have a role to play in supporting capacity needs across the adaptation field, investing in and de-risking innovative solutions, and piloting new approaches.

We also know there are discrepancies across and within regions. In 2022, projects that spanned multiple regions received more than a third of the overall funding tracked by ClimateWorks, yet over 60% of foundation funding directed to a single country or region went to the United States, Canada, and Europe. In comparison, funding directed to the Global South – including Africa, India, and Latin America – represented just 12% of all foundation funding for climate mitigation in 2022 (Desanlis et al. 2023).[3] This trend did not radically change in subsequent reports; foundation funding to Africa, Asia, Oceania, and Latin America grew rapidly, but these regions still received only about 20% of the total foundation funding directed to single countries or regions in 2023 (Esmaeili et al. 2024). More crucially, funding to organizations in low- and middle-income countries received a fraction of core funding compared to their peers in the United States and Europe – just less than 14% of overall flows (Esmaeili et al. 2024).

With this context, we can identify a few clear themes: first, philanthropy can do more, but the call for greater funding is widely heard within the sector (Simpson 2024). Second, there are signs of positive change, which should be encouraged. For instance, regionally, the Arab Foundations Forum launched the Arab Philanthropy Commitment on Climate Change at COP29, marking the first regional commitment

---

2 The author was one of the early co-conveners of this Funder's Coalition. The Adaptation Call to Action (2023) is available online at ClimateWorks Foundation: https://www.climateworks.org/press-release/as-the-climate-crisis-mounts-philanthropy-must-act-to-confront-the-impacts/. ClimateWorks is currently hosting ARC and supporting sector coordination on ways to improve tracking and increase ambition.

3 ClimateWorks data shows that regionally foundation funding increased to Africa by 38% in 2022, more than tripling over the last 5 years. But the author notes that it is unclear whether this funding was reflective of Egypt's hosting of the 27th annual United Nations Climate Change Conference of the Parties (COP27) and the regional spotlight this enabled on the African continent, and how durable this funding trend may be.

within the Philanthropy for Climate Movement. If this pledge translates into material shifts in resources and emboldens a change in practices, it holds tremendous potential for one of the world's most vulnerable climate hotspots, which faces a unique set of transition risks as well as exposure to climate impacts (Arab Foundations Forum 2024).

Situating this current state of play, we further know that philanthropic capital has had a significant influence on shaping several climate-adjacent issues over many decades. Despite the widely held belief that philanthropic capital is finite and difficult to scale, the fact that philanthropic organizations retain high degrees of independence and "hyper-agency" in making funding decisions has allowed the sector to play a disproportionate role in supplementing funding for global public goods. For example, the sector has had a historically large footprint in biodiversity conservation, where more than half of all spending relies on foundation grants (Jung and Harrow 2015; Beer 2023). By 2015, foundation funding for global marine conservation had formally exceeded funding from official development assistance (Betsill et al. 2022). When it comes to building and supporting knowledge, philanthropic contributions to research and innovation are substantial across a range of issues and geographies. In the European Union, for example, philanthropic contributions to the research ecosystem constituted more than half of the annual budget that the European Commission allocated to researchers during the Horizon 2020 program (Aggad 2023).

However, views on philanthropy and its policy-influencing role vary. Critical observers have noted that philanthropies derive much of their power from exchanging one form of capital for another. In the case of private foundations funded by the vast personal fortunes of billionaire founders, it has been argued that the move from the commercial world into the social realm has also enabled other forms of return, whether social, cultural, or symbolic, for those same elites (Kumar and Brooks 2021). Critics contend that philanthropic interventions often rely on technocratic approaches to complex social and political problems, applying minimal scrutiny and preventing the development of "alternative, redistributive solutions" (Kumar and Brooks 2021, 329). Matthew C. Nisbet (2019, 35) warns that as large philanthropies move into the "center of influence on climate change and similarly intractable problems", we are heading toward a future where a few hundred unelected trustees, families, and individuals seek to exercise global power in ways that are accountable to no one. This, according to Nisbet, has led to a form of "insularity", meaning that the climate philanthropic sector has largely favored funding that sends market signals around carbon-energy, rather than investing in other solutions, including climate resilience.

Other research suggests that large foundations have contributed to the development of less contentious civil society movements, as those favored in funding have had to adapt to rationalized models and theories of impact (Cunningham and Dreiling 2021). This resource dependency has further shaped what has been labeled as "inter-organizational isomorphism among donors and recipients", where philanthropic donors and their civil society beneficiaries develop binding social relationships and co-dependent views on the agendas they are working to influence (Cunningham and Dreiling 2021).

These concerns are further amplified by overwhelming evidence of funding gap and biases within philanthropy. For instance, the Philanthropic Initiative for Racial Justice and the Solutions Project suggests that nearly 95% of philanthropic funding directed to climate change is given to white- and male-led climate advocacy groups.[4] The fraction of funding that youth climate movements receive is as low as 0.76%, according to the Youth Climate Justice Study (n.d.). There is also evidence to suggest that for every dollar given toward climate action, only 1 to 2% goes directly to local organizations (Morena et al. 2022). For the communities most vulnerable to climate change and who are routinely at the forefront of preserving ecosystems, the share of philanthropic giving is dismally low – figures suggest that Indigenous and marginalized groups receive less than 1% of the total funds disbursed (Tinoco 2024).

However, in contrast to these criticisms, some views acknowledge philanthropy's positive influence and leadership in improving socio-economic realities across the developing world. Philanthropy creatively leverages resources to amplify grassroots voices and enables the formation of networks such as knowledge-sharing platforms and professional associations. Furthermore, philanthropy takes many forms. Beyond the large-scale philanthropic organizations led by billionaires in the Global North, there is a rapidly changing philanthropic landscape in the Global South, where numerous grant-making institutions work across various scales and geographies. As Maria Netto, Executive Director of Instituto Clima e Sociedade (iCS), a leading philanthropic institution in Brazil working to advance the climate agenda, explained to the author, "There are different ways to talk about philanthropy, and it is not just about billionaires. We need to demystify this idea and understand that the full potential of philanthropy includes a much larger pool of players." Especially in the Global South, regional organizations working directly with communities are leading the way, even if their work is not specifically labeled as "climate" funding. These organizations are addressing the actual impacts of climate change on the ground in ways that demand attention (Señan and Miller 2024).

Viewed through this lens, philanthropy – when organized effectively and equitably – can be a powerful force; it has the capacity to galvanize systemic change, experiment with various theories of impact, and employ a mix of impact investing approaches alongside open and flexible grants (Woodcraft, Munir, and Khemka 2024). There is tremendous variation within the sector. Community foundations that pool resources and funds differ in operations and ideologies from corporate or private foundations, which derive their wealth from companies or affluent families and indi-

---

4 See the Climate Justice Donor Collaborative for further analysis and information. Available online https://climatejusticecollab.org/reports/#:~:text=Of%20the%20philanthropy%20that%20is,(Youth%20Climate%20Justice%20Study).

viduals (Jung and Harrow 2015). Philanthropies also differ in intentions and approaches, often championing multiple perspectives and pursuing long-term agendas, irrespective of political shifts that may push sympathetic governments out of office. When acting as "field-builders", philanthropies are also influenced by their grantees, who exercise significant agency in shaping philanthropic priorities and directing attention to issues that matter most (Betsill et al. 2022). While some funders follow strategic philanthropy principles, others adopt emergent approaches that focus on core, multi-year funding and co-produced evaluation criteria. Additionally, numerous emerging initiatives in the sector aim to shift funding politics and respond to field needs by centering trust-based principles and designing inclusive funding practices.[5]

These debates are beyond the scope of this chapter, but it is important to acknowledge these tensions and bring them into focus when discussing the role philanthropy can play in unlocking climate finance. The main reason to do so is to start from the premise that there are many kinds of philanthropic actors and philosophies. More importantly, it is essential for those with strong expectations of philanthropy's power to shift the realities of climate finance to engage with these critiques. The sector cannot be granted carte blanche as a solution-maker to the global climate finance gap without appropriate institutional accounting that examines the problematic philanthropic role in the financialization of development or without a stocktake of current spending. Philanthropy can indeed be a force to be reckoned with, but we must be cautious in assuming it has greater abilities and reach that do not reflect current realities. Moreover, opaque press releases on major funding decisions made behind closed doors, without transparency on how those decisions were reached, are likely an ill-suited answer to closing a global climate finance gap rooted in and produced by structures of inequality. Observers and champions of philanthropy's positive potential should ultimately dissuade and advise against theories of change based on hierarchical presumptions formed without consultation. Instead, tackling the climate finance conundrum may be best encouraged through collaborative and equitable approaches, some of which already exist and will be explored next.

Tackling the Elephant: Philanthropic Approaches and Tactics

Just as there are many forms of philanthropic organizations, the role philanthropy plays in issues of climate finance is also varied. There are several intervention types,

---

5 Among those examples as Le Cornu et al. (2023) further discuss are initiatives like the Trust-Based Philanthropic Project, the Fund for Shared Insight, the Decolonizing Wealth Project, among many others.

some captured in Figure 16.1, which may be adopted by different philanthropies based on their strategies, operating size, and resources. The same philanthropic organization may also employ many of these strategies at once. While far from a comprehensive typology, this section will explore five identified strategies: working with the private sector to mobilize finance, supporting the creation of capacity platforms and other ecosystem infrastructure, working with grassroots organizations to enable local action, supporting civil society activism and mobilization, and generating evidence and alternative theories of change. These approaches can often be enabled by direct grant-making, but they can also stand as tactics in their own right. Some philanthropic institutions are also more systematically exploring impact investment, expanding their arsenal of tools beyond traditional grantmaking to focus on leveraging all available resources, including efforts to align investments with climate goals (Lewis 2024; Simpson 2024). While this chapter does not cover impact investment in detail, the following discussion offers a snapshot of five core strategies that can be scaled and amplified.

On one end of the spectrum, blended finance capital stacking, and other forms of catalytic investment intended to crowd in private sector finance and de-risk public finance are considered among the main advantages of philanthropic capital. These approaches open the door for larger private investment at later stages and encourage regulatory and policy changes (Beer 2023). When markets do not exist, philanthropy has a role to play in paving the way by investing in solutions that offer demonstration effects and build market appetite. Given the reality that the private sector funds only roughly 14% of green investments in Africa and 35% in all non-OECD countries on average, the need for blended finance models that encourage private sector investment and engagement in the developing world is routinely characterized as an area in which philanthropy can play a key role (Netto and Suchodolski 2023). Proponents of blended finance emphasize that the power of the model lies not simply in mixing different financing structures but in combining nonfinancial resources as well, including convening, market positioning, network creation, and knowledge integration across otherwise siloed players.[6]

The Hewlett Foundation-supported Climate Finance Fund offers a concrete example. Set up to mobilize private capital for climate solutions across China, the European Union, and the United States, the group has earmarked roughly USD 75 million to support financial system change and direct capital to financial products. Describing its mission as one focused on driving change through supporting innovative finance and

---

6 Blended finance has mobilized around USD 198 billion in capital towards sustainable development to date, according to data from Convergence. covering over 1800 unique investors who have participated in one or more blended finance transactions, Convergence also finds that 16% of that blended finance came from philanthropy. The Bill and Melinda Gates Foundation, the Shell Foundation, Omidyar Network, and Oikocredit are those most active in this area (*Figures and data cited in Netto and Suchodolski (2023)*).

the "systemic decarbonization of capital", the fund targets capital allocators across the supply chain. Among the examples of their support, the Fund enabled the Partnership for Carbon Accounting Financials standard to grow its membership from 16 in 2018 to 425 global financial institutions by 2023, with USD 93 trillion in assets under management (Silvi and Kocharekar 2024). The Fund also supported the Principles for Responsible Investment (PRI) in China, allowing it to expand from a handful of signatories in 2018 to over 140 institutions by the time of the Fund's first strategy evaluation (Silvi and Kocharekar 2024).

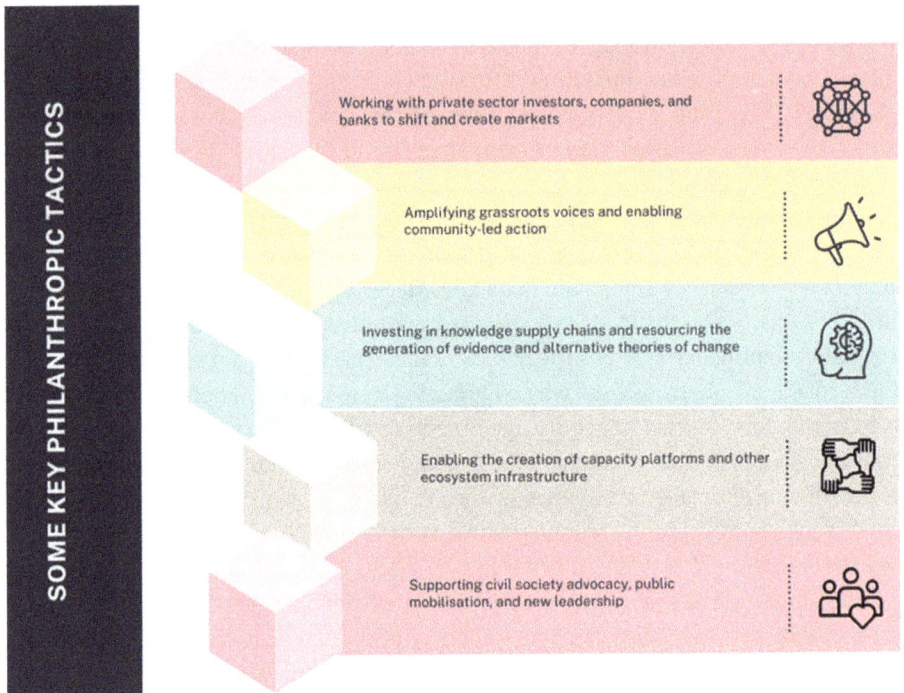

SOME KEY PHILANTHROPIC TACTICS

Working with private sector investors, companies, and banks to shift and create markets

Amplifying grassroots voices and enabling community-led action

Investing in knowledge supply chains and resourcing the generation of evidence and alternative theories of change

Enabling the creation of capacity platforms and other ecosystem infrastructure

Supporting civil society advocacy, public mobilisation, and new leadership

Figure 16.1: Philanthropic strategies and tactics for climate action.
Source: Author.

In the words of Marilyn Waite, Managing Director of the Climate Finance Fund, interviewed for this chapter, part of the logic is to support either market-based interventions in the form of innovation finance or to back critical convening that will allow for myths about incentives to be tackled. "We need to do anything we can to prove to the market that what is perceived as not viable *actually* is" (emphasis in original). "This may be done in multiple ways; it could be about proving that a certain location can bring certain returns, or it can be about investing in showcasing the various ways in which obstacles and barriers are often imagined." When philanthropy backs organizations to drive market-rule change or the rules of financial investment, which are often "skewed towards incumbent economic systems and inertia which are polluting technologies", they can play a strategic role in pushing for the transformation of the systems of finance and the rules that are not working for climate or social justice ends.

Other examples include the recent announcement that the Sustainable Development Goals Loan Fund successfully mobilized over USD 1 billion in investor capital to support the SDGs in emerging and frontier markets. Investors such as Allianz, FMO, and Skandia supported local companies with SDG-aligned loans across Latin America, Asia, Africa, and Eastern Europe, and this funding is guaranteed by the John D. and Catherine T. MacArthur Foundation, which committed a USD 25 million guarantee for credit enhancement. Targeting the energy sector, financial institutions, and agribusiness, the Fund's structure incorporates a "first-loss" investment from FMO and a partial, unfunded guarantee from MacArthur. This blended finance model is intended to support institutional investors who would otherwise not be able to finance high-impact loans in emerging markets (FMO: Entrepreneurial Development Bank 2023).

These approaches require institutional and knowledge infrastructure, and here lies another role that philanthropy plays: resourcing the development of capacity platforms requires intentionality, as does the generation of data required for actors to operate. As an example of the former, Bloomberg Philanthropies, alongside partners from an extensive network of multilateral development banks and international organizations, recently launched the Global Capacity Building Coalition.[7] The Coalition aims to increase the availability of climate finance technical programs for financial institutions in developing countries (Bloomberg Philanthropies 2023).

Philanthropy has played a historically crucial role in funding public goods, like the development of data and research points that can be used to develop informed policy positions and craft key advocacy campaigns. Among numerous examples, organizations like the Climate Policy Initiative, which has played a key role in climate finance debates, have received philanthropic funding. With this focus on the knowledge production supply chain, philanthropy is also serving a core mission. In the words of iCS's Netto, philanthropies can resource the development and design of practical tools that challenge funding patterns and surface blind spots. The most recent work of the Global Adaptation and Resilience Investment Working Group, particularly the release of their important publication identifying the investment opportunity for adaptation, offers a clear example of philanthropic resources and organizations partnering with others to enable agenda-setting thought leadership and the development of taxonomies to support redesigning financial flows (Collins et al. 2024). The investor

---

7 The founding participants of the Coalition include the European Bank for Reconstruction and Development, the African Development Bank, the United Nations Development Programme, the Inter-American Development Bank, among others. Among the initiative's goals is supporting domestic financial institutions with increased capacity to develop credible decarbonization plans as well as climate disclosures.

report and toolkit offer what the authors describe as the first-of-its-kind framework, identifying over 800 publicly traded companies working on resilience and showcasing methods investors can use to find these firms. This kind of knowledge and evidence base is crucial to enable investment.

A third and key role for philanthropy rests on the ability to work with a mix of organizations, especially civil society groups. Yamide Dagnet, Senior Vice President at the National Resources Defense Council and former Environmental Justice Director at the Open Society Foundations, described it to the author: "It is easier for governments to give money to other governments through bilateral cooperation. Philanthropies are expected to fund civil society directly. The issue of access then becomes key, especially as we try to make sure the funding is going to where it is needed the most." Many organizations dedicate their funding to this mission, but in all cases, most philanthropies adopt this strategy within their portfolios. As Dagnet put it, "When philanthropy's social, political, and financial capital is leveraged most effectively, philanthropy can amplify the voices of different kinds of leaders, especially from the Global South and frontline communities."

A crop of funders tackle support to grassroots efforts and initiatives led by frontline communities and explicitly aim to address some of the systemic biases in philanthropy and rectify the historic underspending on leaders from minority racial backgrounds. Efforts to rebalance which kinds of partners are seen as trusted and valuable are underway, with varying degrees of institutional commitments to principles of diversity, justice, equity, and inclusion in grant-making and strategy design (Alongi and Tilghman 2021). Within that fold, the newly established Youth Climate Justice Fund (YCJF) aims to rectify the inadequacy of funding for youth. Launched in 2023, the group is only beginning to set an example of how philanthropy can work differently for youth movements. They aim to create a first-of-its-kind youth-led mechanism to pair funding with youth-to-youth capacity development. Joshua Amponsem, Co-Director at the YCJF, says that "a big part of the philosophy is around transparency in grant-making" and enabling funders to learn from their partners, and not merely the other way around.

The Climate Justice Resilience Fund (CJRF), now led by a practitioner governing board, supports women, youth, and Indigenous Peoples to shape and convey their own lived experiences and practices of climate resilience. Since 2016, CJRF has pooled USD 25 million in funds from philanthropists and private foundations (Climate Justice Resilience Fund n.d). Demonstrating the relevance of this approach, CJRF's Director Heather McGray said in an interview with the author that the "moral authority" of many of the most vulnerable coalitions of countries has itself been elevated through resourcing support from funders, including but not limited to CJRF, who have committed to helping Global South advocates and leaders build coalitions that serve their agendas. "We have seen real creativity and leadership on many of the agendas that matter most to vulnerable countries directly from the Global South", McGray said. The role of philanthropic funding in this context has been to help these groups with both financial and political support, helping bring visibility to the leaders of the Global South so that they can champion their cause to an international audience and on a global stage.

Indeed, the mobilization around the Loss and Damage Fund was supported by a loose coalition of endowed funders and intermediaries, including the Open Society Foundations, the Children's Investment Foundation Fund (CIFF), the Climate Emergency Collaboration Group, Global Greengrants Fund, and CJRF, among others.[8] In the author's own experience, it is clear philanthropic finance and political convening actively contributed to the loss and damage governance debates, across scales, including by supporting the generation of local evidence from Global South communities, as well as resourcing legal and technical support to key negotiation groups. This polycentric approach implies that philanthropies played different roles, at different stages, and for different audiences; for some, they were funders, but for others, they were policy facilitators and strategic thought partners.

Across the spectrum of climate action, a host of intermediary organizations, re-granters, and mid-size family foundations distribute a vast number of relatively smaller grants. Many of these organizations play an outsized role in funding advocacy, strategic communications, the media, and community-led approaches. Individually, they may not be seen as major climate finance players, but together, they constitute a significant source for field-building activities, helping to shape ecosystems, particularly by framing advocacy agendas. The significance of local funds forming collaborative and unified strategies is also worth noting. For example, the recently created *Alianza Socioambiental Fondos del Sur* (Socio-Environmental Funds of the Global South) aims to highlight the role local funds play in supporting grassroots organizations and in making local action and knowledge visible. While these local funds are not often considered at the international policy level, their collective power could be consequential if fully harnessed. Each organization may operate on a small budget, but collectively, this growing and new coalition, as of this writing, comprises 15 local funds operating in 50 countries and has awarded over 9,000 grants, totaling nearly USD 84 million. Alianza is more than just a network; they see themselves, in the words of their Executive Coordinator Juliana Tinoco, as "activist funds, rooted in their communities", and describe their role as not merely about mobilizing funding but about disrupting top-down approaches that treat partners as passive recipients (Tinoco 2024).

These approaches further emphasize another philanthropic value-added: grant-making organizations can engage with nonconventional and experimental forms of understanding impact. For many organizations, particularly those working with local

---

8 At COP26, five philanthropic organizations committed a USD 3 million start-up fund to a prospective loss and damage facility. That funding was later programmed to support diplomatic coordination and civil society advocacy that ultimately helped create some of the key conditions for the negotiation of the historic Loss and Damage Fund in Egypt.

communities, the core additionality of philanthropic capital is providing support for high-risk ventures that defy the traditional conceptualization of what constitutes climate finance. Some projects may not yet have the potential for scalability or replicability, but they require philanthropic support when "learning itself is as important as the potential impact of the project", as Andrés Mogro, Regional Manager of the Climate Action Programme at Fundación AVINA, explained.

Flexible funding, especially for grassroots communities, can highlight the interconnections between climate risks and other forms of socioeconomic interventions. When funding is dedicated to open-ended learning, joint governance processes, and inclusivity, relationships between issues and change pathways can be better developed. Dagnet adds that when philanthropies take risks to "expand the field of partners", they are not only showcasing "where both the real needs are" but also "where under-supported leadership lies".

This principle also applies to resourcing the development of decarbonization technology and supporting capacity-building efforts around such technologies. Experimental learning, essential for the initial stages of research and development, is often difficult to fund through strict public procurement processes and may require billions of dollars in private sector investment to scale. Philanthropic capital can help seed innovation and bridge finance at early stages to support technological advancements and roll-out (McKinsey & Company 2021).

All in all, across these philanthropic tactics, scale is always relative, and the power of philanthropic interventions lies in the multiplicity of approaches. Philanthropy is far from a monolith. But across each of these interventions, there is a common truth: philanthropic capital is most powerful when it mobilizes others, whether that means building new centers of power, nurturing advocacy pathways, or crowding in additional finance. As CIFF's Global Director of Climate, Michael Hugman, put it, "On its own, a billion dollars might not go anywhere. However, the role of philanthropy, through advocacy and grant-making, is to help make the next ten happen. The system needs to be pushed, and philanthropy can help nudge that system forward."

Conclusion

Philanthropy has come a long way in supporting climate action. Coalitions and ecosystems of funders have played a unique role in influencing norms and supporting system learning. This chapter has explored some of the current ways in which philanthropy provides funding for innovative solutions at different scales, all while taking on higher relative risks compared to other players and shaping public agendas through financing movements, diplomatic advisory support, learning, the media, and other tools of mobilization. As Robin Rogers (2011) put it over a decade ago, arguing whether philanthropy is a global public policy player is no longer relevant – it should be accepted as a given.

The funding announcements that often capture the public's attention and media coverage are the millions or billions pledged to large-scale initiatives, routinely committed by extremely affluent individuals and their associated foundations. But this chapter has also argued that philanthropy comes in many forms, and the sector employs a diversity of tactics, each relevant and consequential. De-risking markets often receives disproportionate focus as the primary philanthropic intervention. However, the diversity of tactics discussed in this chapter suggests that de-risking is not the sole role of philanthropy. Even if all institutional funding were diverted exclusively to de-risking markets, it would still be insufficient to unlock the trillions of dollars needed to tackle climate change. More significantly, it would shift funding away from the thousands of civil society organizations that rely on philanthropic capital for their crucial and impactful activities as key actors in policy advances. This would be an incalculable loss. Especially when acting from a place of trust and with a focus on field-building, philanthropic foundations are well-positioned to support institutions and ideas that challenge the status quo.

Funding to local communities through small- to medium-sized grants can also be transformative, particularly in changing the course of community lives or evidencing new data. The latter offers a critical space for experimentation and for developing creative monitoring, evaluation, and learning frameworks – something neither public nor private finance could achieve alone. Both large-scale and community-level partnerships require similar commitments of human resources from philanthropies, which can discourage large, endowed foundations from such small-scale funding. The international community must press philanthropies to do both and not prioritize mega-pledges at the expense of addressing the significant funding gap at the local level. This local gap represents one of the thorniest challenges and is where the greatest global climate finance gap lies.

Philanthropy must do more, and do it faster, all while acknowledging the formal and informal power inherent in its capital and ways of doing business. As a sector, philanthropy is undoubtedly implicated in several power asymmetries. This can be addressed by centering principles of equity in strategy design and conducting a clear-eyed examination of the sector's own funding gaps and history. The philanthropic mobilization around adaptation, for instance, is woefully inadequate and requires a wholesale transformation, especially as climate extremes and impacts intensify.

Climate change presents an institutional and collective challenge of learning in real time. The good news is that philanthropy stands apart due to its comparative agility and capacity to evidence impact. The sector has a tremendous amount of expertise, both within individual organizations and through the ecosystems of policy partners it works with. Yet, there has been insufficient research and attention paid to the diversity within philanthropy and even within single organizations. Little systematic understanding exists regarding how staff, board members, or trustees shape strategies relative to their roles.[9] We must therefore promote greater transparency, research, and accountability within philanthropy itself if the sector is to rise to its potential as a catalyst in socio-economic and political transformation, appropriate to meet the scale of the climate crisis. The time for ambition is now.

References

Aggad, Faten. 2023. "Comparative Multilateral Philanthropy: The Cases of the European Union Commission and the Asian Development Bank on Crisis and Non-crisis Philanthropic Engagements." In *African Philanthropy: Philanthropic Responses to Covid-19 and Development Goals in Africa*, edited by Bhekinkosi Moyo, Mzukisi Qobo, and Nomfundo Ngwenya. Cheltenham: Edward Elgar Publishing.

Alongi, Talia, and Laura Tilghman. 2021. *Time to Act: How Philanthropy Must Address the Climate Crisis*. FSG: Reimagining Social Change.

Arab Foundations Forum. 2024. Arab Philanthropy Commitment on Climate Change (APCCC). November 2024. Accessed December 18, 2024. https://arabfoundationsforum.org/apccc/

Beer, Clare M. 2023. "Bankrolling Biodiversity: The Politics of Philanthropic Conservation Finance in Chile." *Environment and Planning E: Nature and Space* 6 (2): 1191–213.

Betsill, Michele M., Ashley Enrici, Elodie Le Cornu, and Rebecca L. Gruby. 2022. "Philanthropic Foundations as Agents of Environmental Governance: A Research Agenda." *Environmental Politics* 31 (4): 684–705.

Bloomberg Philanthropies. 2023. "UN Agencies, Multilateral Development Banks, Private Sector Finance, and Philanthropy Leaders Unite to Scale Climate Finance Capacity Building." December 1, 2023. Accessed December 18, 2024. https://www.bloomberg.org/press/un-agencies-multilateral-development-banks-private-sector-finance-and-philanthropy-leaders-unite-to-scale-climate-finance-capacity-building/

Climate Justice Resilience Fund. n.d. "About us." Accessed December 18, 2024. https://www.cjrfund.org/about-us

Collins, Lori, Umar Ashfaq, Turbold Baatarchuluu, Erica Downing, Tara Guelig, Jay Koh, and Linda-Eling Lee. 2024. *The Unavoidable Opportunity: Investing in the Growing Market for Climate Resilience Solutions*. Global Adaptation & Resilience Investment Working Group. March 2024. https://unavoidableopportunity.com/climate-change-white-paper/

Cunningham, Jeanine, and Michael C. Dreiling. 2021. "Networks for Environmental Philanthropy: Shaping Environmental Agendas in the Twenty-First Century." *Environmental Sociology* 7 (4): 351–67.

Desanlis, Helene, Narine Esmaeili, Karolina Janik, Tim Lau, and Megan Turnlund. 2023. *Funding Trends 2023: Climate Change Mitigation Philanthropy*. ClimateWorks Global Intelligence. San Francisco: ClimateWorks Foundation.

Esmaeili, Narine, Karolina Janik, Tim Lau, Surabi Menon, Hannah Roeyer, and Megan Turnlund. 2024. *Funding Trends 2024: Climate Change Mitigation Philanthropy*. ClimateWorks Global Intelligence. San Francisco: ClimateWorks Foundation.

FMO: Entrepreneurial Development Bank. 2023. "SDG Loan Fund Mobilizes USD 1.1 Billion of Investor Capital." November 28, 2023. Accessed December 18, 2024. https://www.fmo.nl/news-detail/6fb79fab-ec10-4e7e-9fe8-d908dda30b06/sdg-loan-fund-mobilizes-usd-1.1-billion-of-investor-capital

Gosnell, Greer, and Bruce Tsai. 2021. *Climate Philanthropy Landscape*. Global Health and Development: Research in Brief. Rethink Priorities & Open Philanthropy. San Francisco.

---

9 See Zavaleta et al. (2008) for a discussion on some of these points.

Jung, Tobias, and Jenny Harrow. 2015. "New Development: Philanthropy in Networked Governance Treading with Care." *Public Money & Management* 35 (1): 47–52.

Kempner, Randall. 2023. *Funding Climate Action: Pathways for Philanthropy*. The Aspen Institute and Morgan Stanley Private Wealth Management. Washington D.C

Kumar, Arun, and Sally Brooks. 2021. "Bridges, Platforms, and Satellites: Theorizing the Power of Global Philanthropy in International Development." *Economy and Society* 50 (2): 322–45.

Le Cornu, Elodie, Rebecca L. Gruby, Jeffrey E. Blackwatters, Ash Enrici, Xavier Basurto, and Michele Betsill. 2023. "Conceptualizing Responsible Exits in Conservation Philanthropy." *Conservation Science and Practice* 5 (5): e12868. https://doi.org/10.1111/csp2.12868

Lewis, Ian. 2024. "European Associations Seek Greater Use of Impact Investing in Philanthropy." *Impact Investor*, May 31, 2024. Accessed December 18, 2024. https://impact-investor.com/european-associations-seek-greater-use-of-impact-investing-in-philanthropy/.

McKinsey and Company. 2021. "It's Time for Philanthropy to Step Up the Fight Against Climate Change." *McKinsey Sustainability*, October 21, 2021. Accessed December 18, 2024. https://www.mckinsey.com/capabilities/sustainability/our-insights/its-time-for-philanthropy-to-step-up-the-fight-against-climate-change/

Morena, Edouard, Sofia Arroyo, Asad Rehman, and Dunja Krause. 2022. *Beyond 2%: From Climate Philanthropy to Climate Justice Philanthropy*. Geneva: United Nations Research Institute for Social Development (UNRISD); San Francisco: EDGE Funders Alliance.

Naran, Baysa, Jake Connolly, Paul Rosane, and Dharshan Wignarajah. 2022. *Global Landscape of Climate Finance: A Decade of Data*. Climate Policy Initiative. https://www.climatepolicyinitiative.org/publication/global-landscape-of-climate-finance-a-decade-of-data/

Netto, Maria, and Sergio Gusmao Suchodolski, eds. 2023. *Public Development Banks and Philanthropies: No Longer Strangers*. CEBRI: Centro Brasileiro de Relações Internacionais.

Nisbet, Matthew C. 2019. "Climate Philanthropy and the Four Billion (Dollars, That Is)." *Issues in Science and Technology* 35 (2): 34–36.

Reifsteck, Shawn. 2024. "As the Planet Heats Up, New Trends Drive Climate Giving." *ClimateWorks Foundation*. August 29, 2024. Accessed December 18, 2024. https://climateworks.org/blog/as-the-planet-heats-up-new-trends-drive-climate-giving/

Rockefeller Foundation and Boston Consulting Group (BCG). 2022. *Climate Finance Funding Flows and Opportunities: What Gets Measured Gets Financed*. November 2022. https://www.rockefellerfoundation.org/wp-content/uploads/2022/11/Climate-Finance-Funding-Flows-and-Opportunities-What-Gets-Measured-Gets-Financed-Report-Final.pdf

Rogers, Robin. 2011. "Why Philanthro-Policymaking Matters." *Society* 48 (5): 376–81.

Roeyer, Hannah, Jessica Hitt, Tanisha Reddy, and Megan Turnlund. 2024. "Foundation Funding for Climate Change Adaptation and Resilience." *ClimateWorks Global Intelligence*. November 2024. Accessed December 18, 2024. https://content.climateworks.org/progress-on-foundation-funding-for-climate-change-adaptation-and-resilience.

Señan, Laura, and Erika Miller. 2024. "Global South Leadership on Climate Philanthropy." *Alliance Magazine*, May 30, 2024. Accessed December 18, 2024. https://www.alliancemagazine.org/blog/global-south-leadership-on-climate-philanthropy/.

Silvi, Jennifer M., and Rohan Kocharekar. 2024. *Catalyzing System Change 2018–2023: Climate Finance Strategy Evaluation*. Climate Finance Fund. https://climatefinance.fund/wp-content/uploads/2024/03/CFF-Strat-Eval-V4.pdf

Simpson, Kathleen. 2024. "5 Ways to Redefine Philanthropy's Role in the Fight Against Climate Change." *World Economic Forum*, August 20, 2024. Accessed December 18, 2024. https://www.weforum.org/stories/2024/08/philanthropy-role-climate-action/

Songwe, Vera, Nicholas Stern, and Amar Bhattacharya. 2022. *Finance for Climate Action: Scaling Up Investment for Climate and Development*. London: Grantham Research Institute on Climate Change and the Environment, London School of Economics and Political Science.

Tubiana, Laurence, and Christie Ulman. 2022. "To Meet the Climate Challenge, Philanthropy Must Challenge Itself." *Stanford Social Innovation Review*, April 2022. Accessed December 18, 2024. https://ssir.org/articles/entry/to_meet_the_climate_challenge_philanthropy_must_challenge_itself

Woodcraft, Clare, Kamal Munir, and Nitya Mohan Khemka. 2024. "Introduction." In *Reimagining Philanthropy in the Global South: From Analysis to Action in a Post-COVID World*, edited by Clare Woodcraft, Kamal Munir, and Nitya Mohan Khemka. Cambridge: Cambridge University Press.

Youth Climate Justice Study. n.d. "Why Youth, why now?" Accessed December 18, 2024. https://youthclimatejusticestudy.org/why-youth-why-now-2/

Zavaleta, Erika, Daniel C. Miller, Nick Salafsky, Erica Fleishman, Michael Webster, Barry Gold, David Hulse, Mary Rowen, Gary Tabor, and Jack Vanderryn. 2008. "Enhancing the Engagement of U.S. Private Foundations with Conservation Science." *Conservation Biology* 22 (6): 1477–84.

Part Four: **Climate Finance from Regional and Local Perspectives**

Sagarika Chatterjee

Chapter 17
The Regional Platforms for Climate Projects (RPCP): Lessons Learned for Mobilizing Climate Finance for Tangible Projects

Abstract: This chapter presents the outcomes of the initiative on "Regional Platforms for Climate Projects" (RPCP), which was led by the COP27, COP28 and COP29 Presidencies, the UN Regional Commissions, and the UN Climate Change High-Level Champions in 2022–2024. The platforms were designed to advance the SDGs and Paris Agreement goals by catalyzing capital to flow to climate projects. The initiative included regional forums convening together regional project developers and relevant financiers focused on tangible projects seeking to secure finance. The chapter presents the major findings on what it takes to successfully secure financing for climate projects and the hurdles that emerged from the three editions of the initiative on RPCP. The findings are relevant to implementation of international finance goals to country platforms and financiers.

Keywords: Regional platforms, Blended finance, Private investment, Project pipelines, Investment opportunities, Technical assistance

Introduction

Discussions on climate finance often take place at the international or national level, yet they rarely address regional priorities or highlight specific investment opportunities. At the same time, financial institutions frequently claim they struggle to identify viable projects, while project developers express frustration over the lack of accessible funding. This disconnect has resulted in a persistent impasse that must be resolved. The Regional Platforms for Climate Projects (RPCP) initiative was developed as a means to bridge this gap and facilitate investment in climate projects.

Led by the UN Climate Change High-Level Champions, UN Regional Economic Commissions, and the COP27 Presidency, the RPCP initiative seeks to present a pipeline of investable projects aligned with the Paris Agreement, the United Nations

Note: This chapter is based on UN Climate Change High-Level Champions (2023). This is the Regional Platforms for Climate Projects Report: *Assets to Flows II One Year On. Outcomes and Insights from the Second Edition of the Regional Platforms for Climate Projects Initiative to Accelerate Climate Action and Advance the UN Sustainable Development Goals* launched at COP28.

Framework Convention on Climate Change, and the 2030 Agenda for Sustainable Development. The initiative prioritizes projects that are ready for implementation, expansion, or replication, while actively promoting private-sector participation and streamlining access to project development and financing opportunities.

Through "resource matchmaking sessions", the platforms connect institutional investors and financiers – whether public or private, debt or equity-based, commercial or philanthropic – with governments acting as project proponents. Additionally, the RPCP facilitates dialogue on investment opportunities and advocates for immediate, tangible action in climate finance and the Sustainable Development Goals (SDGs), including mitigation, adaptation, and nature-based solutions.

The platforms also serve as a mechanism for fostering collaboration among a diverse range of regional public and private stakeholders. By engaging these actors, the RPCP accelerates efforts to mobilize both public and private investments in concrete climate initiatives.

The 2023 and 2024 regional shortlists of climate projects were curated through a joint effort by the Climate Champions and UN Regional Commissions, with support from Global Implementation Partners, including SLK Capital and Boston Consulting Group (BCG) Africa. The selection process involved evaluating critical project details, such as ownership, business model, team composition, funding needs, and upcoming milestones. Other key considerations included the potential climate and SDGs impacts, expected financial returns, associated risks, and mitigation strategies. Typically, selection required extensive desk research and at least one in-depth virtual consultation with project developers. To date, climate project developers have secured nearly USD 2 billion in funding, based on data reported to the Climate Champions (UNFCCC 2024).

Refinement of the RPCP Approach over Time

The evolution of the RPCP approach has involved several key phases aimed at enhancing project curation, facilitating financing and strengthening global collaboration.

Initial Phase: Awareness and Proof of Concept (2022)

The first step in refining the RPCP approach was to increase awareness and establish proof-of-concept projects. In 2022, UN Climate Change High-Level Champions, in collaboration with the UN Regional Commissions, launched an initial effort to identify and curate climate initiatives. This process resulted in the identification of over 450 projects, programs, funds, and enterprises, which were compiled into two key documents: the UN Compendium of Climate-Related Initiatives and the supplementary Climate Champions' Extended Compendium of Climate-Related Initiatives (UN Climate

Change High-Level Champions 2023). These resources provided foundational project information to stakeholders, in preparation for COP27.

Second Phase: Focus on Matchmaking and Investment Readiness (2023)

Building on the groundwork established in 2022, the focus in 2023 shifted to facilitating project financing by connecting developers with suitable investors. A rigorous screening process was introduced to assess project readiness for investment, considering factors such as data quality, project maturity, anticipated climate impact, and the credibility of project sponsors.

To enhance matchmaking efforts, investors were categorized based on their geographic interests and funding criteria, which often remained confidential. This segmentation included commercial banks, development finance institutions (DFIs), asset managers, sovereign funds, venture capital firms, and philanthropic entities. The RPCP's regional platform then facilitated matchmaking through project teasers tailored to investor requirements, hybrid regional forums, and bilateral meetings between project developers and financiers.

Expanding Ecosystem Collaboration (2023)

In addition to direct matchmaking efforts, 2023 saw an increased emphasis on integrating RPCP initiatives with broader climate finance networks. This involved engagement with complementary initiatives such as the Independent High-Level Expert Group on Climate Finance, the Sustainable Debt Coalition, the Africa Carbon Markets Initiative (ACMI), and the Climate Policy Initiative (CPI). Furthermore, better coordination was initiated with organizations working on project pipelines, including the International Renewable Energy Agency (IRENA), the Climate Finance Accelerator, Africa50, C40 Cities, the Green Climate Fund, and the NDC Partnership.

RPCP also engaged with financial networks such as the Insurance Development Forum, UNEP Finance Initiative, the Institutional Investors Group on Climate Change (IIGCC), Principles for Responsible Investment (PRI), and the Glasgow Financial Alliance for Net Zero (GFANZ) Africa. These collaborations played a critical role in highlighting the common challenges faced by climate project developers and integrating those concerns into regional and international climate finance dialogues.

Scaling and Strengthening the Project Pipeline Ecosystem (2024)

By 2024, the RPCP initiative had shifted its focus to scaling up efforts by fostering an international ecosystem of organizations specializing in project pipelines. A key development in this phase was the collaboration with Chile-based Ambition Loop[1] and the Capital for Climate platform,[2] which facilitated the creation of the "Climate Investment Engine". This initiative, comprising over ten organizations curating climate project pipelines, was designed to enhance synergy and accelerate climate finance deployment. Notably, the Climate Investment Engine was recognized as a finalist in the World Economic Forum's GAEA Awards.

Capacity building emerged as another priority in 2024, with a stronger emphasis on equipping both project developers and financial institutions with practical tools. This included the launch of a technical assistance directory (UN Climate Change High-Level Champions n.d.) and collaborations with the Global Capacity Building Coalition (Global Capacity Building Coalition n.d.), the UN Economic Commission for Europe's PIERs (United Nations Economic Commission for Europe n.d.), the Capacity-building Alliance of Sustainable Investment (CASI), SLK Capital, and BCG.

Regional Events and Insights

Regional events played a critical role in connecting project developers with financiers while addressing region-specific climate finance challenges. Over the past 3 years, these forums have evolved to improve engagement and effectiveness:

– **2022:** Five regional forums were held in UN regional commission hubs (Bangkok, Addis Ababa, Beirut, Geneva, and Santiago). These events facilitated discussions on priority projects from a UN Member State perspective and engaged financiers in regional issues such as debt and carbon markets.

– **2023:** The approach shifted to holding forums in locations more likely to attract financiers and policymakers. Events were hosted in Bangkok, Abidjan, Dubai, Frankfurt, and Santiago, with a focus on unveiling regional project shortlists and discussing pertinent climate finance challenges. Additional high-level meetings took place at the Africa Climate Summit (Nairobi), the UN Secretary-General's Climate Ambition Summit (New York), COP28 (Dubai), and the UNFCCC's Mitigation Work Programme (Abu Dhabi, Bonn).

– **2024:** The format evolved further, with three targeted project pitch events in New York, Hamburg, and São Paulo. These events facilitated direct engagement between shortlisted investable projects and financiers, including multilateral de-

---

1 See: https://www.ambitionloop.earth/.
2 See: https://www.capitalforclimate.com/.

velopment banks (MDBs), the Green Climate Fund (GCF), DFIs, philanthropic organizations, commercial banks, and institutional investors. The projects showcased spanned sustainable energy, agriculture, nature-based solutions, and climate adaptation.

Additionally, each of COP27, COP28, and COP29 featured high-profile events highlighting climate project developers who had participated in regional forums. During these conferences, investable project lists were released as part of COP Finance Day activities, reinforcing the RPCP initiative's role in scaling climate finance. The 2024 Yearbook of Global Climate Action, presented by non-state actors and the Marrakech Partnership to Paris Agreement signatories, recognized the RPCP as a key effort in mobilizing climate finance (UNFCCC 2024).

In 2023, the RPCP encompassed 63 initiatives from 35 countries across Africa, the Arab region, Asia-Pacific, Europe, and Latin America and the Caribbean. These projects spanned a variety of climate-related themes, including clean energy (23 projects), energy transition (3 projects), e-mobility (9 projects), sustainable agriculture (7 projects), eco-restoration (4 projects), water management (6 projects), and waste management (5 projects). Collectively, these projects required approximately USD 80 billion in capital investment, with the highest demand for funding and financial instruments emerging from the Asia-Pacific and European regions (UN Climate Change High-Level Champions 2023).

As of the latest assessment, more than 30 projects – predominantly from Africa – were engaged in advanced negotiations with financial institutions and investors. Nineteen of these projects had secured partial funding. Institutions involved in financing discussions included commercial banks, asset management firms, and DFIs. The primary sources of funding consisted of venture capital, DFIs, and a limited number of philanthropic contributions.

Given the diverse range of sectors and impacts these projects encompass, identifying a uniform set of success factors is challenging. However, key determinants include a conducive regulatory and economic environment, a well-structured business model, credible stakeholders, and long-term contractual agreements that reassure capital providers.

Several factors were commonly cited as critical to fostering an enabling environment: macroeconomic stability and long-term growth prospects, a supportive policy and regulatory framework, currency stability, active participation of domestic financial institutions, standardized and enforceable contracts, and adherence to high-integrity environmental, social, and governance (ESG) criteria. Additionally, expanding blended finance mechanisms and enhancing the tracking and scaling of adaptation finance emerged as recurring themes.

Insights from the 2023 regional forums, which facilitated dialogue between the UN system, policymakers, and financial institutions, are summarized below. The information provided on projects reflects their status as of October 2023,[3] though specific financing details remain confidential and accessible only to potential investors.

Asia-Pacific

The Asia-Pacific forum convened in Bangkok, Thailand, on May 17, 2023, as part of the 79th Annual Economic and Social Commission for Asia and the Pacific (ESCAP) Summit. The event hosted 40 participants and featured the presentation of 4 projects to over 15 financial institutions and investors, including the Asian Development Bank, Asian Infrastructure Investment Bank, Citi, ClimateWorks Foundation, HSBC, Riverstone, and Standard Chartered Bank. The projects aligned with regional priorities such as a just energy transition, agricultural and food production, civilian infrastructure development, and land restoration. These focus areas were informed by ESCAP's ongoing collaboration with UN member states in the region.

Key Takeaways

The following insights emerged from the discussions:

- Effective collaboration between local governments and private-sector stakeholders is crucial for the success of sustainability-focused initiatives. One illustrative example is a Mongolian project facilitating the transition from charcoal to cleaner energy sources. UNICEF played a pivotal role in securing commitments from local governments and ensuring community ownership, while private-sector partners contributed technical expertise. A neutral facilitator was instrumental in the project's early stages.
- Foundations and nongovernmental organizations (NGOs) play a vital role in the initial development phases of sustainable energy initiatives. At this stage, projects may not yet meet the investment criteria for commercial financiers seeking market-rate returns. Technical expertise is also critical to ensuring climate and Sustainable Development Goal (SDG) impacts. For instance, in Indonesia, a Social Forestry project received grant-based support from foundations to initiate pilot-phase activities. These organizations also provided technical assistance and facilitated community engagement to enhance the project's long-term viability.

---

3 The shortlisted project teasers for 2022, 2023, and 2024 are publicly available on UN Climate Change High-Level Champions n.d., with the 2024 project teasers including project developer contact details to accelerate connections to financiers: https://climatechampions.unfccc.int/system/sponsoring-climate-projects/.

Fairventures Social Forestry (FSF): A Scalable Approach to Reforestation

Project Overview
FSF has developed an investable and scalable model for restoring degraded tropical lands, while preserving existing forests. This initiative is carried out in close collaboration with local communities to foster sustainable, legally compliant income sources, thereby reducing reliance on environmentally destructive practices such as slash-and-burn agriculture and illegal logging. Local community engagement is a cornerstone of FSF's approach, ensuring the long-term viability of restoration efforts. The project utilizes agroforestry systems that integrate fast-growing timber species with agricultural crops, while also generating revenue through carbon sequestration.

Key Milestones
- To date, FSF has rehabilitated 450 hectares of previously degraded land, securing EUR 4.1 million in funding for demonstration projects and an additional EUR 2 million for expansion into new areas.
- FSF has established agreements with three Java-based lightwood timber processors for an annual offtake of over 600,000 cubic meters of timber.
- The organization secured its first impact loan from UBS Optimus Foundation and finalized its first carbon offtake contract with a German mid-sized enterprise.

Financing Needs
FSF seeks impact equity, loans, and grants from investors committed to funding climate solutions with measurable environmental and social benefits. Specific financing requirements are available upon request for interested investors.

Social and Environmental Impact Targets
Economic and Employment Growth
- Currently, FSF has created 50 full-time equivalent (FTE) positions within a local subsidiary and employed 130 field workers.
- By 2032, the project aims to generate 500 direct FTE roles within its special-purpose vehicle (SPV) and provide employment for 5,000 field workers.

Sustainability Goals
- **Carbon Mitigation:** The initiative aims to sequester a certifiable 6 million metric tons of CO_2-equivalent.
- **Land Restoration and Conservation:**
  - By 2032, FSF intends to rehabilitate over 35,000 hectares of degraded land.
  - By 2023, more than 15,000 hectares of existing forest will have been protected.

Community and Inclusivity Goals
- FSF aims to positively impact over 25,000 rural livelihoods by 2032.
- The project expects to create approximately 3,100 jobs for women, based on insights from its pilot initiatives.

Africa 2023 Forum: Highlights

The African Forum, held on June 5, 2023, in Abidjan, Ivory Coast, brought together 130 participants, including representatives from 30 investment organizations and seven project presentations. The event attracted key players from both the private and public sectors, including DFIs such as the African Development Bank and the Africa Finance Corporation, commercial banks, and NGOs. A key feature of the forum was a matchmaking session, facilitating direct engagement between project developers and potential investors. The featured projects spanned multiple climate-related themes, including energy transition, waste management, electric mobility, digital transformation, sustainable food production, and the development of Africa's carbon credit markets.

Key Reflections on Climate Finance in Africa

Challenges in Mobilizing Climate Finance

At the 2023 forum, Jean-Paul Adam, Director of Policy Monitoring and Advocacy at the UN Office of the Special Advisor on Africa, underscored several persistent barriers to climate finance on the continent (UN Climate Change High-Level Champions 2023). These include:

- Political instability and governance challenges
- Complex macro- and microeconomic conditions
- Limited pipelines of bankable projects
- Insufficient technical expertise
- Perceived and actual counterparty risks
- Lack of transparency and accountability.

Addressing these barriers requires targeted interventions in three key areas:

- **Shaping the Narrative** – Stakeholders must move beyond discussions of "energy transition" and instead emphasize economic transformation. This involves shifting Africa's economic model to prioritize value-added industries that generate wealth and alter the global business landscape.
- **Enhancing Stakeholder Support** – Strengthening the role of African regional banks and multilateral development institutions is critical in bridging the gap between governments and private investors. These institutions should facilitate financing, partnerships, and project scalability.
- **Overcoming Market Barriers** – A deeper understanding of market constraints is necessary to unlock private sector investment. This includes not only assessing financial risks but also identifying mechanisms that can de-risk investments and enhance investor confidence.

Debt, Climate Resilience, and Adaptation

Climate resilience projects in Africa are often financed through debt instruments. However, many African nations have faced worsening debt sustainability due to pandemic-related expenditures and inflationary pressures linked to geopolitical events (Bayar, To, and Bale 2023). Recognizing these challenges, COP27 saw the launch of the

Sustainable Debt Coalition, an initiative aimed at restructuring sovereign debt through Key Performance Indicator (KPI)-linked instruments, such as debt-for-nature and climate swaps.

While these instruments offer potential solutions, many African countries lack the technical capacity or political commitment to implement them effectively. In response, institutions like the African Development Bank are working to provide credit under favorable terms, leveraging risk guarantees and technical assistance to create an environment conducive to sustainable investment.

The Role of Insurance in Climate Adaptation

Insurance products will be crucial in supporting Africa's climate transition. However, the development of parametric insurance – policies that provide payouts based on pre-defined climate triggers – requires more comprehensive data collection to be viable.

Carbon Credit Markets in Africa

Africa's carbon credit markets remain largely voluntary, with relatively low pricing, exacerbated by concerns over credit integrity following recent market scandals. Strengthening regulatory frameworks and enhancing transparency will be essential in positioning African carbon credits as a credible asset class in global compliance markets.

Schonau Solar Energy: Advancing Renewable Power in Southern Africa

Project Overview

Schonau Solar Energy is a 116 MW solar photovoltaic (PV) power plant, developed by Emesco in Namibia, with the primary objective of supplying electricity to the Southern African Power Pool (SAPP). By introducing renewable energy into a grid traditionally dependent on fossil fuels, the project aims to reduce carbon emissions, improve energy security, and address the region's electricity shortfall.

This initiative is expected to pave the way for similar renewable energy projects in the region by demonstrating the viability of merchant-based power sales. Schonau Solar Energy will generate and distribute electricity in areas with high solar irradiance, selling power through SAPP's competitive market or via long-term bilateral agreements with member utilities. Since market pricing is subject to supply and demand fluctuations, Emesco has enlisted third-party consultants to assess project feasibility using historical market data.

Key Milestones

– **Regulatory Approvals:** Secured ministerial land and environmental consents, lease agreements, and generation and export licenses

– **Financial Progress:** Received project preparation funding from the Development Bank of Namibia (DBN) and a letter of intent for partial funding
– **Partnerships:** Collaboration with DBN and engagement with potential investors

Financing Requirements
Schonau Solar Energy is seeking investment from DFIs, commercial banks, and financial guarantors. Detailed financing requirements are available for interested investors upon request.

Social and Environmental Impact Goals
Economic Contributions
– The project will supply electricity to the SAPP grid, benefiting nine countries and approximately 350 million people.
– During construction, 400 temporary jobs will be created, with 11 permanent positions available during operations.

Sustainability Goals
– **Annual Carbon Emission Reduction:** 335,429 metric tons of CO_2-equivalent in the first year.
– **Cumulative Reduction by 2030:** 1,525,770 metric tons of CO_2-equivalent.

Community Benefits and Inclusivity
– The project is situated in a region with minimal economic activity, and nearby marginalized communities will directly benefit from employment opportunities.
– One percent of total revenue will be allocated to local community development initiatives.

European Regional Forum: Insights from Frankfurt

On July 4, 2023, the European Regional Forum was held in Frankfurt, Germany, drawing 199 participants and representatives from 120 investment organizations. The event featured four energy transition projects from emerging European markets – Kazakhstan, Turkey, Georgia, and Tajikistan – collectively valued at an estimated USD 4 billion.

These initiatives span multiple sectors, encompassing lithium-ion battery production, energy storage systems, hydrogen projects, wind power, and critical raw material (CRM) supply chains. The forum provided an in-depth exploration of the complexities and investment potential within Europe's evolving energy landscape.

Key Takeaways

- **Holistic Infrastructure Approach:** Experts emphasized that successful clean energy projects require more than just renewable power generation; they must be supported by robust infrastructure, investment in electricity grids, and competitive pricing mechanisms through structured tenders.
- **Financing Challenges:** Rising debt financing costs for renewables—exacerbated by supply chain bottlenecks—necessitate financial risk mitigation tools such as guarantees and concessional financing. The use of sovereign-backed offtake agreements was highlighted as a key strategy.
- **Private Sector Role:** Collaboration between public and private entities is essential for achieving net-zero targets efficiently. Investors and governments must align their sustainability goals to maximize impact.
- **Insurance Market Dynamics:** Political risk insurance should be considered an investment rather than a mere expense, as it plays a crucial role in stabilizing energy project financing.
- **Innovation in Project Structuring:** While investors seek novel approaches, developers remain cautious about oversimplifying financing structures for complex, large-scale projects.

Nigoza Wind Power Plant: Strengthening Georgia's Renewable Energy Sector

Project Overview
The Nigoza Wind Power Plant is a 50-MW onshore wind project in Shida Kartli, Georgia. Currently, in the permitting stage, it is the first privately developed wind energy initiative in the country and aligns with Georgia's national renewable energy strategy.

With favorable wind conditions (Class II wind speeds) and strong site accessibility, the project offers a bankable structure, including a 15-year power purchase agreement (PPA), with potential for export. It follows a Build-Own-Operate (BOO) model, providing long-term revenue stability.

Key Milestones
- **Technical and Environmental Studies:** A full feasibility study – including 4 years of wind data collection – has been completed. An Environmental and Social Impact Assessment (ESIA) and grid connection studies have also been conducted.
- **Regulatory Progress:** The Government of Georgia and the project company were negotiating an implementation agreement at the time of its feature by the Climate Champions.
- **Financial Structure:** USD-indexed 15-year PPA tariff secured.
- **Partnerships:** Collaboration with Tier-I turbine suppliers.

Investment Requirements
- The project seeks renewable energy investments, particularly from independent power producers (IPPs).

Social and Environmental Benefits

Energy Supply and Beneficiaries
- The plant's annual electricity generation will supply clean energy to 50,000–60,000 households in the region.

Job Creation and Economic Growth
- Up to 200 jobs will be created during construction, with 25 permanent positions available post-construction.
- The project will generate additional local revenue through tax payments and land lease agreements.

Sustainability and Climate Goals

Alignment with Georgia's Climate Strategy 2030:
- 35% reduction in total greenhouse gas (GHG) emissions by 2030.
- 15% reduction in GHG emissions in the energy sector by 2023.

Support for Low-Carbon Energy Transition:
- The project is expected to cut emissions by approximately 65,000 metric tons of CO_2 annually.
- Increased wind power capacity will contribute to Georgia's renewable energy targets.

Gender and Social Inclusion
- The project's sponsors adhere to internal policies promoting gender equality and workplace diversity

Latin America and the Caribbean: Regional Forum Insights

The Latin America and the Caribbean Forum took place on September 28, 2023, in Santiago, Chile, with over 400 participants attending both in person and virtually. The event featured a bankability study for a portfolio of 55 energy transition projects, conducted by the Climate Champions, the UN Economic Commission for Latin America and the Caribbean (ECLAC), and other partners.

Additionally, the UN Economic Commission for Europe presented the Global Gateway Investment Agenda for the region, originally introduced during the 2023 EU-ECLAC Summit. A key focus was identifying potential regional financial partners.

Key Takeaways

- **Climate Financial Risk Management:** Discussions explored how regional financial regulators – particularly in Brazil and Mexico – are incorporating climate-related financial risk analysis into policy frameworks, including the development of green taxonomies.
- **Regulatory Advancements:** ECLAC's study provided insights from 10 jurisdictions, outlining how climate finance policies are evolving across the region.

Key Insights

The event highlighted several critical insights related to climate finance, private sector engagement, and sustainable investment strategies.

- **The Role of Ministries of Finance in Green Business Development:** Ministries of Finance play a crucial role in fostering an environment conducive to private-sector participation in sustainable business ventures. However, in many developing economies, these ministries lack the necessary technical expertise. To bridge this gap, capacity-building initiatives should be implemented, alongside enhanced collaboration between government departments and support from international organizations.
- **Corporate Contributions to Debt Issuance and ESG Performance:** Between 2009 and 2021, corporate entities became the leading contributors to debt issuance across the continent. The popularity of green, blue, social, and sustainability-linked bonds has surged, with such instruments accounting for 31% of total debt issuance in 2021. A study presented at the forum analyzed 439 corporations that issued bonds between 2018 and 2022. The findings indicated that companies demonstrating strong ESG performance generally benefited from lower borrowing costs, though country-specific and sectoral factors also influenced these outcomes.
- **Challenges in ESG Reporting and Disclosure:** Another study assessed ESG reporting trends across different regions and sectors. The analysis revealed that disclosure levels remain low, highlighting the need for corporations and regulators to enhance transparency and best practices. Additionally, the proliferation of multiple reporting methodologies and taxonomies presents challenges for regulators. To streamline ESG reporting, stakeholders should work toward adopting internationally recognized frameworks, such as the IFRS Sustainability Disclosure Standards or the Sustainability Accounting Standards Board (SASB) guidelines.

Acción Andina: A Large-Scale Forest Restoration Initiative

Project Overview

Acción Andina is a long-term, large-scale initiative focused on restoring and protecting one million hectares of native high-Andean forest ecosystems. The project spans Argentina, Bolivia, Chile, Ecuador, Peru, and, by 2024, Colombia and Venezuela. This initiative is a joint effort by Global Forest Generation (GFG) and Asociación Ecosistemas Andinos (ECOAN).

To achieve its ambitious targets, Acción Andina aims to secure a combination of private, public, and multilateral investments over the next decade, ensuring that at least 80% of funding is sourced from within the region for long-term financial sustainability. By blending international philanthropic seed grants with regional investments in climate resilience and green infrastructure, the initiative seeks to establish a regional Trust Fund to effectively manage these financial resources.

Key Milestones
- **Operational Goals:** Launch a Trust Fund in 2024 to manage, blend, and distribute private and public investments.
- **Financial Progress:** Secured initial seed funding to establish the Trust Fund and support project implementation across the Andes.
- **Strategic Partnerships:** Collaborations with Salesforce, One Tree Planted, Milkywire, Klarna, Coca-Cola, the World Economic Forum, UNEP, FAO, and the UN Decade on Ecosystem Restoration.

Investment requirements
- The project is seeking funding from impact investors and climate-focused financial institutions.

Social and Environmental Impact Goals

Economic and Community Benefits (by 2030)
- Directly benefits 1 million rural and Indigenous Peoples across seven countries.
- Over 100 million native trees will be cultivated and planted.
- 500,000 hectares of degraded land will be reforested and managed under active restoration programs.
- 200,000 hectares of existing high-Andean forests will be placed under conservation protection.

Sustainability and Climate Resilience
- The initiative enhances climate resilience by improving water and food security, conserving biodiversity, and supporting local livelihoods, thereby reducing urban migration and preventing deforestation in the Amazon.
- Ongoing development of advanced monitoring protocols to assess biodiversity and water security impacts.

Inclusivity and Indigenous Leadership
- Acción Andina operates through a network of local conservation leaders and grassroots organizations with extensive experience working alongside Indigenous communities.

West Asia and North Africa: Key Takeaways from the Regional Forum

The West Asia and North Africa (WANA) forum took place on November 6 in Dubai, UAE, drawing 156 participants from diverse sectors. Attendees included representatives from multilateral financial institutions (such as the European Investment Bank, the European Bank for Reconstruction and Development, and the International Finance Corporation), regional banking groups, corporations, and NGOs.

The forum focused on climate finance solutions for low- and middle-income countries in the region, showcasing projects totaling USD 8.8 billion from Algeria, Egypt, Jordan, Lebanon, Oman, and Tunisia. These projects target green hydrogen production, sustainable urban mobility, water desalination, wastewater treatment, forest management, and land restoration.

Key Insights

Climate Change Impacts and Just Transition: The Arab region is experiencing an increasing number of extreme weather events, including floods and droughts, leading to climate-induced displacement. These challenges highlight the need for a just transition that ensures sustainable development while addressing social and economic inequalities.
- **Uneven Climate Finance Distribution:** Certain countries, such as Egypt and Morocco, have successfully attracted private capital and fostered enabling investment conditions. However, least developed countries like Mauritania, Somalia, Sudan, and Yemen struggle to secure adequate funding. To bridge this gap, more efforts are needed to mobilize climate finance, particularly for small-to-medium enterprises, women, and youth-led initiatives.
- **Strengthening Project Bankability:** To attract investment, projects must be designed with financial sustainability and risk mitigation in mind. The adoption of regional green taxonomies and the use of blended finance mechanisms can support climate action initiatives. Public–private partnerships have proven to be effective in de-risking investments, lowering borrowing costs, and enhancing the bankability of projects in least developed countries.

- **Enhancing Climate Project Pipelines:** Identifying and supporting actionable and investable projects is crucial. Established frameworks such as the NDC Partnership's project alignment checklists can help streamline proposals and improve funding access (NDC Partnership n.d.).

Al Batina Treated Effluent Line

The Omani Water and Wastewater Company is strategically working to enhance the utilization of tertiary treated effluent (TE) due to its environmental and economic value. TE is particularly beneficial for projects such as food security initiatives, as well as various industrial and commercial applications, considering Oman's classification under the water poverty line. This project is recognized as a strategic infrastructure development in Oman and serves as a unique case study in the circular economy. However, the appropriate operational model remains under discussion.

Project Overview

The Al Batina Treated Effluent Line is a project undertaken by the Oman Water and Wastewater Company (OWWSC), operating under Nama Water Services (NWS). This initiative involves constructing a tertiary treated effluent pipeline with a capacity of 40,000 cubic meters per day, extending from the A' Rumais area (Barka) to the Al Maghsar area (Al Musana), covering a distance of 35 kilometers.

OWWSC is committed to maximizing the use of TE due to its significant environmental and economic benefits. The project aligns with national objectives such as food security and sustainable water management, particularly considering Oman's constrained freshwater resources. Key stakeholders in the project include NWS, the Ministry of Agriculture, Oman Food Investment Company, and the Ministry of Economy. While the project is acknowledged as essential infrastructure, discussions are ongoing regarding the optimal implementation model.

By implementing this initiative, the government aims to reduce reliance on desalinated water, cut carbon emissions by 40,000 cubic meters per day, and conserve groundwater as a strategic reserve.

Social Impact Targets

Project Beneficiaries

- 1,100 farmers will benefit from the project, with 40,000 cubic meters of treated effluent per day being sufficient to irrigate approximately 5,600 acres of wheat (assuming 5 acres per farmer).

Employment Creation

- Beyond the direct beneficiaries, multiple job opportunities will emerge along the value chain.

- A projected 30% reduction in groundwater extraction and desalinated water use for non-potable needs in the region will free financial resources that can be redirected toward job creation in other sectors.
- The project will support the establishment of:
  - 10 agricultural/food production facilities
  - 3 municipalities for landscaping purposes
  - 5 industrial facilities utilizing treated effluent
  Sustainability
- Expected mitigation includes a reduction of 2.3 million tons of CO_2 emissions per year.
- 2,240 hectares of barren land will be converted into productive use or protected from degradation.
- The project is expected to save 73 million cubic meters of water over 5 years.
- A 26% increase in green spaces and agricultural production irrigated by treated effluent is anticipated.
- The initiative will contribute to a 10% reduction in GHG emissions for the region, compared to baseline levels.

Key Lessons from the Regional Platform for Climate Projects (RPCP)

Unlocking Climate Finance Through Regional Platforms

Regional Climate Project Platforms play a vital role in mobilizing private investment by facilitating collaboration between governments, financiers, and project developers. Scaling private finance requires an unprecedented level of international and regional cooperation, financial de-risking mechanisms, and public-private dialogue on priorities.

Curating Project Pipelines for Investment Readiness

A well-structured project pipeline is essential for securing funding. The regional forums leading up to COP27, COP28, and COP29 demonstrated that investment opportunities exist, but project developers face challenges in identifying suitable financing mechanisms. A strategic approach to project selection and clustering can catalyze investor interest and improve capital allocation.

Financial Architecture Reform and De-risking Strategies

Both public and private financial institutions must accelerate efforts to scale up climate investment. MDBs should expand their role in risk mitigation, capital cost reduction, and financing large-scale climate projects (Songwe, Stern, and Bhattacharya 2022). Additionally, DFIs should enhance support for green investments, leveraging blended finance models to bridge funding gaps.

Scaling Technical Assistance for Project Development

Technical assistance is critical for supporting early-stage climate projects, particularly in emerging markets and developing economies. Effective technical assistance programs and capacity building help reduce market inefficiencies, improve project design, and enhance sustainability impact assessments. The Climate Champions Initiative has developed a technical assistance directory to connect project developers with relevant resources and expertise.

The transition to a sustainable, climate-resilient economy requires fundamental changes in the global financial system. The RPCP offers a promising framework for scaling climate finance, fostering collaboration, and ensuring that impactful projects receive the funding and support they need.

Conclusion

The global financial system requires substantial reform at international, national, and regional levels to efficiently support climate-related financing in developing countries. At present, the system does not function effectively for climate project developers and financiers. Early-stage initiatives struggle to access capacity-building resources, while those that have secured initial funding often face difficulties obtaining subsequent investment to scale their efforts.

Although the broader financial system continues to evolve, there is an urgent need to strengthen climate project pipelines. During our 2024 forums, financiers repeatedly emphasized the need for a systematic approach to generating and showcasing climate projects throughout the year. However, the current landscape of organizations managing climate project pipelines remains fragmented. Many of these organizations perform critical work but lack the necessary resources to operate at the scale and speed required.

In response, the Climate Champions have partnered with Ambition Loop and Capital for Climate to establish The Climate Investment Engine. This initiative seeks to streamline the process for financiers to discover viable projects, regardless of their origin. Successful implementation of this effort will require the backing of national policymakers, MDBs, and DFIs, and will contribute to expanding the pool of available climate projects.

As efforts intensify to scale climate finance toward 2030, the RPCP presents a promising avenue for channeling funds and technical assistance to viable initiatives. By facilitating real-time collaboration with organizations advancing climate project pipelines, the RPCP can enhance accessibility to funding opportunities.

In the short term, regional platforms aim to:
- continue presenting concrete investment opportunities to financiers at a regional level;
- identify and source new projects, while engaging targeted financiers through external thematic platforms and portals;
- enhance capacity-building efforts to equip climate project developers with the tools needed to access financial resources; and
- foster collaboration with technical assistance providers and experts to support project aggregation and risk mitigation strategies.

References

Bayar, Kifaye Didem, Anthony Tin Yu To, and Ogma Dessirama Bale. 2023. "Slowing Debt Accumulation, Growing Risks: Unveiling the Complexities of Sub-Saharan Africa's Debt Burdens." *World Bank Blog Posts*, March 27, 2023. Accessed December 20, 2024. https://blogs.worldbank.org/en/opendata/slowing-debt-accumulation-growing-risks-unveiling-complexities-sub-saharan-africas-debt

Global Capacity Building Coalition. n.d. "Building Capacity. Unlocking Capital. A World-Leading Platform to Help Financial Institutions Seize the Opportunities of the Transition to Clean and Resilient Economies." Accessed December 18, 2024. https://capacity-building.org/.

NDC Partnership. n.d. "Climate Toolbox: NDC Implementation Readiness Checklist". Accessed December 20, 2024. https://ndcpartnership.org/knowledge-portal/climate-toolbox/ndc-implementation-readiness-checklist.

Songwe, Vera, Nicholas Stern, and Arun Bhattacharya. 2022. *Finance for Climate Action: Scaling Up Investment for Climate and Development*. London: Grantham Research Institute on Climate Change and the Environment, London School of Economics and Political Science.

UN Climate Change High-Level Champions. n.d. "Sponsoring Climate Projects: About the Regional Platforms for Climate Projects." Accessed December 18, 2024. https://climatechampions.unfccc.int/system/sponsoring-climate-projects/.

UN Climate Change High-Level Champions. 2023. *Regional Platforms for Climate Projects: Assets to Flows II One Year On. Outcomes and Insights from the Second Edition of the Regional Platforms for Climate Projects Initiative to Accelerate Climate Action and Advance the UN Sustainable Development Goals*. November. https://capacity-building.org/knowledge-hub/4766ce68-a2cb-4dec-b92b-d372af69f183

United Nations Economic Commission for Europe. n.d. "PPP and Infrastructure Evaluation and Rating System (PIERS): An Evaluation Methodology for the SDGs." Accessed December 18, 2024. https://piers.unece.org/.

United Nations Framework Convention on Climate Change (UNFCCC). 2024. *Yearbook of Global Climate Action 2024: Marrakech Partnership for Global Climate Action.* November. https://unfccc.int/sites/default/files/resource/Yearbook_GCA_2024.pdf.

Patricia Espinosa, Ravi Menon, and Mahmoud Mohieldin

Chapter 18
GFANZ Regional Networks for Africa, Asia-Pacific, and Latin America and the Caribbean

Abstract: The Glasgow Financial Alliance for Net Zero (GFANZ) is an independent, private-sector-led initiative focused on mobilizing capital and removing barriers to investment in the global net-zero transition. To ensure global inclusivity and regional relevance, GFANZ launched Networks in Africa, the Asia-Pacific region (APAC), and Latin America and the Caribbean (LAC), along with local chapters in Brazil, the Caribbean, Hong Kong, and Japan. GFANZ brings together financial sector firms that recognize the opportunities presented by this transition and aims to drive transition finance and unlock private capital at scale by supporting capacity-building and developing innovative financing opportunities and solutions. Each Regional Network is guided by an Advisory Board that provides strategic guidance and advice to the Network. Each Advisory Board is composed of CEOs of financial institutions and experts on transition finance.

This chapter outlines the unique contexts, challenges, priorities, and successes of each Network and showcases how GFANZ is building capacity to enable transition finance to support a just and inclusive transition.

Keywords: Net-zero transition, Financial sector, Private capital, Regional networks, Asia-Pacific, Africa, Latin America and the Caribbean

Introduction

The Glasgow Financial Alliance for Net Zero (GFANZ) is an independent, private-sector-led initiative focused on mobilizing capital and removing barriers to investment in the global net-zero transition. GFANZ brings together financial sector firms – including banks, insurers, asset owners, asset managers, and service providers – that recognize the opportunities presented by this transition. GFANZ aims to help drive transition finance and unlock private capital at scale by supporting capacity building and developing innovative financing opportunities and solutions.

Recognizing that the transition must be globally inclusive while also tailored to regional, national, and local contexts, GFANZ established Regional Networks to expand its global reach and incorporate a broad array of perspectives and expertise. In 2022, GFANZ launched Networks in Africa and the Asia-Pacific region, followed by the Latin America and the Caribbean Network in 2023. It also launched dedicated chapters in Brazil, the Caribbean, Hong Kong, and Japan.

Each Network is led by a region-specific Advisory Board composed of global and regional experts from both the public and private sectors. These Advisory Boards provide strategic direction, regional insights, and expertise. The day-to-day operations of each Network are managed by a Regional Director and a team based in the region, responsible for program development and engagement with relevant local stakeholders.

The main objectives of the Regional Networks include the following:

- Engaging with the financial system through roundtables, workshops, and events to drive understanding, awareness, and knowledge sharing, as appropriate, on key topics such as capital mobilization, transition finance, transition planning, and policy.
- Encouraging greater geographic representation and participation from financial institutions and policymakers in GFANZ's work, ensuring that perspectives from across key regions are reflected in global GFANZ outputs, and that global tools are tailored to meet tailored regional needs.
- Serving as hubs for regionally relevant analysis, research, and knowledge sharing, as appropriate, by connecting stakeholders, amplifying resources, and partnering to provide content aligned with each region's priorities.
- Supporting public–private dialogue on enabling environments to help accelerate financing of the net-zero transition.

This chapter provides an overview of the work and focus of the three GFANZ Regional Networks established to date.

The GFANZ Asia-Pacific Network

Contributing approximately half of global greenhouse gas (GHG) emissions (Figure 18.1) and home to some of the world's largest and fastest-growing economies, the Asia-Pacific (APAC) region is a key strategic area for GFANZ's efforts to help drive climate action and investment in the net-zero transition.

Within APAC, emissions are highly concentrated in four countries – China, India, Japan, and Indonesia – which together account for over 80% of the region's CO_2 emissions. The electricity and heat production sector, along with the industry and buildings sectors, represent the largest sources of emissions (Global Carbon Atlas 2023).[1]

As a leading region in industries central to transition, and with dynamic economies and rising energy demand, developments in Asia will be critical to achieving the goals of the Paris Agreement. The urgency and complexity of the task are heightened by the region's differences in development levels, demographic trends, and technical

---

1 Based on 2023 territorial GHG emissions from fossil fuels (i.e., not land-use change).

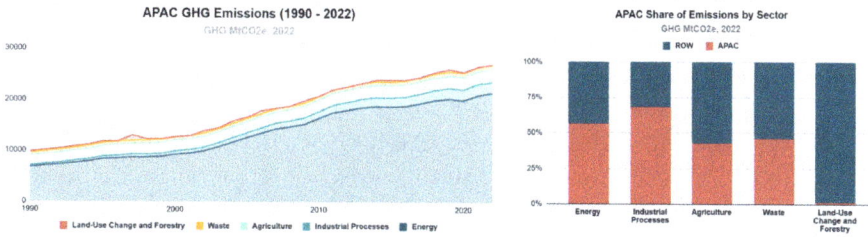

Figure 18.1: Asia's contribution to global carbon emissions.
Source: Climate Watch data – Climate Watch (2024).

and infrastructural challenges – such as ensuring reliable renewable energy sources (IEA 2024). Nevertheless, the transition also presents an opportunity for APAC to lead by example, demonstrating that climate action can align with greater energy security, more resilient infrastructure, and sustainable economic growth.

In response to these challenges and opportunities, the GFANZ Asia-Pacific Network was launched in June 2022 to help accelerate the region's transition. The Network engages financial institutions across both developed and emerging APAC economies, aiming to promote an inclusive global transition. Its mission is to "bring GFANZ to the Asia-Pacific and the Asia-Pacific to GFANZ", contextualizing GFANZ's voluntary global guidance for regional application and incorporating local perspectives into global conversations – ensuring the geographical inclusivity and relevance of GFANZ's work.

Ravi Menon, Singapore's Ambassador for Climate Action and former Managing Director of the Monetary Authority of Singapore (MAS), serves as chair of the Advisory Board, which includes leaders from across the region and sectors. The board's inclusive representation is essential for providing oversight, strategic direction, and local and regional expertise. The Asia-Pacific Network currently engages with nearly 100 financial institutions across the region.

Thematic Focal Areas and Outputs

With regional contextualization and dissemination as a core objective, the Asia-Pacific Network undertakes a broad but targeted range of activities – from thematic reports and capacity building to the launch of Local Chapters[2] aimed at deepening local engagement. The Network's work is guided by four strategic priorities: (1) engagement and outreach to financial institutions, (2) public sector engagement, (3) research and analysis, and (4) capital mobilization into emerging markets and developing economies (EMDEs). These efforts include knowledge exchanges as appropriate,

---

2 Chapters are local offices set up to strategically provide greater local support and engagement.

government engagement, capacity building, and support for country platforms designed to mobilize private finance for the energy transition.

Since its launch in 2022, the Asia-Pacific Network has produced several notable outputs. One such example is the publication *Financing the Managed Phaseout of Coal-Fired Power Plants in Asia Pacific* (Asia-Pacific Network of the Glasgow Financial Alliance for Net Zero 2023), which contextualizes GFANZ's earlier report, *The Managed Phaseout of High-Emitting Assets* (GFANZ 2022a). This publication provides practical, voluntary guidance on key considerations for financial institutions involved in financing the early retirement of coal-fired power plants. It was developed with leadership from regional financial institutions and in consultation with knowledge partners. The report contributed to growing global awareness of managed phaseouts by clarifying what constitutes a credible transaction in the Asia-Pacific context.

Following the development of the GFANZ *Net-Zero Transition Planning Framework*, the APAC Network focused on supporting financial institutions and corporates in strategically planning for the transition. This included capacity-building initiatives and the publication of case study reports that highlight good practice examples of transition plans and implementation strategies from across the region (GFANZ 2022b).

To promote accessibility, the Network has translated both its own resources and global GFANZ documents into regional languages, including Japanese, Korean, and Mandarin Chinese. These translations support broader use in training workshops and capacity-building efforts.

Public engagement is another critical lever used to create an enabling environment for scaling transition finance. While the global regulatory landscape around climate finance is rapidly evolving, it remains relatively nascent in many EMDEs. To address this, the Asia-Pacific Network launched the Southeast Asia Public Policy Workstream in early 2024 as a platform for structured dialogue with governments and policymakers in Malaysia, Thailand, Vietnam, and Indonesia. The workstream consists of an expert group of financial institutions and a consultative group of knowledge partners. It is tasked with identifying enabling public policies on transition planning through various formats, including discussions with regulators and capacity-building activities for financial institutions. By combining policymaker engagement with local capacity building, the Network aims to help promote both consistency within APAC's financial systems and alignment with global financial frameworks – key for mobilizing both domestic and international finance.

Chapters to Deepen Local Engagement

Local Chapters were established to strengthen on-the-ground engagement with key stakeholders, including policymakers, financial institutions, and ecosystem influencers. To date, two chapters have been successfully launched: the Japan Chapter in June 2023 and the Hong Kong Chapter in October 2024. Each chapter has unique objectives and priorities, shaped by the country's level of progress and the political context surrounding climate action.

The Japan Chapter aims to convene local financial institutions through high-level events, such as its inaugural Japan Summit in 2024, where leaders from across the country's financial system discussed the importance of collaboration to help accelerate Japan's transition to net zero. At the summit, 17 organizations signed a joint statement reaffirming the significance of transition planning and highlighting their individual voluntary commitments.

Given Hong Kong's role as a vital bridge between regional capital and transition finance opportunities, the Hong Kong Chapter focuses on fostering engagement and building capacity across Greater China. It emphasizes knowledge sharing, as appropriate, and the use of GFANZ resources to support transition planning and scale transition finance. For both Chapters, support from key regulatory authorities – the Financial Services Agency of Japan (JFSA) and the Hong Kong Monetary Authority (HKMA) – has been pivotal. Their endorsement signals that climate action is a high priority and facilitates alignment between global guidance and local regulations.

Early Retirement of Coal-Fired Power Plants in Asia-Pacific: A Critical Step for Decarbonization

Coal power usage in Asia is projected to continue rising in the coming years due to the region's increasing energy demand. With more than 5,500 active coal-fired power plant (CFPP) generators, the Asia-Pacific region remains heavily dependent on coal, which accounts for nearly half of the region's total energy supply.

The relatively young age of Asia's coal fleet poses economic challenges for early retirement. Nevertheless, early retirement – also known as managed phaseout (MPO) – is one of four core transition finance strategies and is essential for the region to meet climate goals and mitigate the risk of stranded assets. Its success depends on managing a delicate balance among climate impact, energy security, and socio-economic concerns.

Recognizing MPO as a crucial decarbonization tool, the Asia-Pacific Network convened a workstream of leading financial institutions, supported by a consultative panel, to develop technical guidance for credible MPO transactions. The report addresses the critical nexus between transition credibility and financial viability – often a barrier to financial institutions' participation in such deals.

GFANZ's approach to MPO is built on three dimensions: transition credibility, financial viability, and socio-economic inclusivity. In 2023, the final report was launched at COP28. It outlines a three-step process and 10 specific considerations for financial institutions when evaluating MPO transactions, as shown in Figure 18.2. These are designed to ensure thorough evaluation at the government, entity, and asset levels, to enable meaningful climate outcomes and alignment with each institution's net-zero transition plan (GFANZ APAC 2023).

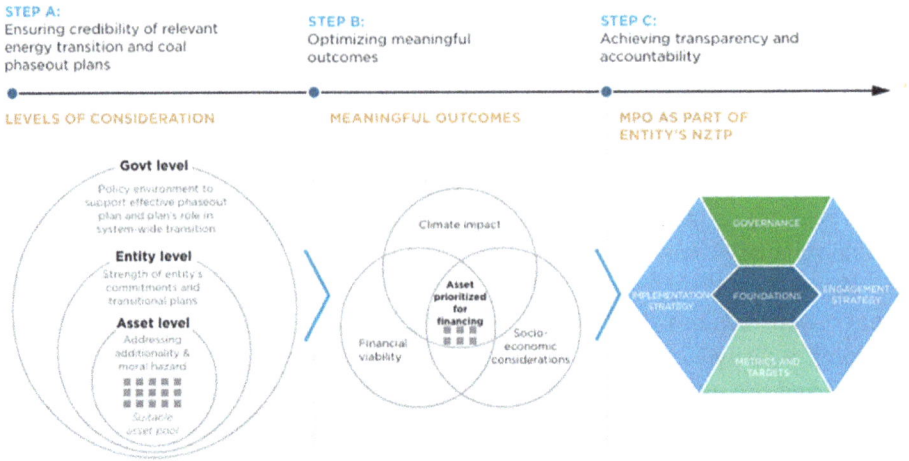

STEP A:
Ensuring credibility of relevant energy transition and coal phaseout plans

STEP B:
Optimizing meaningful outcomes

STEP C:
Achieving transparency and accountability

LEVELS OF CONSIDERATION

MEANINGFUL OUTCOMES

MPO AS PART OF ENTITY'S NZTP

Govt level
Policy environment to support effective phaseout plan and plan's role in system-wide transition

Entity level
Strength of entity's commitments and transitional plans

Asset level
Addressing additionality & moral hazard

Suitable asset pool

Climate impact

Asset prioritized for financing

Financial viability

Socio-economic considerations

GOVERNANCE

IMPLEMENTATION STRATEGY

FOUNDATIONS

ENGAGEMENT STRATEGY

METRICS AND TARGETS

Figure 18.2: Proposed three-step process for consideration of coal phaseout plans.
Source: GFANZ APAC (2023).

Since the report was published, there has been growing willingness and interest among governments, coal plant owners, and financial institutions to support a managed phaseout of coal, with pilot transactions already underway. Following this regional report, the Asia-Pacific Network will undertake further country-specific studies and activities to accelerate capital mobilization across the region.

The GFANZ Africa Regional Network

Delivering a just transition and promoting green growth offer a significant opportunity to provide affordable energy, drive economic development, and create jobs. To ensure that African countries can grow their economies sustainably while maintaining low emissions, large-scale investment in green projects must be unlocked. Inclusive development will also be crucial for the continent's ability to achieve the goals set forth in the Paris Agreement. Africa's high untapped renewable energy potential, relatively abundant land and natural resources, and the world's youngest and fastest-growing labor force position the continent as a key driver of global climate action.

Climate change is already adversely affecting growth in Africa. Projected impacts from global warming exceeding 2 °C – such as heatwaves, droughts, floods, land degradation, biodiversity loss, the spread of pests and invasive species, and increased human morbidity and mortality – are expected to be widespread, with serious consequences for food security and poverty (Trisos et al. 2022).

Despite contributing the least to climate change, Africa is already bearing many of its costs. The continent accounts for only about 4% of global GHG emissions, as shown in Figure 18.3. Agriculture and energy systems are the primary sources of emissions in Africa, with South Africa, Nigeria, and Egypt being the highest emitters on the continent.

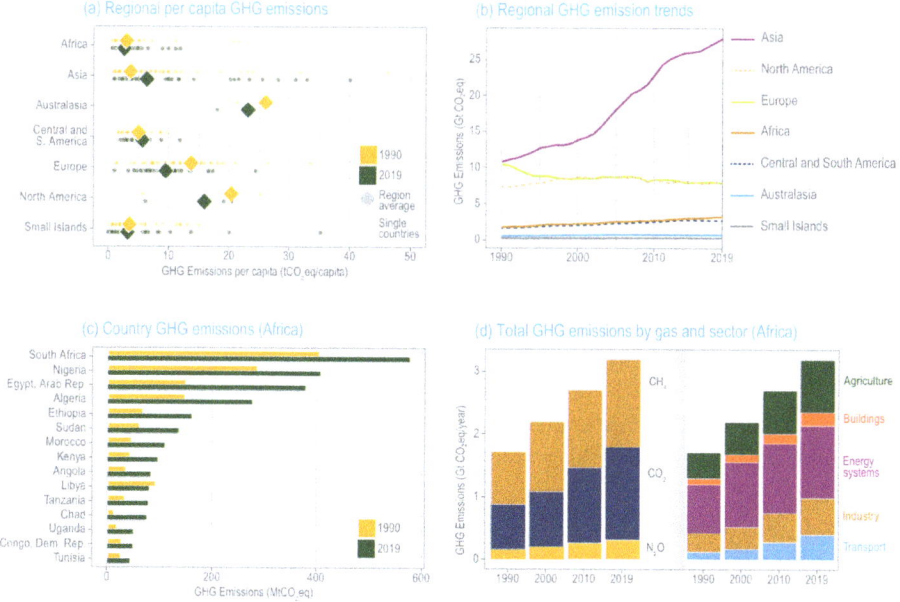

Figure 18.3: Historical greenhouse gas (GHG) emission trends for Africa compared to other world regions. Source: Trisos et al. (2022).

The continent urgently requires action to mitigate emissions growth – such as expanding renewable energy generation capacity and access – and to enhance climate adaptation and resilience, including through new agricultural approaches and inputs to improve food security. Increased private investment is essential to achieving these goals and advancing Africa's Just Transition.

It is estimated that implementing African Nationally Determined Contributions (NDCs) will require more than USD 270 billion[3] in annual financial resources (CPI 2022). However, with current climate-related financial flows amounting to only USD 30 billion per year, there is a pressing need to catalyze a nearly tenfold increase in investment to close the financing gap (CPI 2022). Private investment will be crucial:

---

3 Although Bhattacharya et al. (2024) note that these figures likely fall short of the true requirements as they only encompass NDCs with specific costings, which cover around half of the 5,760 costed and non-costed needs to address climate change identified by 98 developing countries, plus few current NDCs comprehensively cost the investment needs for accelerated energy transition, planned adaptation actions, loss and damage efforts, nature protection and conservation, or the just transition.

approximately 75% of the investment needed for Africa's net-zero and climate-resilient transformation by 2030 is expected to come from the private sector to supplement public financing (UNECA 2023). Yet, private investment currently accounts for just 14% of climate finance in Africa, compared to around 40% in East Asia and the Pacific and 50% in Latin America and the Caribbean. There is substantial potential to use domestic and concessional finance to mobilize international private capital. In some jurisdictions, up to 40% of climate-related private investment is sourced internationally (CPI 2022). This demonstrates a significant opportunity to encourage financing from both international markets and domestic capital for viable projects aligned with the goals of the Paris Agreement.

The GFANZ Africa Network builds on the global work of GFANZ to support the financial system's role in the transition by applying a regional lens to address Africa-specific challenges. Led by African institutions and supported by a regional team, the Network collaborates with African banks, asset owners, asset managers, insurers, and other financial actors. It aims both to bring GFANZ to Africa and to bring Africa to GFANZ, with a central focus on capital mobilization.

To bring GFANZ to Africa, the Network supports the localization of global voluntary guidance and tools, working with key partners to provide the capacity-building needed to scale climate finance among African financial institutions. To bring Africa to GFANZ, the Network ensures that the expertise and perspectives of African financial institutions are incorporated into GFANZ's global outputs.

The GFANZ Africa Advisory Board brings together leaders in finance, government, and climate from across the continent. At its inaugural in-person meeting during COP27 in Sharm El-Sheikh, the Advisory Board, chaired by Dr Mahmoud Mohieldin, approved a work program focused on scaling investment, policy development, knowledge sharing, as appropriate, and collaboration to support Africa's clean growth. Dr Mahmoud Mohieldin, the UN Special Envoy on Financing the SDGs, serves as Chair. The Vice Chair is Dr Mohamed Farid Saleh, Chair of Egypt's Financial Regulatory Authority and Vice Chair of IOSCO. The Board includes leading CEOs, policymakers, and climate leaders from across Africa (GFANZ n.d.a).

The Network takes a systematic approach to analysis and engagement with financial institutions and policymakers to mobilize capital for Africa, working under three overarching objectives:

1. building momentum in transition finance and showcasing African-led climate action;
2. supporting African financial institutions by equipping them with tools and guidance to advance net-zero financing and economies; and
3. unlocking investment in Africa's just transition and sustainable growth.

The GFANZ Africa Advisory Board has approved three flagship initiatives, each supported by working groups chaired by a Board member. These initiatives form part of a multi-year work plan and encompass the following:

A. Supporting the Development of De-risking Instruments and Project Pipelines

This initiative focuses on enhancing the pipeline of investable climate-aligned projects and lowering the cost of private capital, including:

1. Supporting partners working on the UN compendium of climate-related projects (United Nations 2022) and similar initiatives to connect these projects with private financiers.
2. Convening private financial institutions to provide support, advice, and financing for country platforms (e.g., the Senegal Just Energy Transition Partnership and Egypt's NWFE). This includes developing project pipelines, building capacity for bankable project structuring, and facilitating stakeholder engagement.
3. Expanding the availability of de-risking tools such as guarantees, local currency capital market instruments, and FX hedging mechanisms in collaboration with multilateral development banks (MDBs).

B. Providing Capacity Building for Climate Risk and Transition Finance

This initiative seeks to engage regional and national institutions to strengthen climate-related regulations and scale transition finance by:

1. Identifying successful sustainable finance regulatory initiatives and sharing lessons learned;
2. Organizing regional and subregional expert meetings to identify knowledge gaps and shape capacity-building activities;
3. Promoting climate finance awareness and recognition programs across Africa.

C. Driving Interventions to Maximize Carbon Market Benefits for Africa

1. Supporting wider efforts to scale up technical assistance and advisory services supporting carbon market infrastructure, including Article 6 of the Paris Agreement through connecting stakeholders via GFANZ and other networks.
2. Supporting stakeholders in scaling high-integrity carbon credits aligned with the Core Carbon Principles (CCPs), and promoting initiatives such as the Integrity Council for the Voluntary Carbon Market (ICVCM).
3. Building capacity for the Voluntary Carbon Markets Integrity Initiative (VCMI) Access Strategy Toolkit, detailing necessary policy infrastructure for Article 6 and local market regulation.

To implement these objectives, GFANZ Africa has established key partnerships with financial institutions, MDBs, and regulators. It collaborates with the African Development Bank, the African Financial Alliance on Climate Change (AFAC), UNEP FI, and the International Sustainability Standards Board (ISSB), organizing joint capacity-building workshops across the continent. In 2023, GFANZ Africa hosted 11 events, reaching over 500 stakeholders. It also facilitated in-person investor engagements, including a matchmaking session at the 2023 Global Private Investment for Climate Conference, held alongside the Africa Climate Summit in Nairobi, Kenya. Some pipeline projects showcased during the event successfully secured private financing as a result of this engagement.

The GFANZ Latin America and Caribbean Network

Much of Latin America and the Caribbean (LAC) is on the front lines of climate change, facing significant impacts on energy access and supply, food security, and biodiversity. In its most recent assessment report, the Intergovernmental Panel on Climate Change (IPCC) provided a comprehensive evaluation of the region's vulnerabilities, confirming that the adverse effects of the climate crisis are already affecting every LAC country (Castellanos et al. 2022; Mycoo et al. 2022). LAC countries account for between 8% and 10% of global GHG emissions – approximately 3.9 gigatons of CO_2 equivalent ($GtCO_2e$) (Wellenstein and Hickey 2021). The region has a distinctive emissions profile compared to the rest of the world (see Figure 18.4): approximately 44% of emissions originate from agriculture, land use, land-use change, and forestry (LULUCF), while 43% are related to energy – a share significantly lower than the global average of 74% (Ivanova et al. 2021). Notably, 60% of LAC's total electricity production comes from renewable energy sources (IEA 2023).

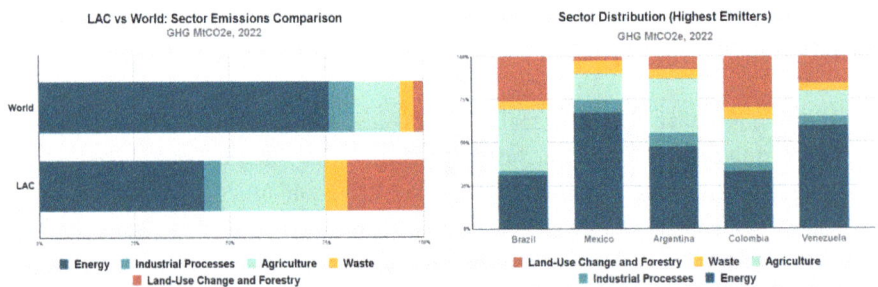

Figure 18.4: Latin America and the Caribbean's emissions compared to global emissions and by sector. Source: Climate Watch data – Climate Watch (2024).

The region's climate vulnerability varies significantly. Countries such as Brazil, Colombia, and Argentina generate most emissions from agriculture and land use, while in Mexico and Venezuela, energy is the dominant source. Vulnerabilities extend beyond physical risks, as many economies rely on climate-sensitive sectors like agriculture, mining, and tourism. These dependencies amplify financial instability and threaten economic growth, with climate-related GDP losses projected to reach up to 23% by 2050 (Zero Carbon Analytics 2024).

Meeting climate goals will require a massive financial effort. By 2030, up to 19% of LAC's GDP – or approximately USD 1.3 trillion annually – is needed to support sustainable growth, including both climate adaptation and mitigation. However, current climate finance flows represent just 0.5% of GDP, necessitating an eight- to tenfold increase to fulfill NDCs. Between 2016 and 2020, LAC received 17% of global climate finance, primarily in the form of loans, further exacerbating regional debt challenges. Nonetheless, private sector involvement in LAC is notable, with nearly equal participation from public and private funding sources (Zero Carbon Analytics 2024).

Despite these challenges, LAC holds immense potential. The region boasts abundant renewable energy resources in wind, solar energy, and bioenergy and is well-positioned to leverage nature-based solutions for emissions reduction. Restoring forests, adopting green technologies, and capitalizing on critical mineral reserves essential for low-carbon innovations – such as copper, lithium, and cobalt – can drive sustainable development and economic resilience. With its renewable energy capabilities and natural assets, LAC is poised to play a pivotal role in addressing global climate challenges. Investments in adaptation, green technologies, and nature-based solutions can unlock economic, social, and environmental benefits, helping to build a more sustainable and resilient future for the region (Ding et al. 2024, 89–101).

The GFANZ LAC Network was launched in October 2023 to address these challenges and unlock the region's potential. By adapting GFANZ global frameworks to regional realities and amplifying LAC perspectives in international discussions, the network aims to mobilize climate finance at scale.

The network is guided by an advisory board composed of leading figures in climate and finance, ensuring that decisions reflect the perspectives and priorities of the region's economies. Patricia Espinosa Cantellano, former executive secretary of the United Nations Framework Convention on Climate Change (UNFCCC) and former secretary of foreign affairs of Mexico, serves as chair of the GFANZ Latin America and Caribbean Advisory Board. Joaquim Levy, director of economic strategy and market relations at Banco Safra and former minister of finance of Brazil, serves as vice chair. They are joined by leading climate finance experts from the private, public, and civil society sectors (GFANZ n.d.b).

The LAC Network engages with a wide range of financial institutions in the region. Many of the region's major institutions are subsidiaries of international firms, while local and regional institutions are often smaller and lack capacity. This underscores the importance of engaging international financial institutions to boost transition finance flows while also building the capacity of local institutions to accelerate their transition planning.

Key Priorities and Outputs

The GFANZ LAC Network is dedicated to catalyzing impactful change across Latin America and the Caribbean on climate finance. With four tailored priorities designed to address the region's unique challenges and opportunities, the network aims to engage a broad range of stakeholders and drive transformative initiatives:

1. **Building Capacity to Support Transition Finance and Planning**
   The network focuses on supporting LAC stakeholders in developing transition plans to manage climate risks and mobilize capital. Key activities include translating resources into Spanish and Portuguese, organizing workshops, and engaging policymakers on sustainable finance. Countries such as Colombia, Mexico, and Panama have launched sustainable finance taxonomies, while Brazil and Chile are developing theirs. Several nations are also beginning to implement ISSB disclosure standards.

2. **Advancing Nature in the Net-Zero Financial Architecture**
   Given the region's dependence on land use and forestry, the network supported regional financial institutions in contributing to GFANZ's 2024 supplemental consultation on voluntary guidance for integrating nature into net-zero transition plans. It also supports guidance on carbon markets for nature-based solutions and collaborates on initiatives such as the Nature Investment Lab (NIL). The network has facilitated dialogue on the climate-nature nexus, including participation at COP16 in Colombia and plans for COP30 in Brazil.

3. **Enabling Capital Mobilization to Address LAC's Investment Gap**
   To address the region's funding shortfall, the Network supports initiatives such as Brazil's Climate and Ecological Transformation Investment Platform (BIP) and Colombia's Climate Finance Leadership Initiative (CFLI), which concluded in October 2024. These initiatives aim to mobilize domestic and international capital by linking local financial institutions with global GFANZ platforms.

4. **Growing the Reach and Tailored Programming of the Network**
   To meet regional needs, the network has launched the Brazil Chapter to deepen engagement with the region's largest economy and emitter and a Caribbean Chapter to address adaptation and resilience. A tailored engagement strategy for Mexico will focus on energy transition opportunities in one of LAC's key economies.

The Brazil Chapter was launched in February 2024, leveraging Brazil's status as the world's sixth largest emitter (EDGAR 2024) and its leadership roles as G20 president and COP30 host in 2025. The chapter convenes climate-focused financial actors to foster awareness, ambition, and collaboration. GFANZ is also advancing capital mobilization through several national initiatives, including:

- **Brazil's Climate and Ecological Transformation Investment Platform (BIP)** – A government-led initiative to mobilize investment in energy, industry, mobility, and nature-based solutions (Government of Brazil n.d.).
- **Nature Investment Lab (NIL)** – An initiative to identify policy and regulatory barriers to investing in nature-based solutions, while developing templates for investment and financing structures.
- **Industrial Transition Accelerator (ITA)** – A program to help finance deep decarbonization in high-emitting industrial sectors through Brazil's Project Support Programme.

The Caribbean Chapter was launched in March 2025; with its rich biodiversity, the Caribbean is well-positioned to help drive capital mobilization initiatives for adaptation, resilience, and nature-based solutions that can help set an example for other regions. The Chapter will also support capacity building for Caribbean financial institutions, helping them strengthen practices around risk management, transition planning, and disclosures. It will help support local financial institutions through workshops and events and work with regional stakeholders such as the Caribbean Climate-Smart Accelerator to connect project developers, policymakers, and governments and create a network of engaged stakeholders.

Conclusion

As the urgency of sustainable development grows, regions are at a critical juncture. With abundant natural resources, renewable energy potential, and the capacity for nature-based solutions, the APAC, Africa, and LAC regions possess unique strengths, which can support global climate action. Aligning financial priorities with climate and sustainability presents a transformative opportunity not only to mitigate environmental and climate risks but also to promote inclusive economic growth while safeguarding ecological heritage for future generations.

References

Asia-Pacific Network of the Glasgow Financial Alliance for Net Zero. 2023. *Financing the Managed Phaseout of Coal-Fired Power Plants in Asia Pacific: Final Report – Guide to Support the Financing of the Early Retirement of Coal-Fired Power Plants as Part of a Just Net-Zero Transition.* December. https://assets. bbhub.io/company/sites/63/2023/11/GFANZ-Financing-the-Managed-Phaseout-of-Coal-Fired-Power-Plants-APAC-December-2023.pdf

Bhattacharya, Amar, Vera Songwe, Eléonore Soubeyran, and Nicholas Stern. 2024. *Raising Ambition and Accelerating Delivery of Climate Finance*. London: Grantham Research Institute on Climate Change and the Environment, London School of Economics and Political Science.

Castellanos, Edwin J., Maria Fernanda Lemos, Laura Astigarraga, Noemí Chacón, Nicolás Cuvi, Christian Huggel, Liliana Miranda, Mariana Moncassim Vale, Jean Pierre Ometto, Pablo L. Peri, Julio C. Postigo, Laura Ramajo, Lisandro Roco, and Matilde Rusticucci. 2022. "Central and South America." In *Climate Change 2022: Impacts, Adaptation and Vulnerability. Contribution of Working Group II to the Sixth Assessment Report of the Intergovernmental Panel on Climate Change*, edited by by H.-O. Pörtner, D. C. Roberts, M. Tignor, E. S. Poloczanska, K. Mintenbeck, A. Alegría, M. Craig, S. Langsdorf, S. Löschke, V. Möller, A. Okem, and B. Rama 689–1816. Cambridge, UK, and New York, NY: Cambridge University Press.

Climate Policy Initiative (CPI). 2022. *The State of Climate Finance in Africa: Climate Finance Needs of African Countries*. June. https://www.climatepolicyinitiative.org/wp-content/uploads/2022/06/Climate-Finance -Needs-of-African-Countries-1.pdf

Climate Watch data: Climate Watch. 2024. *GHG Emissions. Washington, DC: World Resources Institute*. Accessed May 15, 2025. https://www.climatewatchdata.org/ghg-emissions

Ding, Ding, Emilio Fernandez-Corugedo, Alejandro Guerson, and Sònia Muñoz. 2024. "Climate Adaptation in Latin America and the Caribbean: Policy Options." In *Climate Change Challenges and Opportunities in Latin America and the Caribbean*, edited by Anna Ivanova, Julie Kozack, and Sònia Muñoz, 89–101. Washington, DC: International Monetary Fund.

Emissions Database for Global Atmospheric Research (EDGAR). 2024. *GHG Emissions of All World Countries*. European Commission. https://edgar.jrc.ec.europa.eu/report_2024.

Glasgow Financial Alliance for Net Zero (GFANZ). 2022a. *The Managed Phaseout of High-Emitting Assets: How to Facilitate the Early Retirement of High-Emitting Assets as Part of a Just Transition to a Net-Zero World*. June. https://assets.bbhub.io/company/sites/63/2022/06/GFANZ_-Managed-Phaseout-of-High-emitting-Assets_June2022.pdf

Glasgow Financial Alliance for Net Zero (GFANZ). 2022b. *Financial Institution Net-Zero Transition Plans: Fundamentals, Recommendations, and Guidance*. November. https://assets.bbhub.io/company/sites/63/2022/09/Recommendations-and-Guidance-on-Financial-Institution-Net-zero-Transition-Plans-November-2022.pdf

Glasgow Financial Alliance for Net Zero (GFANZ). 2025. "Glasgow Financial Alliance for Net Zero Launches Caribbean Chapter to Support Capital Mobilization Initiatives in the Region." March 13, 2025. Accessed May 7, 2025. https://www.gfanzero.com/press/glasgow-financial-alliance-for-net-zero-launches-caribbean-chapter-to-support-capital-mobilization-initiatives-in-the-region-2/.

Glasgow Financial Alliance for Net Zero (GFANZ). n.d.a "Africa Network". Accessed March 10, 2025. https://www.gfanzero.com/africa-network/

Glasgow Financial Alliance for Net Zero (GFANZ). n.d.b "Latin America & Caribbean Network". Accessed March 10, 2025. https://www.gfanzero.com/latin-america-and-caribbean-network/

Global Carbon Atlas. 2023. "Carbon Emissions." Accessed May 7, 2025. https://globalcarbonatlas.org/emissions/carbon-emissions/

Government of Brazil. n.d. Ministério da Fazenda – Brazil Climate and Ecological Transformation Investment Platform. Accessed March 5, 2025. https://www.gov.br/fazenda/pt-br/acesso-a-informacao/acoes-e-programas/transformacao-ecologica/bip/brazil-climate-and-ecological-transformation-platform

International Energy Agency (IEA). 2023. *Latin America Energy Outlook: World Energy Outlook Special Report*. Executive Summary. https://iea.blob.core.windows.net/assets/1055131a-8dc4-488b-9e9e-7eb4f72b f7ad/LatinAmericaEnergyOutlook.pdf.

International Energy Agency (IEA). 2024. *Global Energy and Climate Model Documentation*. Section 1: Overview of Model and Scenarios. International Energy Agency. https://iea.blob.core.windows.net/as

sets/89a1aa9a-e1bd-4803-b37b-59d6e7fba1e9/GlobalEnergyandClimateModelDocumenta
tion2024.pdf

Ivanova, Anna, Julie Kozack, Jorge Roldós, and Sònia Muñoz. 2021. "Climate Change in Latin America and
the Caribbean: Challenges and Opportunities." *IMF Blog*, October 28. Accessed March 5, 2025.
https://www.imf.org/en/Blogs/Articles/2021/10/28/blog-climate-change-latin-america-the-caribbean-
challenges-and-opportunities#:~:text=The%20energy%20sector%20contributes%20much%20less%
20to%20total,the%20global%20average%20of%20just%20over%201%20percent

Low, Lit Ping, and Daisy Chee. 2023. "Moving Beyond Commitment and Towards Transformation: Asia
Pacific Climate Actions Not on Track." *Asia Pacific Net Zero Economy Index 2023*. December 11, 2023.
PriceWaterhouseCoopers (PwC). Accessed March 10, 2025. https://www.pwc.com/gx/en/issues/esg/
esg-asia-pacific/net-zero-economy-index-asia-pacifics-transition-2023.html.

Mycoo, Michelle, Morgan Wairiu, Donovan Campbell, Virginie Duvat, Yimnang Golbuu, Shobha Maharaj,
Johanna Nalau, Patrick Nunn, John Pinnegar, and Olivia Warrick. 2022. "Small Islands." In *Climate
Change 2022: Impacts, Adaptation and Vulnerability. Contribution of Working Group II to the Sixth
Assessment Report of the Intergovernmental Panel on Climate Change*, edited by H.-O. Pörtner,
D. C. Roberts, M. Tignor, E. S. Poloczanska, K. Mintenbeck, A. Alegría, M. Craig, S. Langsdorf,
S. Löschke, V. Möller, A. Okem, and B. Rama, 043–2121. Cambridge, UK, and New York, NY:
Cambridge University Press.

Trisos, Christopher H., Ibidun O. Adelekan, Edmond Totin, Ayansina Ayanlade, Jackson Efitre, Adugna
Gemeda, Kanungwe Kalaba, Christopher Lennard, Catherine Masao, Yunus Mgaya, Grace Ngaruiya,
Daniel Olago, Nicholas P. Simpson, and Sumaya Zakieldeen. 2022. "Africa." In *Climate Change 2022:
Impacts, Adaptation and Vulnerability. Contribution of Working Group II to the Sixth Assessment Report of
the Intergovernmental Panel on Climate Change*, edited by H.-O. Pörtner, D. C. Roberts, M. Tignor,
E. S. Poloczanska, K. Mintenbeck, A. Alegría, M. Craig, S. Langsdorf, S. Löschke, V. Möller, A. Okem,
and B. Rama, 1285–1455. Cambridge, UK, and New York, NY: Cambridge University Press.

United Nations. 2022. *Towards COP27: Compendium of Climate-Related Initiatives – Opportunities for Climate
Finance and Investments on the SDGs*. New York: United Nations. https://www.un.org/regionalcommis
sionsnyoffice/news/compendium#:~:text=The%20Compendium%20presents%20a%20pipeline,to%2C
%20at%20and%20after%20COP27.

United Nations Economic Commission for Africa (UNECA). 2023. "Climate Finance: Nearly US$3 Trillion
Needed to Implement Africa's NDCs." September 4. Accessed March 5, 2025. https://www.uneca.org/
stories/climate-finance-nearly-us%243-trillion-needed-to-implement-africa%27s-ndcs.

Wellenstein, Anna, and Valerie Hickey. 2021. "10 Key Points on Climate Change Impacts, Opportunities and
Priorities for Latin America and the Caribbean." *World Bank Blogs*,. April 22Accessed March 5, 2025.
https://blogs.worldbank.org/en/latinamerica/10-key-points-climate-change-impacts-opportunities-
and-priorities-latin-america-and#:~:text=%231%3A%20LAC%20contributes%20about%2010,1.33%25%
20of%20global%20emissions%20each.

Zero Carbon Analytics. 2024. *Promises and Reality of Climate Finance Flows in Latin America and the
Caribbean*. November 24. Accessed May 15, 2025. https://zerocarbon-analytics.org/wp-content/up
loads/2024/11/2024-11-Zero-Carbon-Analytics-Briefing-Promises-and-reality-in-climate-finance-for-
LAC.pdf

Hisham Badr

Chapter 19
Mobilizing Local Climate Finance

Abstract: This chapter explores Egypt's National Initiative for Smart Green Projects (NISGP) as an innovative model for localizing climate action and green finance. In response to the urgent need for decentralized and inclusive climate solutions, the NISGP fosters multi-stakeholder collaboration across Egypt's 27 governorates, aligning grassroots innovation with national policy and global climate commitments. The chapter details the initiative's structured and cyclical implementation model, emphasizing its adaptive evaluation framework, capacity-building programs, and strategic public–private partnerships. Through a rigorous selection process and support ecosystem, the NISGP identifies, finances, and scales community-driven green projects across sectors such as renewable energy, sustainable agriculture, waste management, and water conservation.

The chapter highlights the initiative's role in reshaping public perception, mobilizing climate finance, and strengthening institutional capacities through partnerships with local governments, UN agencies, and the private sector. It also examines the initiative's visibility and influence at international climate forums, particularly COP27, COP28, and COP29, where the NISGP emerged as a replicable model of localized climate governance. Finally, the chapter identifies key challenges and outlines a strategic vision for scaling the initiative's impact – both nationally and globally – through expanded capacity building, increased private sector engagement, and the creation of a Green Ecosystem Forum. The NISGP offers a compelling case study in bridging top-down climate policy with bottom-up innovation, advancing Egypt's sustainable development goals while contributing to global climate resilience.

Keywords: Local climate action, Sustainable development, Green economy, Smart green projects, Local government, Replicable climate action model

Introduction

The global response to climate change is, in many respects, a collection of local responses. This is fitting, as climate change vulnerabilities are intrinsically local – shaped by specific environmental, social, and economic dynamics at the community level (Al-Mashat and Mohieldin 2025). A localized approach is therefore necessary for effective, just, and sustained climate action. It ensures that solutions are rooted in local knowledge, that the most affected communities are actively involved, and that the benefits of action are directly felt by those on the front lines of climate impacts (UNDP, UNCDF, and UNEP 2013).

This principle of localizing development and climate action has long been recognized in global development frameworks. As early as 1992, the Earth Summit in Rio de Janeiro acknowledged in *Agenda 21* that many environmental and development challenges originate at the local level, and it mandated a special role for local authorities through Chapter 28 (LA21) (ElMassah and Mohieldin 2020). The Sustainable Development Goals (SDGs), with climate action embedded within them, scale up this ambition by promoting universality while emphasizing the need to localize targets and indicators. Localizing development and climate action entails adapting strategies, monitoring mechanisms, and resource mobilization to subnational contexts – enabling local governments and communities to play an active role in development from the bottom up (ElMassah and Mohieldin 2020). Thus, localization brings decision-making closer to the people, aligning global and national goals with local priorities, increasing transparency, and fostering innovation and investment – especially from the private sector. It also enables more inclusive participation and unlocks economic potential through small- and medium-sized enterprises (ElMassah and Mohieldin 2020).

Egypt's National Initiative for Smart Green Projects (NISGP) stands out as a pioneering model of this approach in action. Launched in 2022, the initiative addresses a key barrier to local climate action: access to finance. It offers a practical framework for identifying, assessing, and financing a pipeline of investable projects for local climate and development priorities across diverse sectors and governorates. The initiative prioritizes highly tailored, context-specific interventions that respond to the unique climate and development challenges of each locality. The NISGP connects these local efforts with national climate objectives – notably by transforming the implementation of Egypt's Nationally Determined Contributions (NDCs) into concrete, localized investment opportunities (Al-Mashat and Mohieldin 2025). It operates through a multi-stakeholder hub that includes UN agencies, multilateral banks, public and private financiers, and the Egyptian government. This structure supports project development and financing while enabling knowledge sharing, technical assistance, and capacity-building.

This chapter discusses the NISGP as a recent model for mobilizing investments in local climate projects. It focuses on improving the delivery of climate finance not through allocations from Egypt's already overburdened national budget, but through innovative financing methods. The chapter draws lessons on how decentralized, participatory, and finance-ready models can help bridge the gap between global climate goals and local realities.

Vision and Objectives of the NISGP

Amid escalating global economic challenges and the intensifying climate crisis, Egypt faces significant development disparities across its governorates. While some regions experience rapid growth, others lag behind – exacerbating the challenge of equitable development. Additionally, access to green finance remains limited, as national priorities continue to focus heavily on infrastructure expansion, education, and sustainability.

At this critical juncture, the NISGP has emerged as a transformative response. This initiative is built on three key pillars: raising awareness about climate change at both national and global levels, educating citizens on strategies to combat its effects, and promoting innovative climate solutions developed by individuals and communities across the country. Through these efforts, the NISGP aims to bridge development gaps and accelerate sustainable progress nationwide.

The launch of the NISGP during Egypt's hosting of COP27 marked a landmark effort to embed sustainable development into the national policy framework. The initiative prioritizes the practical implementation of sustainability by addressing climate change, promoting environmental stewardship, and integrating green innovation into local and national development strategies.

The NISGP's vision is to position Egypt as a regional leader in sustainability by fostering inclusive growth, reducing development disparities, and ensuring equitable access to green technologies and financing. Its objectives include empowering communities to implement climate-resilient projects, supporting the transition to a low-carbon economy, and creating a platform for knowledge exchange and collaboration among citizens, policymakers, and international stakeholders. By aligning with global climate goals and leveraging local ingenuity, the initiative advances Egypt's sustainable development agenda while inspiring other nations in the region.

The initiative represents a collaborative effort between national and international stakeholders to strengthen regulatory frameworks, enhance local capacity, and tailor development priorities to bridge existing development and climate finance gaps. Furthermore, it aligns with the United Nations SDGs and aims to localize these goals by establishing a resilient platform for mobilizing local green funds across Egypt's 27 governorates. This approach ensures that both advanced and underdeveloped regions benefit from climate finance opportunities by developing an inclusive and scalable model that bridges the gap between high-level climate policies and grassroots implementation.

By engaging a broad spectrum of society through its six project categories – large-scale, medium-scale, small-scale projects, start-ups, nonprofit initiatives, and women-led projects – the NISGP fosters a cohesive framework where climate action and economic growth progress hand in hand. Figure 20.1 illustrates how the initiative ensures that the winning projects at the governorate level span all six categories.

The NISGP aims to create synergy among key national and international stakeholders, including government bodies, nongovernmental organizations (NGOs), financial institutions, national entities, and the private sector. Together, they work to advance climate finance and capacity building. This collaborative approach refines the project evaluation process and mobilizes citizens to actively participate in the NISGP – enhancing local engagement and driving the sustainable transformation of Egypt's economy.

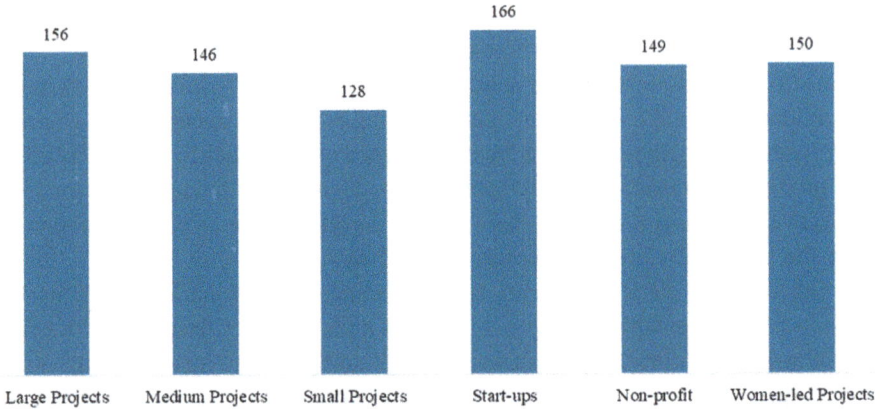

Figure 20.1: Number of governorate-level winning projects across the three rounds of the NISGP by category.
Source: NISGP Database.

The NISGP Timeline

The NISGP follows a structured, cyclical timeline that ensures the initiative remains dynamic, inclusive, and impactful across Egypt's 27 governorates. Each round of the initiative builds on lessons learned from previous cycles, allowing for continuous refinement of processes and stronger alignment with national priorities and global climate objectives.

1. **Preparation Phase**
   Each new round begins with a comprehensive review of the outcomes and feedback from the previous cycle. This reflection phase informs updates to evaluation criteria, outreach strategies, training content, and coordination mechanisms. The Organizing Committee – comprising representatives from collaborating ministries – leads this phase to ensure that each round incorporates best practices and addresses any gaps or challenges previously encountered.

2. **Announcement and Application Launch**
   The initiative officially opens its call for applications across all governorates. Projects are submitted through the NISGP's online portal. A nationwide communication campaign is launched to raise awareness of the initiative's objectives and procedures, encouraging broad participation from diverse communities, institutions, and entrepreneurs.

3. **Outreach and Capacity Building**
   In parallel with the application window, a wide-ranging outreach and capacity-building program is rolled out in collaboration with local governments, relevant

ministries, civil society organizations, the business community, and academic institutions.

Capacity-building sessions are delivered both in person across governorates and online, enabling broad and equitable access. The training covers essential topics such as ideation, business modeling, environmental impact assessment, financing strategies, and project scalability. These sessions are facilitated by experts from the private sector, technical institutions, and past NISGP winners, offering practical guidance to applicants at every stage of project development and implementation.

4. **Evaluation Process**
   Once the call for applications closes, the initiative transitions into a multilayered evaluation process to ensure transparency, rigor, and inclusivity:
   - **Organizing Committee**: Reviews and updates the unified selection criteria and rubric to reflect national priorities and international standards.
   - **System Filtration**: Conducts an initial automated screening to confirm that projects meet baseline eligibility and thematic alignment with the initiative.
   - **Executive Committees (Governorate Level)**: Each governorate forms an executive committee, chaired by the respective governor, to evaluate the filtered projects. Evaluation criteria include innovation, economic feasibility, environmental benefit, and scalability. A unified rubric ensures consistency across governorates while allowing for local prioritization.
   - **Higher Committee**: Composed of experts from UN agencies, ministries, financial institutions, the private sector, and civil society, this committee reassesses the selected projects from each governorate. It identifies the top 10 projects in each of the six thematic categories, based on governance standards and strategic value.
   - **National Judging Committee**: Chaired by Dr Mahmoud Mohieldin, UN Special Envoy on Financing the 2030 Agenda for Sustainable Development, this committee includes senior policymakers, sustainability experts, and industry leaders. They select the top 18 smart green projects (the top three in each category) based on excellence, innovation, and transformative potential.

5. **National Recognition and Global Showcasing**
   The cycle culminates in a National Conference, where the top 18 projects are formally recognized in the presence of key national stakeholders, partners, and media representatives. The event serves as a platform to connect winning teams with government entities, financial institutions, and private sector actors who can support project scalability.

These winning projects are then showcased internationally at the annual United Nations Climate Change Conference (COP), representing Egypt's climate innovation and ambition. This global exposure fosters networking opportunities, investment partnerships, and collaboration with international climate actors – expanding the projects' reach and impact beyond national borders.

Figure 20.2 summarizes the number of projects at each filtration phase across the initiative's three rounds.

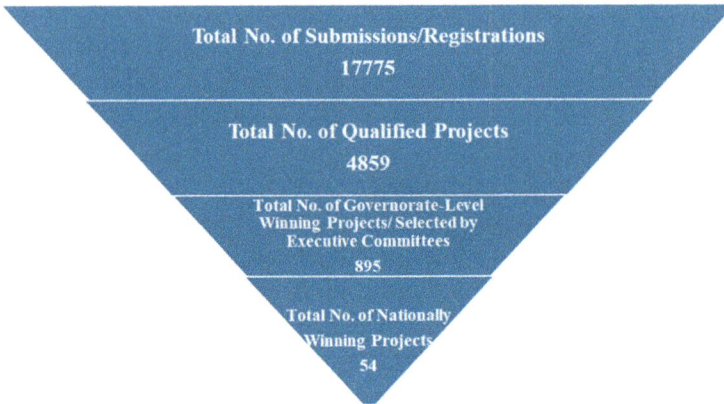

Total No. of Submissions/Registrations
17775

Total No. of Qualified Projects
4859

Total No. of Governorate-Level Winning Projects/ Selected by Executive Committees
895

Total No. of Nationally Winning Projects
54

Figure 20.2: Compiled number of projects across the NISGP filtration phases across its three rounds. Source: NISGP Database.

The Initiative Mechanics

The NISGP is designed with a robust and transparent mechanism to identify, evaluate, and support local innovation at scale. At its core, the initiative provides both digital and institutional platforms through which Egypt's 27 governorates can submit green and smart project proposals. This structure not only facilitates the application process but also contributes to a national database and geographic mapping of sustainable development initiatives, offering a comprehensive overview of emerging green solutions across the country.

A Catalyst for Climate Finance

A key strength of the NISGP is its function as a pre-qualification mechanism for green finance. Through its structured evaluation process, the initiative reduces risk and effort for financiers – whether development banks, UN agencies, or private investors – by identifying investment-ready, high-impact projects that meet stringent environmental, financial, and operational standards.

By curating a national database of vetted projects, the NISGP simplifies due diligence processes and enables financial institutions to engage with confidence. This accelerates the flow of climate finance and ensures that investments are directed toward solutions with measurable and scalable impact.

Projects are assessed using six standardized, nationally adopted evaluation criteria:

1. **Green Component:–** Alignment with environmental sustainability principles and effectiveness in addressing climate change.
2. **Technological Component:–** Use of innovative technologies to enhance efficiency and environmental impact.
3. **Economic Feasibility and Funding Viability:–** Financial soundness, cost-effectiveness, and potential to attract funding.
4. **Scalability and Replicability:–** Potential for the project to expand or be replicated in different contexts.
5. **Developmental Impact:** Contribution to social and economic development, especially in underserved communities.
6. **Empowerment and Equal Opportunity** (specific to the Women's Category): Promotion of inclusivity and women's empowerment.

These criteria guide evaluations at every phase – from local to national – ensuring consistency, transparency, and alignment with Egypt's climate goals.

The evaluation process, as outlined in the initiative's timeline, involves multiple levels of review to ensure a rigorous and equitable selection. Subject matter experts from academia, industry, and NGOs contribute to these assessments, supporting both filtration and final decision-making. Their diverse perspectives ensure that evaluations are multidisciplinary and grounded in real-world challenges of project implementation.

Fostering Collaboration and a Green Mindset

Beyond project evaluation and financing facilitation, the National Initiative for Smart Green Projects plays a transformative role in shifting public perception and behavior toward sustainability. By engaging stakeholders from local governments, civil society, and the private sector, the initiative fosters a collaborative ecosystem that aligns diverse interests around shared climate and development goals.

Through targeted outreach, information sessions, and capacity-building programs, the initiative empowers local communities to actively participate in the green transition. It provides the tools and knowledge needed to move from ideation to execution, bridging the gap between grassroots action and national policy.

Moreover, the initiative functions as a dynamic platform for driving climate finance in Egypt, culminating each round with the National Conference – its flagship event – where winning projects are officially recognized and showcased before key stakeholders. This high-profile gathering includes senior government officials, governors from all 27 governorates, and international partners. At the conference, the Egyptian Prime Minister honors the 18 highest-scoring projects, selected based on their performance according to the initiative's evaluation criteria. These projects span diverse sectors and regions, ensuring inclusive representation of Egypt's sustainable development efforts.

The visibility generated by the conference plays a critical role in mobilizing financial and technical resources needed for project scalability. It also attracts global attention through subsequent presentations at the United Nations Climate Change Conference (COP). This international exposure highlights Egypt's commitment to innovative, localized climate action and positions the initiative as a replicable model for other regions and countries. Widespread media coverage further amplifies the impact, raising awareness of the initiative's success stories and enhancing its reputation among potential collaborators and investors.

By harmonizing stakeholder efforts, streamlining access to funding, and promoting tested climate solutions, the NISGP is building a nationwide movement toward sustainable economic development – where local green innovation is not only encouraged but also strategically supported and internationally recognized.

The Winning Projects

The NISGP projects span sectors such as renewable energy, sustainable agriculture, waste management, and water conservation (see Figure 20.3). These projects offer tangible examples of how local communities are contributing to global climate objectives. By spotlighting localized solutions that respond to specific environmental challenges in Egypt's diverse governorates, the initiative reinforces the value of context-specific interventions in achieving both national and international climate goals.

Among the many green enterprises fostered by the NISGP, several standout projects illustrate the breadth and depth of local ingenuity. For instance, the *Treating Groundwater Contaminated with Iron* project addresses water quality issues in the New Valley governorate. Using an advanced organic method, the initiative removes iron from groundwater, providing safer water for residents. In Ismailia, the *Exergy Project* utilizes geothermal energy to eliminate carbon emissions from gas combustion in poultry farms.

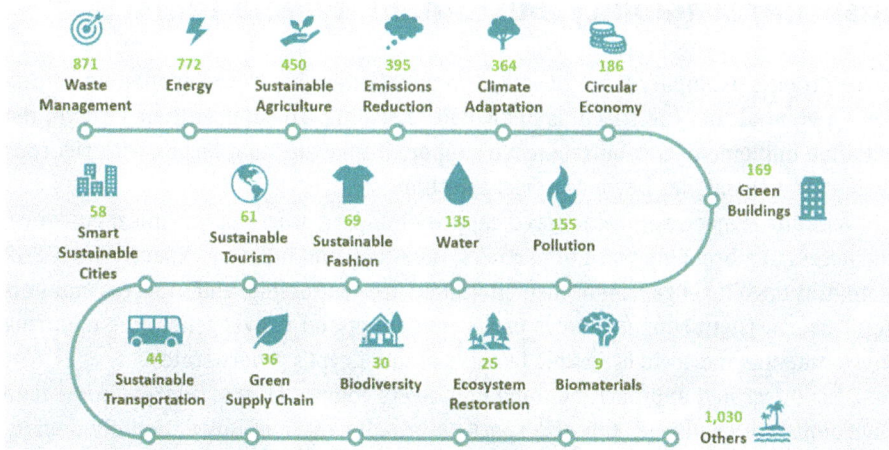

Figure 20.3: Number of qualified projects by sector in the NISGP.
Source: NISGP Database.

Other notable projects include:
- **The Egypt Waste Bank**, which converts agricultural and municipal waste into usable resources. It now recycles used tires into industrial-grade rubber powder and has launched mobile applications to streamline waste collection.
- **Engazaat**, Egypt's first independent power and water producer, generates 15 million cubic meters of water annually, reduces 65,414 tons of CO_2 emissions, and has created 500 jobs through renewable energy investments.
- **Bab Rizq Scrap**, which empowers women – including those with special needs – by training over 25,000 participants to transform scrap materials into marketable products, promoting environmental sustainability and economic inclusion.
- **The 3D Cutter Project**, which tackles e-waste by repurposing discarded electronics into functional machinery such as CNC cutters. This initiative has created 700 sustainable jobs and provides women with critical technical skills.

To ensure long-term impact and scalability, the NISGP complements project visibility with targeted financial and technical support. The initiative collaborates with the Micro, Small, and Medium Enterprise Development Agency (MSMEDA) to offer financing tailored to early-stage and expanding ventures. It also connects winning projects with venture capital firms and private investors, strengthening pathways to commercialization.

Alongside its national support infrastructure, the NISGP partners with international organizations and UN agencies to enhance technical capacities and extend global visibility. At international forums – including COP – the initiative ensures that project representatives engage directly with policymakers, investors, and sustainability leaders, fostering strategic partnerships and international collaboration.

Ensuring Scalability, Sustainability, and Impact

These projects exemplify the innovative potential emerging from Egyptian communities – potential that the NISGP is dedicated to scaling. To support their growth, the initiative implements a comprehensive support framework that begins with rigorous evaluation and extends beyond project selection.

Winning projects receive tailored capacity-building programs, technical guidance, and access to a broad network of partners, investors, and industry experts. The NISGP maintains ongoing engagement through follow-up, mentorship, and progress monitoring. This consistent support allows projects to adapt and thrive, generating enduring environmental and socio-economic benefits across Egypt's governorates.

This integrated approach not only empowers communities to address immediate environmental challenges but also sparks a broader wave of innovation. By demonstrating the value of coordinated financial and technical backing, the NISGP offers a replicable model for scaling grassroots climate solutions – bridging the gap between local innovation, national policy, and global impact.

Partnerships and Capacity Building: Two Pillars of Success

The NISGP places strategic partnerships and capacity building at the center of its model for sustainable impact. From the outset, it has embraced collaboration, establishing a support ecosystem that unites international organizations, UN agencies, financial institutions, the private sector, and government entities. These partnerships provide visibility, technical expertise, funding opportunities, and institutional support, helping projects scale and succeed. The NISGP ensures that Egypt's green innovation landscape is not only vibrant but also resilient, inclusive, and prepared to meet both national and global climate goals.

A. Multifaceted and Dynamic Partnerships

International and National Collaborations

At the heart of the NISGP is the belief that collective action is essential to address the complex challenges of climate change. The initiative serves as a platform for inclusive, scalable, and sustainable climate action by engaging a broad range of stakeholders – including government bodies, civil society, financial institutions, and international organizations.

The initiative's collaborative model has helped elevate local innovations to global recognition. In particular, it has developed strong partnerships with UN agencies in Egypt, such as UNDP, WFP, UN Women, FAO, ILO, UNIDO, UN-Habitat, and IFAD. These agencies offer technical assistance to winning projects, amplify their visibility, and facilitate access to expertise, funding, and knowledge exchange.

Through these partnerships, NISGP-backed projects participate in international forums, engage with global policymakers and investors, and showcase their innovations on world stages. These opportunities help position Egypt as a leader in community-driven climate action and raise the profile of local projects that might otherwise remain unseen.

By acting as a bridge between grassroots innovation and global systems, the NISGP ensures that local solutions are celebrated, supported, and scaled. This collaborative structure – grounded in inclusivity, capacity-building, and international engagement – has proven essential to the initiative's success and Egypt's broader climate action strategy.

Governmental Collaboration

The NISGP works in close coordination with Egypt's governors, who serve as essential links between the initiative and local enterprises. Their involvement ensures alignment with each governorate's green sector priorities and provides critical insights that help address specific environmental and economic needs on the ground.

The initiative also maintains ongoing engagement with relevant ministries to continuously enhance its operational model. This includes refining evaluation criteria, reviewing implementation performance, and identifying areas for improvement. The collaborative and adaptive approach extends to the evaluation process itself, reinforcing transparency and diligence in project selection.

To bolster financial support for green projects, the NISGP partners with MSMEDA to proactively reach out to winning projects and offer tailored financial and technical assistance. The initiative also collaborates with national banks – such as Banque Misr – which contributes by providing expert-led online training sessions and sponsoring key NISGP activities. Industry leaders, including Egypt Post and Misr Insurance, further support the initiative through event sponsorship and outreach efforts. These partners play a vital role in advancing the initiative by providing financial and logistical resources that contribute to operational sustainability.

A strategic partnership with the National Training Academy strengthens the capacity of both applicants and the technical teams of executive committees in each governorate. These efforts ensure that relevant actors are equipped with the necessary skills to effectively implement the NISGP's framework and objectives.

In line with its commitment to inclusivity, the NISGP collaborates with the National Council for Persons with Disabilities to promote the participation of individuals with disabilities in all aspects of the initiative. Youth engagement is also a key priority, with strong partnerships formed with schools, universities, STEM institutions, and government agencies such as the Ministry of Higher Education and the Ministry of Youth and Sports, helping to nurture a new generation of climate-conscious leaders and innovators.

Private Sector Engagement

Recognizing the private sector as a critical driver of climate action, the NISGP engages private enterprises as active contributors to Egypt's green transition. The initiative adopts a multifaceted approach – raising awareness, building private sector capacity, encouraging project submissions, and inviting companies to act as sponsors or collaborators within the NISGP ecosystem.

Private sector involvement spans a wide spectrum – from established corporations to youth-led startups – each playing a unique role in scaling green innovation. Some companies, such as Canal Sugar Company, have contributed through sponsorships, particularly in the domain of sustainable agriculture. Others have provided direct support through:

- **Technical Assistance**: Offering advisory support to improve project implementation.
- **Training Programs**: Delivering capacity-building sessions for entrepreneurs and private entities.
- **Awareness Campaigns**: Promoting green innovation and encouraging public participation.
- **Operational Support**: Enhancing the NISGP's ability to scale its activities.

Strategic partnerships with institutions such as the Federation of Egyptian Industries and the Alexandria Businessmen Association further enable green projects to access sector-specific guidance and networking opportunities, helping integrate them into market ecosystems.

Through these sustained collaborations, the NISGP reinforces its commitment to inclusive climate action – positioning the private sector not merely as beneficiaries but as essential partners in Egypt's sustainable development.

B. Strengthening Capacities Across the Green Ecosystem

Capacity Building for Local Government Officials

As part of its inclusive implementation strategy, the NISGP conducts targeted capacity-building sessions for local government officials. These trainings equip participants with tools to identify and support green projects in their regions. Officials are trained in selection criteria, application procedures, and evaluation methodologies, enabling them to conduct initial assessments aligned with unified national standards. These efforts are coordinated with relevant ministries and sectoral experts to ensure fairness and transparency in the evaluation process.

Capacity Building for Applicants

The NISGP underscores the power of localized action. Through workshops held in youth centers, universities, and schools across all 27 governorates, the initiative has engaged a wide cross-section of society. This approach localizes SDGs, embedding them in regional priorities and community-led efforts.

Training programs cover a broad range of topics, including project management, environmental assessment, data analysis, and monitoring and evaluation. Delivered both in-person and online, these sessions enhance accessibility and participation. They are facilitated by private sector experts, associations, and former NISGP winners, allowing applicants to benefit from technical and practical knowledge.

The NISGP at COPs

The NISGP's debut at COP27 marked a turning point, showcasing how national efforts can be effectively decentralized to support local climate action. Its continued presence at COP28 and COP29 expanded its international network, attracting attention from governments, financial institutions, development agencies, and civil society organizations.

These forums elevated the initiative's visibility and credibility, connecting winning projects with investors and technical partners. The presence of NISGP-backed projects demonstrated real-world success and progress in climate finance. At each COP, representatives participated in panels, workshops, and roundtables with global experts and policymakers, gaining insights and tools to improve initiative outcomes.

Participation in these conferences positioned the NISGP as a thought leader in localized climate finance. Its representatives shared a compelling vision of how diverse actors – from local governments to grassroots entrepreneurs – can be empowered to drive climate action through well-supported frameworks.

Challenges

Despite notable progress, the NISGP faces several challenges that must be addressed to enhance its impact:

- **Enhancing Grassroots Engagement**: More inclusive outreach is needed to increase participation from remote and underserved communities.
- **Strengthening Capacity-Building Systems**: Developing more structured, needs-based training programs will enhance resilience and investment-readiness.
- **Deepening Private Sector and Investor Engagement**: Greater involvement from corporate actors and financiers will unlock new resources and partnerships.
- **Fostering Green Entrepreneurship and Innovation**: Engaging start-ups, incubators, and innovation hubs can scale sustainable solutions.
- **Expanding Global Visibility and Influence**: Continued participation in global forums will strengthen the NISGP's international reputation and attract new funding and policy influence.

Way Forward

The NISGP offers a pioneering model for improving the delivery of climate finance at the local level through innovative financial mechanisms. Localized responses are essential to addressing climate challenges, but they must be embedded within coherent national policy frameworks. The initiative bridges the gap between top-down policies and bottom-up innovation.

Internationally recognized for its impact, the NISGP was highlighted by the World Economic Forum (WEF) as one of the most impactful sustainable practices in the MENA region, citing its high scalability and measurable outcomes. Among its achievements:

- Conversion of 50 million tons of waste into valuable resources
- Creation of over 27,000 direct and indirect jobs in green sectors

Its presence at COP27, COP28, and COP29 further connected winning projects with funding and technical support networks.

Looking ahead, the initiative envisions evolving into a fully integrated platform supporting Egypt's green transition. Planned expansions include broadening the project database, increasing inclusivity in project categories, and intensifying climate education across governorates.

A strategic next step is the development of a Green Ecosystem Forum, convening stakeholders across the green economy to foster partnerships, exchange knowledge, and drive investment. Efforts are also underway to package the NISGP model into a replicable framework for adaptation in other national contexts, positioning it as a scalable global model for inclusive and impactful climate action.

References

Al-Mashat, Rania, and Mahmoud Mohieldin. 2025. "Localizing Climate Action in Egypt: A Novel Model for Development Finance." *World Economic Forum*. January 20, 2025. Accessed April 30, 2025. https://www.weforum.org/stories/2025/01/localizing-climate-action-egypt-model-development-finance/.

ElMassah, Suzanna, and Mahmoud Mohieldin. 2020. "Digital Transformation and Localizing the Sustainable Development Goals (SDGs)." Ecological Economics 169: 106490. https://doi.org/10.1016/j.ecolecon.2019.106490.

United Nations Development Programme (UNDP), United Nations Environment Programme (UNEP), and United Nations Capital Development Fund (UNCDF). 2013. *Financing Local Responses to Climate Change: Implications of Decentralisation on Responses to Climate Change*. Bangkok, Thailand.

Mahmoud Mohieldin, Mona Elbahtimy, and Miral Shehata
Towards Sufficient, Efficient, and Just Climate and Development Finance

Abstract: This chapter underscores the urgency of adopting a new growth model that is sustainable, low-carbon, climate-resilient, and nature-positive. It reflects on the high cost of inaction, which risks locking countries into carbon-intensive development pathways and escalating the financial burden of climate response. Emphasizing the need for an integrated approach to development, discusses the false dichotomy between climate and development finance and investments, which often frames climate and development priorities as competing or mutually exclusive, and calls for holistic, long-term strategies that align mitigation, adaptation, and development priorities through inclusive, country-specific pathways.

The chapter synthesizes the book's central argument for systemic transformation, built on a theory of change anchored in strong institutions and regulatory frameworks on the global, regional, national, and local levels; technological innovation and diffusion; and a climate finance framework grounded in the principles of sufficiency, efficiency, and fairness. It discusses the pillars of this transformation and calls for coordinated, context-sensitive development strategies that empower emerging markets and developing economies (EMDEs) to leapfrog toward inclusive and resilient green growth.

Keywords: Sustainable development goals, Institutions, Regulatory frameworks, Technological innovation, International financial architecture, Climate resilience

Introduction

Science is clear about the reality of climate change, which is already taking an economic toll across all countries. If global temperatures continue to rise, and mitigation and adaptation efforts remain constrained, lives and livelihoods could suffer, and the world economy could incur long-term losses comparable to the most severe recessions in history. Warming of around 4 °C by 2100 could reduce annual global GDP by 10–23%[1] (O'Neill et al. 2022, 2459). These economic risks are expected to be especially

---

[1] There is a consensus on the global economic damages from climate change and that they tend to grow non-linearly with higher levels of temperature. However, identifying a single range of estimates for the size of these damages is challenging due to the existence of a wide range of global estimates, which depend on incomparable methodologies. For a full discussion, see O'Neill et al. 2022, pp. 2495–2499.

significant in developing countries due to the nonlinear impact[2] of rising temperatures on economic output (Acevedo et al. 2020). On the other hand, by 2030, advancing climate action could deliver economic gains equivalent to 15–18% of global GDP (Bhattacharya et al. 2024, 5).

Throughout its chapters, this book examines the barriers to sufficient, effective, and fair climate and development finance, recognizing that current global efforts fall short of achieving the Paris Agreement and the Sustainable Development Goals (SDGs). It acknowledges the lack of a viable growth model as a fundamental challenge driving the development and climate crisis in most emerging markets and developing economies (EMDEs). The latter constitute the largest share of the investments required to transition to low-carbon energy and resilience building, face the greatest risks from climate change, and house most of the world's natural and biodiversity resources. Hence, the book calls for a big investment push in these countries, informed by growth arithmetics, highlighting the need for greater investments in human capital, infrastructure, nature, and resilience. These are crucial components of a successful growth strategy, yet they are often missing. Such a strategy has the merit of setting countries toward a high-growth, green, resilient, and inclusive development trajectory through leveraging integrated country-specific approaches (Kharas and Mohieldin 2025; World Bank Group 2023). It calls for this investment push amidst a changing development landscape as geopolitical tensions, pressures on aid, high debt burdens, and shifting perspectives on trade, industrial policy, multilateralism, and the public sector have challenged conventional development strategies.

The book advocates for a systemic transformation, guided by a comprehensive theory of change that spans multiple levels, actors, and sectors to tackle climate and development challenges at the necessary scale. Informed by Duflo (2022), the effective implementation of this theory of change rests on two foundational pillars: effective institutions and regulatory frameworks at global, regional, national, and local levels that guide behavior and decision-making; and technological innovation and diffusion, all anchored in sufficient, efficient, and just finance.

An Integrated Approach to Development

Climate change poses a significant challenge for realizing sustainable development, with far-reaching social, economic, political, and environmental consequences, particularly for marginalized communities. Recognized as a critical pillar of the 2030

---

2 According to Burke, Hsiang, and Miguel (2015) and Acevedo et al. (2020), economic productivity tends to decline sharply as temperatures rise above a certain threshold. Since developing countries generally have higher baseline temperatures, they are disproportionally affected by the impacts of climate change.

Agenda (SDG 13: Climate Action), climate change can slow or even reverse progress on many SDG targets (Nature 2023; UN DESA and UNFCCC 2023). For example, climate change's impacts on agriculture in Sub-Saharan Africa have deeply hindered efforts toward poverty and hunger alleviation (SDG 1 and SDG 2) (UN DESA and UNFCCC 2023).

There has been a false dichotomy between climate and development finance and investments, often framing climate and development priorities as competing or mutually exclusive. However, in reality, with careful and well-rounded design, climate policies and investments can directly support sustainable development. They help, inter alia, to improve public health, reduce air pollution, lower agricultural emissions, and enhance food and water security – while reducing vulnerability to climate risks and ultimately boosting global economic growth (UN DESA and UNFCCC 2023). Translating climate mitigation into clean energy projects to advance the energy transition directly contributes to SDGs 3, 7, and 11, while progress on SDGs 9 and 12 is essential to support low-carbon industrialization and sustainable consumption and production. At the same time, adaptation is equally critical to achieving the SDGs. Estimates suggest that reaching nearly 70% of the SDGs by 2030 will require widespread adaptation measures, particularly in urban areas and fragile ecosystems (Fuldauer et al. 2022). Investments in climate adaptation and resilience – as captured in the Sharm el-Sheikh Adaptation Agenda, which emphasizes action across key impact systems such as food and agriculture, water and nature, coastal and ocean systems, human settlements, and infrastructure – bring direct progress toward SDGs 2, 3, 6, 11, 14, and 15, reinforcing the role of adaptation as a development accelerator.

Similarly, failing to account for trade-offs between SDG 13 and the broader set of SDGs – along with insufficient attention to the principles of a just transition – can undermine the effectiveness of development policies and programs in achieving their intended goals, potentially resulting in negative impacts on employment and economic growth. For instance, transitioning to a low-carbon (SDG 13) and resource-efficient economy (SDG 12) could create 100 million new jobs globally by 2030, but may also jeopardize nearly 80 million existing jobs (ILO 2019, 184). However, well-designed policies that support education, training, lifelong learning (SDG 4), and social protection (SDG 1.3) can help workers transition smoothly between sectors and occupations (ILO 2019).

The Expert Group on Climate and SDG Synergy identifies several barriers to tapping the potential synergies between climate action and the SDGs. These include a lack of integrated and long-term economic planning, fragmented funding mechanisms for both agendas, insufficiency of climate and development finance, and unbalanced finance flows disproportionately favoring high-income countries. This results in four major failures: (i) inadequate and fragmented investment in both climate action and the SDGs, (ii) insufficient investments in key sectors such as climate-resilient infrastructure, food systems, healthcare, and social needs, (iii) limited investment in areas of adaptation and the priorities of lower-income countries, and (iv) inadequate support for the most vulnerable regions, with a broader failure to ensure investment quality (Glemarec et al. 2024, 8).

Approaching the 2030 Agenda and the Paris Agreement with a holistic, integrated approach can reduce the investment gaps confronting both agendas and enhance the efficiency and cost-effectiveness of climate and development investments. However, many investments in low-carbon economy, climate adaptation, and climate mitigation overlook the broader value of the SDGs and the benefits of green investments, which in turn limit the flow of climate finance, particularly from the private sector (UN DESA and UNFCCC 2023). Failing to factor climate risks into economic development and investment decisions can lead to maladaptation and weaken the overall impact of climate finance on socioeconomic progress (Glemarec et al. 2024). As argued in the chapter *"Different paths, same goals: A transition approach to climate and development finance"*, advancing toward climate mitigation, adaptation, and development also requires acknowledging that countries differ in their priorities across these three imperatives as well as in their capacities and access to finance; thus, enabling country-specific transition pathways is essential to achieving inclusive, sustainable development and maximizing impact across all three goals with the necessary urgency.

Institutions and Regulatory Frameworks

The current international financial architecture is highly fragmented and not fit for purpose to meet the scale, speed, and complexity of the ongoing climate and development crises. A comprehensive, system-wide reform should redefine the roles, mandates, and governance structures of the various organizations in the international ecosystem, including multilateral development banks (MDBs), multilateral climate funds, bilateral agencies, private investors, and philanthropies. Enhancing transparency is at the heart of the necessary reform to identify resource gaps and foster accountability and trust. The reform should also address the multiplicity of financing mechanisms operating under different mandates and access modalities, which hinders access and undermines effective climate action (G20 2024). This fragmentation, particularly in governance, not only creates inefficiencies but also systematically favors countries with stronger institutional capacity and experience in navigating complex funding mechanisms, leaving the most vulnerable countries underserved and exacerbating inequality. A meaningful solution requires a dedicated coordinating platform with the authority to steer climate finance institutions toward more specialized, complementary roles, supported by governance structures tailored to the needs of fragile and capacity-constrained countries, sustained investment in institutional capacity, and a more equitable distribution model (Rastogi 2025).

Despite some efforts, the global financial "system" lacks the coherence and integration that define a "system" (Mohieldin 2023) and still fails to account for the impact of nature loss and insufficient adaptation to climate change, as argued in the chapters on *"Financing a Global Nature-Positive Economy"* and *"Financing the New Adaptation Economy"*. The goal is to have the global system function as truly implied by the term: "a set of interconnected elements that together form a whole, with all the components working together in an interconnected manner according to certain principles, mechanisms, and procedures" (Mohieldin 2025). Then, this global system would be capable of scaling up finance, accelerating its mobilization, improving its quality, fostering international cooperation in trade and technology, and strengthening governance to ensure balanced representation for developing countries. The urgent task is to build this new and inclusive architecture amidst a multipolar world, recognizing that the old economic order, shaped originally by the victors of World War II, has been receding (Mohieldin 2025).

Given the recent inclination to undermine global multilateralism, marked by tariff wars and shifting alliances that undermine longstanding global dynamics, regional cooperation becomes critical for climate and development action. Many neighboring countries share common climate and development priorities, and climate change impacts are often regional, particularly in shared ecosystems or natural resource areas. Regional platforms can facilitate the testing of new models of cooperation in governance, trade liberalization, and sustainable development, while enabling the pooling of financial resources, the sharing of knowledge and expertise, the harmonization of policies, and the leveraging of collective negotiating power in international forums (Mbeva 2025). Advancing mitigation through clean, efficient, and secure energy often demands regional cooperation. For example, electricity grids operate most efficiently when supported by regional transmission capacity, and ensuring backup support for variable wind and solar power is best managed through regional cooperation (Abuov, Linn, and Sabyrova 2023).

Similarly, many ecosystems and natural resources, such as water, span multiple nations, making joint management of water, agriculture, disaster response, and infrastructure more effective than individual efforts. Collaborative planning and pooled expertise also alleviate climate cascading transboundary risks, often many times larger than domestic risks (Harris and Klein 2024). However, realizing the strength of regional cooperation necessitates the presence of robust regional institutions and frameworks. As shown in the respective chapters, initiatives such as the Regional Platforms for Climate Projects (RPCPs) and the regional networks developed under the Glasgow Financial Alliance for Net Zero (GFANZ) illustrate how regional cooperation can tailor project pipelines, financing frameworks, and investment priorities to specific regional contexts, ensuring that both climate and development goals are addressed in a coherent and context-sensitive manner. The Association of Southeast Asian Nations (ASEAN) is an inspiring example of regional cooperation and coordination in trade, investment, and technology, facilitating intra-bloc collaboration and collective engagement with global partners.

National institutions and regulatory frameworks are critical for securing the scale of investments and systemic changes necessary for a low-carbon, climate-resilient, nature-positive, and sustainable growth model. These institutions are expected to play a dual role: implementing the necessary expenditure and revenue reforms to strengthen domestic resource mobilization (DRM) and developing long-term climate and development strategies. Such strategies should include articulated investment and financing scenarios that assess funding needs and balance state budgets with external financing. They ensure a commitment to green and sustainable growth despite short-term political cycles and fiscal pressures. These strategies should then be translated into investment programs and project pipelines. Integrated National Financing Frameworks (INFFs) can support this process by outlining how the national sustainable development strategy will be financed and implemented, coordinating public, private, domestic, and international financial resources (Mohieldin et al. 2023, 45; Noureldin and Morsy 2022). This process requires strengthening institutional capacity, improving coordination, and fostering collaboration among governments, the private sector, and development finance institutions (DFIs).

Governments should lead efforts to co-develop investment programs and expand initiatives that connect prepared projects with investors. Country platforms should efficiently allocate investment opportunities, using public finance to address non-commercially viable priorities, while mobilizing private capital where feasible. Successful implementation also depends on strong and sustained policy and institutional reforms to create an enabling environment for investment. Transitions in key sectors, such as energy and food, require a combination of policy tools, including carbon pricing, regulations, subsidies, strategic public investments, and reforms to the financial system (Bhattacharya et al. 2023).

Climate and development crises are most acutely felt at the local level, and any solutions that ignore the local dimension are incomplete. Global climate and development action consists of local responses to these challenges. Local institutions possess knowledge of local contexts and can ensure that climate and development strategies are culturally appropriate, socially inclusive, and that interventions meet the respective communities' needs and values. However, the current climate and development landscapes have not given enough attention to these local institutions, particularly as decision-makers for planning and implementation. For example, in many developing countries, local governments do not have authority over key planning and service delivery functions, cannot mobilize the necessary resources to fulfill their mandates, and face capacity constraints (Mohieldin et al. 2023, 118). Similarly, despite the Paris Agreement's emphasis on the importance of local knowledge systems in climate action, local communities are yet to be fully integrated into the climate and development decision-making process. Strengthening the climate and development response requires adopting a localization approach, enhancing multi-level governance coordination, embedding local knowledge into project design, and facilitating access to finance at the local level. This includes establishing initiatives and platforms that support the identification of pipelines of local climate projects and securing financing arrangements to help launch and scale these projects, as demonstrated in the chapter on *"Mobilizing Local Climate Finance"*, which discusses Egypt's National Initiative for Smart Green Projects.

Technological Innovation and Diffusion

Technological innovation, development, and transfer are key drivers of economic development and growth. Estimates show that differences in the technological adoption rate across countries can explain approximately 75% of the income gap between developed and developing countries over the past 200 years (Comin and Mestieri 2018). With the growing risks posed by climate change, technology has become a key pillar of the Paris Agreement, playing a central role in enabling the shift to a low-carbon, climate-resilient future. Cutting emissions necessitates developing cleaner energy sources, increasing energy efficiency, adopting new modes of production and consumption, and diffusing such low-carbon solutions. This green innovation and diffusion have the dual benefit of advancing climate goals, while driving economic development, unlike degrowth approaches (World Bank Group 2023). Climate change is also altering modes of life and the natural and physical assets on which various populations depend, necessitating reliance on technologies that increase societies' adaptation and resilience to extreme and slow-onset events. Climate technologies not only contribute to achieving climate goals but also unlock solutions in key areas of sustainable development, including secured access to energy, sustained agricultural productivity, and better, risk-informed decision-making.

Climate technologies have witnessed significant progress over the last decade. The unit costs of several climate technologies, particularly low-carbon technologies, have declined sharply, making their widespread adoption more feasible. Over the last ten years, solar photovoltaic costs have declined by 90%, onshore wind by 70%, and battery prices by more than 90% (Ritchie 2024). The International Energy Agency (2023, 13) estimates that current technologies can meet more than 80% of the emissions reductions required by 2030 to be on track for the 1.5 °C goal. Numerous technologies have also been deployed to support climate adaptation in areas such as climate-smart agriculture and forestry, water preservation and coastal protection, and climate-adapted and resilient cities (WIPO 2022). However, as argued in the chapter titled *"Working Together to Promote Greener and Better Technologies for All"*, realizing the potential of climate technologies to achieve global climate goals hinges on their widespread adoption. Data reveal a significant concentration of climate technologies in developed countries. High-income countries accounted for 80% of all low-carbon technological inventions between 1990 and 2015 (Pigato et al. 2020, xxi), but the transfer of these technologies to developing countries remains limited. Approximately 71%

of all patent transfers occurred between high-income countries compared to 23% from high-income to middle-income countries, and almost no transfers to low-income countries between 2010 and 2015 (Pigato et al. 2020, 67). A similar pattern is observed for patented climate adaptation technologies (Dechezleprêtre et al. 2020, 6–7). This suggests that the innovation and diffusion of adaptation technologies are not driven by the adaptation needs of countries but rather by the recipient countries' absorptive capacity. This is concerning, as developing countries, where adaptation needs are more urgent and critically important, often have weaker technological and absorptive capacities.

Climate technology transfer includes the transfer of physical equipment, technical know-how, and the required capabilities to understand, choose, operate, and adapt technologies to local conditions, as well as the institutional and policy frameworks that support technological uptake and foster local innovation (IPCC 2000). Technology transfer is a collaborative and learning process that requires human, physical, financial, and organizational capital (Pigato et al. 2020, ix). Nevertheless, in many developing countries, human capital, technological literacy, and the quality and effectiveness of governing bodies and organizations responsible for managing and implementing technology-related policies are limited. This explains the barriers that constrain technology transfer to developing countries. Moreover, as discussed in the chapter on *"Financing Mitigation, including Just Energy Transitions"*, climate technologies require high upfront investment costs over long tenors. Developing countries generally face higher financing costs than developed countries and usually cannot access long-term financing in capital markets. This can severely limit the deployment of climate technologies, even when they are, in principle, the most cost-effective solution for achieving mitigation or adaptation outcomes. Many climate technologies, particularly in mitigation, require adequate complementary infrastructure and a well-developed regulatory environment. Uncertainty about climate policies and regulations can lower the return on climate investments, leading to suboptimal investment levels in climate technology (UNEP Copenhagen Climate Centre 2022).

Governments in developing countries should strengthen their regulatory frameworks and provide clear and credible policy directions to reduce investment and social risks and build investors' confidence. Government commitment to climate policies, along with public investment and procurement choices, sends signals to the private sector about the market size for clean technologies, stimulating research and investment efforts toward clean technologies. Investing in human capital – through greater investment in education and strategic public-private partnerships in technical development – is crucial for strengthening countries' absorptive capacity and enabling a shift from basic technology adoption to endogenous innovation. International development cooperation can provide multifaceted support for developing countries to address the barriers that slow down technology transfer.

Development cooperation institutions can support public and private institutions by providing technical assistance and capacity building to increase their capacity to absorb and deploy new technologies. Through their country programs, development institutions support governments in developing countries to strengthen national policies, regulatory frameworks, and innovation ecosystems (UNEP Copenhagen Climate Centre 2022). MDBs and DFIs are the main sources of long-term, concessional financing for developing countries, and they can directly finance hard technology transfer and necessary supporting infrastructure. They need to leverage and catalyze private investments in climate technologies by lowering the investment risks that increase the cost of capital in developing countries. Greater attention should be given to facilitating the diffusion of adaptation technologies by enhancing knowledge sharing and capacity building. Since the technologies prioritized in countries' Technology Needs Assessments are largely mature, the main barriers to their uptake are less about affordability (UNEP Copenhagen Climate Centre 2022). Development cooperation should, therefore, focus on supporting information dissemination, building local capacity, and tailoring technologies to local needs and conditions.

Climate technology transfer to developing countries is key to unlocking low-carbon, climate-resilient economic growth. The demand for energy in EMDEs is rapidly increasing, and these countries are at a crossroads regarding how they will fulfill this demand. Missing the opportunity to benefit from low-carbon technologies would lock developing countries into a carbon-intensive development path, substantially increasing the cost of decarbonization. This is particularly concerning, given that estimates indicate that approximately 90% of investments that would become stranded from the early retirement of coal-fired power plants are tied to recently commissioned coal plants in EMDEs (World Bank Group 2023, 15). An investment boost in energy efficiency, renewables, and adaptation means that developing countries can leapfrog to cleaner and greener technology. These countries have latecomer advantages over developed countries due to the absence of legacy infrastructure and, to a large extent, deep vested interests. New technologies can positively impact productivity growth and other development objectives. The primary challenge is no longer just climate technology innovation, but ensuring that climate solutions are accessible, equitably distributed, deployed at the scale and speed needed for effective climate action, and adapted to local contexts. This involves reducing costs, strengthening international technological cooperation, and establishing conditions for the widespread adoption of green technologies, especially in countries with limited financial, institutional, and industrial capacity.

An Integrated Approach to Finance

Mobilizing the scale and quality of finance to support the significant investment push toward green and sustainable growth requires an integrated approach that harnesses all pools of finance. This approach should tap into the distinct advantages of various finance sources and capitalize on their complementarities to enhance overall leveraging capacity.

Domestic public finance is critical for funding the big investment push, recurrent spending, and maintaining creditworthiness. Estimates show that around 60% of the climate- and nature-related spending requirements would come from DRM (Bhattacharya et al. 2023, 14). Bhattacharya et al. (2022, 9) further estimate that meeting the incremental financing required for development, climate, and nature implies an incremental DRM equivalent to 2.7% of EMDEs' GDP. As elaborated in the chapter on *"Domestic Resource Mobilization"*, improving DRM requires enhancing tax capacity and efforts as well as spending efficiency and effectiveness. With developing countries facing an average tax gap of 9% of GDP (IMF 2024, 4), tax reforms such as broadening the tax base, increasing progressivity, improving compliance through administrative measures, and leveraging digital tools hold significant potential for revenue growth. These measures need to be accompanied by reforms in carbon pricing, carbon taxation, and the phasing out of harmful subsidies. Taxation should serve as both a revenue-generating mechanism and an incentive to change business and consumer behavior. Many EMDEs have significant room to enhance spending efficiency and effectiveness. Low-income countries lose 53% of their investment returns due to management inefficiencies such as weak project design, evaluation, and selection, while emerging markets lose about 34% (Baum, Mogues, and Verdier 2020, 35). Climate and development goals should be reflected in national budgets, as budgets function as economic, legal, political, and accountability tools that sustain policy objectives beyond electoral cycles while addressing short- and long-term priorities (Mohieldin et al. 2023, 51).

The transition to a green and sustainable growth model entails higher upfront investment needs. Debt is a crucial instrument that enables governments to finance investments beyond their budgetary constraints. If governments borrow responsibly and invest in productive projects, they can stimulate economic growth and make debt service more manageable. Several factors determine the debt sustainability, including its volume, what it finances, the interest rate charged, inflation, and the economic growth rate. Hence, changing economic conditions can render sustainable debt unsustainable. Slower economic growth and rising interest rates can induce heavy debt repayments and spending cuts that further weaken growth and revenue generation, creating a cycle of indebtedness, as argued in the chapter on *"Managing Debt Vulnerabilities to Allow for Climate Action"*. This scenario has played out in many low- and middle-income countries over the past three years (Jacobs, Getzel, and Colenbrander 2024, 29–30). Many developing countries witnessed a decline in their creditworthiness in 2023 and 2024, making it harder to access global capital markets. As a result, no developing country issued a new bond in 2023 (Bhattacharya et al. 2024, 29). Climate and natural disasters further worsen the debt crisis, feeding into a vicious cycle of debt, climate, and nature (The Expert Group on Debt, Nature & Climate 2024). Frequent environmental shocks and stresses force countries to borrow to finance disaster response and recovery, but these shocks make borrowing more expensive and slow economic growth, making debt repayment even costlier. High debt burdens constrain countries' fiscal space and their ability to pursue low-carbon and climate-resilient development paths, thus increasing their vulnerability to such damaging episodes.

Several reforms have been proposed to address the debt crisis faced by EMDEs. The chapter on *"Connecting the Virtuous Circle: From Debt-for-Development Swaps to Sustainability-Linked Sovereign Finance"* examines how innovative debt restructuring and reprofiling instruments that have emerged in recent years must be deployed, including sustainability-linked bonds and loans, use-of-proceeds bonds, and debt swaps, while recognizing their limitations. For instance, debt swaps are not a comprehensive solution for debt relief. They are typically small in scale and often inefficient for environmental action and debt reduction. For countries facing unsustainable debt, swaps alone cannot restore solvency unless implemented on a large scale, and should not replace necessary debt restructuring (IMF and World Bank 2024). Proposals have also been made to provide temporary liquidity to countries at risk of debt distress. Diwan, Kessler, and Songwe (2024) propose a framework in which MDBs would channel more funding for new investments, debtor countries would commit to enhancing macroeconomic stability, and creditors would agree to reschedule their claims. Countries facing extreme climate-related events should benefit from debt relief. This can be achieved through climate- or disaster-contingent debt clauses allowing for the temporary suspension of debt repayments when the debtor experiences a predefined shock. Several countries also call for improving the Common Framework in terms of faster timelines for negotiations, better coordination and information sharing, and debt service suspension at the beginning of negotiations (Chen and Hart 2025).

Public finance alone is insufficient to meet climate and development investment needs. Achieving the SDGs, the Paris Agreement, and the Kunming-Montreal Global Biodiversity Framework goals requires tapping into private finance. Bhattacharya et al. (2023, 15) estimate that EMDEs, excluding China, will need at least USD 1 trillion a year in private capital by 2030 to achieve their climate and development objectives. However, private capital mobilization in EMDEs has been significantly limited in speed and scale. Most EMDEs lack the enabling environment and necessary capacity to attract private investors. These challenges are further compounded by significant investor-perceived risks, particularly macroeconomic risks – sovereign, political, and currency risks – that drive up the cost of capital.[3] These barriers indicate that EMDEs often lack both creditworthy entities with a history of reliably servicing debt and a pipeline of bankable projects suitable for investment. EMDEs need to start by improv-

---

3 In addition to these macroeconomic risks that drive the overall cost of capital, EMDEs also face climate investment risk premium, especially for solar projects. IEA (2024) finds that the weighted cost of capital for solar Photovoltaic investments in EMDEs, excluding China, was at least twice as high as in advanced economies.

ing their investment environment through defining clear, credible, and actionable transition pathways, standards, and robust regulatory frameworks, while eliminating regulatory uncertainty and definitional ambiguities. EMDEs should also revamp and deepen their domestic financial systems to unlock domestic private capital, leveraging approximately USD 17 trillion in domestic financial resources, including household savings, pension funds, corporate capital, and local bank financing (Bhattacharya et al. 2023, 16). Tackling the high cost of capital in EMDEs calls for various measures at both international and country levels to lower actual and perceived risks, both at the macroeconomic and project levels. The design, composition, and structure of blended finance and other risk-sharing and de-risking mechanisms will depend on factors such as the project's development phase, scale, technology maturity, capital market development, and macroeconomic conditions. Country-level policies and measures are essential to strengthen macroeconomic stability, enhance the investment climate, develop domestic capital markets, and establish effective regulatory and legal frameworks.

The big investment push also necessitates the active involvement of MDBs and DFIs. MDBs' business model and engagement with countries position them to be sources of low-cost finance, technical knowledge, and policy advice, and to catalyze private finance. However, the MDBs' role in climate finance has been below their potential. This has led to proposals to reform MDBs, particularly by the Independent Expert Group on Strengthening MDBs (2023). The reforms call for a new country engagement model in which MDBs support EMDEs in designing and delivering their climate and development strategies. This shift moves away from a project-centered model toward a more coordinated, country-driven framework that promotes collective action among MDBs. The chapter on *"Multilateral Development Banks Support for Climate Action – A Story of Evolution, Rather than Revolution"* focuses on the MDBs' catalytic role in mobilizing climate finance, arguing that MDBs are also required to scale up their lending and enhance their ability to mobilize private-sector finance. Estimates show that MDBs mobilized only USD 17 billion in private finance in EMDEs in 2022 compared with a total lending of USD 80.6 billion for climate action (Bhattacharya et al. 2023, 18).

MDBs have struggled to foster private investment due to a lack of strategic alignment with sector- and country-specific needs. Instead, MDBs often compete for low-risk projects rather than facilitating private-sector participation. They also lack the necessary tools to effectively share risk and lower the cost of capital. This latter point has induced calls for MDBs to take more informed risks and provide risk-sharing tools. There is pressure on MDBs to increase the use of guarantees and currency hedging mechanisms to more effectively contribute to lowering the cost of capital and mobilizing climate finance. Foreign exchange risk is addressed in detail in the chapter on *"De-risking Macro-Finance and Unblocking the Green Transition in Emerging Economies"*, which also highlights the Eco Invest initiative – a collaborative effort between the G20 Brazilian Presidency and the Inter-American Development Bank – as a promising step toward hedging currency risks associated with climate-related investments. MDBs are also expected to play a greater role in advancing climate adaptation, as elaborated in the chapter on *"The Role of Multilateral Development Banks in Climate Adaptation"*, which calls for MDBs to scale up adaptation finance, offer technical and capacity-building support, promote inclusive and community-driven approaches, and drive structural reforms that enhance access, equity, and effectiveness in adaptation efforts, particularly in developing countries.

The reality of the finance landscape and the conditions faced by developing countries necessitate a significant increase in concessional finance. Investing in adaptation, building resilience, addressing loss and damage, fostering a nature-positive economy, and advancing a just transition might not be as attractive to private investors and require funding that exceeds developing countries' fiscal capacity. While developed countries must take the lead in expanding concessional finance, meeting the overall needs requires more predictable funding through international taxation, specialized funds (as discussed in the *"Financing Loss and Damage"* chapter), tapping into carbon markets, and leveraging contributions from the corporate sector and philanthropy. For instance, voluntary carbon markets (VCMs) have the potential to generate as much as USD 50 billion over the medium term (Bhattacharya et al. 2023, 22), but as argued in the chapter on *"Voluntary Carbon Markets: Promise or Peril in Global Climate Action"*, realizing this potential requires integrating regulatory innovation, stakeholder coordination, and alignment with international standards. The chapter titled *"Shaken or Stirred? Mobilizing Philanthropy for Climate Finance"* demonstrates that philanthropic capital holds a unique advantage in taking on high-risk investments, piloting innovative technologies and approaches, and operating in climate-vulnerable regions. Moreover, philanthropy possesses network capital and the ability to shape and influence policy and investment agendas.

Finance represents a key anchor to the theory of change required to unlock the growth story of the twenty-first century. The climate and development finance framework outlined in the book recognizes that the sufficiency of finance depends on mobilizing diverse sources of capital, harnessing their complementarities, and leveraging their catalytic potential. It recognizes that channeling climate finance to developing countries requires strengthening national institutions, advancing regulatory reforms, and identifying a pipeline of investable projects. But these national reforms should be complemented by deep reforms in the international financial architecture anchored in enhanced integrity and transparency to hold different parties accountable for their commitments, as outlined in chapters on *"A Compass to Guide Climate Finance Integrity"* and *"Enhancing Transparency and Accountability in Climate Finance Mobilization from Developed to Developing Countries"*. These reforms aim to improve the scale and quality of finance, strengthen the role of DFIs and MDBs, and break the vicious cycle of debt, nature, and climate facing many developing countries. The framework also advocates for a more balanced approach across mitigation, adaptation, loss and damage, and nature finance by aligning each strand of finance with the characteristics of different areas of climate action. It also recognizes that an efficient climate finance system depends on stronger coordination and coherence across various climate funding mechanisms, as well as simplifying access to these resources, particularly during times of crisis.

Unlocking the Twenty-First-Century Growth Story

A new growth model is essential – one that is sustainable, climate-resilient, low-carbon, and nature-positive. The cost of inaction is high and will place increasing pressure on the scale of financial resources required by countries to meet mitigation targets, adapt to the impacts of climate change, address loss and damage, and restore degraded ecosystems that sustain livelihoods.

Failure to act risks locking countries into carbon-intensive development pathways, resulting in outdated infrastructure and large volumes of stranded assets. However, the journey toward sustainable development is not uniform – particularly for EMDEs. Each country's path is shaped by a unique combination of geography, natural endowments, income levels, economic diversification, infrastructure stock, human capital, institutional and governance frameworks, and social capital.

Advancing this new growth paradigm requires a clearly defined theory of change. This must be anchored in effective, resilient institutions at the global, regional, national, and local levels, with technological innovation and the widespread diffusion of climate solutions at its core. These elements are vital to ensuring that all actors within the ecosystem make informed decisions that enable developing countries to leapfrog carbon-intensive development and transition directly to green growth models.

This book advocates for such a theory of change, emphasizing that finance is the primary enabler of its realization. It presents a climate and development finance framework based on the principles of sufficiency, efficiency, and fairness. The framework is grounded in the transparent and quantifiable assessment of investment needs across sectors and climate action areas, and it is supported by enhanced mechanisms to track financial contributions from various sources.

References

Abuov, Kenzhekhan, Johannes F. Linn, and Lyaziza Sabyrova. 2023. "A Regional Platform for Climate Action: The Case of CAREC for the Greater Central Asia Region." *Brookings*, November 30, 2023. Accessed April 17, 2025. https://www.brookings.edu/articles/a-regional-platform-for-climate-action-the-case-of-carec-for-the-greater-central-asia-region/.

Acevedo, Sebastian, Mico Mrkaic, Natalija Novta, Evgenia Pugacheva, and Petia Topalova. 2020. "The Effects of Weather Shocks on Economic Activity: What Are the Channels of Impact?" *Journal of Macroeconomics* 65: 103207. https://doi.org/10.1016/j.jmacro.2020.103207

Baum, Anja, Tewodaj Mogues, and Geneviève Verdier. 2020. "Chapter 3: Getting the Most from Public Investment." In *Well Spent: How Strong Infrastructure Governance Can End Waste in Public Investment*, edited by Gerd Schwartz, Manal Fouad, Torben Hansen, and Geneviève Verdier. Washington, DC: International Monetary Fund.

Bhattacharya, Amar, Meagan Dooley, Homi Kharas, Charlotte Taylor, and Nicholas Stern. 2022. *Financing a Big Investment Push in Emerging Markets and Developing Economies for Sustainable, Resilient, and Inclusive Recovery and Growth*. London: Grantham Research Institute on Climate Change and the Environment, London School of Economics and Political Science; Washington, DC: Brookings Institution.

Bhattacharya, Amar, Vera Songwe, Eléonore Soubeyran, and Nicholas Stern. 2023. *A Climate Finance Framework: Decisive Action to Deliver on the Paris Agreement – Summary*. London: Grantham Research Institute on Climate Change and the Environment, London School of Economics and Political Science.

Bhattacharya, Amar, Vera Songwe, Emmanuel Soubeyran, and Nicholas Stern. 2024. *Raising Ambition and Accelerating Delivery of Climate Finance*. London: Grantham Research Institute on Climate Change and the Environment, London School of Economics and Political Science.

Burke, Marshall, Solomon M. Hsiang, and Edward Miguel. 2015. "Global Non-linear Effect of Temperature on Economic Production." *Nature* 527: 235–39. https://doi.org/10.1038/nature15725.

Dechezleprêtre, Antoine, Samuel Fankhauser, Matthieu Glachant, Jan Stoever, and Sarah Touboul. 2020. *Invention and Global Diffusion of Technologies for Climate Change Adaptation: A Patent Analysis*. Washington, DC: The World Bank.

Duflo, Esther. 2022. *Good Economics for Warmer Times: Evidence for Effective and Equitable Climate Action*. Presentation, World Bank. Accessed May 22, 2025. https://thedocs.worldbank.org/en/doc/98ac38b95ebcddfba3ea640fdeed693d-0080012022/original/GEFT-Climate-WorldBank-EDuflo.pdf.

Chen, Yunnan, and Tom Hart. 2025. "Common Framework, Uncommon Challenges: Lessons from the Post-COVID Debt Restructuring Architecture." *ODI Global Insight*, February 21. Accessed March 5, 2025. https://odi.org/en/insights/common-framework-uncommon-challenges-lessons-from-the-post-covid-debt-restructuring-architecture/.

Comin, Diego, and Martí Mestieri. 2018. "If Technology Has Arrived Everywhere, Why Has Income Diverged?" *American Economic Journal: Macroeconomics* 10 (3): 137–78. https://doi.org/10.1257/mac.20150175

Diwan, Ishac, Martin Kessler, and Vera Songwe. 2024. *A Bridge to Climate Action: A Tripartite Deal for Times of Illiquidity*. Policy Note 14. Finance for Development Lab, January 14. Accessed February 15, 2025. https://findevlab.org/a-bridge-to-climate-action/

Fuldauer, Lena I., Scott Thacker, Robyn A. Haggis, Francesco Fuso-Nerini, Robert J. Nicholls, and Jim W. Hall. 2022. "Targeting Climate Adaptation to Safeguard and Advance the Sustainable Development Goals." *Nature Communications* 13 (1): 3579. https://doi.org/10.1038/s41467-022-31202-w

G20. 2024. *2024 G20 Sustainable Finance Report*. https://g20sfwg.org/wp-content/uploads/2024/10/2024-G20-Sustainable-Finance-Report.pdf

Glemarec, Yannick, Barbara Buchner, Luis Gomez Echeverri, Meagan Fallone, and Soumya Swaminathan. 2024. *Seeking Synergy Solutions: A New Financial System to Enable Both Climate and SDG Action*. Expert Group on Climate and SDG Synergy. New York: United Nations.

Harris, Katy, and Richard Klein. 2024. "The Collective Advantage: Understanding Transboundary Climate Risks in Southeast Asia and Charting a Path Forward." *Adaptation Without Borders*, November 7, 2024. Accessed April 17, 2025. https://adaptationwithoutborders.org/knowledge-base/adaptation-without-borders/the-collective-advantage-understanding-transboundary-climate-risks-in-southeast-asia-and-charting-a-path-forward/.

International Energy Agency (IEA). 2023. *Net Zero Roadmap: A Global Pathway to Keep the 1.5 °C Goal in Reach*. Paris: IEA.

International Energy Agency (IEA). 2024. *Reducing the Cost of Capital: Strategies to Unlock Clean Energy Investment in Emerging and Developing Economies*. https://www.iea.org/reports/reducing-the-cost-of-capital.

Independent Expert Group on Strengthening MDBs. 2023. *Strengthening Multilateral Development Banks: The Triple Agenda*. Volume 1. https://www.cgdev.org/publication/strengthening-multilateral-development-banks-triple-agenda.

International Labour Office (ILO). 2019. *Skills for a Greener Future: A Global View Based on 32 Country Studies*. Geneva: ILO.

International Monetary Fund (IMF). 2024. *G20 Note on Alternative Options for Revenue Mobilization*. Accessed February 15, 2025. https://www.imf.org/external/np/g20/pdf/2024/062424.pdf

International Monetary Fund. Strategy, Policy, & Review Department, and World Bank. 2024. *Debt for Development Swaps: An Approach Framework*. Policy Papers 2024, 038. Accessed February 15, 2025. https://www.imf.org/en/Publications/Policy-Papers/Issues/2024/08/05/Debt-for-Development-Swaps-An-Approach-Framework-553146

Intergovernmental Panel on Climate Change (IPCC). 2000. *Methodological and Technological Issues in Technology Transfer: A Special Report of IPCC Working Group III*. Summary for Policymakers. https://www.ipcc.ch/site/assets/uploads/2018/03/srtt-en-1.pdf.

Jacobs, Michael, Bianca Getzel, and Sarah Colenbrander. 2024. *International Development and Climate Finance: The New Agenda*. London: Overseas Development Institute.

Kharas, Homi, and Mahmoud Mohieldin. 2025. "Four Priorities for Success at the Sevilla Fourth International Conference on Financing for Development." Working Paper #192. Brookings Center for Sustainable Development. https://www.brookings.edu/articles/four-priorities-for-success-at-the-sevilla-fourth-international-conference-on-financing-for-development/

Mbeva, Kennedy. 2025. "Why Regional Initiatives Are Key to Addressing the Catastrophic Risks of Climate Change and Underdevelopment." *Forum on Trade, Environment, and the SDGs (TESS)*. March 17, 2025. Accessed April 17, 2025. https://tessforum.org/latest/why-regional-initiatives-are-key-to-addressing-the-catastrophic-risks-of-climate-change-and-underdevelopment.

Mohieldin, Mahmoud. 2023. "Paris Summit: A New Financial Architecture?" *Ahram Online*, July 4, 2023. Accessed May 22, 2025. https://english.ahram.org.eg/NewsContentP/4/504138/Opinion/Paris-Summit-A-new-financial-architecture.aspx.

Mohieldin, Mahmoud. 2025. "The End of the Post-War 'Order'". *Ahram Online*, May 14, 2025. Accessed May 22, 2025. https://english.ahram.org.eg/NewsContentP/4/546180/Opinion/The-end-of-the-postwar-;order;.aspx

Mohieldin, Mahmoud, Sameh Wahba, Maria Alejandra Gonzalez-Perez, and Miral Shehata. 2023. *Business, Government and the SDGs: The Role of Public-Private Engagement in Building a Sustainable Future*. Cham: Palgrave Macmillan.

Nature Editorial. 2023. "The Science Is Clear: Sustainable Development and Climate Action Are Inseparable." *Nature*, August 29, 2023. Accessed February 15, 2025. https://www.nature.com/articles/d41586-023-02686-3.

Noureldin, Diaa, and Reham Morsy. 2022. "Integrated National Financing Framework." In *Financing Sustainable Development in Egypt Report*, edited by Mahmoud Mohieldin, 46–71. Cairo: League of Arab States.

O'Neill, Brian, Maarten van Aalst, Zelina Zaiton Ibrahim, Lea Berrang Ford, Suruchi Bhadwal, Halvard Buhaug, Delavane Diaz, Katja Frieler, Matthias Garschagen, Alexandre Magnan, Guy Midgley, Alisher Mirzabaev, Adelle Thomas, and Rachel Warren. 2022. "Key Risks Across Sectors and Regions." In *Climate Change 2022: Impacts, Adaptation and Vulnerability. Contribution of Working Group II to the Sixth Assessment Report of the Intergovernmental Panel on Climate Change*, edited by H.-O. Pörtner, D.C. Roberts, M. Tignor, E.S. Poloczanska, K. Mintenbeck, A. Alegría, M. Craig, S. Langsdorf,

S. Löschke, V. Möller, A. Okem, B. Rama, 2411–2538. Cambridge, UK and New York: Cambridge University Press.

Pigato, Miria, Simon J. Black, Damien Dussaux, Zhimin Mao, Miles McKenna, Ryan Rafaty, and Simon Touboul. 2020. *Technology Transfer and Innovation for Low-Carbon Development*. International Development in Focus. Washington, DC: World Bank. http://hdl.handle.net/10986/33474.

Rastogi, Archi. 2025. "Climate Finance Needs a Conductor." *Project Syndicate* . June 10, 2025. Accessed June 12, 2025. https://www.project-syndicate.org/commentary/fragmented-finance-landscape-hinders-effective-climate-action-by-archi-rastogi-2025-06.

Ritchie, Hannah. 2024. "Solar Panel Prices Have Fallen by Around 20% Every Time Global Capacity Doubled." *Our World in Data*. Accessed February 17, 2025. https://ourworldindata.org/data-insights/solar-panel-prices-have-fallen-by-around-20-every-time-global-capacity-doubled

The Expert Group on Debt, Nature & Climate. 2024. *Interim Report of the Expert Review on Debt, Nature & Climate: Tackling the Vicious Circle*. https://d1leqfwiwfltz5.cloudfront.net/documents/Tackling_the_Vicious_Circle.pdf.

United Nations Department of Economic and Social Affairs (UN DESA) and United Nations Framework Convention on Climate Change (UNFCCC). 2023. *Synergy Solutions for a World in Crisis: Tackling Climate and SDG Action Together. Report on Strengthening the Evidence Base*. First Edition 2023. New York: United Nations.

UNEP Copenhagen Climate Centre. 2022. *Technology Transfer for Climate Mitigation and Adaptation: Analysing Needs and Development Assistance Support in Technology Transfer Processes*. Policy Brief. October. https://unepccc.org/wp-content/uploads/2023/06/tech-transfer-policy-brief-oecd.pdf

World Intellectual Property Organization (WIPO). 2022. *Green Technology Book 2022: Solutions for Climate Change Adaptation*. Geneva: World Intellectual Property Organization.

World Bank Group. 2023. *The Big Push for Transformation through Climate and Development: Recommendations of the High-Level Advisory Group on Sustainable and Inclusive Recovery and Growth*. Washington, DC: World Bank.

Index

www.ingramcontent.com/pod-product-compliance
Lightning Source LLC
Chambersburg PA
CBHW061750260326
41914CB00006B/1054